JOHN CATT'S

Which School? for Special Needs 2015/16

24th Edition
Editor: Jonathan Barnes

JOHN
CATT
EDUCATIONAL
LIMITED

Published in 2015 by
John Catt Educational Ltd,
12 Deben Mill Business Centre,
Woodbridge, Suffolk IP12 1BL UK
Tel: 01394 389850   Fax: 01394 386893
Email: enquiries@johncatt.com
Website: www.johncatt.com
© 2015 John Catt Educational Ltd

**A CIP catalogue record for this book is available from the
British Library.**

ISBN: 978 1 909717 33 6

Contacts
Editor
Jonathan Barnes

Advertising and School Profiles
Tel: +44 (0) 1394 389850
Email: sales@johncatt.com

Distribution/Book Sales
Tel: +44 (0) 1394 389863
Email: booksales@johncatt.com

Contents

Introduction

by Jonathan Barnes, Editor

Welcome to the 2015/16 edition of *Which School for Special Needs?*

Our intention for this guidebook is to provide a one-stop service for families looking for the right school for their children. It's hard to think of a more important decision to make than choosing a school for a child with special needs, and if we can help make that decision-making process a little easier, then we will have achieved our aim!

We also intend to give the guide a 'yearbook' feel, providing a snapshot of the SEN sector. The most important aspect of this, I believe, is trying to explain the latest position regarding legislation and Government reforms, which can be complicated and confusing. And for that reason we have again invited some experts in the field to give their thoughts on the latest issues affecting children with special needs and their families. You can read their thoughts in the editorial section, starting with Claire Dorer's foreword on page 9.

Finding an establishment that will address the needs of your child is extremely important, as it will have a significant impact on their development, the level of independence they are able to achieve and the opportunities they are able to embrace in life. The search for the right school can be a complex and emotional journey and so, to help the reader, we have tried to make this guide as informative, interesting and easy to use as possible.

This guide also provides the reader with detailed information about the range of provision for children with SEN, helping you to make an informed, confident choice of school or college according to your child's individual needs. As well as featuring listings and information of independent schools and colleges we also provide up-to-date details of all the maintained special schools in the UK. With each new edition we do our best to ensure that our resource is up-to-date with current data, research, classification and opinion, and that each special needs sector is fairly and accurately represented in the guide. We welcome, however, suggestions from readers as to how we could further improve this resource. We hope you enjoy the new edition.

Melton, Suffolk, April 2015

How to use this guide

Here are some pointers on how to use this guidebook effectively

Which School? for Special Needs is divided into specific sections:

1. Editorial

This includes articles, written by experts in their fields, explaining various aspects of special needs education. There are also case studies and other interesting articles.

2. Profiles

Here the schools and colleges have been given the opportunity to highlight what they feel are their best qualities in order to help you decide whether this is the right school for your child. They are presented in sections according to the needs they specialise in:

- social interaction difficulties (autism, ASD & ASP)
- emotional, behavioural and/or social difficulties.
- learning difficulties (including dyslexia/SPLD)
- sensory or physical impairment

Within these sections, schools and colleges are listed by region in alphabetical order.

3. Directory

Here you will find basic up-to-date information about every independent or non-maintained special needs school and college, and further education colleges, in England, Northern Ireland, Scotland and Wales, giving contact details, size of school and which specific needs are catered for. (You will find a key to the abbreviations at the start of each directory section) The directory is divided into four sections:

- social interaction difficulties (autism, ASD & ASP)
- emotional, behavioural and/or social difficulties.
- learning difficulties (including dyslexia/SPLD)
- sensory or physical impairment

Within these sections, each establishment is listed by region in alphabetical order and those that have entries in the profiles section are cross-referenced to allow you to find further detailed information. Against each entry you will find a number of symbols indicating any SEN speciality, including an icon to indicate if the school is DfE approved.

4. Useful associations and websites

In this section we provide a list of useful organisations and websites relevant to special educational needs, which may be useful to parents looking for specific help or advice.

5. Maintained schools

Here we have included basic details of all maintained special schools in England, Northern Ireland, Scotland and Wales. They are listed according to their Local Authority.

6. Index

Page numbers preceded by a D indicate a school appearing in the directory, those without will be found in the profiles section.

How to use this guide effectively
John Catt's *Which School? for Special Needs* can be used effectively in several ways according to the information you are looking for. For example, are you looking for:

A specific school? If you know the name of the school but are unsure of its location simply go to the index at the back of the guide where you will find all schools listed alphabetically.

A particular type of school? Both the profiles and directories are divided into sections according to the type of provision. **See also the appendix on page 147**, which lists specific special needs and the schools that cater for them.

A school in a certain region? Look first in the relevant directory. This will give you the basic information about the schools in each region, complete with contact details and which specific needs are catered for. More detailed information can be found in the profiles section for those schools who have chosen to include a full entry.

More information on relevant educational organisations? At the end of the directories you will find a list of useful organisations and websites relevant to special educational needs.

Please note: regional divisions
To facilitate the use of this guide, we have included the geographical region 'Central & West'. This is not an officially designated region and has been created solely for the purposes of this publication.

One final thing, on the next page you will find a list of commonly used SEN abbreviations. This list can be found repeated at various points throughout the guide.

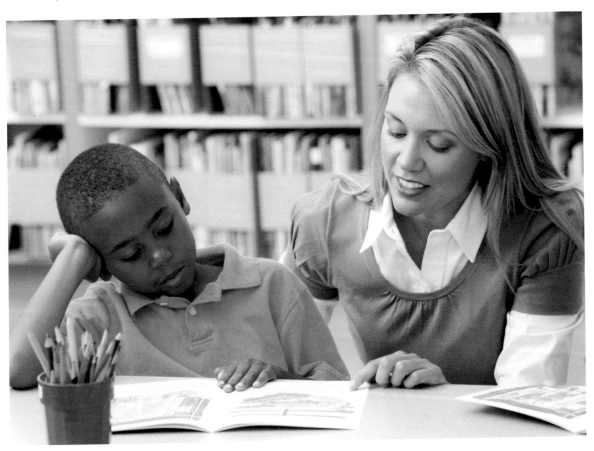

Abbreviations – a full glossary can be found at page 283

ACLD	Autism, Communication and Associated Learning Difficulties	HI	Hearing Impairment
ADD	Attention Deficit Disorder	LD	Learning Difficulties
ADHD	Attention Deficit and Hyperactivity Disorder	MLD	Moderate Learning Difficulties
		MSI	Multi-sensory Impairment
ASD	Autistic Spectrum Disorder	OCD	Obsessive Compulsive Disorder
ASP	Asperger Syndrome	PD	Physical Difficulties
AUT	Autism	PH	Physical Impairment
BESD	Behavioural, Emotional and Social Difficulties	Phe	Partially Hearing
		PMLD	Profound and Multiple Learning Difficulties
CCD	Complex Communication Difficulties	PNI	Physical Neurological Impairment
CLD	Complex Learning Difficulties	SCD	Social and Communication Difficulties
CP	Cerebral Palsy	SCLD	Severe to Complex Learning Difficulties
D	Deaf	SEBD	Severe Emotional and Behavioural Difficulties
DYS	Dyslexia		
DYSP	Dyspraxia	SEBN	Social, Emotional and Behavioural Needs
EBD	Emotional and Behavioural Difficulties	SLD	Severe Language Difficulties
EPI	Epilepsy	SLI	Specific Language Impairment
GLD	General Learning Difficulties	SPLD	Specific Learning Difficulties
HA	High Ability	SP&LD	Speech and Language Difficulties
		VIS	Visual Impairment

The reforms are finally here – now the hard work starts!

Claire Dorer, chief executive of the National Association of Independent Schools and Non-Maintained Special Schools (NASS) says it will take time for new legislation to bed in

It's a great pleasure to be writing the foreword to this guide for the third time. After two years of writing about impending legislation and policy reform it's also something of a relief to finally be able to talk about the arrival of the SEND Reforms! The reforms signaled in the Children and Families Act and new SEND Code of Practice went live on 1st September 2014 and we are now knee-deep in the joys of implementation!

For children and families entering the SEN system for the first time, there has been much promised. Instead of Statements of SEN, children and young people are being issued with Education, Health and Care Plans, which promise a more holistic, child-centred and outcomes-focused approach to assessing and meeting Special Educational Needs. There are new duties on local authorities and clinical commissioning groups to work together to ensure that services are available to meet needs. Parents also have new powers to express a preference for a much wider range of schools – including the majority of the schools that appear in this guide.

For children already within the SEN system there is a transitional period where Statements of SEN will be transferred to Education Health and Care Plans (EHCP). Consequently, there are currently two legal systems for SEN in operation. At the moment, the plan is for all statements to be transferred to Plans within three years with young people transferring between phases of education made a priority for transfer. For some families this will mean waiting for some time before they are part of the new SEN system, which creates potential for confusion and frustration. Some support has been built into the new system. Local authorities are making 'Independent Supporters' available to parents negotiating the new SEN system to help ensure that parents have access both to information and someone on 'their side' to help with the practicalities of assessment and the issuing of the Plan.

The SEN Reforms present particular challenges for local authorities. In addition to the commissioning duties and transfer responsibilities mentioned above, each local authority must produce a 'local offer' of education, health and social care services that they expect to be available to people from their area. Searching for your home authority's local offer online should take you to lots of information about what is available in your area, including schools, health services and short breaks services. It should also include more specialist services outside the authority's boundaries that they make use of. This should include a list of schools that have been approved by the Secretary of State to take children with SEN (sometimes known as the 'S41 list') and Non-Maintained Special Schools used by the authority.

In practice, many authorities are still getting up to speed with the reforms. Whilst every local authority has a local offer, not all are fully up to speed yet. Specialist special school provision is one of the areas least likely to be included, which creates the risk of parents missing out on finding the best possible placement for their child. That's why there is still such value in having guides like this one, where you can find a wide range of schools in one place. As noted above, the Children and Families Act strengthens parent's right to choose a specific school

Whilst the country faces a year of political change, the indications are that all the major political parties have committed to allowing the SEN reforms time to bed-in. This will be welcome news to all – we all feel there is more than enough flux to be negotiating at the moment!

for their child. In the past, this only extended to state-maintained schools but, where a child has an EHCP, parents now have the same right to express a preference for a special academy, Non-Maintained Special School and Secretary of State Approved Independent Schools. There is a new conditional duty on local authorities to meet parental preference for school placements. The only grounds for turning this down are if the school cannot meet the child's needs or if the authority can prove the placement is a poor use of resources. In theory, it should now be easier for parents to secure placements at the schools that appear in this guide. In practice, there has been little testing out of this to date. It's not always easy for parents to know where they might be missing out on information or their rights and there is still a reliance on parents challenging when they are unhappy with what is being presented to them. The Government set out to build a system that was less confrontational. Whilst that is still the great hope of all who work in SEN, we are still in a period where the new legislation is being tested out and challenged – sometimes in court. The establishment of case law is an important part of the bedding-in of any

new legislation but this is still daunting for parents faced with being the first to raise a challenge.

On the ground, special schools are working hard to ensure that parents can easily access information about their services. If you follow-up entries in this guide with a visit to school websites you should be able to get a real feel, both for what is provided and what the school 'feels' like. Many schools now have videos on their websites to help give you a much more instant sense of the school. Most schools are open to parents visiting to get a better sense of whether the school might be the right place for their child.

Whilst the country faces a year of political change, the indications are that all the major political parties have committed to allowing the SEN reforms time to bed-in. This will be welcome news to all – we all feel there is more than enough flux to be negotiating at the moment! The work of implementing the reforms is going to be carried out over several years and whilst we may have all wished for a magic wand to be cast on the 1st September the reality is more a case of everyone rolling up their sleeves and digging in for the long haul.

Forty years of change and learning

We turn the spotlight on Phil Champion, the Operations Manager (Schools and Colleges) at Hesley Group, who has enjoyed a long career in special education

Reflecting on a career that started in 1973 at a teacher training college in North-West England, Phil Champion (pictured right) identifies three key attributes which have helped throughout this time, namely stamina, a sense of humour and an ability to "think outside the box". We focus on teaching, as we consider the intervening years which have passed so quickly.

Retaining an interest outside work, in addition to being very much a family man has been very important. Originally a physical education teacher (and a footballer of no mean ability, independent report has indicated), Phil is a life-long Liverpool football club supporter. He was often buoyed, through any difficult times in the first half of his career, by the success of the team. He admits he more frequently had to look elsewhere for inspiration in the second half. While he might possibly be moving towards extra time in career-terms, Phil retains enthusiasm for all things education-related, as well as for Liverpool.

Phil has worked through a period of huge change in special education. He cites the Warnock Report of 1978 and the subsequent 1981 Education Act, as having had particular impact, with the formal introduction of the notion of "special educational needs" (SEN) and of "statements", the emphasis on integration and inclusion and the identification of common educational goals for all children – independence, enjoyment and understanding – whatever the nature or level of their abilities or disabilities. Phil notes the development of the National Curriculum, further to the 1988 Education Act, had specific effects on education for children with complex needs and disabilities and on the wider context in which provision evolved and was viewed, with for example, the impact on schools of league tables and potentially associated issues such as inclusion policy.

Latterly, the Children and Families Act of 2014 has the potential Phil feels, to have over time, the same seismic influence as did the Warnock Report, if all parties can embrace a number of particular opportunities he believes it offers: firstly, a renewed emphasis on every child, whatever their start in life, having an equal chance to reach for their full potential; secondly, of families receiving greater and more consistent support to remain positively involved for the long term in – and contributing to – the lives of children with complex and potentially challenging needs; and thirdly, of actively and fully supporting for

longer, children and young people who need more time to learn.

It is in the context of legislative change, considerable economic and political flux and changing fortunes for Liverpool Football Club, that Phil has pursued his career. Initially the focus for Phil was on working with young people with emotional and behavioural disorders. Over time this focus became one of autism, learning disabilities and associated complex needs.

In 1974 while studying for a dual teacher and youth leader qualification, a summer opportunity arose for Phil, in a small assessment and treatment service, to work as a relief residential social worker and teach P.E. and General Subjects to young offenders. He loved the work

HESLEY HELPED ME TO HELP MYSELF.

We're one of the UK's leading independent providers of residential services, schools and colleges supporting people with autism and complex needs.

Our highly trained staff provide the highest quality, person-centred approach. Giving those who use our services the support, skills and tools they need to be as independent as possible.

Our unique Hesley Enhancing Lives Programme (HELP) is a big part of this.

Combining the latest techniques and practices, HELP is our successful value-based positive behaviour support programme. Based on the principles of Therapeutic Crisis Intervention which is accredited by the British Institute of Learning Disabilities, HELP reduces the need for high-risk interventions by taking an empathic and proactive approach. We focus on how our actions can positively shape the emotional well-being of all those who use our services. It's why all our staff are given HELP training to make sure it works in practice as well as theory.

Find out more about the Hesley Enhancing Lives Programme visit **www.hesleygroup.co.uk** or call us **0800 055 6789**.

1975
2015
Hesley Group
Celebrating 40 years

Established in 1975, Hesley Group, through its schools and colleges support 8 to 25 year olds with a highly experienced and expert multidisciplinary educational, care and therapeutic staff resource, in high quality purpose built settings. We're focused on positive outcomes and progress towards sustainable independence.

and the challenges and responsibility that went with it. When he qualified as a teacher in 1976, Phil joined what was then a residential Community Home with Education, staying in this job for eight fulfilling years. One highlight of this time was co-founding a regional Residential Schools Sports Association, involving nine special schools in a range of regular sporting activities, which had not been tried in that geographical area before, in particular for boys who presented the range of needs and challenges that they did. The overall initiative – and the individual fixtures – proved highly successful, with staff committing actively and with far fewer problems occurring than some predicted. There were many positive outcomes, including in relation to team-work, an exposure to winning - and losing - well; and some great fun, for the young people – and staff – involved.

At this point – in the aftermath of the Warnock Report and the subsequent 1981 Education Act – Phil was seconded by National Children's Homes, who ran the school, to do an Honours Degree in Special Education, which greatly helped draw theory and practice together, forming a key foundation stone in his further career development.

Stamina, a sense of humour and "thinking outside the box" all helped Phil enjoy this part of his career as much as he did. When on duty one break-time, Phil "lost" "half" of the 66 boys at the school, who absconded only to return one-by-one, in a way guaranteed to stretch his nerves and the amusement of the boys and some more experienced colleagues, to the maximum.

Phil moved on to become, for five years, a senior teacher and Acting Deputy Head of a local authority residential school for children with moderate learning difficulties (as described at that time), which helped hone his managerial skills and during which time he supported local mainstream schools with the integration agenda.

In 1989 Phil joined the Hesley Group, as Deputy Head at a school near Doncaster, with a remit to revise educational provision there, for boys aged 5-13 years with emotional and behavioural disorders, in line with the newly emergent National Curriculum. Around this time, Hesley was developing its first schools for children and young people with Autism. In January 1994 Phil moved to Fullerton House School near Doncaster, as Head, to lead a new senior management team, in the development of a service for 8-19 year olds with autism, learning disabilities and complex needs, including behaviour which challenged. He was involved in developing the first care modern apprenticeships of the current era and loved, as ever, the opportunity to see – and help – young people and staff progress positively.

Phil has had a number of senior roles within the Hesley Group since this time, including his current Operational Lead role for Children's and College Services. Though the option of retirement has offered itself, it seems that Phil is intent on extra time and passing on his experience, expertise and passion for positive education, for a while yet to come.

For more information on Hesley Group schools, see page 30

New SEN system is 'a work in progress...'

Douglas Silas, Principal of Douglas Silas Solicitors, gives some thoughts on the the new SEN legal framework

Gosh - I can't believe that it's been seven months already (or more by the time you read this)...

When I wrote an article for 'Which School for Special Needs' at about this time last year, we were still awaiting the Children and Families Bill to be given Royal Assent to allow for a new SEN framework to apply from September 2014.

My concerns a year ago

Last year I said: 'I do not have a crystal ball to be able to look into the future and see what will happen...' But, with only a few months left to go, I expressed the following concerns even at that late stage:

- About there still not being clear guidance to schools and Local Authorities (LAs);
- About the language and structure of the (already by then 2nd draft) Code of Practice still seeming inaccessible to parents of children with special educational needs (SEN) and young people with SEN; and
- About there still not being a clear, detailed and unambiguous framework for Education, Health and Care (EHC) assessments and plans (which were due to replace Statements of SEN).

I also expressed a fear that this system could again lead to another 'postcode lottery' if there was no national set of standards.

Fortunately, the Government subsequently issued a revised final draft of the Code of Practice and made some amendments to the Bill before it received Royal Assent and a new Code of Practice was issued at the end of July 2014 (after schools had already broken up for the summer) to come into effect in September 2014. To many people's great concern, the Government only produced a revised version of its 'Transitional Guidance' at the end of August 2014, just a few days before the new law came into effect.

A year on

Well, here we are a year on and I now have the advantage of talking about what I have seen during the past seven months or so. I am pleased to say that the whole SEN system did not come to a standstill on 1 September 2014, but it does seem to me that there has already been a lot of confusion and anxiety generated amongst both parents and professionals during these first few months.

The definitions of SEN and special educational provision (SEP) remain roughly the same as they were before. However, as well as children, 'young people' are now referred to in their own right if they are over 16 years of age (at least at the end of the academic year in which they turn 16). It is again still not SEN if a child or a young person has a different home language as before, although now health and care provision can be considered as special educational provision, where it is provided for educational or training purposes.

Part 3 of the Children and Families Act 2014 covers things like:

- Education, Health and Care (or EHC) provision, including the need for integration between services and the joint commissioning of services;
- The need for cooperation and assistance (both internally and externally) to do this;
- The provision of information and advice;
- The procedures for EHC needs assessments and the making of EHC plans following assessments;
- Information about appeals, mediation and dispute resolution processes; and
- Functions of LAs and schools, etc.

I am pleased to say that the whole SEN system did not come to a standstill on 1 September 2014, but it does seem to me that there has already been a lot of confusion and anxiety generated amongst both parents and professionals during these first few months.

One of the main concerns expressed before the new SEN framework came into effect was the structure of EHC plans. Now that there is more flexibility and 'localism' to be able to do things in their own way (as opposed to before when things were more prescribed by law), each LA has taken advantage of this fact and seems to be doing things a bit differently to the next. This means that we now have up to 152 different types of EHC plans!

Now, rather than having the same six parts as a Statement had...

- Part 1 - Personal Details
- Part 2 - Special Educational Needs
- Part 3 - Special Educational Provision
- Part 4 - School or Other Placement
- Part 5 - Non-educational Needs
- Part 6 - Non-educational Provision

... EHC plans have a minimum of 12 statutory sections...

- Section A -Views/Interests/Aspirations of the child/ young person (and his or her parents);
- Section B - Special Educational Needs;
- Section C - Health Needs (which relate to the SEN);
- Section D - Social Care Needs (which relate to the SEN);
- Section E - Outcomes;
- Section F - Special Educational Provision(required to meet the SEN described);
- Section G Health Provision (reasonably required by the SEN or disability);
- Section H1 - Social Care Provision (made under the Chronically Sick and Disabled Persons Act 1970);
- Section H2 - Other Social ;Care Provision (reasonably required by the SEN or Disability);
- Section I - Placement (which includes both the name and type of school/nursery/post-16 or other

institution). Section I is left blank in a draft EHC Plan to allow parents/young people to express a preference for an educational institution to be named

- Section J - Personal Budget (if agreed, including any arrangements that have been made for any direct payments);
- Section K - Advice/Information used to prepare the EHC plan (referred to previously as the 'Appendices' to a Statement).

I am all for this new more comprehensive structure. However, parents have been very surprised and angry to find out that they can still only appeal about the SEN, the SEP and school/institution that is named in, respectively, sections B, F and I (as opposed to parts 2, 3 and 4 of Statements). So, although EHC plans now have new sections about Health 'needs and provision' and Care 'needs and provision' (both H1 and H2) and, even more importantly, dedicated sections about 'Outcomes' (section E) and 'Personal Budgets (section J), parents cannot appeal against these new sections.

The whole theme behind the new SEN framework was to try and resolve disputes as early as possible and start 'working together towards mutually agreed outcomes'; but parents have been shocked to find out that 'Outcomes' in an EHC plan cannot be appealed against if they are disputed (unlike with the 'Objectives' in statements). Instead, they have to be agreed during the EHC needs assessment or as a result of the Annual Review of the EHC plan. I have already heard parents complaining: "They have given with one hand and taken back with the other".

Also, although, theoretically, EHC plans now go from 0-25, practically, there is no automatic expectation or entitlement that they will continue until then, only if the 'Outcomes' on them (which I have said cannot be challenged) have not yet been achieved. There is already a fear on behalf of children/young people with SEN that some LAs will put low achieving 'outcomes' in EHC plans so that they can later argue that the 'Outcomes' in the plan have been achieved and it is therefore no longer necessary to maintain it. This is very worrying.

There is now a duty to admit a child or young person, not only to a maintained school named in an EHC plan, but also to other types of schools or institutions that may be named in it, such as an academy, a further education (or FE) institution, a non-maintained special school, or a 'Section 41 approved' independent institution.

There is just too much detail in the new SEN Code of Practice, so I would not be able to do it proper justice here in such a short article. Although, as before, in relation to statutory assessments for Statements of SEN, a request for an EHC needs assessment can still be made by parents or a school; a request for an EHC needs assessment can now also be made by a young person themselves, or if a child is brought to the attention of the LA by another body, such as a health or care agency.

Overall, there seem to be lots of 'teething' difficulties as would normally be expected but I have already seen that, although the aim was to try and make EHC plans more 'understandable, accessible, clear and concise' than Statements, many EHC plans that I have seen, are running to about 15-20 pages. I have even been told by one legal colleague that she has seen an EHC plan of over 50 pages!

Conclusion

I have noticed that Statements have become lengthier and more detailed over the years, so are we again overcomplicating things? How does this sit with what we are used to and what we are aiming for now? Perhaps this is the difference between 'theory' and 'practice'? The Children and Families Act says that the new SEN Code of Practice must be revised from time to time. Believe it or not, as I write this at the beginning of April 2015, a new version has just been issued.

I often say that it took us 10-20 years to get used to the old system, but we now seem to be starting again. The main thing to realise is that it will take time to effect proper cultural change. Are EHC plans really just 'E' plans with a bit of 'H' and 'C' tagged on? Are we going to be able to change things from a 'fight' culture between 'warrior parents' and LA 'bureaucracy' to now 'working together towards agreed outcomes'? Are we going to see a lot of inter-agency disputes? How are we going to square the concept of 'best possible' outcomes with the previous requirement to only provide an 'adequate' education and the fact that no pupil is entitled to a 'Rolls Royce' education?

Although the House of Lords approved the final version of the Code of Practice at the end of July 2014, in June 2014, when the final draft of the Code of Practice was issued, its Scrutiny Committee stated that: 'There is a 'real risk' that [the Code of Practice] may imperfectly achieve its glossy objectives'

I truly hope that SEN provision will not prove again to be a 'postcode lottery'. I think that we now need to take a more pragmatic approach and work with what we have. Importantly, we always need to remember the child or young person. I know that this seems obvious, but it is very easy to forget the child or young person sometimes, with too much focus on policies, rights, funding and the law. We must also remember that children, young people and their families have now been put at the 'heart' of the process. As I said last year, EHC plans are not meant to be just statements by another name that now go up to 25.

I guess it is still early days for everyone and we should just look at things as a 'Work In Progress'...

Douglas Silas Solicitors are the only solicitors specialising exclusively in SEN, whose website is www.SpecialEducationalNeeds.co.uk

Douglas is also the author of 'A Guide To The SEN Code of Practice (What You Need To Know)' which is available for all eBook readers. For further information visit: www.AGuideToTheSENCodeOfPractice.co.uk

Special Education: research into practical skills therapeutic learning

Dr Mandy Nelson, Director of Research and Collaboration at Ruskin Mill Land Trust, outlines a new MA to start in September 2015

Over the last 6 months, colleagues at the Ruskin Mill Land Trust have been working closely with colleagues at Lillehammer University College in Norway to develop an innovative Masters programme in Special Education. The programme focuses specifically on Practical Skills Transformative Learning which embodies the Ruskin Mill Trust approach to special needs education (Practical Skills Therapeutic Education). In December 2014, we received the exciting news that the proposed Masters had been approved by Lillehammer University College.

The impulse for the creation of this new and innovative Masters was the need to re-think special education in light of the evidence of failure within traditional educational systems, as demonstrated by disengagement and drop out, and the growth in the number of learners with learning difficulties and/or emotional problems. As a result, the Masters seeks to explore pedagogic approaches to learning in order to ensure that they are fit for purpose and meet the needs of both evolving educational systems and society.

The Masters programme is about exploring and enhancing alternative pedagogic approaches to special needs education through the medium of practical skills. The use of practical skills in learning creates the potential for transformation in young people, as learners. It focuses on the importance of increasing the prominence of practical and aesthetic traditions and giving them renewed vigour and status within current pedagogies. Special needs educators will benefit from being educated and trained to adopt pedagogic processes which embed sensory participation and practical skills. Through this, they can become agents of change, as social entrepreneurs, creating insights and developing skills through using resources from outside the traditional classroom in the facilitating transformative learning.

Through the combination of theoretical, practical and experiential approaches, the Masters seeks to facilitate the development and evaluation of new and innovative approaches in the area of education, with specific reference to [children and] young people with learning disabilities and/ or special needs. In this it will focus upon, problematise and provoke existing perspectives in the area of special needs education.

> The use of practical skills in learning creates the potential for transformation in young people, as learners. It focuses on the importance of increasing the prominence of practical and aesthetic traditions and giving them renewed vigour and status within current pedagogies.

The programme is aimed at individuals with an interest in exploring alternative approaches to special needs education. It will give programme participants the opportunity to research and experience practical skills as a form of transformative learning within the context of a pedagogic laboratory. Through conducting research within the field and exploring and evaluating existing practice (practice informed research), it seeks to further develop and enhance practice (research informed practice).

By agreement with the government of Norway, as the Masters is an award of Lillehammer University College, there are currently no student course fees attached (other than a small annual administration fee) for EU students.

The programme will be delivered over two years through a series of residential blocks located at Ruskin Mill Trust's Field Centre in Nailsworth (UK) and Lillehammer University College (Norway). It will combine theoretical studies and philosophical debate with reflection through practical application and experiential learning, within the context of craft skills, biodynamic ecology and transformative movement. The programme will be delivered through a combination of lectures, seminars and workshops and will provide an additional opportunity for students to engage in research within the context of a real-world laboratory.

Some Challenges Need
Ambitious and Innovative Solutions!

Work Experience:
Ben delivering organic produce he helped to grow, harvest and account for, to a local shop

Ruskin Mill Trust transforms lives for people with ASD including Asperger Syndrome, learning difficulties and differences, mental health issues and challenging behaviour

"It is brilliant here because I can come out of my shell. Here I am treated as a person and as a grown-up. I love working with my hands and having a challenge. I feel a lot calmer!" Ben, 1st-year, Coleg Plas Dwbl

re-imagining potential

Our young people learn and achieve through practical, real-life activities and accredited courses to progress onto greater independence, further education, training and employment.

Ruskin Mill Trust's *Practical Skills Therapeutic Education* draws on the understanding that developmental delay can be addressed by the intentional re-connection of head, hand and heart. An integrated programme of practical skills, contemporary apprenticeship and home-care, enables learners and residents to undertake their own journey to re-imagine their potential.

To find out more about our innovative, holistic and personalised curriculum for day and residential students, delivered by trained and expert staff, contact our nearest provision or visit our website: www.rmt.org

Ruskin Mill Trust draws its inspiration from the insights of Rudolf Steiner, John Ruskin and William Morris. Charity No: 1137167

Why research practice-based learning?

Will Mercer, from Ruskin Mill Trust, explores some current thinking on why practical skills programmes are considered beneficial for those in special education.

There is increasing interest and research into the effects of learning through practical skills programmes that are driven by relationship-centred and contemporary apprenticeship models. The current focus on an academic qualification to populate the modern workforce leaves a considerable amount of people outside of mainstream educational options with subsequent ongoing, and often life-long, negative ramifications. Specialist provision has stepped in and pioneered bespoke methods to enable a wide spectrum of disempowered learners to have options of moving forward with their lives.

At the heart of these specialist methods, is an overriding belief that the brain can be worked with and developed throughout life and that it has the capacity to overcome areas of damage, trauma or developmental delay such as that diagnosed in Autism, ADHD, injury or a range of other syndromes. The question therefore arises: Is the brain plastic, able to regenerate in adulthood and re-programme itself by developing new channels of

transmission that bypass normal pathways and synapses that appear blocked or damaged?

For those engaged in the field the answer is a resounding yes and one of the key pieces of research concerns the relationship between the brain and the hand, where it is proposed that brain development is influenced by sophisticated and sensitive information received from the hand engaged in real-time, productive activity (Frank R Wilson). Interaction with the environment through hands-on activity is therefore seen as the means to encourage brain plasticity and development capacity previously considered impossible or unlikely.

This relationship between qualitative physical activity and cognitive development to promote renewed self-confidence, improved social and communication skills, adaptability to change and greater social effectiveness, is the goal for all providers of special education whose vision is to maximise the potential for each individual. This approach supports a host of practical programmes

Entertaining a holistic approach to development should include a healthy combination of head, heart and hand or thinking, feeling and doing

and cultural and social scenarios whose focus is to feed, nourish and re-programme the brain.

This symbiotic and inter-related dynamic between head and hand is further nurtured by the support and enthusiasm of those engaged in teaching and caring. From parent and family, to school, social groups and friendships, the sense of warmth and wellbeing can only be engendered if positive support underpins the education and development of an individual. For many children and young people who suffer from negative role models, adding the socially binding ingredients of support and warmth to the positive boundaries and creative resistance met through practical activities and their multi-transferable skills, promotes wholesome attitudes and outcomes.

Entertaining a holistic approach to development therefore, should include a healthy combination of head, heart and hand or thinking, feeling and doing. It is hoped that the forthcoming MA in Special Education will complement and add to ongoing research into the relatedness of the human organism, and the effectiveness of pioneering approaches to enhance the quality of people's lives. For further information visit: www. thefieldcentre.org.uk/ma

For more information about the Ruskin Mill Trust, see page 34

Multi-sensory classroom is 'a revelation' for pupils with severe learning difficulties

Nicola Stephens reports on an exciting new development at Kisimul School

In September 2014, Kisimul Schools supported the investment of a fully integrated, immersive sensory classroom at their lower school Swinderby site in Lincolnshire. The Kisimul Group supports pupils with severe learning difficulties and challenging behaviour, generally with a diagnosis of autism. Pupils at the Swinderby School are aged between eight and sixteen and currently have access to a wide and varied curriculum supporting life skills, functional skills and promoting independence and the development of communication.

The rationale behind such an innovative development for the school was to offer our pupils a multi-sensory, interactive environment in which pupils are fully immersed in a particular theme through the medium of ICT and sensory play. The intention is that pupils are to

be given the opportunity to explore a topic by having available to them a multitude of sensory play activities, sensory stories, an interactive floor, themed lighting, sounds and projections.

Sessions are intended to be mainly pupil-led and the focus for them are interaction and engagement in either a one to one or a small group to enhance learning opportunities and communication. In addition, it was hoped that pupils would benefit from intensive interaction opportunities and from sensory stimulation based around weekly topic areas linked to the school's overall termly topic.

The reactions to the interactive sensory classroom, and the popularity of it amongst our pupils since its install, has been incredibly positive. From giving pupils the opportunity to find themselves in the middle of a snow covered, scented, pine wood amongst the characters from 'The Gruffalo's Child', to allowing them to take a journey into 'Space' and act out role-play adventures dressed as astronauts while zapping rockets and aliens on the interactive floor, the pupils have been enlightened and astounded by the potential available to them.

Pupils have been involved in a lively Chinese New Year street parade. They have enjoyed an explosive Bonfire Night party, using an iPad to project large images of fireworks onto the wall. Pupils have been able to engage with images of fireworks on the interactive floor in order to hear them zooming and whizzing as they seemingly disappear beneath their touch.

Students have explored 'Autumn' through the use of sensory stories, adapted to include accessible, interactive ICT software. They have also celebrated 'Australia Day' using themed props and lighting, observing iconic Australian scenes projected onto walls whilst being able to use interactive maps of Australasia on the interactive floor, not to mention, relaxing in the company of a didgeridoo therapist.

Pupils have been encouraged to discover their environment independently to create a pupil-led session of exploration and realisation, supported by a teacher to oversee, guide and support the pupils to participate positively in the activities they choose to do.

Our multi-sensory classroom has been pivotally important in being able to support our sensory pupils who require an immersive, practical and varied learning environment in order to thrive. The interactive floor offers opportunities to develop an understanding of cause and effect, as does the interactive iPad system, which pupils can use to change the lighting in the room at the press of a button or the roll of an interactive dice. Our pupils can relax on the vibro-acoustic bed while having their feet and hands massaged along with feeling the vibrations of their preferred music, or perhaps listening to a sensory story handling topic-related objects and sharing the experience with staff.

This development and addition to our school has offered our pupils the chance to experience different ways of communicating with others. Turn taking and sharing can be developed and promoted by using various parts of their body to scatter stars or leaves on the interactive floor or to 'swim' through an ocean, wiping away waves to reveal different sea creatures along the way. Seeing the pupils' reactions to revealing an

> It was a joy to witness the excitement and amazement of one of our pupils, as he, with guidance from staff, was able to use software to edit the strip lights, spotlights and bubble wall to colours of his choosing.

autumnal photograph of themselves, beneath a cover of leaves that they themselves can wipe away using their hands or feet has been magical. It was a joy to witness the excitement and amazement of one of our pupils, as he, with guidance from staff, was able to use software to edit the strip lights, spotlights and bubble wall to colours of his choosing.

By offering such a range of activities and experiences to our pupils, we have witnessed a pupil shed a tear at being able to hear his own voice, projected through the use of a microphone beamed from the speakers around the room; pupils' confidence in transitioning has progressed; a pupil, prior to visits to the multi-sensory classroom, was reluctant to accept sharing personal space, will now share sensory stories and scent bottles while exploring the seasons.

Still somewhat in its infancy, our multi-sensory classroom has so far been a revelation. Pupils have developed in confidence, their ability to interact and communicate with others has progressed and regardless of ability level, the pupils have flourished in this immersive, multi-sensory environment. Due to the success of this venture, Kisimul Group intends to install further multi-sensory immersive classrooms at both our Upper School site, Acacia Hall, near Market Rasen in Lincolnshire, and at our Woodstock school site in Surbiton, Surrey. It is anticipated that these limitless innovations to our school's learning environments will continue to enhance our pupils' learning and encourage positive interactions and experiences for new and current pupils alike.

For more information about Kisimul schools, see page 32

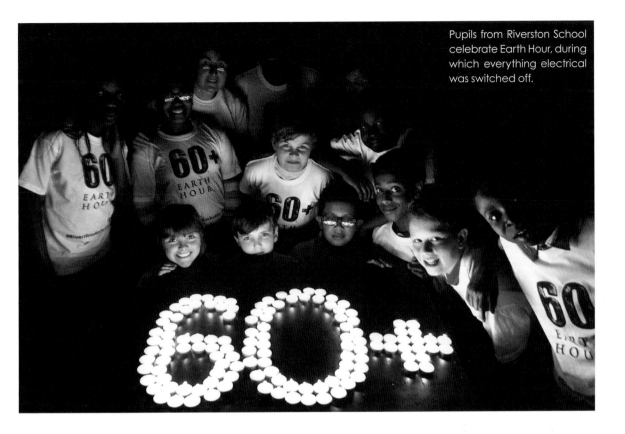

Connecting with the world around us

James D Allen, Deputy Headmaster of Riverston School, on a week of learning and fun designed to change understanding and attitudes

In every school, the curriculum and the school's over-arching aims and goals that underpin its ethos continue on a daily, weekly and termly basis. Sport, extra-curricular activities and curriculum options reinforce a school's attitudes towards education, its pupils and what is important in preparing children for life beyond school. It is predictable, routined and comfortable, exactly as it should be to enable pupils to succeed within a structured and familiar environment.

This predictable pattern is punctuated by equally predictable events which break that routine, bring pupils off-timetable, further enabling the school to deliver what is considered to be important beyond the curriculum. A service of remembrance to commemorate the Centenary of WWI, a day spent dressed as your favourite book character for World Book Day, or a cake sale to raise money for Red Nose Day are all examples of how the school's daily routine is interspersed – and enhanced – by

foreseeable activities. Unpredictable events (often less positive and uplifting) present a necessary opportunity to teach, learn, explain, consider and discuss.

January's events that followed the terrorist attacks in Paris, subsequent unity marches across France and the ensuing Charlie Hebdo publication, whilst shocking and disturbing, provided the very real chance for pupils to understand the impact of actions around the globe. Discussions for older students centred on the meaning of freedom of speech and expression; should the resulting impact of that freedom have any bearing on the action? During that week of 'living history' it is critical that, as a school, no view or opinion is expressed by staff, but rather all sides of a debate are presented to allow pupils to consider their own views. These questions are considered and pupils supported in their understanding of such events within the context of a structured and familiar routine.

Riverston School

Recently, the country has celebrated British Science Week – a chance to celebrate anything and everything scientific – to wow, to engage, to impress and to enable enquiry. With the end of term approaching, immediately followed by the WWF's worldwide Earth Hour, an opportunity appeared to present itself to engage the whole of Riverston School in a final week of learning and fun that would be remembered and, it is hoped, would in some small part, change understanding and attitudes. And so, it was agreed...British Science Week and Earth Hour would combine in a tumultuous timetable of activities that would conclude the spring term in the most dramatic and erudite fashion, culminating in the school's very own Earth Hour shut-down.

Our team of scintillating scientific specialists astounded and wowed us on a daily basis with lesser-known facts, feats of the impossible and experiments to help us to question and to comprehend. Science assemblies opened the week and, following a trip to Homebase for the essentials, our younger pupils began the process of creating their own mini bio-domes, as Year 7 and 8 students Skyped with a group of students from Urbnisi School in Georgia.

The middle of the week brought the opportunity for mufty as pupils across the school arrived in their own clothes, not only bringing a pound for the privilege. The day was to present so much more than simply fund raising. The previous two weeks had seen the school's foyer turned into an extract from The X-Factor as break times became an ever-present chance to practise those critical moves that would create the final piece on Wednesday afternoon. Bedecked in specially-designed t-shirts and led by one teacher's unstoppable enthusiasm, the whole school from year 6 to year 13 walked from Lee to Blackheath to perform an imaginative and energetic flashmob dance to attract the attention of the local community. Pedestrians stopped in awe of the spectacle, bus travellers were seen waving in support of this worthy cause, and local walkers joined in with this most unique of impromptu gatherings. Of course it might be considered that to include a group of teenaged boys, dress them in attention-grabbing t-shirts, put them in public and ask them to dance, something of a tall order at best, and a risk at worst! However, the school rose to the occasion as upwards of sixty students and staff danced their global socks off, with the rest of the school in hand-clapping support. It was a spectacle, it was an achievement and it raised the profile of this global occasion for students and staff, their families, and the local community and beyond.

As this most global of weeks forged ahead, the school was fortunate to have representatives from the Lush Company to talk to and work with the students on creating sustainable bags from scarves. Practical, hands-on activities to enhance their learning and understanding of what British Science Week and Earth Hour are all about. As Friday arrived, the students enjoyed the Science Olympiad, a triad of challenging experiments to design floating vessels, three-dimensional spaghetti structures and the largest bubble. With hands-on learning at the heart of the entire week, this couple of hours was no different. Whilst some hands were getting wet with water, sticky with marshmallow and creative with tinfoil, others were similarly resourceful with a sewing machine in support of the official launch of the Riverston bag for life. Bags-for-Life is a whole school upcycling initiative which aims to inspire students and the wider community to think creatively about waste. All bags are made from materials destined to end up in a land fill – donated fabric remnants, trimmings and surplus garments. Each bag is unique and made individually by hand bearing our own 'Handmade@Riverston' label. All proceeds from the bags will contribute to tree-planting next term, reducing our environmental impact and further raising the profile of this cause.

And finally...twenty-four hours ahead of Saturday's global Earth Hour, this unique of weeks climaxed with the school's very own electrical shutdown. Lights, computers, monitors, projectors and screens, telephones, cookers and sewing machines, were switched off between two and three o'clock. In Food Technology, pupils in year 9 cooked miniature pancakes using recycled tin cans, a candle and a lot of patience! Those in year 6 created catwalk dresses and accessories from bin liners and clothing cast-offs. After five days of high-energy activity, learning and unique events, British Science Week at Riverston School finished in the calmest of ways with an hour without power.

Bags for life and a Skype link with a Georgian school...exploding corks, mini bio-domes and a flashmob dance in Blackheath, assemblies, experiments and a conclusion to the week switching off from everything that has become familiar and accustomed. Not a bad way to immerse us all in learning, launching us into the Easter holidays full of scientific enquiry and engagement with the world around us.

For more information about Riverston School, see page 41

The pursuit of value

Clare King, Headmistress at The Moat School, says a new assessment technique could hold the key to measuring a school's performance

What is the role of an educator? When you peel back the layers of bureaucracy and buzz-words that exist in the increasingly competitive schools sector, this remains the ever-present question we should ask ourselves as head teachers, teachers, SENCOs and parents. The role of 'teacher' in education goes beyond the responsibility of passing along information. The primary function of the teacher includes teaching a variety of facts and skills to pupils but, additionally, the teacher encourages a sense of value and meaningfulness intended to stimulate a child's social development. The aim is to produce well-rounded, articulate and inquisitive young people who are able to question the world around them, and confident in their ability to analyse their own learning along the

way. But how do you measure a school's effectiveness at doing this?

Traditionally schools have been measured against each other using simple results and league tables. From the point at which exams were standardised we had an accurate measure of how one student fared against another and therefore how to quantify the success of a school. So how do you compare a gritty urban comprehensive with a prestigious boarding school, for example, when schools with selective entry can cherry pick the highest achievers and compete on a very unfair playing field?

The Centre for Evaluation and Monitoring (CEM) is an independent not-for-profit organisation with over thirty years of experience in pioneering value-added assessments. As part of Durham University, CEM are the leading body on measuring effectiveness and provide feedback to schools to improve their delivery of learning. It is CEM's MidYIS (Middle Years Information System) assessment (taken in year 7, 8 or 9) which forms the basis of interesting data that can serve to more accurately illustrate a school's relative performance.

The assessment measures 'developed ability' – a student's underlying raw learning potential, free of the influence of curriculum-based teaching. To establish a baseline, each student takes a test in four parts - vocabulary, maths, non-verbal and skills – which contribute to an overall curriculum-free measurement. The tests are intended to gauge aptitude for learning rather than achievement and allows a teacher to accurately determine areas for improvement in their students.

These baseline figures can be used to predict achievement and GCSE grades for an individual and, from these predictions, it is possible to see where a school has added 'value' to a child's schooling. When a school increases students' achievement level relative to other schools, this relative advantage is called value-added. Once students have taken GCSE or have KS3 teacher assessed grades, their results are collected for value-added analysis.

Choosing the right school for your child can be one of the most daunting tasks a parent will ever undertake. This can be considerably more overwhelming if the child has specific learning difficulties (SpLD). We all dream of our children excelling at school – in maths, English, sport or music, but for some children, just getting through the normal school day can be challenging enough. With a bit of luck, a pupil's school will flag up any learning difficulties around Year 2 and suggest an assessment, although many children with SpLD can remain undiagnosed for much longer. Parents may have suspected their child

was not keeping up, even though his or her intelligence appeared 'normal', otherwise it could come as a bolt out of the blue. It is at this stage that parents usually wonder what they should be doing.

Increasingly, for the parents of a child with a specific learning difficulty, the measure of a school's success and subsequent suitability comes from outside the traditional measures of achievement and, although the GCSE results of a particular school will definitely be of interest to a prospective parent, more often the pastoral care and nurturing learning environment that a school encourages forms the basis of any decision.

Specialist schools provide children diagnosed with a SpLD the opportunity of receiving an academic education in a safe and supportive learning environment up to GCSE for children between the ages of 11 to 16 years. It comes as no surprise to parents that their children often possess extraordinary talents and creativity and it is an important goal for these schools to identify and foster this by providing additional courses in non-traditional subjects such as creative and performing arts, food technology, computer technology, art and design, media studies and design technology. Pupils will need individual timetables that address their needs and classes must be small with a high teacher/ pupil ratio. A school may often offer an enrichment programme that enhances the pupil's skills academically, emotionally and socially. It is well known that the progress of pupils at these type of holistic specialist schools is typically outstanding. This reinforces the belief that, given the opportunity and resources at the right age, despite their difficulties, these children can make meaningful improvements to the quality of their lives and their contributions to society.

The MidYIS assessment, and subsequent value-added scores, could hold the key to truly understanding how well a student has achieved and how successful a school has been in helping them on their journey.

Clare King is Headmistress at The Moat School.

The Moat School is an independent secondary day-school for pupils with specific learning difficulties. CEM reported that despite increasingly complex cohorts, average value added data over 3 years shows The Moat School performing in the top 5% of schools nationally

For more information about The Moat School, see page 68.

Choosing a special needs school

Educational psychologist and author Ruth Birnbaum offers practical advice on seeking effective education for children with special educational needs

No-one is prepared for having a special needs child and developmental difficulties know no boundaries. Parents are often in a quandary about whether a school is appropriate and suitable for their individual child and even whether they should travel the mainstream or special school route.

In writing my book, Choosing a School for a Child with Special Needs (2010), I hoped to demystify the process and empower parents to ask questions of schools when they visit, so that a more balanced view can be reached and an objective decision can be made. Parents need to work together with schools and other professionals to decide what their child needs and how their strengths can be realised in a school context. While parents live with their child every day and have much to offer, they also have to listen to advice. Weighing up what really matters is possible and choices can be made on the best evidence available.

Choosing a school is such an important decision that it cannot be left to chance.

Here are some helpful pointers:

1. Look at the primary area of need
The 2014 Code of Practice sets out four areas of special educational needs:
- Communication and Interaction
- Cognition and Learning
- Social, Emotional and Mental Health
- Sensory and Physical

2. Understand the Background
Understand the role of psychological assessment and draw up a list of schools which state they can meet the assessed need and then obtain the documents that will help you restrict your list to those schools that need to be visited.

3. Set up a Visit
Make sure a visit is set up with the right people; look at the general physical school environment, as well as the classroom environment. Make a record of the school visit. Look at the Local Offer in your Local Authority.

4. Look at Specific Provision/Intervention
Consider the type of provision in both mainstream and special schools. Probe and analyse what is available in reality and the professional support the child will receive.

What are the qualifications needed? What type of intervention could be available? Does the school offer help with Specific Learning Difficulties/Sensory Needs/Autistic Provision; are different therapies available; eg Art Therapy; Music Therapy; Drama Therapy; Play Therapy or Psychotherapy. Does the school offer Counselling and Mentoring? Can the child access Speech and Language Therapy, Occupational Therapy and Physiotherapy?

5. Consider other important issues
Levels of Integration and Inclusion; Religious Beliefs; Co-Education; School Size; Small Classes; Transition; Equality and Discrimination. In all cases, there will be practical questions to ask.

6. Think about other School Models available
There can be a range of different school models to consider, depending on the need; such as mainstream, special units in mainstream, special schools, dual-placements, pupil referral units, residential schools, home education, hospital schools, studio schools and virtual schools.

7. Summarise your thoughts
Evaluate findings on a spreadsheet with your own comments and compare school visits. Trust your first impressions and feelings but be open to other views. Use websites, resources and organisations in the area you are researching. The Local Offer should help you understand

Parents need to work together with schools and other professionals to decide what their child needs and how their strengths can be realised in a school context. While parents live with their child every day and have much to offer, they also have to listen to advice. Weighing up what really matters is possible and choices can be made on the best evidence available.

what education, health and social care services can provide for your child.

Perhaps, a few selective questions from my book will offer some examples:

- A key question, when looking at special schools, is to determine whether all teachers share the specialism, or only some of them; eg if a child is placed in a specialist dyslexic school, will the child receive lessons in History and Geography at secondary level from specialist teachers in their subject area, who have also undertaken SpLD training? If not, one must consider whether the value of attending such a school outweighs a mainstream experience.
- What happens to the class work that the child misses when they are in the special unit? How do they catch up or will they be following the same curriculum in the unit? If the unit has a number of different aged children, are lessons taught across the age ranges in the unit or will children be taught separately?
- Is the Occupational Therapist trained or certified in the use of any standardised diagnostic tools that are used to assess children who might have sensory processing disorder?
- How often is the Speech and Language Therapist in school? Is the focus on individual or group therapy? Does the SaLT spend time in the classroom? How much time?
- In a special school, how many staff have a recognised qualification in the area of need? eg ASD.
- Is there any special equipment already being used in specific subjects; such as Food Technology, Maths, Science, PE, etc?
- In the classroom, note the class sizes and the physical space. Is there room for additional resources; eg a work station or wheelchair? Are the goals and objectives of the lessons clearly set out in a visual format and do the children understand them? Are different strategies used for children who cannot access the usual format?

By making a decision, based on factual evidence where possible, a parent should be able to accept or reject a school on the basis of impartial evaluation.

Using the combination of this guidebook and Choosing a School for a Child with Special Needs, parents will be able to make an informed choice and act as advocates for their child who may not be able to speak for themselves. The new Code of Practice (2014) now extends education for young adults up to 25 years and there is a clearer focus on the views, wishes and feelings of the child and young person and on their role in decision making, so take them on visits and ensure their views are heard whenever possible. It is important that the young person remains at the centre of decision making so that the best possible educational outcomes are achieved.

Ruth Birnbaum is an Educational Psychologist in independent practice with over 30 years' experience in education. She is a registered psychologist with the Health and Care Professions Council. She visits schools across the UK to consider provision and advise parents and consultants on which schools are most appropriate for which children. Website: www.ruthbirnbaum.co.uk

School groups

Hesley Group

**Central Services, Hesley Hall, Tickhill
Doncaster DN11 9NH
Tel: 01302 866906
Fax: 01302 861661
Email: enquiries@hesleygroup.co.uk
Website: www.hesleygroup.co.uk**

Fullerton House College

Tickhill Square, Denaby, Doncaster, South Yorkshire DN12 4AR
Tel: 01709 861663
Fax: 01709 869635
Email: enquiries@hesleygroup.co.uk
Website: www.hesleygroup.co.uk
FOR MORE INFORMATION SEE PAGE 80

Fullerton House School

Tickill Square, Denaby, Doncaster, South Yorkshire DN12 4AR
Tel: 01709 861663
Fax: 01709 869635
Email: enquiries@hesleygroup.co.uk
Website: www.fullertonhouseschool.co.uk
FOR MORE INFORMATION SEE PAGE 81

Wilsic Hall College

Wadworth, Doncaster, South Yorkshire DN11 9AG
Tel: 01302 856382
Email: enquiries@hesleygroup.co.uk
Website: www.hesleygroup.co.uk
FOR MORE INFORMATION SEE PAGE 80

Wilsic Hall School

Wadworth, Doncaster, South Yorkshire DN11 9AG
Tel: 01302 856382
Fax: 01302 853608
Email: enquiries@hesleygroup.co.uk
Website: www.wilsichallschool.co.uk
FOR MORE INFORMATION SEE PAGE 82

I CAN

8 Wakley Street
London EC1V 7QE
Tel: 0845 225 4073
Fax: 0845 225 4072
Email: info@ican.org.uk
Website: www.ican.org.uk

helps children
communicate

REGISTERED CHARITY 210031

I CAN'S Dawn House School

Helmsley Road, Rainworth, Mansfield, Nottinghamshire
NG21 0DQ
Tel: 01623 795361
Fax: 01623 491173
Email: dawnhouse@ican.notts.sch.uk
Website: www.dawnhouseschool.org.uk or www.ican.org.uk
FOR MORE INFORMATION SEE PAGE 66

I CAN's Meath School

Brox Road, Ottershaw, Surrey KT16 0LF
Tel: 01932 872302
Fax: 01932 875180
Email: meath@meath-ican.org.uk
Website: www.meathschool.org.uk or www.ican.org.uk
FOR MORE INFORMATION SEE PAGE 69

Kisimul

**The Old Vicarage, Swinderby
Lincoln LN6 9LU
Tel: 01522 868279
Email: enquiries@kisimul.co.uk
Website: www.kisimul.co.uk**

Cruckton Hall

Cruckton, Shrewsbury, Shropshire SY5 8PR
Tel: 01743 860206
Fax: 01743 860941
Email: marcia.garnett@cruckton.com
Website: www.cruckton.com
FOR MORE INFORMATION SEE PAGE 48

Kisimul School

The Old Vicarage, 61 High Street, Swinderby, Lincoln, Lincolnshire
LN6 9LU
Tel: 01522 868279
Fax: 01522 866000
Email: admissions@kisimul.co.uk
Website: www.kisimul.co.uk
FOR MORE INFORMATION SEE PAGE 64

Kisimul School – Woodstock House

Woodstock Lane North, Long Ditton, Surbiton, Surrey KT6 5HN
Tel: 020 8335 2570
Fax: 020 8335 2571
Email: admissions@kisimul.co.uk
Website: www.kisimul.co.uk
FOR MORE INFORMATION SEE PAGE 70

Kisimul Upper School

Acacia Hall, Shortwood Lane, Friesthorpe, Lincoln, LN3 5AL
Tel: 01673 880022
Fax: 01673 880021
Website: www.kisimul.co.uk

RNIB
105 Judd Street
London WC1H 9NE
Website: www.rnib.org.uk

supporting blind and
partially sighted people

RNIB College Loughborough

Radmoor Road, Loughborough, Leicestershire LE11 3BS

Tel: 01509 611077

Fax: 01509 232013

Email: hannah.wharton@www.rnib.org.uk

Website: www.rnib.org.uk/rnibcollege

FOR MORE INFORMATION SEE PAGE 87

RNIB Pears Centre for Specialist Learning

Wheelwright Lane, Ash Green, Coventry, West Midlands CV7 9RA

Tel: 024 7636 9500

Fax: 024 7636 9501

Email: pearscentre@rnib.org.uk

Website: www.rnib.org.uk/pearscentre

FOR MORE INFORMATION SEE PAGE 97

RNIB Sunshine House School and Residence

33 Dene Road, Northwood, Middlesex HA6 2DD

Tel: 01923 822538

Fax: 01923 826227

Email: shsadmin@rnib.org.uk

Website: www.rnib.org.uk/sunshinehouse

FOR MORE INFORMATION SEE PAGE 88

Ruskin Mill Trust

**Old Bristol Road, Nailsworth
Stroud GL6 0LA
Tel: 01453 837 500
Email: enquiries@rmt.org
Website: www.rmt.org**

Brantwood Specialist School

1 Kenwood Bank, Nether Edge, Sheffield, South Yorkshire S7 1NU
Tel: 0114 258 9062
Email: admin@brantwood.rmt.org
Website: www.rmt.org
FOR MORE INFORMATION SEE PAGE 56

Clervaux

Clow Beck Eco Centre, Jolby Lane, Croft on Tees, North Yorkshire DL2 2TF
Tel: 01325 729860
Email: info@clervaux.org.uk
Website: www.clervaux.org.uk
FOR MORE INFORMATION SEE PAGE 57

Coleg Plas Dwbl

Mynachlog-ddu, Clunderwen, Pembrokeshire SA66 7SE
Tel: 01994 419420
Email: info@plasdwbl.rmt.org
Website: www.rmt.org
FOR MORE INFORMATION SEE PAGE 84

Freeman College

Sterling Works, 88 Arundel Street, Sheffield, South Yorkshire S1 2NG
Tel: 0114 252 5940
Fax: 0114 252 5996
Email: enquiries@fmc.rmt.org
Website: www.rmt.org
FOR MORE INFORMATION SEE PAGE 79

Glasshouse College

Wollaston Road, Amblecote, Stourbridge, West Midlands DY8 4HF
Tel: 01384 399400
Fax: 01384 399401
Email: enquiries@ghc.rmt.org
Website: www.rmt.org
FOR MORE INFORMATION SEE PAGE 76

Ruskin Mill College

The Fisheries, Horsley, Gloucestershire GL6 0PL
Tel: 01453 837500
Fax: 01453 837506
Email: enquiries@rmc.rmt.org
Website: www.rmt.org
FOR MORE INFORMATION SEE PAGE 60

School profiles

Schools and colleges specialising in social interaction difficulties (Autism, ASD & ASP)

Prior's Court School

(Founded 1999)

Hermitage, Thatcham, West Berkshire
RG18 9NU
Tel: 01635 247202
Fax: 01635 247203
Email: mail@priorscourt.org.uk
Website: www.priorscourt.org.uk
Director of Education and Learning:
Sue Piper

Appointed: September 2011
School type: Independent Special School
Age range of pupils: 5–19
No. of pupils enrolled as at 01/01/2015: 59
Boys: 48 **Girls:** 11 **Sixth Form:** 24
No. of boarders: 56
Fees per annum as at 01/01/2015:
On application

Prior's Court School is an independent special school for students with autism aged from 5 to 19 years. The School offers day, weekly and termly places with 38, 44 and 52 week options. Students are on the autistic spectrum have moderate to severe learning difficulties and complex needs. They may have additional associated diagnoses. Some students exhibit challenging behaviours. All are working within P scales to lower national curriculum levels.

The School was opened in 1999. It is managed by Prior's Court Foundation, a registered, non-profit making charity which also runs a young adult provision and specialist autism training centre on the same site.

As an autism-specific school, Prior's Court is able to focus on meeting the special needs of its students in the most effective and consistent way to support their learning:

• A meaningful and functional curriculum with individualised learning programmes used throughout the waking day is built around students' interests and skills.

• The environment is adapted to meet students' needs – it is highly structured, calm, low-arousal, safe and secure with space and physical exercise a key feature providing opportunities to learn, exercise, socialise and relax onsite. Set in over 50 acres, facilities include a stable yard and paddocks for

approach, the school aims to achieve the highest level of progress for each individual enabling them to self-manage behaviour, communicate, manage transitions, develop independent living and social skills, choice-making and advocacy and progress to building vocational skills and undertaking work-placement activities. Skills once taught and practiced onsite can then be generalised and undertaken successfully offsite. Frequent access to the nearby villages, towns and community facilities enable students to work towards inclusion as far as possible.

"The outstanding curriculum is highly personalised. It provides rich opportunities for high-quality learning and promotes pupils' personal development extremely well."

Most recent Ofsted inspection (Education)

"The quality of care provided to young people is outstanding."

Ofsted Inspection October 2014

"I am absolutely delighted with the progress being achieved. Teaching and house staff are superb, broadening our child's skills and experience. Improvement in speech and language has been very impressive, as has the ability to self-manage behaviour."

Parent at Prior's Court School

animal husbandry, a walled garden with greenhouse and polytunnel for horticulture, sensory swimming pool, trampolines, trim trail, zip wire, swings, activity track and outdoor gym.

- The school's strong focus on training means that staff are experienced in using a range of methodologies and strategies to support each individual's needs and development in all settings throughout the waking day.
- A large onsite multi-disciplinary team including Occupational therapy, Speech & Language therapy, Clinical Psychologists and Nurses as well as dedicated horticulture, animal husbandry, swimming, activities and ICT

instructors provide support throughout the school day and in residential settings as well as out in the community where appropriate. All staff (education, residential, night, multi-disciplinary and therapeutic as well as a team of flexible workers who provide cover for absence or injury) are trained from induction onwards ensuring the highest levels of knowledge and expertise. These dedicated staff work closely with families and professionals to create a co-ordinated and consistent programme of education and care whose success is recognised worldwide.

By combining autism expertise and best practice with a person-centred

Potterspury Lodge School

(Founded 1956)
Towcester, Northamptonshire NN12 7LL
Tel: 01908 542912
Fax: 01908 543399
Email: mail@potterspurylodge.co.uk
Website: www.potterspurylodge.co.uk

Principal: Mr John W D Brown
Appointed: September 2004
School type: Boys' Termly Boarding,
Weekly Boarding and Day
Age range of boys: 8–18
No. of pupils enrolled as at 01/01/2015: 46

Sixth Form: 11
No. of boarders: 10
Fees per annum as at 01/01/2015:
Day: £51,330
Weekly Boarding: £76,989
Termly Boarding: £82,125

Potterspury Lodge is a charitable trust, which offers high quality education for boys aged between eight to eighteen years who have autistic spectrum disorders and a variety of emotional, social and behavioural difficulties and associated learning difficulties.

We teach the full National Curriculum, with the exception of a modern foreign language. Class sizes are kept to around eight or nine students and in addition to the subject teachers there are also learning support assistants in every class.

For boarders, the accommodation is organised so that they live in small groups of five or six in self contained houses, with them all enjoying the benefit of their own care staff and sharing in the day to day living arrangements, as one would in a family.

From year ten, pupils follow a life skills programme. In year eleven, some students are able to take part in work based training and all year 10 and year 11 students undertake two week-long periods of work experience.

We have provision for students in years 12 and 13 in The Stables Further Education Centre. Education and Residential support managers enable students to follow programmes of education and training according to their individual needs, using our own resources and those of local colleges, amenities and workplace training providers.

The School enables children to develop and grow in a caring and supportive atmosphere, and gives them the perfect opportunity to socialise and enjoy life. We organise trips for the pupils on a regular basis, including skiing holidays in Italy and outdoor pursuits expeditions in the UK and France. All pupils are given the opportunity to be fully included in activities.

The grounds are wonderful for sports and outdoor games, particularly when the weather is nice. The children are also encouraged to join in the wide number of after school clubs, which include such diverse activities as Badminton, Pottery, Football, Computers and Technology as well as our own Scout Group. We make full use of local recreational and Leisure facilities and some students are members of the local Sea Cadets Corps.

Statement for VAT exemption: *Potterspury Lodge School is a registered charity, which exists to provide pupils with Special Educational Needs with a wide range of opportunities to experience success. These are designed to help them progress towards being better integrated into society and then to go on to meet the demands of independent adult life.*

Charity No 1103356

Riverston School

Riverston

(Founded 1926)

63-69 Eltham Road, Lee Green, London, SE12 8UF

Tel: 020 8318 4327

Fax: 020 8297 0514

Email: office@riverstonschool.co.uk

Website: www.riverstonschool.co.uk

Headmistress: Mrs S E Salathiel

School type: Independent Non-Selective Day School

Age range of pupils: 9 months–19 years

No. of pupils enrolled as at 01/01/2015: 215

Boys: 155 *Girls:* 60

Fees per annum as at 01/01/2015:

On application

Making the significant move away from mixed games to separate boys and girls was always going to have its own challenges. To insist that all sixty boys take part in rugby could be argued that the school was stuck in the dark ages, building up towards the traditional masters versus boys end-of-term match, something akin to Monty Python's Meaning of Life, as under-nourished boys are trampled into the mud, beaten into submission and left feeling broken and worthless. Readers will be delighted to hear that the reality was very different!

Breaking down the myths associated with rugby, teaching new skills, developing teamwork and instilling a passion for the game were at the heart of the staff delivering this bold new move. Given the additional needs of many of its pupils, was this a risk too great? Teaching the skills necessary to ensure safe play was essential, resulting in a contact tackle not even being considered in the first six weeks. In order to change attitudes, teaching had to be gentle, understanding and safe, whilst also exciting those who wanted to learn the tough stuff.

Despite the understandable concerns, progress has been steady, not only in the development of skills but in the changing outlook of so many of the children. Those who had previously thought of rugby as a treacherous game played by fearsome Welshmen have come to realise the poetic majesty of the game. Boys who had become accustomed to kicking the familiar round ball around the playground have swapped the traditional pig skin for the more beautifully-shaped oval of a Gilbert size 5. Six Nations fever, whilst not quite reaching Barclays Premiership levels, has taken a hold of our pupils and understanding is higher when we celebrate the efforts of every team on Super Saturday.

Whilst there remain some who do not like the game, opinions have been shifted and every one of those sixty has learned new skills and made inroads into the development of a sport that they had previously believed to be inaccessible.

As the strains of Bach's Toccata and Fugue drift across the playing fields, boys will be grateful to have been learning rugby today and not in the Python-inspired days of the 1970s.

Rainbow School
for Children and Young People with Autism (Part of BeyondAutism)

RainbowSchool
Part of **Beyond**Autism

(Founded 2000)
The Tram House, 520 Garratt Lane,
London, SW17 0NY

48 North Side Wandsworth Common,
London, SW18 2SL
Tel: 020 3031 9700
Email: admin@beyondautism.org.uk
Website: www.beyondautism.org.uk
Head Teacher: Lesley Love

Appointed: September 2013
School type: Independent Special School
Age range of pupils: 4–19 (Early Years/
Primary, Secondary and 6th Form)
Fees per annum as at 01/01/2015:
Available on request

Rainbow School is an Approved Independent Special School for children and young people aged 4-19 years with autism and related communication disorders. We provide an education which sees each child and young person grow in confidence and autonomy. We make sure they feel safe and secure in their school environment and achieve their maximum potential.

The school is run by BeyondAutism, a registered non-profit making charity which also runs outreach, training and consultancy services for parents, carers, professionals and schools.

Rainbow School has two sites (primary and secondary) in Wandsworth, South West London. Pupils are currently placed with us by 14 Local Authorities across London. The school offers 1:1 and small group teaching from 9.15am to 3.15pm at the primary school and from 9.30am to 3.30pm at the secondary school for approximately 39 weeks per year. The school day follows a structured timetable. This includes group sessions and individual programme sessions to develop functional language skills in many areas of the curriculum. Outdoor playtime, assembly, horse-riding, art, music and PE are all part of the Rainbow School week. We also have a school choir – "Song Club" that sings at special events.

How we teach
We use the principles of Applied Behaviour Analysis (ABA) and B F Skinner's Analysis of Verbal Behaviour (VB) to structure our programme. ABA/VB has taught children diagnosed with autism successfully for 40 years. It helps us to work out what motivates a child to learn and then breaks every task down into small achievable steps. We apply ABA/VB in teaching core skills from speech and language, self-care

and motor skills right through to reading and writing.

Teaching with ABA/VB also reduces challenging behaviour and helps pupils to build on their social, play and independence skills. By teaching functional communication skills and reducing challenging behaviour we're able to guarantee children access to a broad, balanced and specialised curriculum that is tailored to their educational needs. The curriculum that we use is within the framework of the National Curriculum and Early Years Foundation Stage Curriculum. Our teaching team also work closely with the Speech and Language Therapist and the Occupational Therapist and our pupils' communication and sensory needs are

worked on daily across the curriculum.
Working together
We work closely with our pupils' families so we can build their aspirations and specific targets into our education and therapy programmes. We always keep parents informed, reporting daily on the progress their child makes. Parents are encouraged to do the same, letting our specialists know how their child is behaving at home. Rainbow School also offers parents support at home to help them reduce or adapt specific behaviours which impact on their family's lives.

Admissions
To be eligible for admission to Rainbow School pupils must:
- Have a diagnosis of autism or a related communication disorder.

- Have a Statement of Special Educational Needs or an Education, Health and Care Plan (EHCP), or are in the process of gaining one.
- Have agreement (in writing) from the LA or another source to fund the placement.
- Have the appropriate age, skills and behaviour for the vacancy that exists.

About BeyondAutism

BeyondAutism was founded by parents of children with autism in 2000 to give children diagnosed with autism the best opportunities and a positive outlook on life. We know that a specialist education for autism and communication disorders is vital and we understand that autism doesn't stop after leaving school. That's why we have developed a range of outreach services which utilise the knowledge and experience of our highly skilled staff to deliver life changing outcomes for children and young people with severe autism in other schools and at home.

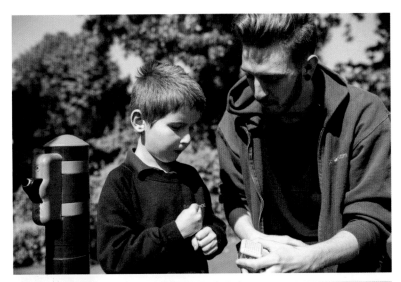

School Outreach

We can bring our support to you. BeyondAutism staff can make regular visits to other schools who are struggling to support children with severe autism. We can deliver programmes to specific members of staff or train large groups in INSET training.

We also make individual visits to children in various settings. These can last throughout a child's time in school and beyond. In some cases, children may need help and support at home.

Training

We offer training programmes to parents and carers so they can assist in their child's education. They cover topics such as:

* Managing challenging behaviour
* Teaching communication skills
* Eating Difficulties
* Sleeping difficulties
* Toilet training

BeyondAutism also runs day courses for professionals, including specialist ABA training. Our training team is made up of highly qualified BCBA Consultants and Teachers who are experts in the field of ABA and VB.

For further information on our outreach and training services please email info@beyondautism.org.uk for a brochure or call 020 3031 9705. We are able to tailor all of our services to suit individual needs.

The Holmewood School

The Holmewood School
London

(Founded 2010)

88 Woodside Park Road, London, N12 8SH
Tel: 020 8920 0660
Fax: 020 8445 9678
Email: enquiries@thsl.org.uk
Website: www.thsl.org.uk

Head of School: Lucia Santi
School type: Coeducational Day
Age range of pupils: 7–19
Fees per annum as at 01/01/2015:
On request

The Holmewood School London caters for students who have speech, language and social communication difficulties and those associated with high functioning autism and Asperger's syndrome.

Our school offers a successful alternative to mainstream education. Class sizes are small with a high staffing ratio. Comprehensive programmes are planned and delivered by specialist staff to meet each child's needs.

Teaching ensures all learning styles are met and addresses our kinaesthetic, visual, auditory and multi-sensory learners so that maximum individual potential is achieved. A structured and tailored environment ensures students are supported and challenged in their learning and development.

The curriculum is designed using the National Curriculum up to GCSE. For those students more vocationally oriented we support a range of courses that develop interests, strengths and skills providing valuable career related experiences and qualifications.

Mainstream experiences with our link schools support teaching and learning. The Holmewood School is part of a global network of schools within the Dwight family of schools offering an international perspective.

Learning is enhanced through our social skills and life skills curriculum. Planning and reflection time built into each day emphasises the importance that we place on students' personal development. Our whole school focus on celebrating student achievement is reflected in our approach to positive behaviour and rewards.

Therapies and practice are cutting edge and delivered by our multidisciplinary team. Comprehensive programmes are designed and integrated within our curriculum. The school benefits from a unique sensory integration clinic.

Located in North London the school has access to the rich cultural and educational experiences that the capital provides. Excellent local transport services makes learning in the community accessible for our students. Educational visits and offsite activities are incorporated within our programmes so students can consolidate and generalise the learning that takes place in the classroom.

If you think The Holmewood School would be the right place for your child, please contact our admissions team on 020 8920 0660 or enquiries@thsl.org.uk.

Royal College Manchester

Seashell Trust, Stanley Road, Cheadle, Cheshire SK8 6RQ

Tel: 01616 100100
Fax: 01616 100101
Email: admissions@seashelltrust.org.uk
Website: www.seashelltrust.org.uk
School type: Coeducational Day & Boarding

Age range of pupils: 19–25
No. of pupils enrolled as at 01/01/2015: 70
Fees per annum as at 01/01/2015:
Available post-assessment

Royal College Manchester, awarded 'Outstanding' in our most recent Ofsted inspection, shares a 90-acre site in the beautiful Cheshire countryside with Royal School Manchester and is committed to supporting young people with complex communication and learning needs to achieve positive outcomes such as progression into supported living or personalised day services, further learning or supported employment depending on their individual needs and ambitions.

In addition to courses delivered in the college and with our community partners, we also have a supported internship programme for students to develop their work skills in preparation for future employment. We use our expertise in communication and person-centred thinking to enable students to participate in shaping their individual programmes of study by expressing their views and making choices about particular activities which they find motivating.

A personalised pre-admission assessment forms the basis of each student's individual learning programme. The rich and varied curriculum focuses on relevant and meaningful opportunities to develop communication, independence, life skills and consider progression into supported employment. Students have access to a range of work experience opportunities onsite and in the community, and continue to benefit from the support of our job coach after leaving the college. We also support a range of employers to identify opportunities and create varied and meaningful work placements for our young people.

Our multidisciplinary team of teaching staff, physiotherapists, occupational therapists, speech and language therapists, assistive technologists, audiologists and nursing staff ensure that all our young people receive holistic care according to their needs.

Our facilities include our onsite hydrotherapy and swimming pools, a fully inclusive fitness suite, a state-of-the-art audiology clinic and our media suite. We believe that all young people should be supported to work towards their aspirations and participate in making decisions and planning their lives.

Royal School Manchester

Seashell Trust, Stanley Road, Cheadle,
Cheshire SK8 6RQ

Tel: 01616 100100
Fax: 01616 100101
Email: admissions@seashelltrust.org.uk
Website: www.seashelltrust.org.uk
School type: Coeducational Day &
Boarding

Age range of pupils: 2–19
No. of pupils enrolled as at 01/01/2015: 45
Fees per annum as at 01/01/2015:
Available post-assessment

Royal School Manchester, judged 'Outstanding' in our most recent Ofsted inspection, shares a 90-acre site in the beautiful Cheshire countryside with Royal College Manchester and provides a safe and secure environment for children and young people with complex learning and communication needs. Our teaching staff hold mandatory qualifications in MSI, VI, HI and Autism teaching, and our Learning Support Assistants include trained Intervenors for students with MSI. Our provision is Autism Accredited and we are a licensed Duke of Edinburgh Award Scheme Hub.

Onsite facilities include an audiology clinic where our resident audiologists perform hearing assessments as well as routine managing and fitting hearing aids, an accessible swimming pool and hydrotherapy pool, a number of sensory rooms, several adapted bicycles and a fully accessible fitness suite accredited by the Inclusive Fitness Initiative. In the Medical Centre, a registered nurse-led service, which includes a mental health nurse, works as part of the multidisciplinary team to provide holistic care for each student according to their needs.

Our team of specialist staff includes physiotherapists, speech and language therapists, occupational therapists and assistive technologists who work collaboratively with school staff, residential care and families in order to help every student achieve their potential.

Royal School Manchester adopts a person-centred approach to the delivery of each student's individualised curriculum. Children and young people benefit from a broad and balanced curriculum which includes Music (and the use of our Gamelan orchestra), Communication, Mathematical Development and ICT. From Key Stage 3, students attend Careers lessons, and students have opportunities for work experience placements from Key Stage 4.

Particular priority is given to promoting communication, independence, life skills and physical development and wellbeing. Our vision is that all our students are safe and happy, achieve the best possible outcomes and are valued and valuable members of their communities.

West Kirby Residential School

(Founded 1881)

Meols Drive, West Kirby, Wirral, Merseyside
CH48 5DH
Tel: 0151 632 3201
Fax: 0151 632 0621
Website: www.wkrs.co.uk
Principal: Mr Gareth Williams OBE

School type: Coeducational Day & Weekly Boarding
Age range of pupils: 5–19
No. of pupils enrolled as at 01/01/2015: 95
Fees per annum as at 01/01/2015:
On application

Changing Children's Lives, Building Better Futures

WKRS is a Non Maintained Special School for pupils with a wide range of complex social, emotional and behavioural difficulties often linked with conditions such as Autism, learning difficulties and communication problems.

The school prides itself on being able to help some very complex young people access the National Curriculum and work towards appropriate accreditation in all subjects including Open Awards, GCSEs and AS Levels. Staff are highly skilled in the understanding of the social and emotional needs of the pupils, as well as being able to personalise the academic work accordingly and provide high levels of support.

We believe the views of the pupils are paramount to success and the school offers opportunities for this through school council and individual discussion. Every pupil has an 'individual support plan' which they and staff contribute to. Differentiation and small classes with high levels of adult support have proven successful. We have excellent facilities, particularly for sport, music and other practical subjects. Pupils also have a voice through the School Council.

The school has its own integrated Services department which provides additional 'therapy' and educated support often necessary for the pupils to access the National Curriculum and fulfil their academic and personal potential. This department consists of: an Educational Psychologist, SALT, Physiotherapist, Behaviour and Reading support specialists/teams, a Learning Mentor and a Family Liaison Officer.

We have the option of day provision or flexible boarding provision on a termly basis, with pupils staying between one and four nights per week. Residential units include two houses in the locality and all are maintained to a high standard, with individual bedrooms and common areas for dining and recreation.

We hold the International School Award and have forged strong links with schools in South Africa and China and an orphanage in India, where exchange visits have taken place over a number years now, real experiences which most of our pupils would have considered beyond their reach.

Post 16 is based in an off-site annex. Each pupil has a study programme tailored to their individual needs, involving academic study, work related skills and further development of social and communication skills.

Staff are experienced at assisting pupils in the difficult process of transition from school to adult life. All pupils benefit from the strong pastoral ideal that runs through the school, to be aware both of themselves as individuals and within a group, increasing their respect for others, their self-esteem, emotional stability and acceptability.

Our staff are well qualified, experienced professionals. Recruitment procedures are rigorous with exemplary professional development available for all, as evidenced through our Investors in People Silver award. Continued professional development is supported through an extensive range or partnerships with local schools, universities and other agencies.

Most recently the school has achieved Autistic Accreditation through the National Autistic Society.

'This is an Outstanding School in all areas', (Ofsted 2013) which takes children further and enjoys their success.

WKRS is a registered charity no. 207790.

Cruckton Hall
(part of the Kisimul Group)

(Founded 1981)

Cruckton, Shrewsbury, Shropshire SY5 8PR

Tel: 01743 860206

Fax: 01743 860941

Email: marcia.garnett@cruckton.com

Website: www.cruckton.com

Head Teacher: Marcia Garnett

School type: Boys' Residential

Age range of boys: 8–19

No. of pupils enrolled as at 01/01/2015: 80

Fees per annum as at 01/01/2015:

On application

Curriculum

For those pupils who are resident at Cruckton we provide a 24-hour approach. All boys at the school have an Individual Education Plan (IEP), a Placement and Care Plan, Health Plan and, from Year 9, a Transition Plan. The respective parts of these plans are discussed between the professionals at the school, the boy and his parents/carers. The school has a full range of specialist rooms to support all National Curriculum subjects. All pupils are prepared for GCSE examinations in English, maths and science. They can also choose to study for GCSE in history, geography, French, German, computer studies, art, home economics and design technology. In addition, we also offer ECDL, AQA Skills for Life Awards and a variety of Entry Level certificates.

Assessment and entry requirements

Entry is by interview and assessment. The multi-disciplinary team of professionals will carry out a baseline assessment on each student within the first six weeks of admission. Cruckton has a visiting consultant child and adolescent psychiatrist who visits the boys on a regular basis, as required. The multi-disciplinary team consists of a consultant educational psychologist, systemic psychotherapist, two speech and language therapists, occupational therapist and two paediatric nurses. They provide a variety of interventions and therapies to minimise the anxieties and maximise the development of our young people.

The wider environment

The hall is a listed building surrounded by ten acres of gardens that include woods, playing fields and play areas. The site is located within a friendly rural community, in beautiful countryside, four miles from the market town of Shropshire. The Welsh Marches provide a stunning backdrop and a rich source of options for our regular trips and adventures. The town of Shrewsbury offers excellent amenities for the school and is now linked to the motorway network of the West Midlands, greatly improving access.

Residential environment and activities

The structure that provides success for the boys in the classroom environment is replicated in the residential area and boys have a range of recreational activities provided, which reflect their needs and encourage their specialisms. Many boys choose an active leisure programme. This can be provided by activities such as skateboarding, swimming, football and cricket, and in the summer the Adventure Camp encourages team work amongst our student group through activities such as orienteering, mountain biking, rock climbing and raft building. For the more studious, a range of activities from *Warhammer* to chess club are provided. Links with local clubs and societies include the local stables, local army cadet force, Jiu Jitsu, Laser Quest, bowling alley, street dancing and swimming are well-established. The links between the IEP targets are shared across the 24-hour approach, both in the home and education setting, with a huge variety of enrichment activities and programmes. Forest school, Lego therapy, robotics, stable management, mountain biking, Blists Hill Museum and work experience are all part of the enrichment programme.

Behaviour management

It is accepted that many boys come to

Cruckton Hall School exhibiting both difficult and challenging behaviour. The structural consistency of various approaches, combined with a consistent nurturing environment, has a track record of providing the boys with the ability to be accepted within social settings of their choice. The basis of the approach is to foster the following qualities: self-respect, respect for other students, respect for staff, courtesy, politeness, patience, tolerance and motivation to work. Boys will be encouraged and supported to meet as many of these expectations as is possible. Attendance at school is a non-negotiable requirement of a boy's placement at Cruckton Hall. School uniform is always worn.

Aims and philosophy

Cruckton Hall School aims to provide a warm, structured and caring learning environment in which each boy feels safe and secure, can succeed, is treated as an individual and is able to develop his skills and talents in order that he leaves school as an active participant in, and a positive contributor to, society.

'Cruckton Hall provides a good quality of education and offers good, "seamless", boarding provision.'

'It is outstanding in promoting pupils' personal development and does exceptionally well in "opening doors" for pupils, enabling them to learn, and preparing them for life after school in employment, college, university or in more sheltered environments.'

'The school's curriculum is outstanding and creates in pupils an excitement about learning which they have not experienced previously.'

'A key strength of the school is the way it supports pupils' transition, whether this is into the school, into courses or adult life. Pupils are particularly well informed through the wide range of support they receive, as well as formal careers guidance.'

Ofsted report 23rd November 2012.

Independent Specialist Colleges

(Founded 2013)

Fullerton House College

Tickhill Square, Denaby, Doncaster, South Yorkshire DN12 4AR

Tel: 01709 861663

Fax: 01709 869635

Wilsic Hall College

Wadworth, Doncaster, South Yorkshire DN11 9AG

Tel: 01302 856382

Fax: 01302 853608

Email: enquiries@hesleygroup.co.uk

Website: www.hesleygroup.co.uk

Head: Jeff Cox

Appointed: December 2013

School type: Independent Specialist Residential College

Age range of pupils: 18–25

No. of pupils enrolled as at 01/01/2015: 9

Fees per annum as at 01/01/2015:

On request

Specialist residential colleges offering flexible education care and support for up to 52 weeks per year for young adults aged 18-25, who have complex needs including behaviour that may challenge and a learning disability, often in association with autism.

At Wilsic Hall College, young people live within a beautiful rural setting with ready community access and at Fullerton House College in the heart of the community, in an urban setting with many local facilities including a sports centre, restaurants and shops.

Mission

Our Independent Specialist Colleges (ISCs) support young adults with their transition into adult life by focusing on their specific needs, capabilities and aspirations.

Education: Everybody has a highly personalised programme of learning, equipping them with skills they will need for adult life.

Extended learning: During evenings, weekends and college holidays a wide range of extra-curricular activities are on offer to ensure people are fully engaged with stimulating experiences both on and off site providing further, meaningful learning opportunities.

Professional services: A dedicated multi-disciplinary therapeutic team including college tutors, college support workers, consultant clinical psychologist, consultant psychiatrist, applied behaviour analysts, speech and language therapists, occupational therapists, registered manager, care and support staff work together to support each individual's progress.

High quality accommodation: College accommodation includes individualised bedrooms, quality living spaces that promote independence and progressive skills development assisted by the appropriate use of specialist/adaptive technology. We also have a range of on-site and off-site facilities that offer progressive learning opportunities for young adults with a range of needs and wishes.

Keeping in contact: We work to develop relationships between staff and families that are strong, positive and mutually respectful. People are supported to be in contact with their friends and family; we welcome visits to the colleges at any time. Everyone has a plan that will include the best means for them to maintain this contact whether by 'phone, letter, email or Skype.

Fullerton House School

 **Hesley** Group

(Founded 1990)

Tickill Square, Denaby, Doncaster, South Yorkshire DN12 4AR

Tel: 01709 861663
Fax: 01709 869635
Email: enquiries@hesleygroup.co.uk
Website: www.fullertonhouseschool.co.uk
Head: Jeff Cox
Appointed: December 2013

School type: Independent Specialist Residential School
Age range of pupils: 8–19
Capacity: 40
Fees per annum as at 01/01/2015: Available on request

A specialist residential school offering flexible education and care, which can include day and respite provision, for up to 52-weeks-per-year for young people aged 8-19, all of whom have complex needs including behaviour that may challenge and a learning disability, often in association with autism.

Fullerton House School is situated in the heart of the village of Denaby Main, near Doncaster. Its central location provides easy access by road, rail or air. Our mission is to enhance the lives of the young people entrusted to us by focusing on their specific needs, capabilities and aspirations.

Education: Each young person has a carefully designed Individual Learning Plan based on their specific needs in line with the National Curriculum, which supports their positive progress in a range of areas.

Extended learning: During evenings, weekends and school holidays a wide range of extra-curricular activities are on offer to ensure that young people are fully engaged with stimulating and meaningful experiences both on and off-site.

Professional services: A dedicated on-site team including carers, teachers, tutors, communication, behaviour and occupational therapy , psychology and other specialists ensure that young people have ready access to the services they require.

High-quality accommodation: Single person and small group occupancy of high-quality accommodation is provided at Fullerton House School. Every young person has their own bedroom, the majority of which have en-suite bathrooms. We also have a range of on-site facilities to complement and enrich the lives of those who come to live and learn with us.

Keeping in contact: We understand that while we may offer a very positive option for the young person, we may not be on your doorstep. Keeping in touch with loved ones is essential. Everyone has a plan to support optimum contact with family/carers and friends whether this be by phone, letter, email or Skype.

Wilsic Hall School

(Founded 1996)

Wadworth, Doncaster, South Yorkshire

DN11 9AG

Tel: 01302 856382

Fax: 01302 853608

Email: enquiries@hesleygroup.co.uk

Website: www.wilsichallschool.co.uk

Head: Geoff Turner

Appointed: September 2008

School type: Independent Specialist Residential School

Age range of pupils: 11–19

Capacity: 33

Fees per annum as at 01/01/2015: Available on request

A specialist residential school offering flexible education and care, which can include day and respite provision, for up to 52-weeks-per-year for young people aged 11-19, all of whom have complex needs including behaviour that may challenge and a learning disability, often in association with autism.

Wilsic Hall School is situated in its own 14-acre site approximately five miles south of Doncaster. Its central location provides easy access by road, rail or air. Our mission is to enhance the lives of the young people entrusted to us by focusing on their specific needs, capabilities and aspirations.

Education: Each young person has a carefully designed Individual Education Plan based on their specific needs in line with the National Curriculum, which supports their positive progress in a range of areas.

Extended learning: During evenings, weekends and school holidays a wide range of extra-curricular activities are on offer to ensure that young people are fully engaged with stimulating and meaningful experiences both on and off-site.

Professional services: A dedicated team including carers, teachers, tutors, behaviour, communication and occupational therapy, psychology and other specialists ensure that each young person has ready access to the services they require.

High-quality accommodation: Single person and small group occupancy of high-quality accommodation is provided at Wilsic Hall School. Every young person has their own bedroom, the majority of which have en-suite bathrooms. We also have a range of on-site facilities to complement and enrich the lives of those who come to live and learn with us.

Keeping in contact: We understand that while we may offer a very positive option for the young person, we may not be on your doorstep. Keeping in touch with loved ones is essential. Everyone has a plan to support optimum contact with family/carers and friends whether this be by phone, letter, email or Skype.

Schools and colleges specialising in emotional, behavioural and/or social difficulties (EBSD)

Appletree Treatment Centre provides high quality care and education for girls and boys aged between 6 and 12 with emotional, health, social and associated learning difficulties.

Over 20 years experience has allowed us to develop a superb clinical programme. Qualified and experienced psychologists and therapists provide individual therapy for our children, clinical input for the children's individual programmes and clinical consultation and training for our care, teaching and support teams.

Our high staff ratios enable us to provide a structured, therapeutic, twenty-four hour programme which focuses on helping children to form positive relationships. These enable the children to increase their self-esteem, which in turn allows them to acquire the skills they need to succeed at home, in school and in life. All homes and schools are registered with Ofsted and have good or outstanding judgements.

appletree
treatment centre
growing & learning together
www.appletreeschool.co.uk

Successful reintegration to families

After an average of just 2 years and 6 months with us 91% of our leavers in the last 5 years were able to leave residential care/special school provision and return to families or foster families and day schools. The remaining 9% of our leavers continued in residential care to facilitate increased and appropriate contact with their families.

Only planned moves onwards

Girl who left us in 2005 (recent letter sent to us)
The day I came back to see you I didn't want to go. Appletree is home, the only place I can call home. I had my bad times and really good ones, which I will never forget. I miss you all so much and wish I could come home, but I have grown up now. Hope I hear from you really soon. xxx

20 years proven record with good staff retention levels

We work alongside adoptive, foster and birth families

Parent said

"I feel my son is now happy, safe, and is learning in school. This is the first time this has happened in 4 years and he has only been there 6 months"

"I speak with the house tutors once a week and meet with Rob or Clair once a week. This is great and we get to talk about any new developments"

"I get to speak with my son's therapists regularly. This is useful and they tell me about progression or issues"

"I'm very happy with the placement"

Close to 100% attendance in education with no unauthorized absence

All children engage in individual therapy, most continue throughout their stay with us

Social worker said

"This placement has been a resounding success for the young person I'm responsible for"

"The psychological input from therapists has been great. It hasn't been superficial like some homes, it has added great value to the development of X"

"Communication has been great throughout the length of the placement"

"I'm very happy and have no concerns"

Psychology support for our teams working with children

Our children are usually able to return to families and day schools before they reach their teenage years, for the few who need continued support we have a small home to help guide them through their teenage years with personalised education

Appletree Treament Centre has three children's homes, Appletree and Fell House and Willow Bank
We help children with emotional, health, social and associated learning difficulties

Appletree and Fell House provides high quality care and education for girls and boys aged between 6 and 12. We help children who are vulnerable and require a nurturing environment.

Appletree is home for up to 12   Fell House is home for up to 8

Appletree and Fell House each have their own school on site

Consistentcy and stability are ensured for the few teenagers who continue under our umbrella. This is vitally important through these challenging years and helps in developing and gaining life skills for independence.

Willow Bank is home for up to 4

Willow Bank's education is tailored to the individual

tel 015395 60253 - Natland, Kendal Cumbria LA9 7QS - **email clair.davies@appletreeschool.co.uk**

Everyone within Appletree Treatment Centre has a responsibility for, and is committed to, safeguarding and promoting the welfare of children and young people and for ensuring that they are protected from harm.

Philpots Manor School

(Founded 1959)
West Hoathly, East Grinstead, West Sussex
RH19 4PR
Tel: 01342 810268
Email: info@philpotsmanorschool.co.uk

Website: www.philpotsmanorschool.co.uk
Education Co-ordinator:
Ms Linda Churnside BEd
School type: Coeducational Boarding
Age range of pupils: 7–19

No. of pupils enrolled as at 01/01/2015: 34
Boys: 22 **Girls:** 12
Fees per annum as at 01/01/2015:
Day: £65,000
Weekly Boarding: £65,000

Founded in 1959 and set in the heart of the Sussex countryside, Philpots Manor School is an independent residential school and training centre offering an academic and social education to children and young adults from 7 to 19 years of age.

The emotional, behavioural, social and communication problems that most of our students display may stem from a learning difficulty, social deprivation, abuse or from a recognised clinical condition, such as epilepsy, a development disorder or autism. Students need to have the potential to function in a social situation. Because of this we do not admit students with severe learning difficulties, severe psychological problems, or with extreme behavioural problems.

Classes usually contain a maximum of six students with one class teacher and at least one class assistant. Our residential units can accommodate either up to six or nine residential students, depending on the size of the unit. We also cater for day students. We offer a 36 week curriculum with residential children returning home at weekends. As well as offering a wide range of academic subjects we also offer horse-riding, pottery, gardening, weaving, art and music. Most pupils are entered for examination at GCSE or Entry Level in English, Maths, Science and Art at a time that is appropriate for each. Up to six GCSE subjects are offered.

OCN courses for Post-16 pupils accredit a wide range of subjects that most pupils study. Continuous assessment by the teachers avoids examinations for those pupils who least benefit from additional stress in their lives. Current courses include stable management and land-based studies.

We have play therapy, counselling, speech, music, Eurythmy and Bothmer Gym as well as a visiting osteopath.

For further information, please visit our website at:
www.philpotsmanorschool.co.uk
or telephone 01342 810268

Brantwood Specialist School

1 Kenwood Bank, Nether Edge, Sheffield,
South Yorkshire S7 1NU
Tel: 0114 258 9062
Email: enquiries@brantwood.rmt.org
Website: www.rmt.org

Headteacher: Constantin Court
School type: Independent
Coeducational Day & Residential
Age range of pupils: 7–19 years

Brantwood is an independent specialist school for children and young people aged 7-19 with complex behavioural, emotional and social difficulties (BESD), Autistic Spectrum Disorder including Asperger Syndrome, attachment disorder, ADHD and those deemed 'hard to engage'. The school offers daytime and residential provision up to 52 weeks and respite care subject to availability. Graded as 'Good' by Ofsted (2012), Brantwood's Social Care Report by Ofsted in 2014 was Graded as 'Outstanding'. The school is set in a quiet neighbourhood with secure grounds.

Curriculum

The curriculum has four distinct strands:

Steiner Waldorf Education: A holistic and inclusive approach to the development of the young person which emphasises the importance of the distinct ways in which humans relate to the world through their intellectual, emotional and physical activity.

Practical Skills Therapeutic Education (PSTE): PSTE enables people to develop transferable skills through real-life purposeful activities, gain confidence through achievement in school, engage in the wider community and achieve a wide range of qualifications according to their interests and skills.

The National Curriculum: Students can achieve appropriate nationally recognised qualifications from NOCNs and BTECs to GCSEs.

Individual Therapies: Speech and Language, Movement (Eurythmy), Massage, Art and Occupational Therapies are incorporated into each young person's education plan as appropriate. The school doctor and therapists work closely with staff and parents/carers at all times.

Brantwood Specialist School provides:

- Small class sizes and house groups of five students or fewer according to a student's ability and need

- Healthy organic food and nutritional education
- Engagement with the local community and help in planning leisure time and outdoor activities
- Involvement in festivals, other celebrations and social and cultural events
- Opportunities to develop and improve living skills for both day and residential students

Residential

Residential provision is in the school's central location and the local community providing consistency, warmth and positive role modelling that young people need to develop their skills and potential. Students are actively engaged in developing leisure activities, community participation and planning and cooking a healthy organic diet. The Children's Home Outstanding Ofsted Report 2014 quotes: *'Young people's lives significantly improve from living at this home'*. One parent commented *"It is small and homely here; they really care for my child."*

Admissions

For enquiries contact Admissions on 0114 250 0036 or email admissions@brantwood. rmt.org

Referrals are taken throughout the year. *Brantwood Specialist School Registered No: 373/6002. Children's Home Registered No: SC423753. Ruskin Mill Trust is an educational charity No: 1137167.*

Clervaux

Clow Beck Centre, Jolby Lane, Croft-on-Tees, North Yorkshire DL2 2TF
Tel: 01325 729860
Email: info@clervaux.org.uk
Website: www.clervaux.org.uk

Strategic Lead: Bonny Etchell-Anderson
School type: Coeducational Day & Residential
Age range of pupils: 16–25+

Clervaux offers day and residential places to young people and adults with complex learning and behavioural difficulties, mental health issues, complex social needs and ASD including Asperger Syndrome. Clervaux provides unique opportunities to learn and develop transferable skills through Ruskin Mill Trust's Practical Skills Therapeutic Education method which engages people in meaningful, hands-on and real-life activities.

Clervaux's rich personalised programme enables students and service users to develop their vocational, personal and social skills to make positive contributions to society. The wide-ranging provision is based on its 110-acre biodynamic farm in Croft-on-Tees, North Yorkshire and at its artisan café, bakery and shop in the centre of Darlington.

Curriculum

The workshops and vocational training programmes offer students both personal and vocational opportunities to develop skills. The rural setting of the Clow Beck Centre farm provides workshops and sessions in weaving, textiles, green woodwork, catering and stained glass as well as delivering land work, biodynamic agriculture and horticulture, animal husbandry and woodland management. In nearby Darlington, there are opportunities for students and trainees to apply for supported work placements within catering, through the bakery or front of house positions in the artisan bakery and café. This allows young people to work and train in a social enterprise, bring quality local and organic food to Darlington and engage with community life.

Residential provision

Our residential provision, Clervaux Life, carries the Trust's vision to a whole-life approach providing 24-hour care. All people have the ability to grow and develop to their potential and Clervaux Life seeks to harness and nurture that potential by providing a rich and varied lifestyle to those wishing to expand their capabilities. This holistic approach provides the stability to build confidence, make positive lifestyle choices and develop meaningful relationships based on mutual respect. Provision is offered both to those leaving full-time specialist education who are in need of additional one or two years' independence training, and to those benefitting from long-term care.

Clervaux takes referrals throughout the year and offers up to 52-week placements, as well as respite care.

Admissions

For all initial enquiries please contact: Ruth Bright, Admissions manager:
Email: ruth.bright@fmc.rmt.org
Telephone: 0114 252 5940

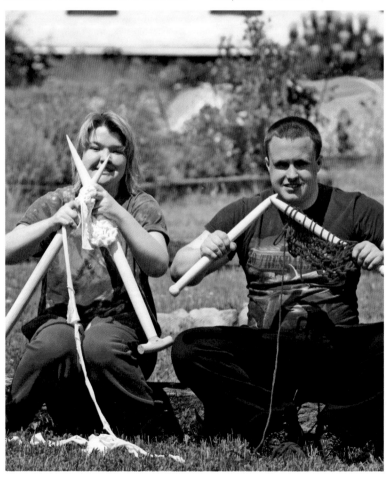

Schools and colleges specialising in learning difficulties (including dyslexia/SPLD)

Ruskin Mill College

The Fisheries, Horsley, Gloucestershire
GL6 0PL
Tel: 01453 837500
Fax: 01453 837506
Email: enquiries@rmc.rmt.org

Website: www.rmt.org
Principal: Dan Alipaz
School type: Coeducational Day &
Residential
Age range of pupils: 16–25

Ruskin Mill College, a long standing and successful independent college in Gloucestershire, offers over 100 places to young people with complex learning and behavioural difficulties, mental health issues and autistic spectrum disorders including Asperger Syndrome.

Practical Skills Therapeutic Education

Set in 140 acres including a biodynamic farm, woodlands and a fishery, the college is one of four operated by Ruskin Mill Trust (Argent College, Birmingham, opens September 2015, see Glasshouse College), whose internationally renowned Practical Skills Therapeutic Education method offers young people a unique opportunity to learn and develop transferable skills through meaningful, hands-on, real-life activities and accredited courses. Our experienced Pathways team will work with each student assisting them to undertake work experience and prepare each student for their transition back into their respective communities.

The college provides an extensive range of nutritional, therapeutic and medical support, as required. Each core element of the educational cycle is designed to establish active and positive relationships with nature, people and the community through a holistic approach to human development. At Gables Farm and the market garden, students help to grow and harvest healthy organic food, and prepare meals in the college canteens, café and households.

Integrated Learning for Living and Work

The college offers a personalised pre-entry assessment leading to an individualised learning and development programme. A rich and varied curriculum offers exciting opportunities to develop communication, social, work and living skills. Activities include practical land-based and traditional craft activities, animal husbandry, fish farming, woodland management, horticulture, catering and hospitality, music, art and drama, with communication and functional skills embedded throughout the day and residential provision.

Accreditation and Transition

Courses are accredited through the Qualification and Credit Framework and students will also prepare for work competency through a wide range of internal and external work experience. Qualifications include NVQs and BTECs, as well as GCSE and AS levels delivered in partnership with local providers. The college's cultural programme offers students further opportunities to develop their social and work skills. In their final year, students work with a dedicated transition team and engage with their acquired transferable skills to prepare for life after college.

Residential Provision

Students live in family or team houses in the local community which offer the consistency, warmth and positive role modelling that some young adults need to develop their living skills, achieve greater independence and re-imagine their potential. Students can progress onto placements in training flats or semi-independent living, where they have the opportunity to take greater responsibility for themselves.

Ruskin Mill College takes referrals throughout the year and offers up to 52-week placements.

Admissions

For all initial enquiries please contact the Admissions Team on 01453 837501 or by email: admissions@rmc.rmt.org

Ruskin Mill Trust is an educational charity and draws its inspiration from the insights of Rudolf Steiner, John Ruskin and William Morris. Charity No: 1137167

St Christopher's School

St Christopher's School
(Bristol)

(Founded 1945)

Carisbrooke Lodge, Westbury Park, Bristol, BS6 7JE

Tel: 0117 973 6875

Fax: 0117 974 3665

Email: info@st-christophers.bristol.co.uk

Website: www.st-christophers.bristol.sch.uk

Principal: Ms Orna Matz BEd, MEd(Autism)

Appointed: April 2013

Head of Care: Karen Horseman

School type: Coeducational Boarding

Age range of pupils: 5–19

No. of pupils enrolled as at 01/01/2015: 42

Boys: 32 **Girls:** 10

Fees per annum as at 01/01/2015: On request

We are an Independent Special School and Registered Children's Home providing 40-52 week residential provision for children and young people with severe and complex learning difficulties, including autism and behaviour difficulties. The well-being of pupils is at the heart of St Christopher's. We provide specialist care, education and therapy for our pupils, inspired by the holistic principles of Rudolf Steiner. We have had Autism Accreditation since 2007.

St Christopher's specialises in providing a therapeutic environment for its pupils – we believe the surroundings, quality of food and social interaction all contribute to the pupils' development. We have a team of highly skilled therapists who work alongside the School and Care staff to provide individualised learning programmes and positive behaviour support. Our staff are all trained in understanding attachment difficulties. We work closely with families. We also make excellent use of a wide range of strong community ties.

All this enables our pupils to make good progress in achieving their potential and enjoying a very full life. We pride ourselves on the levels of independence our pupils achieve whilst they are with us and on the constructive way in which we support transitions.

St Christopher's School is set in beautiful grounds in Bristol, south-west England.

It's the ethos at St Christopher's that makes it such a special place – we believe that beyond any learning, physical or emotional difficulties that any child has, there is always an intact human spirit and individuality that shines through. This ethos shows to everyone who attends and visits the school, with Ofsted saying in our latest school inspection report (Dec 2012):

"The school's spiritual ethos is at the heart of pupils' outstanding spiritual, moral, social and cultural development."

The Unicorn School

(Founded 1991)

20 Marcham Road, Abingdon,
Oxfordshire OX14 1AA
Tel: 01235 530222
Email: info@unicornoxford.co.uk
Website: www.unicornoxford.co.uk
Headteacher: Mr. Andrew Day BEd (Hons)
University of Wales (Cardiff)

School type: Coeducational Day
Age range of pupils: 6–14
No. of pupils enrolled as at 01/01/2015: 68
Fees per annum as at 01/01/2015:
Information on application

An 'outstanding' independent specialist school for dyslexic, dyspraxic and dyscalculic children (Ofsted Feb 2012)

- Provides specialist education for children from both independent and maintained schools to teach strategies and skills to enable them to return to mainstream as soon as possible.
- Structured multisensory, individualised programme with emphasis on synthetic phonic approach.

- Specialist dyslexia teachers, differentiated National Curriculum, daily individual tuition and small classes (maximum 12). Extensive use of computers and encouragement to develop creative talent.
- Speech therapy, occupational therapy, art therapy and instrumental tuition available on site.
- Educational and emotional needs met on an individual basis as well as

through friendly atmosphere and community spirit.

The Unicorn School is a registered charity, which exists to provide full-time education for children with specific learning difficulties who require specialist tuition. (Charity no. 1070807 CReSTeD category SP)

Egerton Rothesay School

(Founded 1923)
Durrants Lane, Berkhamsted, Hertfordshire
HP4 3UJ
Tel: 01442 877060
Fax: 01442 864977

Email: admin.dl@eger-roth.co.uk
Website: www.eger-roth.co.uk
Headteacher: Mr Colin Parker BSc(Hons),
Dip.Ed (Oxon), PGCE, C.Math MIMA
Appointed: September 2013

School type: Coeducational Day
Age range of pupils: 6–19
No. of pupils enrolled as at 01/01/2015: 143
Fees per annum as at 01/01/2015:
Day: £14,310 – £20,370

A Very Different Education

ERS is a school especially for the child who can benefit from additional support. This means delivering the best possible education for each child whilst providing them with a genuinely supportive framework that will help them to achieve their full potential.

We are an inclusive school, welcoming children with a wide range of abilities and from all cultures and faiths. We believe that learning should be enjoyable and holistic – so it is about preparing each child for life after school, as much as academic subjects and exams.

ERS focuses on students who have found, or would find, it difficult to make progress and to succeed within another school. We have a range of specialist support, teachers and therapists who provide for a range of children whose additional needs may include dyslexia, dyspraxia or speech and language issues, Asperger syndrome

and high functioning autism. Classes are grouped for individual requirements.

The school has an accepting atmosphere in which children feel understood and in which they do not 'feel different'. This boosts self-confidence and aids in the enrichment of learning.

Our aim is always to see what we can do for your child – and then to work with our resources and your support so that we can help them be successful. Our input can be for the child's whole school career, through to GCSE or simply on an interim basis to help re-focus their progress, depending on their needs.

In September 2012 we launched our new 'Sixth Form' Provision. For students who will continue to mature beyond the age of 16 and require an additional amount of support and time in order to enable them to transfer successfully into a further education establishment or employment. The school is developing

both one-year and two-year educational programmes within a high quality, secure and supportive environment in which students are able to continue to mature, develop and learn.

All learning and social activities take place within an environment offering exceptional pastoral care and whole person development that is driven and informed by the school's Christian foundation.

ERS is also more than just a local school – students travel to the school from all directions, many using the comprehensive minibus service that the school runs over a 35 mile radius.

You are most welcome to come to the school to see if you think our approach would be right for your child. To arrange a visit please contact Liz Martin (01442 877060 or liz.martin@eger-roth.co.uk) or see our website: www.eger-roth.co.uk for more information.

Kisimul School

(Founded 1977)

The Old Vicarage, 61 High Street, Swinderby, Lincoln, Lincolnshire LN6 9LU
Tel: 01522 868279
Fax: 01522 866000
Email: admissions@kisimul.co.uk
Website: www.kisimul.co.uk
Director of Education:

Mr Danny Carter BA(Hons), MA, MEd
School type: Coeducational
Independent Residential Special School
Age range of pupils: 8–19
No. of pupils enrolled as at 01/01/2015: 60
Fees per annum as at 01/01/2015:
On application

Kisimul School is one of the UK's leading independent residential special schools, offering a homely and safe environment for children who have severe learning difficulties, challenging behaviour, autism and global developmental delay.

Kisimul School offers residential education, care and leisure programmes at both our upper and lower school, for up to 52 weeks of the year, for pupils aged 8 to 19 years. The school is registered with the Department for Education and Ofsted. Limited day placements are also offered at both school sites.

The name Kisimul, pronounced 'kishmul', was taken from Kisimul Castle, which overlooks one of the safest harbours in the British Isles. Like its namesake, Kisimul School offers a safe haven, providing care and protection for its pupils whilst preparing them for the journey ahead into adulthood.

Kisimul School was founded in 1977 in a comfortable Georgian house (known today as the Old Vicarage) set in four acres within the small Lincolnshire village of Swinderby. Facilities at the Old Vicarage include an indoor heated swimming pool, large playground, soft play areas with ball pool and multi-sensory rooms for relaxation and stimulation.

In 2003, our upper school, Acacia Hall opened, offering the same standard of exceptional care and education within grounds adapted and utilised in a way to reflect the older age group. Acacia Hall offers riding stables, an adventure playground, collection of small farm animals and an area dedicated to horticulture.

Kisimul School has opened an additional school, Woodstock House, in Long Ditton, Surrey. Woodstock House received its first pupils in April 2008, and

again offers the same quality of care and education for pupils aged 8 to 19 years. Kisimul School has developed this site to be a mirror image of its existing school operations, using the same teaching methods and ethos.

Kisimul School's mission is to continuously strive for excellence in the care and education of its pupils, with a vision to have the best assisted living environment.

The school provides a caring, consistent, safe and supportive environment in which its young people can flourish and develop their skills in order to fully realise their individual potential. Residential and school staff work closely together to enable the pupils to progress in their personal development and learning. The 24-hour approach incorporates a wide range of activities to enrich the learning experiences of all pupils, helping them to learn to communicate and cooperate more effectively with others and enabling them to grow in confidence, self-esteem and independence.

The highly structured school curriculum aims to address the very specific needs of our pupils, by providing every opportunity for them to enjoy their education and develop their skills, knowledge and understanding through practical and functional learning experiences.

Classes are small and staffed at a ratio of at least 1:1. The integrated developmental curriculum incorporates the National Curriculum (lower school) or Adult Pre-Entry Curriculum Framework (Post-16) and a wide range of therapeutic programmes, collectively designed to meet the diverse sensory needs of our pupils. These include speech and language therapy, music therapy, aromatherapy, play development, HANDLE (Holistic Approach to Neuro-Development and Learning

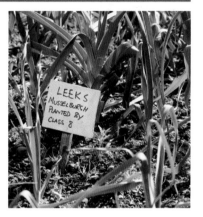

Efficiency) and EASIE (Exercise and Sound in Education).

A key priority is to develop our pupils' communication skills and since many are non-verbal we teach the alternative and augmentative systems of Makaton signing and PECS (Picture Exchange Communication System) alongside vocalisations and speech.

External accreditation is gained through a wide variety of ASDAN 'Towards Independence' programmes and the Duke of Edinburgh's Award Scheme.

Kisimul School works closely with the parents, carers and professionals from its placing authorities to ensure the highest possible standards of care and education.

Kisimul School is committed to the view that all people are entitled to equality of opportunity regardless of ability or disability, gender or chosen gender, age, status, religion, belief, nationality, ethnic origins or sexual orientation.

For further information, including exciting job opportunities within Kisimul School, please visit our website at www. kisimul.co.uk or contact us at the address above.

I CAN'S Dawn House School

helps children
communicate
REGISTERED CHARITY 210031

(Founded 1974)

Helmsley Road, Rainworth, Mansfield,
Nottinghamshire NG21 0DQ
Tel: 01623 795361
Fax: 01623 491173
Email: dawnhouse@ican.notts.sch.uk
Website: www.dawnhouseschool.org.uk
or www.ican.org.uk

Principal: Angela Child
School type: Coeducational Day &
Residential
Age range of pupils: 5–19
No. of pupils enrolled as at 01/01/2015: 75
Fees per annum as at 01/01/2015:
On request

I CAN's Dawn House School is a specialist speech, language and communication school for children and young people aged 5-19 years. We are committed to the highest quality education, therapy and care for pupils with severe and/or complex speech, language and communication difficulties or Asperger's Syndrome.

At Dawn House School the pupils receive the specialist intensive support that they need. We are able to cater for a number of other difficulties which are commonly associated with communication difficulties, including: learning difficulties, behavioural difficulties, problems with attention and memory, motor dyspraxia, sensory difficulties, autistic spectrum difficulties and emotional problems.

Pupils' individual needs are assessed and addressed through curriculum planning and assessment and IEP planning. Speech and language therapists and teachers plan lessons that meet two sets of targets: curriculum learning objectives and specific speech and/or language aims. For pupils who need more specific focused work to develop their speech and language skills, individual or small group sessions are timetabled during the school day.

Our school makes use of Makaton to support children's learning. The school also promotes the use of a range of voice output devices to support individual pupil's communication.

A full-time Occupational Therapist and OT assistants work within some lessons and with individual pupils on more focused, intensive work where necessary. The Family and Community Liaison Worker supports pupils' families and is a key link between home and school.

Residential Care at Dawn House School aims to ensure the emotional and physical well-being of our boarding pupils through an extended curriculum. The school can provide opportunities for non-residential young people to benefit from extended days and overnight stays. The care staff organise a range of activities out of school hours.

Dawn House was rated as an 'Outstanding' school by Ofsted in March 2014 and January 2015. The inspectors found pupils at the school achieve exceptionally well and all pupils make outstanding progress whatever their individual needs or disabilities.

The Further Education department caters for students (16-19 years) who have a communication difficulty or Asperger's Syndrome. The provision is based at the Dawn House site but has very close partnerships with Vision West Notts and Portland two local FE colleges, local employers and training providers.

Dawn House School is part of I CAN, the children's communication charity (www. ican.org.uk).

Pield Heath House School

(Founded 1901)

Pield Heath Road, Uxbridge, Middlesex
UB8 3NW
Tel: 01895 258507
Fax: 01895 256497
Email: admin@pieldheathschool.org.uk
Website: pieldheathschool.org.uk
Principal: Sister Julie Rose

School type: Coeducational Day & Boarding
Age range of pupils: 7–19
No. of pupils enrolled as at 01/01/2015: 78
Fees per annum as at 01/01/2015:
On application

Established in 1901 Pield Heath House is a non-maintained school in Uxbridge, West London for young people aged 7-19 with special educational needs. Judged 'Outstanding' by Ofsted at our last three inspections we offer day, residential and respite provision for those with moderate to severe learning difficulties, complex learning needs including autistic spectrum disorders, and associated speech, language and communication difficulties.

Our highly skilled and deeply committed staff are passionate in their work with our students to encourage their progress, celebrate their achievements and inspire confidence in their futures, in close partnership with parents and carers. We provide a holistic approach to education within a caring, spiritual environment where every young person is of equal importance, valued for what they are and encouraged to reach their maximum potential.

Each of our students has a personalised education programme which addresses their specific needs to live a fulfilled life in a challenging and changing world. Our multi-disciplinary team facilitates the learning process both in classroom settings and in the home environment for those who are resident.

A team of experienced therapists work alongside educational and residential staff in supporting the development of our students who are also encouraged to participate in a range of extra-curricular activities.

A comprehensive programme based on the National Curriculum is offered at Key Stage 2 and 3. Small class groups, with a high level of staff support, enable our students to access a suitably individualised curriculum. Statutory requirements at Key Sage 4 include the core subjects of English, Maths, ICT, RE, Citizenship and Science.

For students aged 14-19, the curriculum is structured to enable them to acquire the necessary skills to develop independence in their adult lives. Programmes are designed to promote their personal, social and vocational skills, and they have the opportunity to access nationally accredited programmes.

Pield Heath House School accommodates a wide range of learning requirements; the provision is flexible and tailored to optimise individual rates of progress and attainment. This encourages the development of confident, well adjusted, sensitive and independent young people able to live life to the full.

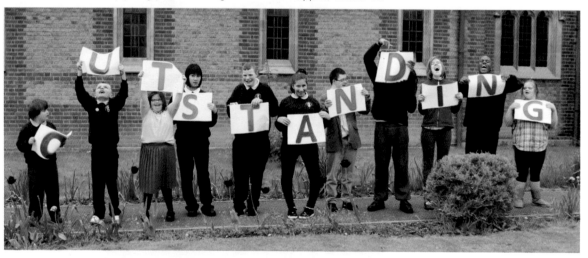

The Moat School

The MOAT SCHOOL
All dyslexic children can be helped to achieve

(Founded 1998)

Bishops Avenue, Fulham, London,

SW6 6EG

Tel: 020 7610 9018

Email: office@moatschool.org.uk

Website: www.moatschool.org.uk

Head: Ms Clare King

Appointed: January 2013

School type: Coeducational Day

Age range of pupils: 11–16

No. of pupils enrolled as at 01/01/2015:

Boys: 64 *Girls:* 20

Fees per annum as at 01/01/2015:

Day: £26,349

An aspirational London day school for children with specific learning difficulties

Founded in 1998, The Moat School is London's first co-educational secondary day school for children with specific learning difficulties (primarily dyslexia). We offer an intensive and structured learning programme teaching the National Curriculum.

A fundamental aim of The Moat is to identify and nurture talent to enable pupils to flourish, experience success and fulfil their potential. Teachers at The Moat School are not only subject specialists but also hold a post graduate specialist qualification in teaching pupils with SpLDs. In addition to our teaching staff and Learning Support Assistants, we have a team of experienced therapists including Speech and Language, Occupational Therapy and a School Counsellor. The Moat School is an ISA school and CReSTeD registered and has been described as the 'Gold Standard' in SpLD education.

The Moat School Offers

- A whole-school approach to learning for pupils aged 11 to 16 years (year groups 7-11)
- Specialist teaching with highly-trained staff
- Structured and individual learning programmes
- Class sizes based on a maximum of 10 pupils with individual and smaller group teaching as appropriate
- An embedded, whole-school therapeutic approach
- Development of organisational and study skills, and advanced use of Information & communication Technology (ICT)
- Access to the National Curriculum and GCSE qualifications
- A wide range of sporting and extra-curricular enrichment activities

In terms of adding value, The Moat School has continued to perform in the top 5% of schools nationally since 2005 – *Analysis of MidYIS by the Durham University's Centre for Evaluation and Monitoring*

The Good Schools Guide says: '*Something special. Not for children wanting to be cosseted and comforted, but a hardworking haven for bright, determined dyslexics and dyspraxics who know what they want from life and will achieve when given a chance.*'

The Moat School, come and see for yourself!

I CAN's Meath School

helps children
communicate

REGISTERED CHARITY 210031

(Founded 1982)

Brox Road, Ottershaw, Surrey KT16 0LF
Tel: 01932 872302
Fax: 01932 875180
Email: meath@meath-ican.org.uk
Website: www.meathschool.org.uk
or www.ican.org.uk
Headteacher: Janet Dunn OBE, MA,

AdvDipSpecEduc
Appointed: September 2003
School type: Coeducational Day &
Residential
No. of pupils enrolled as at 01/04/2015: 54
Fees per annum as at 01/01/2014:
On request

I CAN's Meath School is a residential (weekly) and day school providing teaching, therapy and care to children aged 4-11 years, whose primary difficulty is speech, language and communication, including Asperger's Syndrome. Meath School is a unique, nurturing, specialised learning community. The school and care settings have been recognised by Ofsted as 'outstanding' since 2008 and are on the Ofsted Outstanding Providers list.

Children with associated difficulties including some degree of learning difficulty, attention control, fine and gross motor co-ordination problems, mild visual and/or hearing impairments, medical needs and social interaction problems may also benefit from the provision.

Learning and achieving

All pupils are taught within a broad, balanced and relevant curriculum, including the new National Primary Curriculum for 2014 (except Modern Foreign Languages) which is differentiated, modified and tailored for pupils with severe and complex speech, language and communication needs. Strong processes for assessment, planning, teaching and reviewing ensure that each pupil makes the maximum progress in learning.

Classes are primarily based on pupils' language comprehension skills, also taking account of curriculum attainments, learning and social needs. In this way we know behaviour and progress are maximised.

Class groups can include between eight and twelve pupils, across year groups and Key Stages.

Each class has a core team of teacher, speech and language therapist and at least one learning support assistant. The speech and language therapy team and

occupational therapists are an important part of the pupils' education. Specialist teaching is offered in music, art, craft, design and PE.

Partnership with parents

Meath School staff collaborate closely with parents, sharing successes and helping with any concerns or difficulties at home. The Family Support Worker acts as a link between home and school and will visit families where needed.

The School

Meath School is housed in fine Victorian buildings and the site includes a modern

teaching block, gym, music, art and cookery rooms, ICT suite, small swimming pool, school field, activity play areas and woodland. The school has a programme of after school clubs and a summer holiday club.

Meath School is part of I CAN, the children's communication charity (www. ican.org.uk), and is an integral part of the I CAN Centre in Surrey. The Centre and School offer flexi placements and holistic multi-disciplinary independent two day specialist assessments.

Kisimul School – Woodstock House

(Opened 2008)

Woodstock Lane North, Long Ditton,
Surbiton, Surrey KT6 5HN
Tel: 020 8335 2570
Fax: 020 8335 2571
Email: admissions@kisimul.co.uk
Website: www.kisimul.co.uk
Director of Education:

Mr Danny Carter BA(Hons), MA, MEd
School type: Coeducational
Independent Residential Special School
Age range of pupils: 8–19
No. of pupils enrolled as at 01/01/2015: 40
Fees per annum as at 01/01/2015:
On application

Kisimul School is one of the UK's leading independent residential special schools, offering a homely and safe environment for children who have severe learning difficulties, challenging behaviour, autism and global developmental delay.

Kisimul School offers residential education, care and leisure programmes at both our upper and lower school, for up to 52 weeks of the year, for pupils aged 8 to 19 years. The school is registered with the Department for Education and Ofsted. Limited day placements are also offered at both school sites.

The name Kisimul, pronounced 'kishmul', was taken from Kisimul Castle, which overlooks one of the safest harbours in the British Isles. Like its namesake, Kisimul School offers a safe haven, providing care and protection for its pupils whilst preparing them for the journey ahead into adulthood.

The original Kisimul School was founded in 1977 in a comfortable Georgian house (known today as the Old Vicarage) set in four acres within the small Lincolnshire village of Swinderby. Facilities at the Old Vicarage include an indoor heated swimming pool, large playground, soft play areas with ball pool and multi-sensory rooms for relaxation and stimulation.

In 2003, our upper school, Acacia Hall opened, offering the same standard of exceptional care and education within grounds adapted and utilised in a way to reflect the older age group. Acacia Hall offers riding stables, an adventure playground, collection of small farm animals and an area dedicated to horticulture.

Woodstock House received its first pupils in April 2008, and again offers the same quality of care and education for pupils aged 8 to 19 years. Kisimul School has

developed this site to be a mirror image of its existing school operations, using the same teaching methods and ethos.

Woodstock House is situated within 8.1 acres of tranquil countryside, offering space to develop in a safe and secure environment. Woodstock House is within easy access from the M25 via the A3.

Kisimul School's mission is to continuously strive for excellence in the care and education of its pupils, with a vision to have the best assisted living environment.

The school provides a caring, consistent, safe and supportive environment in which its young people can flourish and develop their skills in order to fully realise their individual potential. Residential and school staff work closely together to enable the pupils to progress in their personal development and learning. The 24-hour approach incorporates a wide range of activities to enrich the learning experiences of all pupils, helping them to learn to communicate and cooperate more effectively with others and enabling them to grow in confidence, self-esteem and independence.

The highly structured school curriculum aims to address the very specific needs of our pupils, by providing every opportunity for them to enjoy their education and develop their skills, knowledge and understanding through practical and functional learning experiences.

Classes are small and staffed at a ratio of at least 1:1. The integrated developmental curriculum incorporates the National Curriculum (lower school) or Adult Pre-Entry Curriculum Framework (Post-16) and a wide range of therapeutic programmes, collectively designed to meet the diverse sensory needs of our pupils. Our sensory integration programmes include speech and language therapy, music therapy,

aromatherapy, occupational therapy, educational psychology input and EASIE (Exercise and Sound in Education).

A key priority is to develop our pupils' communication skills and since many are non-verbal we teach the alternative and augmentative systems of Makaton signing and PECS (Picture Exchange Communication System) alongside vocalisations and speech.

External accreditation is gained through a wide variety of ASDAN 'Towards Independence' programmes and the Duke of Edinburgh's Award Scheme.

Kisimul School works closely with the parents, carers and professionals from its placing authorities to ensure the highest possible standards of care and education.

Kisimul School is committed to the view that all people are entitled to equality of opportunity regardless of ability or disability, gender or chosen gender, age, status, religion, belief, nationality, ethnic origins or sexual orientation.

For further information, including exciting job opportunities within Kisimul School, please visit our website at www. kisimul.co.uk or contact us at the address above.

St Catherine's School

St Catherine's School
For Speech, Language and Communication Needs

(Founded 1983)
Grove Road, Ventnor, Isle of Wight
PO38 1TT

Tel: 01983 852722
Fax: 01983 857219
Email: general@stcatherines.org.uk
Website: www.stcatherines.org.uk
Principal: Dr B Carleton
Appointed: September 2011

School type: Coeducational Boarding
Age range of pupils: 7–19
No. of pupils enrolled as at 01/01/2015: 46
Boys: 35 **Girls:** 11 **Sixth Form:** 28
No. of boarders: 33

At St Catherine's we offer specialist education, therapy and residential care to young people aged 7 to 19 with **speech, language and communication needs** and **associated conditions** such as **autism, Asperger Syndrome, dyspraxia** and **dyslexia**. In 2014, Ofsted rated St Catherine's education provision as Good and its care provision as Outstanding.

Our students – who are a mixture of day students, and weekly or termly boarders – come from across the UK and abroad. Students are taught a modified curriculum in small classes, with high staff-to-student ratios incorporating a teacher, a speech and language therapist and a learning support assistant. Each student has his/her own individual educational and care programme, which integrates speech and language therapy and occupational therapy.

Students have the opportunity to gain a range of vocational and academic qualifications according to individual abilities and preferences including GCSEs and BTECs. From age 14 we provide students with a range of work-related experiences including accredited courses at our vocational training unit, work experience and taster courses at our local college.

Our therapy team are integral to St Catherine's and support the school's Total Communication approach including the use of sign-supported English. The speech and language and occupational therapists provide in-depth assessments, individualised therapy programmes, small group therapy sessions, intervention in the classroom and residential support.

Each of our residential students has their own bedroom and is supported to pursue leisure activities as well as learn independence skills. We are actively involved in our local community, which provides a nurturing setting for practising life skills including independent travel.

Across all activities there is an emphasis on personal development, independence skills and emotional maturity supporting each student to gain the skills they will need for their journey to adulthood.

Places at St Catherine's can be funded by local authorities or privately.

St John's School & College

ST. JOHN'S

EMPOWERING VOICE. ENABLING CHOICE

Business Centre, 17 Walpole Road,
Brighton, East Sussex BN2 0AF
Tel: 01273 244000
Fax: 01273 602243

Email: admissions@st-johns.co.uk
Website: www.st-johns.co.uk
Principal & Chief Executive:
Mr Mark Hughes
Appointed: September 2010
School type: Coeducational Boarding
& Day

Age range of pupils: 7–25
No. of pupils enrolled as at 01/01/2015: 97
Boys: 78 **Girls:** 19
No. of boarders: 47
Fees per annum as at 01/01/2015:
Day: £50,000 approx
Full Boarding: £95,000 approx

Situated in Brighton and Seaford in East Sussex, St. John's is a Special Educational Needs School and Specialist College that provides education, care and medical therapy to young people aged 7-25.

We welcome learners who have a wide range of complex learning disabilities, those with autism and related autism spectrum conditions and young people who have special needs resulting from behavioural, emotional and social difficulties.

Our school learners (pre-19) focus on the core skills of literacy, numeracy and IT and also undertake a comprehensive PSHE programme. At the college (post-19) there is a strong focus on work-based learning, with learners being given the opportunity to gain practical work experience in a number of enterprises both within the organisation and externally.

Our dedicated in-house medical and therapy service provides speech and language therapy, occupational therapy, counselling, nursing services and behaviour support. All of these services work holistically with the education service in order to unlock the full potential of all our learners in their day to day learning and activities.

St. John's also offers residential placements to young people attending our School and College. We have 7 dedicated residential homes, with 4 located in Seaford and 3 in Brighton. Each house is unique, providing high quality, person centred care and support to our diverse population of learners.

More than anything else, St. John's is about transforming lives – making a real and practical difference to the young people who access our services and embracing the unique diversity they present. Our core mission is to enable them to achieve their goals and aspirations; to reach out and achieve the possible and to live their lives to the full.

St Joseph's Specialist School & College

Christ in Our Lives
No Limits ... Just Possibilities

(Founded 1950)

Amlets Lane, Cranleigh, Surrey GU6 7DH

Tel: 01483 272449

Fax: 01483 276003

Email: admissions@
st-josephscranleigh.surrey.sch.uk

Website:
www.st-josephscranleigh.surrey.sch.uk

Principal: Mrs Mary Fawcett

Appointed: Sept 2005

School type: Coeducational Day &
Residential

Age range of pupils: 5–19

No. of pupils enrolled as at 01/01/2015: 73

Fees per annum as at 01/01/2015:

Day: Range from £57,905

Full Boarding: Range from £83,898

The School

St. Joseph's Specialist School & College is recognised by Ofsted as an "Outstanding", well-established day & residential school catering for children and young people with special needs from ages 5 to 19 years across 52 weeks of the year.

Currently with 85% of learners on the Autistic Spectrum we also specialise in a range of complex needs including Speech & Language difficulties, moderate to severe learning difficulties, social communication disorders and challenging behaviours. Autism Accredited by the National Autistic Society, St Joseph's is a proven solution for both families and Local Authorities seeking the next step for education, care and therapy.

With Specialisms in Communication, Interaction and the Creative Arts, we offer tailor made teaching and learning styles, environment, therapies and professional

standards to meet all the needs of ASD learners through personalised learning programmes based on an integrated curriculum, functional communication, visual structure and positive behaviour management. These programmes incorporate a number of methods recognised for working with ASD leaners: TEACHH, Intensive Interaction; PECS; Social Stories and MAKATON signing and symbols. By focusing on learning and behavioural needs, as well as personal preferences, ensures a truly bespoke and personalised approach is taken to ensure success. Information is carefully gathered from a wide range of sources including: the statement of special needs; the diagnosis; developmental history; educational records and assessments; medical records; parents, care staff and observations.

The school is situated close to Cranleigh Village, which retains a great sense of 'community' with a range of amenities including a Leisure Centre, library, shops, cafes, arts centre, churches, sports and social clubs. With good transport links to both Horsham and Guildford where more leisure and social facilities including cinemas, theatre and indoor bowling can be found. The school is an active member of the local community and all learners are encouraged to take an active part in community life, to maximise their potential and engage with local people.

Strong leadership, teaching, care and therapeutic intervention combine to deliver positive outcomes to meet high expectation and aspirations of both learners and families. A calming environment takes into account a wide variety of complex sensory issues and uses a variety of techniques – photographs,

symbols and visual cues – children feel comfortable in their surroundings and cope easily with daily routines.

We specifically adapt the curriculum to meet each child's individual needs and focus on the development of personal, social and communication along with independent living skills, especially for those aged 16+ years.

By maintaining routines within a structured environment and promoting functional communication we enable learners to stay motivated, maximise their potential and work towards positive learning outcomes, whilst seeing a reduction in both anxiety and challenging behaviours.

Therapies

We have our own dedicated team of therapists who enhance and complement the education and care of all learners. A Head of Therapies co-ordinates and leads a department which includes Speech and Language, Occupational Therapy, Music, Arts Physiotherapy, Equine and Drama.

We believe communication underpins successful learning, self-esteem, positive behaviour and opportunities for life. All learners are assessed and a therapy programme devised based on their individual needs. To ensure learning is transferred to real life situations, our therapists accompany our children and young people into the community on a regular basis to access local facilities and activities.

Flexible Residential Options

Recently registered as a Children's Home, we provide care, education and therapies for up to 52 weeks a year. Alternatively we can offer a variety of flexible Residential options to meet the needs of Local Authorities, learners and families.

We offer an environment where each learner is supported and able to develop those skills needed to maximise personal independence. Each residential group is staffed on an individual basis well equipped to give a homely atmosphere. Our last Ofsted Inspection judged our Quality of Care as "outstanding". By maintaining a waking day curriculum we believe our learners benefit greatly from a consistency of approach.

Fully integrated into our community we ensure all our learners' skills are transferred and managed in realistic settings and reflects their levels of need. A Speech and Language therapist also visits all the residential groups to ensure consistency across the day.

Supported Living

We recently extended our provision to young people aged 19+ in need of independent supported living. "Springvale" in Cranleigh and Long Barn in Beare Green offer accommodation for adults with learning difficulties where each young person has their own tenancy and is supported by a tailored support package reflecting their own lifestyle choices and activities.

Glasshouse College

Wollaston Road, Amblecote, Stourbridge,
West Midlands DY8 4HF
Tel: 01384 399400
Fax: 01384 399401
Email: enquiries@ghc.rmt.org

Website: www.rmt.org
Principal: Paul Gawdan
School type: Coeducational Day &
Residential
Age range of pupils: 16–25

Glasshouse College, awarded 'Good' by Ofsted, offers over 90 places to young people with a wide range of complex learning and behavioural difficulties, mental health issues and ASD including Asperger Syndrome.

Practical Skills Therapeutic Education

Set in the heritage glassmaking district of Stourbridge with a 36-acre farm and 10-acre woodlands nearby, the college is one of four operated by Ruskin Mill Trust (see Admissions for Argent College opening in Birmingham in September 2015), whose internationally renowned Practical Skills Therapeutic Education method offers young people a unique opportunity to learn and develop transferable skills through meaningful real-life activities and accredited courses in both the day and residential settings.

The college provides an extensive range of nutritional, therapeutic and medical support, as required. Each core element of the educational cycle is designed to establish active and positive relationships with nature, people and the community through a holistic approach to human development. At Vale Head Farm, students help to grow and harvest healthy organic food, and then prepare meals in the college canteens, café and households.

Integrated Learning for Living and Work

A personalised pre-entry assessment leads to an individualised learning and development programme. A rich and varied curriculum offers exciting opportunities to develop communication, social, work and living skills and two newly refurbished state-of-the-art visitor centres, the Glasshouse Arts Centre and the Ruskin Glass Centre, offer students exceptional opportunities to develop social and vocational skills in professional and public environments.

Activities include traditional glassmaking, land-based and traditional craft activities, animal husbandry, woodland management, bow making, archery, mountain biking, catering, working a narrowboat, music, art, drama and maskmaking, with numeracy, communication and functional skills embedded throughout the day and residential provision.

Accreditation and Transition

Courses are accredited through the Qualification and Credit Framework and include OCNs, NVQs, BTECs, and GCSE and AS levels in partnership with local providers. Work competency is gained through a wide range of internal and external work experience. In their final year, students work with a dedicated team to consolidate their transferable skills and prepare for transition.

Residential Provision

Students live in family or team houses in the local community offering the consistency, warmth and positive role modelling that some young adults need to develop living skills, achieve greater independence and re-imagine their potential. Training flats offer even more opportunities to take greater responsibility for themselves.

Glasshouse College takes referrals throughout the year and offers 36, 40, and 52-week placements, as well as respite care.

Admissions

For all initial enquiries please contact the Admissions Team on 01384 399437 or by email at: admissions@ghc.rmt.org including for **Argent College** Birmingham OPENING September 2015

Ruskin Mill Trust is an educational charity and draws its inspiration from the insights of Rudolf Steiner, John Ruskin and William Morris. Charity No: 1137167

Overley Hall School

(Founded 1979)
Overley, Wellington, Telford, West
Midlands TF6 5HE
Tel: 01952 740262
Fax: 01952 740262

Email: info@overleyhall.com
Website: www.overleyhall.com
Headteacher: Mrs Beverley Doran
Appointed: September 2013
School type: Coeducational Residential

Age range of pupils: 8–19
No. of pupils enrolled as at 01/01/2015: 20
Boys: 16 **Girls:** 4
No. of boarders: 20

Overley Hall School is an independent, residential special school and Children's Home, providing education and care to children and young adults aged from eight to 19 years who have a wide range of complex needs including autism, epilepsy and severe learning disabilities. The school is committed to offering each child a wide range of good quality experiences; this occurs through partnerships with parents/carers, teachers and therapists in the delivery of a waking day curriculum by a dedicated team.

In-house speech and language and occupational therapies are offered regularly to each child.

The school/residential home is set in a quiet, rural location which provides a calm and nurturing learning and living environment for young people in our care. Our school building, alongside the residential house, stands in 13 acres of lawn, walled kitchen garden and woodland.

Other facilities within the campus and grounds include a lifeskills room, indoor sensory hydropool, soft play space, art and craft workshops, sensory rooms, recreational and relaxation areas.

Our registered 'Forest School' operates within the woodland areas, and is led by qualified practitioners from Overley Hall School; this offers pupils opportunities for multi-sensory outdoor learning and recreation experiences throughout the seasons.

Sunfield School

WORKING TOGETHER TRANSFORMING LIVES

(Founded 1930)

Clent Grove, Woodman Lane,
Stourbridge, West Midlands DY9 9PB
Tel: 01562 882253
Fax: 01562 883856
Email: referrals@sunfield.org.uk
Website: www.sunfield.org.uk
Principal: Caroline Bell

School type: Independent
Coeducational Residential & Day Special
School
Age range of pupils: 6–19
Fees per annum as at 01/01/2015:
Available on request

Sunfield is an independent residential special school and charity in the West Midlands, with over 80 years of experience in supporting children and young people with complex learning needs such as autism.

Working together

Sunfield offers flexible 38 to 52 week residential placements and day places, as well as an assessment and outreach service. Our specialised provision uses personalised, innovative and responsive approaches in care, education, psychology, therapies, health and family services. We work together, with young people, their families, and other supporting professionals, to make a meaningful difference – often where children have been unable to thrive elsewhere.

"You won't find a better special school who will take care of your child and really try and give them a sense of purpose and education. This is a really great place with great people who can help your child and the whole family." **Parent**

Sunfield has 58 acres of parkland with nature trails, play areas and a farm with animals and pets. Our extensive facilities, with state-of-the-art equipment and dedicated professionals, include 12 residential houses with personalised bedrooms and 24/7 care teams, accommodation for visiting families, a sensory integration suite, and an on-site multi-disciplinary psychology and therapy team.

"Individually tailored systems result in young people making significant personal educational and social progress. This is expertly facilitated by well informed, professional staff." **Ofsted**

Transforming lives

Education at Sunfield begins by creating an environment in which children feel secure; where they feel their needs are met, their feelings can be safely expressed and their communication is understood. Here, they will discover and demonstrate their strengths and develop their self-esteem. In our experience, this is the point at which they start to engage with their learning and living; the start of an exciting transformation – for young people and their families.

Freeman College

Sterling Works, 88 Arundel Street, Sheffield,
South Yorkshire S1 2NG
Tel: 0114 252 5940
Fax: 0114 252 5996
Email: enquiries@fmc.rmt.org

Website: www.rmt.org
Principal: Bonny Etchell-Anderson
School type: Coeducational Day &
Residential
Age range of pupils: 16–25

Freeman College, awarded 'Good' by Ofsted, offers over 90 places to young people with complex learning and behavioural difficulties, mental health issues and ASD including Asperger Syndrome.

Practical Skills Therapeutic Education
Based in the illustrious metalworking district of Sheffield, the college is one of four operated by Ruskin Mill Trust (Argent College, Birmingham, opens September 2015, see Glasshouse College), whose internationally renowned Practical Skills Therapeutic Education method offers young people a unique opportunity to learn and develop transferable skills through meaningful real-life activities and accredited courses in both the day and residential programmes.

Freeman College provides an extensive range of nutritional, therapeutic and medical support, as required. Each core element of the educational cycle is designed to establish active and positive relationships with nature, people and the community through a holistic approach to human development. Healthy organic food is grown and harvested at the college's 8-acre market garden and prepared with students in the canteens, café and households.

Integrated Learning for Living and Work
A personalised pre-entry assessment leads to an individualised learning and development programme. A rich and varied curriculum is designed to offer opportunities to develop lifelong communication, social, work and living skills. Activities include traditional metal crafts such as spoon forging, copper and pewter work, gilding and jewellery, as well as land-based and traditional crafts, animal husbandry, horticulture, catering and hospitality, music, art and drama, with communication and functional skills embedded throughout the day and residential provision.

Accreditation and Transition
Courses are accredited through the Qualification and Credit Framework and include OCNs, NVQs, BTECs, as well as GCSE and AS levels delivered in partnership with local providers. Work competency is gained through a wide range of internal and external work experience including through its arts and crafts shop, the Academy of Makers, cultural and events programmes, workshops and award-winning café. In their final year, students collaborate with a dedicated transition team to hone their transferable skills and prepare for life after college.

Residential Provision
Students live in family or team houses in the local community, which offer the consistency, warmth and positive role modelling that some young adults need to develop their living skills, achieve greater independence and re-imagine their potential. Students can progress onto placements in training flats where they have the opportunity to take greater responsibility for themselves.

Freeman College takes referrals throughout the year and offers up to 52-week placements.

Admissions
For all initial enquiries please contact the Admissions Team on 0114 252 5953 or by email: admissions@fmc.rmt.org

Ruskin Mill Trust is an educational charity and draws its inspiration from the insights of Rudolf Steiner, John Ruskin and William Morris. Charity No: 1137167

Independent Specialist Colleges

 Hesley Group

(Founded 2013)

Fullerton House College
Tickhill Square, Denaby, Doncaster, South Yorkshire DN12 4AR
Tel: 01709 861663

Fax: 01709 869635

Wilsic Hall College
Wadworth, Doncaster, South Yorkshire DN11 9AG
Tel: 01302 856382
Fax: 01302 853608
Email: enquiries@hesleygroup.co.uk
Website: www.hesleygroup.co.uk

Head: Jeff Cox
Appointed: December 2013
School type: Independent Specialist Residential College
Age range of pupils: 18–25
No. of pupils enrolled as at 01/01/2015: 9
Fees per annum as at 01/01/2015:
On request

Specialist residential colleges offering flexible education care and support for up to 52 weeks per year for young adults aged 18-25, who have complex needs including behaviour that may challenge and a learning disability, often in association with autism.

At Wilsic Hall College, young people live within a beautiful rural setting with ready community access and at Fullerton House College in the heart of the community, in an urban setting with many local facilities including a sports centre, restaurants and shops.

Mission

Our Independent Specialist Colleges (ISCs) support young adults with their transition into adult life by focusing on their specific needs, capabilities and aspirations.

Education: Everybody has a highly personalised programme of learning, equipping them with skills they will need for adult life.

Extended learning: During evenings, weekends and college holidays a wide range of extra-curricular activities are on offer to ensure people are fully engaged with stimulating experiences both on and off site providing further, meaningful learning opportunities.

Professional services: A dedicated multi-disciplinary therapeutic team including college tutors, college support workers, consultant clinical psychologist, consultant psychiatrist, applied behaviour analysts, speech and language therapists, occupational therapists, registered manager, care and support staff work together to support each individual's progress.

High quality accommodation: College accommodation includes individualised bedrooms, quality living spaces that promote independence and progressive skills development assisted by the appropriate use of specialist/adaptive technology. We also have a range of on-site and off-site facilities that offer progressive learning opportunities for young adults with a range of needs and wishes.

Keeping in contact: We work to develop relationships between staff and families that are strong, positive and mutually respectful. People are supported to be in contact with their friends and family; we welcome visits to the colleges at any time. Everyone has a plan that will include the best means for them to maintain this contact whether by 'phone, letter, email or Skype.

Fullerton House School

(Founded 1990)

Tickill Square, Denaby, Doncaster, South Yorkshire DN12 4AR

Tel: 01709 861663
Fax: 01709 869635
Email: enquiries@hesleygroup.co.uk
Website: www.fullertonhouseschool.co.uk
Head: Jeff Cox
Appointed: December 2013

School type: Independent Specialist Residential School
Age range of pupils: 8–19
Capacity: 40
Fees per annum as at 01/01/2015:
Available on request

A specialist residential school offering flexible education and care, which can include day and respite provision, for up to 52-weeks-per-year for young people aged 8-19, all of whom have complex needs including behaviour that may challenge and a learning disability, often in association with autism.

Fullerton House School is situated in the heart of the village of Denaby Main, near Doncaster. Its central location provides easy access by road, rail or air. Our mission is to enhance the lives of the young people entrusted to us by focusing on their specific needs, capabilities and aspirations.

Education: Each young person has a carefully designed Individual Learning Plan based on their specific needs in line with the National Curriculum, which supports their positive progress in a range of areas.

Extended learning: During evenings, weekends and school holidays a wide range of extra-curricular activities are on offer to ensure that young people are fully engaged with stimulating and meaningful experiences both on and off-site.

Professional services: A dedicated on-site team including carers, teachers, tutors, communication, behaviour and occupational therapy , psychology and other specialists ensure that young people have ready access to the services they require.

High-quality accommodation: Single person and small group occupancy of high-quality accommodation is provided at Fullerton House School. Every young person has their own bedroom, the majority of which have en-suite bathrooms. We also have a range of on-site facilities to complement and enrich the lives of those who come to live and learn with us.

Keeping in contact: We understand that while we may offer a very positive option for the young person, we may not be on your doorstep. Keeping in touch with loved ones is essential. Everyone has a plan to support optimum contact with family/carers and friends whether this be by phone, letter, email or Skype.

Wilsic Hall School

(Founded 1996)
Wadworth, Doncaster, South Yorkshire
DN11 9AG

Tel: 01302 856382
Fax: 01302 853608
Email: enquiries@hesleygroup.co.uk
Website: www.wilsichallschool.co.uk
Head: Geoff Turner
Appointed: September 2008

School type: Independent Specialist Residential School
Age range of pupils: 11–19
Capacity: 33
Fees per annum as at 01/01/2015:
Available on request

A specialist residential school offering flexible education and care, which can include day and respite provision, for up to 52-weeks-per-year for young people aged 11-19, all of whom have complex needs including behaviour that may challenge and a learning disability, often in association with autism.

Wilsic Hall School is situated in its own 14-acre site approximately five miles south of Doncaster. Its central location provides easy access by road, rail or air. Our mission is to enhance the lives of the young people entrusted to us by focusing on their specific needs, capabilities and aspirations.

Education: Each young person has a carefully designed Individual Education Plan based on their specific needs in line with the National Curriculum, which supports their positive progress in a range of areas.

Extended learning: During evenings, weekends and school holidays a wide range of extra-curricular activities are on offer to ensure that young people are fully engaged with stimulating and meaningful experiences both on and off-site.

Professional services: A dedicated team including carers, teachers, tutors, behaviour, communication and occupational therapy, psychology and other specialists ensure that each young person has ready access to the services they require.

High-quality accommodation: Single person and small group occupancy of high-quality accommodation is provided at Wilsic Hall School. Every young person has their own bedroom, the majority of which have en-suite bathrooms. We also have a range of on-site facilities to complement and enrich the lives of those who come to live and learn with us.

Keeping in contact: We understand that while we may offer a very positive option for the young person, we may not be on your doorstep. Keeping in touch with loved ones is essential. Everyone has a plan to support optimum contact with family/carers and friends whether this be by phone, letter, email or Skype.

The New School

The New School

BUTTERSTONE

(Founded 1992)
Butterstone, Dunkeld, Perth & Kinross

PH8 0HA
Tel: 01350 724216
Fax: 01350 724283
Email: info@thenewschool.co.uk
Website: www.thenewschool.co.uk
Head of School: Mr Scott Gordon
Appointed: January 2015
School type: Coeducational Day & Boarding

Age range of pupils: 11–19
No. of pupils enrolled as at 01/01/2015: 26
Boys: 19 **Girls:** 7
No. of boarders: 18
Fees per annum as at 01/01/2015:
Day: £40,085
Weekly Boarding: £51,571

Our vision is very clear – we want every young person to leave us thoroughly prepared for life in the 21st century. We have high expectations and the relaxed, flexible and supportive environment of The New School encourages our young people to feel comfortable with who they are, and to flourish as individuals.

We are a school with a specialism. Our provision is aimed at those young people who find mainstream education difficult to access. The New School specialises in education for fragile learners in general, for young people with Aspergers/Autistic Spectrum condition, ADHD, Tourette's syndrome and Foetal Alcohol syndrome. Skilled teaching and care staff support young people who have had interrupted learning, dissatisfying school experiences, or simply those who learn differently. We are a truly inclusive school.

The New School curriculum is broad, coherent and highly varied – meeting the different needs of each and every one of our young people. Our classes are small, with an average of five. Our students are encouraged to follow interests – making the learning motivating, relevant and meaningful for them, regardless of academic ability. We deliver a full menu of SQA accredited courses, from Curriculum for Excellence National 2 up to Higher level in most subjects. ASDAN accreditation system units and courses are offered to some students, helping them to develop independence, skills for work and skills for life. Speech and language therapy is offered to all students, if required. Our sector-leading 'Showcase' eprofile recording system ensures that the student population recognise and celebrate their own achievements – both academic and more broadly throughout their time here,

evidence is gathered across the 24-hour curriculum. We are passionate about outdoor learning, and utilise the beautiful

school situation to promote this in various ways. Our trained staff deliver full Duke of Edinburgh's Award up to Gold level.

Coleg Plas Dwbl

Mynachlog-ddu, Clunderwen,
Pembrokeshire SA66 7SE
Tel: 01994 419420
Email: info@plasdwbl.rmt.org
Website: www.rmt.org

Principal: Dan Alipaz
School type: Coeducational Day &
Residential
Age range of pupils: 16–25

Coleg Plas Dwbl offers places to young people with complex learning and behavioural difficulties, mental health issues and autistic spectrum disorders including Asperger Syndrome.

Practical Skills Therapeutic Education

Coleg Plas Dwbl is based in 100 acres of biodynamic farm and woodlands. It is one of four colleges operated by Ruskin Mill Trust (Argent College, Birmingham, opens September 2015, see Glasshouse College), whose internationally renowned Practical Skills Therapeutic Education method offers young people a unique opportunity to learn and develop transferable skills through meaningful real-life activities and accredited courses, helping them to prepare for adulthood.

The college provides a range of nutritional, therapeutic and medical support. Each core element of the educational cycle is designed to establish active and positive relationships with nature, people and the community through a holistic approach to human development. Students help to work the farm producing, harvesting and preparing healthy organic food, and supplying local outlets.

Integrated Learning For Living and Work Programme

Coleg Plas Dwbl offers a personalised pre-entry assessment leading to an individualised learning and development programme. A rich and varied curriculum offers exciting opportunities to develop communication, social, work and living skills. Activities include practical land-based and traditional craft activities, animal husbandry, woodland management, horticulture and catering, with social, communication and functional skills embedded throughout the day and residential curriculum.

Accreditation and Transition

Courses are accredited through the Qualification and Credit Framework and students will also prepare for work competency through a wide range of internal and external work experience. Qualifications include NVQs and BTECs; other options are available in partnership with local providers. The curriculum is also supported by additional sessions and activities which help students to understand and explore the culture and history of the area and try local crafts. In their final year, students are supported by staff to focus on transition and engage with the many transferable skills acquired to prepare for life after college.

Residential Provision

Students live in family houses or team houses which offer the consistency, warmth and positive role modelling that some young adults need to develop their living skills, achieve greater independence and re-imagine their potential. When appropriate, students can then progress to placements in training flats where they have the opportunity to take greater responsibility for themselves.

Coleg Plas Dwbl takes referrals throughout the year and offers placements up to 52 weeks.

Admissions

For all initial enquiries please contact the Admissions Team on 01994 419420 or by email at: admissions@plasdwbl.rmt.org

Ruskin Mill Trust is an educational charity and draws its inspiration from the insights of Rudolf Steiner, John Ruskin and William Morris. Charity No: 1137167

Schools and colleges specialising in sensory or physical impairment

Penn School

Church Road, Penn, High Wycombe,
Buckinghamshire HP10 8LZ
Tel: 01494 812139
Fax: 01494 811400
Email: office@pennschool.bucks.sch.uk
Website: www.pennschool.bucks.sch.uk

Headteacher: Mary-Nest Richardson
School type: Coeducational Boarding
Age range of pupils: 11–18
No. of pupils enrolled as at 01/01/2015: 29
Boys: 18 **Girls:** 11

At Penn School we offer specialist education, therapy and care to young people with communication difficulties associated with Speech, Language and Communication Needs, Autistic Spectrum Conditions and Hearing Impairment.

The school has a highly qualified, experienced and dedicated staff and this is reflected in the friendly and happy atmosphere which is evident to all visitors.

The school provides a rich and stimulating environment in which all members of the community work towards achieving their potential in academic, social and independent living terms. Our students are motivated and hard-working and achieve well in a range of accreditation from Entry Level to GCSE and BTEC.

Current statistics indicate that 92% of our students are making Good or better progress in KS3 and KS4 (as at 06/01/2015).

Our Vision

Penn School provides a happy, secure and stimulating learning environment where everyone is inspired to achieve their personal best.

Our Aims

- To educate and care for our young people with communication difficulties enabling them to become successful learners who make progress and achieve.
- To celebrate, recognise and value each individual's achievement thus building confidence and self-esteem.
- To equip our young people with the skills required to live fulfilling lives as responsible citizens who make a positive contribution to life in modern Britain with an emphasis on employability and work-related learning.
- To foster an inclusive community of all students, parents, carers and friends of the school which values trust, honesty, diversity and mutual respect in favour of equal opportunities and access for all.
- As British citizens, to value our freedom, to promote tolerance and respect for rule of law and British institutions and promote belief in personal and social responsibility.

RNIB College Loughborough

RNIB College Loughborough

(Founded 1989)
Radmoor Road, Loughborough,
Leicestershire LE11 3BS
Tel: 01509 611077
Fax: 01509 232013
Email: hannah.wharton@rnib.org.uk

Website: www.rnib.org.uk/rnibcollege
Principal: June Murray
School type: Coeducational College and residence
Age range of pupils: 16–65
No. of pupils enrolled as at 01/01/2015: 109

RNIB College Loughborough is a specialist college that supports people aged 16 to 65 with a wide range of disabilities, medical and health conditions. Our programmes are designed to develop independence skills for involvement in community life. Our bespoke residential and day programmes and active learning environment create a vibrant community in which young people flourish.

Education and Skills

All learners have an individual learning plan, with targets and goals agreed between themselves and their tutor. Progress is regularly monitored to ensure learners achieve their potential.

Our in-house programmes support people at Foundation Level to Level 1 through our innovative enterprise-led curriculum. Along with skills development and therapies, learners can progress on to independent or supported living, further education, supported employment, voluntary work or involvement within the community.

We can also support learners to access mainstream courses at Loughborough College. Learners have specialist support provided by RNIB and have access to RNIB College's purpose-built residential accommodation.

Living and Leisure

The Stan Bell Centre provides modern, purpose built, safe accommodation for learners and is situated very close to the college building. The Centre has ten flats each with six en-suite bedrooms. Within the building there is a shared TV lounge, three further lounges, a small gym, a games room and a computer room.

Learners are encouraged to be as independent as possible; however we recognise that some people will always need a little more support. Our residence is staffed 24 hours a day and support is available from staff at all times.

The college is based in Loughborough, near the town centre which has a good has a good selection of shops, cafes, bars and entertainment.

Visit us!

The best way to find out more about the college is to come and have a look round. Call us today to arrange your visit!

RNIB Sunshine House School and Residence

33 Dene Road, Northwood, Middlesex
HA6 2DD
Tel: 01923 822538
Fax: 01923 826227
Email: shsadmin@rnib.org.uk
Website: www.rnib.org.uk/sunshinehouse

Head: John Ayres
School type: Coeducational
Age range of pupils: 2–14
Fees per annum as at 01/01/2015:
Enquire for details

RNIB Sunshine House School and Residence, in Northwood, Middlesex, is a specialist school, children's home and service for families supporting blind and partially sighted children with significant learning difficulties and disabilities.

Boasting a range of specialist indoor and outdoor facilities, Sunshine House provides a safe and supportive environment for children to meet their full potential.

Education and Curriculum

Everyone at Sunshine House is treated as an individual with their own specific needs and learning goals. Working together with parents and specialists we ensure that achievements go beyond the classroom into everyday life.

Our specialist school educates children and young people from two to 14 years who have a range of physical, learning and sensory needs. Children follow an individually tailored curriculum supporting their special education needs. Most children are working between P levels 1 and 8. Each class has no more than eight children with a minimum support ratio of two adults for every three children.

Therapies and Healthcare

Our team of in-house therapists combine their work with a child's learning, making therapies a part of everyday school life. We also have a paediatric community nurse who ensures that all health needs are met.

Short Stays

Our children's home offers a range of flexible day care, overnight and short stay options, where children and young people aged between two and 16 years can stay up to four nights per week (Monday to Thursday) for up to 50 weeks per year during the school term and holidays. We welcome children who attend school elsewhere, providing we can meet their needs.

Visit us!

The best way to find out more about the school and residence is to come and have a look round. Call us today to arrange your visit!

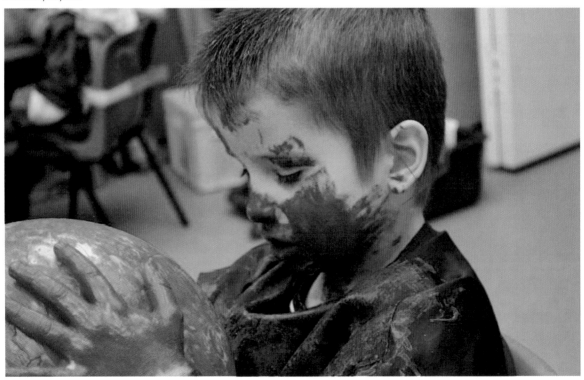

Chailey Heritage School

(Founded 1903)
Haywards Heath Road, North Chailey,

Lewes, East Sussex BN8 4EF
Tel: 01825 724444
Fax: 01825 723773
Email: office@chf.org.uk
Website: www.chf.org.uk
Charity Chief Executive: Helen Hewitt
Headteacher: Simon Yates
Director of Social Care: Denise Banks

School type: Coeducational Boarding & Day
Age range of pupils: 3–19
Plus Futures@Chailey Heritage for young adults aged 19–25
No. of pupils enrolled as at 01/01/2015: 73
Fees per annum as at 01/01/2015:
Please contact the school for details

Chailey Heritage School is a non-maintained special school for children and young people aged 3 to 19 with a wide range of complex physical, communication, sensory and learning difficulties and health needs.

Chailey Heritage School was judged to be outstanding by Ofsted in October 2014, for a third consecutive time.

Chailey Heritage Residential is a registered children's home and offers flexible care packages for up to 52 weeks of the year.

Education

The school offers a broad and balanced curriculum adapted to each pupil according to age and ability. This is alongside integrated therapy from a highly skilled team that includes expert teachers, paediatric medical consultants, speech and language therapists, physiotherapists, occupational therapists, nurses and rehabilitation engineers. This holistic approach ensures that learning programmes can be designed to suit each individual.

The school is divided into three departments: Pre-School/Primary Department (PSP) for nursery age children up to 11 years old; Secondary Department (11-16 years); 16+ Department for students up to 19 years old. For some pupils the school can set up and support dual placements with pupils' local mainstream schools.

Flexible residential care

Chailey Heritage Residential offers purpose-built, residential bungalows designed for young people who require residential provision in order to attend school. Each bungalow can accommodate young people for flexible boarding packages from overnight/short breaks right up to 52-week care. We also specialise in post-operative care and convalescence.

The residential department is led by a Registered Children's Home Manager supported by individual House Managers who lead and manage highly trained staff, providing 24-hour care, together with NHS nurses.

On site clinical support

Chailey Heritage School shares its location with Chailey Heritage Clinical Services (CHCS) – a specialist clinical team and part of the Sussex Community NHS Trust. Pupils' clinical needs are overseen by specialists in paediatric conditions, neurological problems and long-term disabilities. Therapists from CHCS make up part of the school's multidisciplinary team, which offers a unique combination of education, residential, therapy and health services on a single site.

Transition

Chailey Heritage Futures is a transition provision for young adults aged 19-25. For more information visit www.chf.org.uk

Chailey Heritage School and Futures@ Chailey Heritage are part of Chailey Heritage Foundation. Registered Charity Number 1075837. Registered in England as a Charitable Company limited by Guarantee No. 3769775

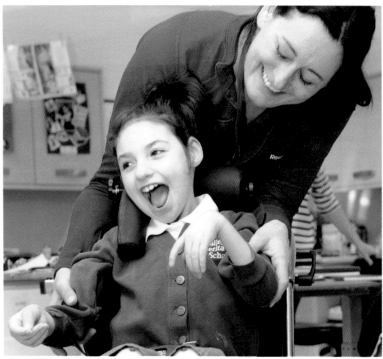

Moor House School & College

(Founded 1947)

Mill Lane, Hurst Green, Oxted, Surrey
RH8 9AQ
Tel: 01883 712271
Fax: 01883 716722
Email:
admissionsteam@moorhouseschool.co.uk
info@moorhouseschool.co.uk

Website: www.moorhouseschool.co.uk
Principal: Mrs H A Middleton
School type: Coeducational Day &
Residential
Age range of pupils: 7–19
No. of pupils enrolled as at 01/01/2015: 107
Fees per annum: On request

"Quality of teaching: Outstanding"-Ofsted 2014

Moor House is a special school and college for children and young people with language difficulties and related communication difficulties. Students come to Moor House from our local area as well as from across the UK. Their fees are paid by their Local Authorities.

The school, believed to be the first of its kind, has provided inspiration for other schools both in the UK and abroad, and continues to lead in areas of specialist education, therapy and research. Moor House shares its expertise and research findings to support children in the wider community and professionals at Moor House publish their work to share our innovative and evidence based methods internationally.

"…. Pioneering work in many areas of speech and language therapy and in teaching methods continues to place Moor House School at the forefront of research, development and practice in the education of children with severe, specific speech and language impairments." The Bercow Report

Learning

Students are empowered to reach their potential in classroom learning and independence, and to develop communication skills, friendships and self-belief. We offer a highly specialist, safe, caring and stimulating learning environment. Students are taught in small classes by teachers with experience of working with children with language difficulties. Adapted language and visual approaches are used so that children can understand and develop the language that they need for learning.

Speech and language therapists (SLTs) work closely with teachers to understand

and support each child's difficulties and strengths. Taking a holistic approach to learning, the teachers and SLTs plan and deliver English and Science lessons collaboratively, to ensure that children gain maximum benefit.

The curriculum

An adapted National Curriculum is taught at Moor House, with the core curriculum of English, Maths, Science and ICT being taught along with Geography, History, Art (including 3D Design), Music, Design & Technology, Food Technology, PSHCE, P.E. and Religious Education.

Progress and Qualifications

Our results show that overall our students make excellent progress. Students take qualifications that match with their skills and level of development. Many students take GCSE qualifications, which we offer in English Language, English Literature,

Mathematics, Science, ICT, History, Fine Art and Ceramics. We also offer Functional Skills qualifications in English and Maths, vocational qualifications such as Home Cooking Skills at Levels 1 and 2, the AQA Unit Award Scheme in Science, and Entry Level qualifications in subjects such as English, Maths, ICT, DT and Music.

Therapy

Speech and language therapy is an essential part of a student's week at Moor House and is integrated throughout their day. The SLTs work with students individually, in groups, as well as in the classroom where lessons such as English are jointly planned and delivered.

All students are supported through the school by occupational therapy programmes which include functional class support in PE, Art, Food Studies, life skills training and self-care support.

For some students who have more specific occupational therapy needs, we provide additional weekly individual, paired or group work delivered by an Occupational Therapist (OT).

Residential Care

Our Residential Care has been classed as Outstanding by Ofsted in each of the last four years. The Care team work to provide our students with a homely environment whilst they stay with us. The team also works closely with the teaching and therapy staff to ensure that each child receives the support needed.

College (Sixth Form) Curriculum

"The sixth form is outstanding and prepares students exceptionally well for the next stage in their adult lives" – Ofsted 2014

The College's objective is to support each student to gain vocational qualifications, make confident and appropriate life choices and to be prepared for the next stage of their adult life. Students are supported by the Moor House specialist staff to enable them to access our local link FE college courses. Students also access our specialist support to achieve additional qualifications in Maths and English and develop important skills for life and employment. Teaching and residential care staff work jointly with SLTs and OTs to provide individual study programmes and after college support.

Learning at the Partnership Colleges

Students can access vocational courses on offer at the partnership colleges such as painting and decorating, child care, media studies, art and design, catering, sport and active leisure and animal management. Achievement ranges from Foundation and Level 1 in Year 12 to as high as Level 3 at the end of Year 14. As well as providing support directly to the students, the MHC Therapy department offers training and student specific advice to teaching staff running the link college courses.

St Mary's School & 6th Form College

(Founded 1922)

Wrestwood Road, Bexhill-on-Sea, East Sussex TN40 2LU
Tel: 01424 730740
Fax: 01424 733575
Email: admin@stmarysbexhill.org
Website: www.stmarysbexhill.org

CEO & Principal:
Dr Sharon Menghini Doctorate, PGCE, SpID Diploma, M.Ed (SEN), Cert.Ed
School type: Coeducational Boarding & Day
Age range of pupils: 7–19
No. of pupils enrolled as at 01/01/2015: 104

Making a difference

We are an inspirational School and 6th Form College for young people aged 7-19 with speech, language and communication disabilities, many of whom have other complex needs. We are committed to providing integrated therapy, education and care tailored to each young person's abilities and aspirations.

The children and young people are taught in small groups and follow an exciting broad and balanced curriculum, which is adapted to meet individual needs and is delivered by highly qualified teachers and support staff with the integrated support of therapists for a truly holistic approach.

Children receive individual therapy programmes which may include specialist support from: Speech and Language Therapists, Physiotherapists, Occupational Therapists, Well-being Team and Educational Psychologist.

Other specialist professionals include an Audiologist and Teacher of the Deaf, Sign Language Tutors, Social Worker, visiting Doctor (GP) and onsite Nursing Team.

Here at St Mary's, we support each child to develop and maximise their communication skills. Parent signing classes are offered on site or via Skype to ensure families can communicate with their child as effectively as possible.

At St Mary's our residences are warm and caring places, creating a 'home from home' feel. In nurturing and stimulating environments we work with our children and young people to develop life skills and encourage everyone to learn and live with each other. Opportunities to take part in a wide range of activities are available every day, with children and young people accessing the local community on a daily basis.

Our fantastic facilities include:
- Sensory Room
- Physiotherapy Room
- Adventure Playground
- Swimming and Hydrotherapy pool
- Sensory Integration Room
- Traversing Wall
- Nature Trail
- Music & Drumming Room
- Outdoor Tennis Courts
- Science Lab
- ICT Suite
- Horticultural area & Polytunnel

The Children's Trust School
Non-Maintained Special School

The Children's Trust
For children with brain injury

(Founded 1985)

Tadworth Court, Tadworth, Surrey
KT20 5RU
Tel: 01737 365810
Fax: 01737 365819
Email: school@thechildrenstrust.org.uk
Website:
www.thechildrenstrust.org.uk/school

Interim Head: Pam Walden
School type: Coeducational Boarding
Age range of pupils: 3–19
No. of pupils enrolled as at 01/04/2015:
Boys: 24 **Girls:** 25
Fees per annum as at 01/01/2015:
On application

The Children's Trust School, formerly known as The School for Profound Education, is one of the few special schools in the UK that works exclusively with learners with profound and multiple learning difficulties (PMLD) and complex health needs.

Our aim
At The Children's Trust School our aim is to provide a caring and happy environment where we use our expertise to meet each child's special educational needs and celebrate their achievements.

As a non-maintained residential special school, we pride ourselves on delivering education, therapy and care for children and young people with profound and multiple learning difficulties and complex medical needs. We have our own team of therapists, a doctor and small team of nurses, all onsite.

We work with children with a range of conditions including cerebral palsy, Rett syndrome and acquired brain injury. We provide day and residential education for learners aged three upwards. Residential care is available for up to 52 weeks a year.

Learning
We offer a wide range of learning opportunities to help each individual develop, thrive and grow, with an extensive team of teaching, therapy and nursing care staff. Using our specially designed 24-hour curriculum, The Profound Education Curriculum, we focus on the precursors to learning, intentional communication and interaction, to help our pupils understand the world around them.

Facilities
We have a state of the art hydrotherapy pool, residential accommodation only a walk away from the school building, and even a wheelchair accessible tree house!

Why choose us?
Our expertise is providing the best opportunities and quality of life for children with very high levels of need. It is about putting our pupils first.

The school is part of The Children's Trust, the UK's leading charity for children with brain injury. Registered charity number 288018.

Treloar School

Enabling Education

(Founded 1908)

Holybourne, Alton, Hampshire GU34 4GL
Tel: 01420 547400
Email: admissions@treloar.org.uk
Website: www.treloar.org.uk
Head: Jo McSherrie
Principal: John Stone
School type: Coeducational Boarding & Day

Age range of pupils: 2–19
No. of pupils enrolled as at 01/09/2015: 95
Boys: 50 **Girls:** 45 **Sixth Form:** 31
No. of boarders: 54
Fees per annum as at 01/09/2015:
As per assessment

Treloar Nursery and School provide education, care, therapy, medical support and independence training to children and young people from 2 to 19 years of age with complex physical disabilities. Provision is both day and residential and we accept students from across the UK and overseas. In addition our College, based on the same site, offers continued education and care up to the age of 25 years. Our aim is to prepare physically disabled young people for adult life, giving them the confidence and skills they need to achieve their full potential, and also become socially and economically active in their communities.

We have an on site medical centre and weekly doctors surgeries in addition to on site provision for occupational therapy, physiotherapy, speech and language therapy, educational psychology, visual and hearing impairment, assistive technology plus dieticians and counsellors. Timetables are integrated with classroom and daily living activities to ensure the most beneficial use of the student's time.

Entry Requirement

Admission is considered on the basis of the particular student's needs following discussion and assessment with education, medical, therapy and care staff. All offers are tailor made to provide the maximum benefit for each student and we strive to be flexible. Part time placements, limited time placements and respite for day students are all available. We pride ourselves on our strong parental links

and have been awarded the nationally recognised Leading Parent Partnership Award.

Life on Campus

We are situated in a beautiful rural location on the edge of Alton in Hampshire with a good road and rail network. We ensure a varied range of out of school activities including sports, art, drama, clubs and

extensive visits off site utilising our own specialist fleet of vehicles. On site facilities include a swimming pool, all weather sports facilities, a hydrotherapy pool and social club.

Treloar Trust is a registered charity which supports Treloar School and College (Charity No 1092857).

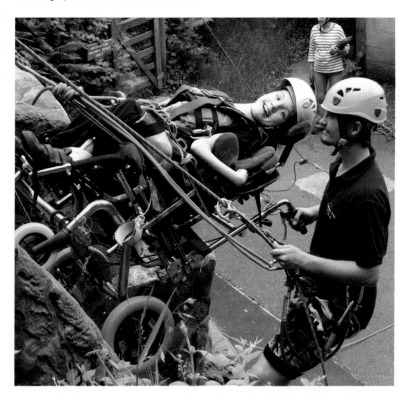

WESC Foundation – The Specialist College for Visual Impairment

The Specialist College for Visual Impairment

(Founded 1838)

Countess Wear, Exeter, Devon EX2 6HA

Tel: 01392 454200

Fax: 01392 428048

Email: info@wescfoundation.ac.uk

Website: www.wescfoundation.ac.uk

Principal: Mrs Tracy de Bernhardt-Dunkin

School type: Non-maintained Special School and College

Age range of pupils: 16+

Fees per annum as at 01/01/2016:

On request

WESC Foundation provides a wide range of post-16 academic and vocational courses and specialist training and support to help young people with a visual impairment make a successful transition to adult life. Many pupils from the school move directly to the college.

Tailored to the needs of the individual, our courses contain employability and work experience modules and are supported by work placements in our own social enterprise firms (shops and eBay centre) or with partner organisations.

We also work in partnership with other colleges of further education to provide our students with a unique academic and vocational experience.

The college offers:

- Specialist support tailored to the needs of each student
- A challenging curriculum
- A wide range of nationally accredited awards and qualifications
- A virtual learning support
- Work placements with local employers
- Professional specialists: speech and language therapists, physiotherapists, occupational therapists, music therapists, mobility tutors, qualified nurses and care staff
- Qualified and experienced teachers of the visually and multi-sensory impaired
- Individual learning plans
- High staff:learner ratio
- Purpose-built accommodation: from fully supervised to self-contained houses
- Day and residential placements
- Broad-based leisure programmes
- Specialist sensory environments

College accommodation comprises of comfortable bedrooms with well-equipped areas for socialising with friends and visitors. Maple Lodge and Ash Lodge benefit from larger bedrooms and extra wide access for wheelchairs. Lodges feature adjustable height kitchen and bathroom appliances, talking kitchen equipment and an accessible laundry. The latest technologies, equipment and fittings help develop and support independent living skills. Campus facilities include: pool, gym, library, bar and social area.

Situated on the outskirts of Exeter – city in the country by the sea – the campus offers access to a huge range of activities and experiences. Extended curricular activities include trips to the beach, park, ten pin bowling and even residential trips abroad.

Please call or email for more information on assessment and admissions quoting WHM/16.

Registered charity no. 1058937.

WESC Foundation – The Specialist School for Visual Impairment

The Specialist School for Visual Impairment

(Founded 1838)

Countess Wear, Exeter, Devon EX2 6HA
Tel: 01392 454200
Fax: 01392 428048
Email: info@wescfoundation.ac.uk
Website: www.wescfoundation.ac.uk
Chief Executive: Mrs Tracy de Bernhardt-Dunkin

School type: Non-maintained Special School and College
Age range of pupils: 5–16
Fees per annum as at 01/01/2016: On request

WESC Foundation specialises in meeting the needs of young people with visual impairment, including many with complex needs. The school offers an excellent academic curriculum that follows the National Curriculum. Each pupil receives mobility and therapy sessions where a need has been identified (occupational therapy, physiotherapy, speech and language therapy, music therapy, etc.). Specialist ICT equipment and adapted access technology is tailored for each pupil.

The school residences offer homely, comfortable accommodation for weekly boarders and those wishing to stay occasionally. Accommodation comprises of comfortable bedrooms and areas for socialising with friends and visitors. Groundfloor areas are wheelchair accessible and suitable adaptations are made for individuals.

Our 14-acre campus provides space for pupils to enjoy the sensory garden, swimming pool, gym and adapted playing areas. Situated on the outskirts of Exeter – city in the country by the sea – the campus offers access to a huge range of activities and experiences. Extended curricular activities include trips to the beach, park, ten pin bowling and even residential trips abroad.

Pupils are totally involved in planning for their future with many of them continuing their studies and development at our college, which is situated on the same campus.

Candidates for both the school and college need to come for an assessment. This is free and is usually held over a period of two days. The assessment process is an opportunity for you to take an in-depth look at what we have to offer and allows our specialist staff to determine how best to meet a young person's needs. Please call or email for more information on assessment and admissions quoting WHM/01/16.

Registered charity no. 1058937

RNIB Pears Centre for Specialist Learning

RNIB Pears Centre

(Founded 1957)

Wheelwright Lane, Ash Green, Coventry, West Midlands CV7 9RA
Tel: 024 7636 9500
Fax: 024 7636 9501
Email: pearscentre@rnib.org.uk
Website: www.rnib.org.uk/pearscentre

Executive Headteacher: Andy Moran
Appointed: September 2007
School type: Coeducational day school and Children's Home
Age range of pupils: 2–19
No. of pupils enrolled as at 01/01/2015: 29

RNIB Pears Centre offers individually tailored education, care and therapies to children and young people with multiple disabilities and complex health needs who are blind or partially sighted, from pre-school up to the age of 19.

We offer a stimulating and supportive purpose-built environment for children and young people, enabling them to reach their full potential for fulfilment. Our education and care are both graded "Outstanding" by Ofsted. Our nursing care for children with additional medical needs is also fully compliant with Care Quality Commission (CQC) standards.

Education and curriculum

Our broad, balanced and relevant curriculum is differentiated to meet individual needs and learning styles. Class groups are arranged considering not just age but developmental and sensory need. Each class has usually no more than seven pupils, with a staff team of a teacher, senior teaching assistant and at least two additional teaching assistants. Our curriculum delivery is supported with input from other specialists such as speech and language therapists and physiotherapists.

We offer a newly established early years education provision in our well-staffed specialist nursery known as The Orchard.

Our specialist outreach service called "Periscope" offers practical support to individual pupils and educational advice and guidance to professionals and parents. Our team can also carry out a range of assessments, reviews and reports to facilitate and improve learning, such as functional vision assessments.

Living and leisure

Our children's home offers up to 52-week care. We also offer specialist care as a step-down from hospital for children and young people with high health and medical needs (including long-term ventilation or life threatening or life-limiting conditions).

Our comfortable and homely environment is both stimulating and supportive. Each young person living with us has their own bedroom, which is made safe and personal to them. Children and young people plan and choose their social and leisure activities, like pop concerts and swimming. This enhances their self-esteem and sense of identity.

Therapies and healthcare

Our in-house therapy team offers specialist expertise including learning disabilities, physiotherapy, speech and language therapy, behaviour management and mobility/habilitation. Water and music therapies, clinical psychology and occupational therapy are also part of our provision.

Visit us!

The best way to find out more about the school and children's home is to come and have a look round. Call us today to arrange your visit!

The Royal National College for the Blind (RNC)

Great Britain's leading specialist college for people who are blind or partially sighted

Education, employment and empowerment

(Founded 1872)
Venns Lane, Hereford, Herefordshire
HR1 1DT

Tel: 01432 265725
Fax: 01432 842979
Email: info@rnc.ac.uk
Website: www.rnc.ac.uk
Principal: Ms Sheila Tallon
School type: Coeducational Boarding & Day
Age range of pupils: 16–65

Students from all over the UK
No. of pupils enrolled as at 01/01/2015:
No. of boarders: 150
Fees per annum as at 01/01/2015:
Funded via Local Authorities (younger students) or Department for Work and Pensions (adults)

The Royal National College for the Blind (RNC) is the UK's leading specialist residential college of further education for people over the age of 16 with a visual impairment.

At RNC we have created a vibrant and supportive community, valuing personalised learning plans that help each student to achieve their future ambitions while building and developing their self-confidence and independence.

We offer a wide range of study programmes at levels to suit each individual including A Levels, BTECs, ITECs, NVQs and OCRs in subjects from humanities, massage and languages to IT and media production.

RNC is home to the UK's first VI Sports Academy and Cisco Networking Academy, offering tailored training in both the sporting and technology industries. Students also gain independence and mobility skills to support their transition to adulthood.

Many students go on to university or into employment or self-employment, having engaged not just academically but socially in a safe yet dynamic environment. Among the many clubs and activities on offer are Duke of Edinburgh Awards, crafts, angling, Young Enterprise, performing arts, horticulture and sports including football and goalball.

In 2011, Ofsted awarded RNC 'outstanding' as a specialist residential provider. In 2013 we maintained our 'good' with outstanding elements rating as a Further Education and Skills provider. Teachers were praised as being skilled at providing an accessible learning environment in which students with little or no sight participate fully.

RNC also offers services to a diverse audience including businesses, universities and other education providers, and to professionals working with visually impaired people.

Prospective students can visit the College and speak with specialist staff, or attend a free Have a Go weekend, trying out different courses in a relaxed atmosphere. Contact Student Enquiries for more information on 01432 376 621 or visit www.rnc.ac.uk.

Doncaster School for the Deaf

Doncaster School for the Deaf

(Founded 1829)

Leger Way, Doncaster, South Yorkshire DN2 6AY

Tel: 01302 386733

Fax: 01302 361808

Email: principal@ddt-deaf.org.uk

or secretary@ddt-deaf.org.uk

Website: www.deaf-trust.co.uk

Executive Principal: Mr Alan W Robinson

School type: Non-maintained (Special)

Coeducational Boarding and Day

Age range of pupils: 3–19

No. of pupils enrolled as at 01/01/2015: 27

Boys: 18 *Girls:* 9

No. of boarders: 4

Fees per annum as at 01/01/2014:

Fees on request

We offer a broad and balanced curriculum which is accessible to all our pupils, providing smooth progression and continuity through all Key Stages.

The language and communication policy at Doncaster School for the Deaf is a pupil-centred approach, based on their method of preferred communication. We aim to meet the needs of pupils who communicate through British Sign Language (BSL) or English.

The School has a full-time Audiologist, Speech and Language Therapist and a team of Teaching Assistants as well as an on-site fully qualified Nurse. Most teachers are experienced and qualified teachers of the deaf.

Provision for resident pupils is in a modern comfortable house sympathetically converted to provide high standards of living accommodation.

Qualifications include A Levels, AS Levels, GCSE, Entry Level Certificate of Achievement, ASDAN and Signature (BSL). The school believes that the school curriculum should be broad, balanced and personalised in order to reflect the needs of each pupil and to nurture a lifelong desire to learn. In addition to curriculum subjects pupils access speech therapy, BSL lessons and Deaf Studies. Some KS4 and KS5 pupils are able to access vocational courses as part of the 14-19 curriculum.

The School works in partnership with Little Learners Day Nursery and Communication Specialist College Doncaster (formerly Doncaster College for the Deaf) which share the same campus.

We have close links with parents, and other professionals.

The school occupies a large, pleasant site. A superb sports hall, heated indoor swimming pool and extensive playing fields. The school welcomes visitors.

St John's Catholic School for the Deaf

(Founded 1870)
Church Street, Boston Spa, Wetherby,
West Yorkshire LS23 6DF
Tel: 01937 842144
Fax: 01937 541471

Email: info@stjohns.org.uk
Website: www.stjohns.org.uk
Headteacher: Mrs A Bradbury BA(Hons),
MSc, NPQH
School type: Coeducational Boarding & Day

Age range of pupils: 4–19
No. of pupils enrolled as at 01/01/2015: 68
Fees per annum as at 01/01/2015:
On application

St John's is a non-maintained residential and day school offering bespoke education to deaf, multi-sensory impaired (MSI) and language impaired children. We were founded almost 150 years ago and although the school is based on a Catholic ethos, we welcome children from other faiths or none. Some pupils have additional and complex needs which may include dyslexia, dyspraxia, learning difficulties, ASD, ADHD, and physical disabilities. Our pupils are aged from 4 to 19 years and come to us from all parts of the UK.

St John's is an oral school, where pupils are taught by specialist teachers of hearing impaired children. We place great emphasis on developing each child's potential for understanding and using spoken and written language, as well as reading and writing. Our unique approach has gained us a national and international reputation for promoting linguistic, academic and personal growth, enabling pupils to make their contribution to a wider world.

In our Speech and Language Department we have specialist therapists so pupils can receive intensive individual speech therapy. Our teachers are qualified teachers of hearing impaired children with additional qualifications in areas such as MSI and dyslexia and we also have qualified intervenors. Close liaison and joint planning across staff teams helps to provide well-coordinated provision, including support from the York Deaf CAMHS team.

We offer a vibrant curriculum with a wide range of qualifications that include GCSEs as well as creative and vocational courses, to meet the needs of the individual pupils.

The development of communication skills has special emphasis at St John's and we have a dedicated Expressive Arts Centre which is designed for drama, music, and dance. We have specialist

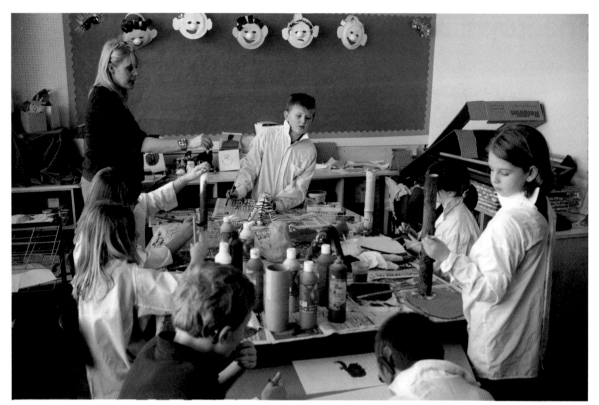

music and drama teachers, one to one music tuition and have a soundproof recording booth for pupils to create their own compositions.

Our other facilities include three different sensory rooms to support pupils with dual or multi sensory impairments to maximise their use and integration of all their senses.

Our Post 16 students attend mainstream colleges, supported by our own note takers and a teacher of the deaf. Students receive additional tutorial support at school as well as continuing with speech therapy and courses in English and Maths.

Residential life at St John's supports pupils' communication, social and life skills. Students grow in confidence and maturity,

leaving St John's so well prepared for adult life that Ofsted has judged the care pupils receive as outstanding.

If you would like to visit and experience first-hand, the education and care we offer our pupils, please contact our Pupil Admissions Co-ordinator Mandy Dowson on 01937 842144 or email info@stjohns.org. uk.

The Royal Blind School

THE ROYAL BLIND SCHOOL

(Founded 1835)

43-45 Canaan Lane, Edinburgh, EH10 4SG

Tel: 0131 446 3120

Fax: 0131 447 9266

Email: office@royalblindschool.org.uk

Website: www.royalblind.org/education

Head Teacher: Elaine Brackenridge (BEd)

School type: Coeducational, National

Grant Aided Special School

Age range of pupils: 5–19

No. of pupils enrolled as at 01/01/2015: 44

Fees per annum as at 01/01/2015:

Available on request

The Royal Blind School is Scotland's only residential school specialising in the care and education of visually impaired children and young people, including those with complex needs and visual impairment. The school is situated in the Morningside area of Edinburgh.

We offer day and weekly residential places. Our residential houses are fully accessible and designed to be a home from home.

We enrol pupils from P1 to S6. There is a free pre-school playgroup held weekly for children who are visually impaired, including those with complex needs.

The Royal Blind School has a high ratio of staff to pupils. Each child follows an individualised education programme underpinned by the Curriculum for Excellence and Getting It Right for Every Child (GIRFEC). We deliver a broad general education and offer qualifications and accreditation by the Scottish Qualifications Authority (SQA), Junior Awards Scheme Scotland and ASDAN.

Our approach is inclusive and pupil-centred, providing many opportunities for experience and achievement. We strive to make learning enjoyable, fun, challenging and self-affirming. Subjects offered include art, drama, outdoor education and craft, design and technology.

We deliver independent living skills, mobility and orientation to ensure that all pupils become as independent as possible.

The Royal Blind School was founded on compassionate and forward thinking principles in 1835. It is run by Scotland's largest visual impairment charity, Royal Blind, and is regulated by Education Scotland and the Care Inspectorate. We are a grant aided special school supported by the Scottish Government.

Places are paid for through fees from local authorities or privately.

Outreach Support

We also provide an education outreach service offering support, training, resources and advice to staff in mainstream schools who are working with visually impaired pupils.

For more information please visit our website www.royalblind.org/education or telephone 0131 446 3120, or email office@royalblindschool.org.uk.

Scottish Charity No. SC017167.

Directory

Schools and colleges specialising in social interaction difficulties (Autism, ASD & ASP)

Abbreviations

ACLD	Autism, Communication and Associated Learning Difficulties
ADD	Attention Deficit Disorder
ADHD	Attention Deficit and Hyperactive Disorder (Hyperkinetic Disorder)
ASD	Autistic Spectrum Disorder
ASP	Asperger Syndrome
AUT	Autism
BESD	Behavioural, Emotional and Social Difficulties
CCD	Complex Communication Difficulties
CLD	Complex Learning Difficulties
CP	Cerebral Palsy
D	Deaf
DEL	Delicate
DYS	Dyslexia
DYSP	Dyspraxia
EBD	Emotional and Behavioural Difficulties
EBSD	Emotional, Behavioural and/or Social Difficulties
EPI	Epilepsy
GLD	General Learning Difficulties
HA	High Ability
HI	Hearing Impairment
HS	Hospital School
LD	Learning Difficulties
MLD	Moderate Learning Difficulties
MSI	Multi-sensory Impairment
OCD	Obsessive Compulsive Disorder
PD	Physical Difficulties
PH	Physical Impairment
Phe	Partially Hearing
PMLD	Profound and Multiple Learning Difficulties
PNI	Physical Neurological Impairment
PRU	Pupil Referral Unit
SCD	Social and Communication Difficulties
SCLD	Severe and Complex Learning Difficulties
SEBD	Severe Emotional and Behavioural Disorders
SEBN	Social, Emotional and Behavioural Needs
SLD	Severe Learning Difficulties
SLI	Specific Language Impairment
SPLD	Specific Learning Difficulties
SP&LD	Speech and Language Difficulties
SLCN	Speech Language & Communication Needs
VIS	Visually Impaired

Key to Symbols

Type of school:

(♂)	Boys' school
(♀)	Girls' school
🌍	International school

School offers:

(A)	A levels
(🏢)	Boarding accommodation
(16+)	Entrance at 16+
(⚙)	Vocational qualifications
(✎)	Learning support
(✔)	This is a DfE approved independent or non-maintained school under section 342 or 347(1) of the 1996 Education Act

Please note: Unless otherwise indicated, all schools are coeducational day schools. Single-sex and boarding schools will be indicated by the relevant icon.

Central & West

Bristol

NAS Anderson School
Rookery Lane, Pilning,
Bristol BS35 4JN
Tel: 01454 632532
Head of Education: Simon
Cartwright
Age range: 10–19
No. of pupils: 20
Special needs catered for:
ASD, ASP, AUT
♿ 16+ ✓

Oxfordshire

LVS Oxford
Spring Hill Road, Begbroke,
Oxfordshire OX5 1RX
Tel: 01865 595170
Head Teacher: Ms Jane Straw
Age range: 11–19
Special needs catered for:
ASD, ASP, AUT
♿ 16+

Swalcliffe Park School Trust
Swalcliffe, Banbury,
Oxfordshire OX15 5EP
Tel: 01295 780302
Principal: Mr Kiran Hingorani
Age range: B11–19
No. of pupils: 45
Special needs catered for: ADHD,
ASD, BESD, DYS, DYSP, MLD, SP&LD
♿ 16+ ✓

West Berkshire

PRIOR'S COURT SCHOOL
For further details see p. 38
Hermitage, Thatcham,
West Berkshire RG18 9NU
Tel: 01635 247202
Email: mail@priorscourt.org.uk
Website: www.priorscourt.org.uk
**Director of Education and
Learning:** Sue Piper
Age range: 5–19
No. of pupils: 59 VIth24
Special needs catered for:
AUT, CLD, EPI, MLD, SCLD
♿ ✓

Wiltshire

Farleigh Further Education
College Swindon
Fairview House, 43 Bath Road, Old
Town, Swindon, Wiltshire SN1 4AS
Tel: 01793 719500
Principal/Manager: Mr
Martin Bentham
Age range: 16–25
No. of pupils: 63
Special needs catered for: ASP, LD
16+ ♿

Stratford Lodge
4 Park Lane, Castle Road,
Salisbury, Wiltshire SP1 3NP
Tel: 0800 288 9779
Head: Sue King BA(Hons), PGCE
Dip in Adv Ed Studies SEN, NPQH
Age range: 16–19
Special needs catered for:
ADHD, ASD, ASP
♿ 16+

East

Cambridgeshire

Gretton School
High Street, Girton, Cambridge,
Cambridgeshire CB3 0QL
Tel: 01223 277438
Headteacher: Lyndsey Stone
Age range: 5–19
Special needs catered for:
ASD, AUT, LD
16+ ✓

On Track Training Centre
Enterprise House, Old Field Lane,
Wisbech, Cambridgeshire PE13 2RJ
Tel: 01945 580898
Headteacher: Mrs Sharon Claydon
Age range: 11–18
Special needs catered for:
ADHD, ASP, EBD
16+ ✓

Park House
Wisbech Road,
Thorney, Peterborough,
Cambridgeshire PE6 0SA
Tel: 01733 271187
Head: Mr Alan Crossland
Age range: 4–16
Special needs catered for: AUT
✓

Essex

The Yellow House School
1 Alderford Street, Sible
Hedingham, Halstead,
Essex CO9 3HX
Tel: 01787 462504
Age range: 13–17
No. of pupils: 11
Special needs catered for:
ADHD, ASP, EBD
✓

Hertfordshire

NAS Radlett Lodge School
Harper Lane, Radlett,
Hertfordshire WD7 9HW
Tel: 01923 854922
Principal: Jo Galloway
Age range: 4–19
No. of pupils: 55
Special needs catered for:
ASD, ASP, AUT
♿ 16+ ✓

Norfolk

Acorn Park School
Mill Road, Banham, Norwich,
Norfolk NR16 2HU
Tel: 01953 888656
Head Teacher: Mr John Shaw
BEd(Hons), DipEdMan
Age range: 4–19
Special needs catered for:
ASD, AUT, CLD, EPI, LD, MLD,
SCD, SCLD, SLD, SPLD
♿ 16+

St Andrews School
Lower Common, East Runton,
Cromer, Norfolk NR27 9PG
Tel: 01263 837927
Headteacher: Ms Gillian
Baker BSc(Hons), BA, CertEd,
PGC-Asperger Syndrome
Age range: 6–17
No. of pupils: 17
Fees: Day £40,000
Special needs catered for:
ADD, ADHD, ASD, ASP, AUT, DYS,
DYSP, SCD, SLD, SP&LD, SLI
✓

East Midlands

Derbyshire

High Grange School
Hospital Lane, Mickleover,
Derby, Derbyshire DE3 0DR
Tel: 01332 412777
Headteacher: Marisa Kelsall
Age range: 8–19
Special needs catered for:
ASD, ASP, AUT
16+ ✓

Leicestershire

Sketchley Horizon
Manor Way, Sketchley, Burbage,
Leicestershire LE10 3HT
Tel: 01455 890023
Principal: Ms Sarah-Jane Astbury
Age range: 8–19
No. of pupils: 30
Special needs catered for:
ASD, ASP, AUT
16+ ✓

Northamptonshire

Alderwood
302 Wellingborough Road,
Rushden, Northamptonshire
NN10 6BB
Tel: 01933 359861
Head: Mrs Jacqueline Wadlow
Special needs catered for: ASD, AUT
♿ 16+ ✓

Hill Farm College
c/o The Manor House,
Squires Hill, Rothwell,
Northamptonshire NN14 6BQ
Tel: 01536 711111
Principal: Jo Morris
Age range: 14–19
No. of pupils: 12
Special needs catered for:
ADHD, ASD, ASP
♿ 16+

POTTERSPURY LODGE SCHOOL
For further details see p. 40
Towcester, Northamptonshire
NN12 7LL
Tel: 01908 542912
Email: mail@
potterspurylodge.co.uk
Website:
www.potterspurylodge.co.uk
Principal: Mr John W D Brown
Age range: B8–18
No. of pupils: 46 VIth11
Fees: Day £51,330 WB £76,989
Special needs catered for:
ADD, ADHD, ASD, ASP, AUT,
DYS, DYSP, EBD, SCD, SP&LD
(♿)(🏫)(16+)(✔)

Greater London

Kent

Baston House School
Baston Road, Hayes,
Bromley, Kent BR2 7AB
Tel: 020 8462 1010
Principal: Steve Vincent
Age range: 3–19
Special needs catered for: ASD
(16+)(✔)

Middlesex

NAS Sybil Elgar School
Havelock Road, Southall,
Middlesex UB2 4NR
Tel: 020 8813 9168
Principal: Chloe Phillips
Age range: 4–19
No. of pupils: 99
Special needs catered for:
ASD, ASP, AUT
(🏫)(16+)(✔)

Surrey

'the little group'
c/o St Josephs Catholic
Primary School, Rosebank,
Epsom, Surrey KT18 7RT
Tel: 01372 720218
Head Teacher: Judy Gilham
Age range: 2–5+
Special needs catered for: ASD, AUT

London

London

North London

Kestrel House School
104 Crouch Hill, London N8 9EA
Tel: 020 8348 8500
Headteacher: Kerry Harris
Age range: 4–16
Special needs catered for: ASP, AUT
(✔)

THE HOLMEWOOD SCHOOL
For further details see p. 44
88 Woodside Park Road,
London N12 8SH
Tel: 020 8920 0660
Email: enquiries@thsl.org.uk
Website: www.thsl.org.uk
Head of School: Head
of School Lucia Santi
Age range: 7–19
Special needs catered for:
ASP, AUT, DYS, DYSP, SP&LD
(IB)(16+)(✔)

TreeHouse School
Woodside Avenue, London N10 3JA
Tel: 020 8815 5424
Head: Julie O'Sullivan
Age range: 3–19
No. of pupils: 67
Special needs catered for: ASD, AUT
(16+)(✔)

South-East London

RIVERSTON SCHOOL
For further details see p. 41
63-69 Eltham Road, Lee
Green, London SE12 8UF
Tel: 020 8318 4327
Email: office@
riverstonschool.co.uk
Website:
www.riverstonschool.co.uk
Headmistress: Mrs S E Salathiel
Age range: 9 months–19 years
No. of pupils: 215
Special needs catered for:
ASD, ASP, AUT, LD
(♿)(£)(🔗)(✔)

South-West London

RAINBOW SCHOOL
For further details see p. 42
The Tram House, 520 Garratt
Lane, London SW17 0NY
Tel: 020 3031 9700
Email: admin@
beyondautism.org.uk
Website:
www.beyondautism.org.uk
Head Teacher: Lesley Love
Age range: 4–19 (Early
Years/Primary, Secondary
and 6th Form)
Special needs catered for:
ASD, ASP, AUT, SCD
(✔)

The Chelsea Group of Children
The Hall, Waynflete Street,
London SW18 3QG
Tel: 020 8946 8330
Director: Libby Hartman
Age range: 4–8
Special needs catered for: ADHD,
ASP, AUT, LD, MLD, SP&LD, SPLD
(✔)

The Priory Lodge School
Priory Lane, London SW15 5JJ
Tel: 020 8392 4410
Principal: Pancho Martinez
Age range: 7–19
No. of pupils: 40
Special needs catered for:
ASD, ASP, AUT, LD
(16+)(✔)

North-East

Durham

Priory Hurworth House
38 The Green, Hurworth-on-Tees,
Darlington, Durham DL2 2AD
Tel: 01325 720424
Principal: Mr John Anderson
Age range: 7–19
No. of pupils: 30
Special needs catered for:
AUT, BESD, EBD
(16)

Tyne & Wear

ESPA College
6-7 The Cloisters, Ashbrooke,
Sunderland, Tyne & Wear SR2 7BD
Tel: 0191 510 2600
Principal (Acting): Mrs C Pickup
Age range: 16–25
No. of pupils: 100
Special needs catered for:
ASD, ASP, AUT
(金)

Thornhill Park School
21 Thornhill Park, Sunderland,
Tyne & Wear SR2 7LA
Tel: 0191 514 0659
Head Teacher: Margaret Burton
Age range: 4–19
No. of pupils: 74
Fees: Day £33,752–£45,806
FB £117,433–£204,986
Special needs catered for:
ASD, ASP, AUT
(金) (16) (✓)

North-West

Cheshire

ROYAL COLLEGE MANCHESTER
For further details see p. 45
Seashell Trust, Stanley Road,
Cheadle, Cheshire SK8 6RQ
Tel: 01616 100100
Email: admissions@
seashelltrust.org.uk
Website:
www.seashelltrust.org.uk
Age range: 19–25
No. of pupils: 70
Special needs catered for:
ASD, D, MSI, PD, PMLD, VIS
(金)

ROYAL SCHOOL MANCHESTER
For further details see p. 46
Seashell Trust, Stanley Road,
Cheadle, Cheshire SK8 6RQ
Tel: 01616 100100
Email: admissions@
seashelltrust.org.uk
Website:
www.seashelltrust.org.uk
Age range: 2–19
No. of pupils: 45
Special needs catered for:
ASD, D, HI, MSI, PMLD
(16)

Cumbria

Lindeth College
The Oaks, Lindeth, Bowness on
Windermere, Cumbria LA23 3NH
Tel: 01539 446265
Principal/Manager: Ms
Shirley Harrison
Age range: 16–25
No. of pupils: 30
Special needs catered for: ASP, LD
(16) (金)

Greater Manchester

Fairfield House School
59 Warburton Lane, Partington,
Manchester, Greater
Manchester M31 4NL
Tel: 0161 7762827
Headteacher: Ms Melanie Sproston
Age range: 8–19
Special needs catered for: ASD
(16) (✓)

Inscape House Cheadle
Schools Hill, Cheadle, Greater
Manchester SK8 1JE
Tel: 0161 283 4750
Headteacher: Liz Loftus
Age range: 5–16
No. of pupils: 55
Special needs catered for: AUT
(✓)

Lancashire

Bracken School
1 Harbour Lane, Warton,
Preston, Lancashire PR4 1YA
Tel: 01772 631531
Headteacher: Paul Addison
Age range: G11–16
No. of pupils: 5
Special needs catered for:
ADHD, DYS, MLD
(金)

Oliver House
Hall Gate, Astley Village,
Chorley, Lancashire PR7 1XA
Tel: 01257 220011
Principal: Ms Wendy Sparling
Age range: 6–19
No. of pupils: 28
Special needs catered for:
ASD, ASP
(金) (16) (✓)

Red Rose School
28-30 North Promenade,
St Annes on Sea, Lytham St
Annes, Lancashire FY8 2NQ
Tel: 01253 720570
Principal: Colin Lannen
Age range: 5–16
Special needs catered for:
ASD, DEL, SPLD
(✓)

Rossendale School
Bamford Road, Ramsbottom,
Bury, Lancashire BL0 0RT
Tel: 01706 822779
Principal: Mr David Duncan
Age range: 7–18
Special needs catered for: ADD,
ADHD, ASD, ASP, AUT, BESD, CLD,
DYS, DYSP, EBD, EPI, HA, SEBD, SLD
(A) (金) (✓)

Trax Academy
Riverside Park, Wallend Road,
Preston, Lancashire PR2 2HW
Tel: 01772 731832
Head: Mr Rodger Davies
Age range: 11–18
No. of pupils: 12
Special needs catered for:
ADHD, EBD
(16) (✓)

Westmorland School
Weldbank Lane, Chorley,
Lancashire PR7 3NQ
Tel: 01257 278899
Head Teacher: Mrs S M Asher
BSc (Hons), PGCE, NPQH
Age range: 5–11
No. of pupils: 44
Special needs catered for:
ADHD, ASD, ASP, AUT, BESD,
MLD, SP&LD, SPLD
(✓)

Merseyside

Arden College
40 Derby Road, Southport,
Merseyside PR9 0TZ
Tel: 01704 534433
Principal/Manager: Mr
Mark Musselle
Age range: 16–25
No. of pupils: 53
Special needs catered for: ASP, LD
(16) (金)

Lakeside School
Naylors Road, Huyton, Liverpool,
Merseyside L27 2YA
Tel: 0151 4877211
Head Teacher: Mrs V I Size
BEd(Hons), MEd(Autism)
Age range: 5–13
No. of pupils: 24
Special needs catered for: ADD,
ADHD, ASD, ASP, AUT, BESD, CLD,
DEL, DYS, DYSP, EPI, HA, HI, LD, MLD,
PH, SCD, SP&LD, SPLD, SLI, VIS
(✓)

Peterhouse School for Pupils with Autism & Asperger's Syndrome
Preston New Road, Southport,
Merseyside PR9 8PA
Tel: 01704 506682
Headteacher: Janet Allan
Age range: 5–19
No. of pupils: 51 VIth20
Fees: Day £38,190
WB £90,896 FB £120,045
Special needs catered for:
ASD, ASP, AUT
(金) (16) (✓)

WEST KIRBY RESIDENTIAL SCHOOL
For further details see p. 47
Meols Drive, West Kirby, Wirral,
Merseyside CH48 5DH
Tel: 0151 632 3201
Website: www.wkrs.co.uk
Principal: Mr Gareth
Williams OBE
Age range: 5–19
No. of pupils: 95
Special needs catered for:
ADD, ADHD, ASD, ASP, AUT,
BESD, CLD, DYSP, SCD, SP&LD
(金) (✓)

Social interaction difficulties (Autism, ASD & ASP)

South-East

Berkshire

Heathermount, The Learning Centre
Devenish Road, Ascot, Berkshire SL5 9PG
Tel: 01344 875101
Headteacher: Ms Ruth Bovill
Age range: 5–19
No. of pupils: 25
Special needs catered for: ASD, ASP, AUT
16+ ✔

NAS Thames Valley Free School
Conwy Close, Tilehurst, Reading, Berkshire RG30 4BZ
Tel: 0117 9748 430
Principal Designate: Fiona Veitch
Age range: 5–16
Special needs catered for: ASP, AUT

East Sussex

Rookery Hove
22-24 Sackville Gardens, Hove, East Sussex BN3 4GH
Tel: 01273 202 520
Principal/Manager: Mr Loz Blume
Age range: 18–35
No. of pupils: 13
Special needs catered for: ASD, ASP
16+ ⊕

Step by Step School for Autistic Children
Neylands Farm, Grinstead Lane, Sharpethorne, East Sussex RH19 4HP
Tel: 01342 811852
Headteacher: Mrs Faye Palmer
Age range: 4–11
No. of pupils: 12
Special needs catered for: AUT
✔

Hampshire

Grateley House School
Pond Lane, Grateley, Andover, Hampshire SP11 8TA
Tel: 0800 288 9779
Head: Mrs Sue King BA(Hons), PGCE, DAE (SEN) NPQH
Age range: 9–19
Special needs catered for: ASD, ASP
⊕ 16+ ✔

Hill House School
Rope Hill, Boldre, Lymington, Hampshire SO41 8NE
Tel: 0800 288 9779
Head of School: Ms Kate Landells BSc (open), CertSocSci(open) NVQ3 HSC, PTLLS(L4)
Age range: 11–19
Special needs catered for: ASD, AUT, SCD, SCLD, SLD
⊕ 16+ ✔

Southlands School
Vicars Hill, Boldre, Lymington, Hampshire SO41 5QB
Tel: 0800 288 9779
Head: Ms Naomi Clarke BEd DipEd, SEN, AMBDA
Age range: B7–16
Special needs catered for: ASD, ASP
♀ ⊕ 16+ ✔

Tadley Horizon
Tadley Common Road, Tadley, Basingstoke, Hampshire RG26 3TB
Tel: 01189 817720
Principal: Phil Jonas
Age range: 5–19
No. of pupils: 67
Special needs catered for: ASD, ASP, AUT
⊕ 16+ ✔

Kent

Blue Skies School
126 Maidstone Road, Chatham, Kent ME4 6DQ
Tel: 01634 357770
Head of School: Mr Jonathan Higgins
Age range: 11–19
No. of pupils: 17
Special needs catered for: ASD, ASP, AUT
16+ ✔

NAS Helen Allison School
Longfield Road, Meopham, Kent DA13 0EW
Tel: 01474 814878
Executive Principal: Dr Jacqui Ashton Smith
Age range: 5–19
No. of pupils: 70
Special needs catered for: ASD, ASP, AUT
⊕ 16+ ✔

The Quest School
Church Farm, Church Road, The Old Stables, Offham, Kent ME19 5NX
Tel: 01732 522700
Headteacher: Mrs Anne Martin
Age range: 4–14
No. of pupils: 8
Special needs catered for: AUT, EBD
✔

Surrey

Eagle House School (Mitcham)
224 London Road, Mitcham, Surrey CR4 3HD
Tel: 020 8687 7050
Head Teacher: Alan Simons
Age range: 4–11
Special needs catered for: ASD, ASP, AUT, MLD, SCD, SLD
✔

Eagle House School (Sutton)
95 Brighton Road, Sutton, Surrey SM2 5SJ
Tel: 020 8661 1419
Head Teacher: Mr Tom Coulter
Age range: 11–19
Special needs catered for: AUT
16+ ✔

Jigsaw CABAS® School
Building 20, Dunsfold Park, Stovolds Hill, Cranleigh, Surrey GU6 8TB
Tel: 01483 273874
Executive Head: Ms Kate Grant
Age range: 4–19
No. of pupils: VIth17
Fees: Day £49,900–£52,732
Special needs catered for: ASD, AUT
16+ ✔

Papillon House
Pebble Close, Tadworth, Surrey KT20 7PA
Tel: 01372 363663
Headteacher and Director: Mrs Gillian Hutton
Age range: 4–16
Fees: Day £45,000
Special needs catered for: ASD, AUT
✔

Unsted Park School
Munstead Heath Road, Godalming, Surrey GU7 1UW
Tel: 01483 892061
Principal: Mr Steve Dempsey
Age range: 7–19
No. of pupils: 55
Special needs catered for: ASD, ASP, AUT
⊕ 16+ ✔

West Sussex

LVS Hassocks
London Road, Sayers Common, Hassocks, West Sussex BN6 9HT
Tel: 01273 832901
Head Teacher: Kira Brabanec
Age range: 8–19
Special needs catered for: ASD, ASP, AUT
16+

South-West

Cornwall

Three Bridges Education Centre
East Hill, Blackwater, Truro, Cornwall TR4 8EG
Tel: 01872 561010
Headteacher: Rebecca Edwards
Age range: 11–19
No. of pupils: 8
Special needs catered for: ASD, ASP, AUT
16+ ✔

Devon

Cheltham Senior School
Bere Alston, Yelverton, Devon PL20 7EX
Tel: 01822 840379
Principal: Mr John Steward
Age range: 7–19
No. of pupils: 63
Special needs catered for: ADHD, ASD, ASP, AUT, BESD, CLD, EBD, GLD, MLD, SCD, SCLD
⊕ 16+ ✔

Coombe House
Coleford, Crediton, Devon EX17 5BY
Tel: 01363 85910
Principal: Pat Dingle
Age range: 16–30
No. of pupils: 16
Special needs catered for: ASD
16+ ⊕

Dorset

Portfield School
Parley Lane, Christchurch, Dorset BH23 6BP
Tel: 01202 573808
Headteacher: Mr Tyler Collins
Age range: 3–19
No. of pupils: 59
Special needs catered for: ASD, AUT
⊕ 16+ ✔

Purbeck View School
Northbrook Road, Swanage,
Dorset BH19 1PR
Tel: 0800 288 9779
Head: Susan Harvey CQSW
Ex Dip in Management
Age range: 7–19
Special needs catered for: ASD, AUT
🏛 16+ ✔

The Forum School
Shillingstone, Blandford
Forum, Dorset DT11 0QS
Tel: 0800 288 9779
Head: Mr Adrian J A Wylie
BED PG DIP (Autism) NPQH
Age range: 7–19
Special needs catered for: ASD, AUT
🏛 16+ ✔

The Wing Centre
126 Richmond Park Road,
Bournemouth, Dorset BH8 8TH
Tel: 0800 288 9779
Head: Janette Morgan MA, BA,
NPQH, PGCert in AS, CM CIPD
Age range: B16–19
Special needs catered for:
ASD, ASP
🧍 🏛 16+

Somerset

3 Dimensions
Chardleigh House, Chardleigh
Green, Wadeford, Chard,
Somerset TA20 3AJ
Tel: 01460 68055
Education Manager: Ms Nita Ellul
Age range: B11–16
No. of pupils: 5
Special needs catered for:
ADHD, AUT, EBD
🧍 🏛 ✔

Farleigh College Mells
Newbury, Nr Mells, Frome,
Somerset BA11 3RG
Tel: 01373 814980
Principal: Ms Sharon Edney
Age range: 11–19
No. of pupils: 52
Special needs catered for: ADD,
ADHD, ASD, ASP, AUT, DYS, DYSP
🏛 16+ ✔

Farleigh Further Education College Frome
North Parade, Frome,
Somerset BA11 2AB
Tel: 01373 475470
Principal/Manager: Mr
Alun Maddocks
Age range: 16–25
No. of pupils: 87
Special needs catered for: ASP, LD
16+ 🏛

North Hill House
Fromefield, Frome,
Somerset BA11 2HB
Tel: 01373 466222
Principal: Ms Sharon Edney
Age range: B7–18
No. of pupils: 62
Special needs catered for:
ADD, ADHD, ASD, ASP, AUT
🧍 🏛 16+ ✔

West Midlands

Shropshire

CRUCKTON HALL
For further details see p. 48
Cruckton, Shrewsbury,
Shropshire SY5 8PR
Tel: 01743 860206
Email: marcia.garnett@
cruckton.com
Website: www.cruckton.com
Head Teacher: Marcia Garnett
Age range: B8–19
No. of pupils: 80
Special needs catered for:
ADD, ADHD, ASP, AUT,
DYS, EBD, PMLD, SPLD
🧍 Ⓐ 🏛 ✔

Higford School
Higford Hall, Higford, Shifnal,
Shropshire TF11 9ET
Tel: 01952 630600
Headteacher: Anne Adams
Age range: 8–19
Special needs catered for:
ASD, AUT, CLD, DYS, DYSP, EPI,
GLD, HA, LD, MLD, MSI, PMLD,
SCLD, SLD, SP&LD, SPLD
🏛 16+ ✔

Staffordshire

Priory Highfields
9 & 11 Highfields Road, Chasetown,
Burntwood, Staffordshire WS7 4QR
Tel: 01543 672 173
Principal: Ms Joan Pearson
Age range: 18–25
No. of pupils: 10
Special needs catered for: ASD
16+ 🏛

Rugeley Horizon
Blithbury Road, Blithbury, Rugeley,
Staffordshire WS15 3JQ
Tel: 01889 504400
Principal: Ms Joan Pearson
Age range: 5–19
No. of pupils: 48
Special needs catered for:
ASD, ASP, AUT
🏛 16+ ✔

Strathmore College
Unit 7 Imex centre, Technology
Park, Bellringer Road, Trentham
Lakes South, Stoke-on-Trent,
Staffordshire ST4 8LJ
Tel: 01782 647384
Principal/Manager: Ms Kate Ward
Age range: 16–25
No. of pupils: 37
Special needs catered for: ASP,
BESD, CLD, GLD, LD, MLD, SLD
16+ 🏛

Warwickshire

Avon Park School
St John's Avenue, Rugby,
Warwickshire CV22 5HR
Tel: 01788 524448
Head Teacher: Sophie Garner
B.Ed, M.Ed (Oxon), NPQH
Age range: 6–16
No. of pupils: 19
Special needs catered for: ADD,
ADHD, ASD, ASP, BESD, CLD,
DYSP, LD, SCD, SEBD, SP&LD

West Midlands

The Island Project School
Diddington Hall, Diddington Lane,
Meriden, West Midlands CV7 7HQ
Tel: 01675 442588
Principal: Jacqui Walters-Hutton
Age range: 6–19
Special needs catered for: ASD, AUT
✔

Worcestershire

AALPS Midlands
The Rhydd, Hanley Castle,
Worcestershire WR8 0AD
Tel: 01684 312610
Registered Manager: Darren
Goodwin
Age range: 16–25
Special needs catered for: ASD
16+ 🏛 16+

Yorkshire & Humberside

Lincolnshire

Barton School
Barrow Road, Barton-upon-
Humber, Lincolnshire DN18 6DA
Tel: 01652 631280
Headteacher: Mark Eames
Age range: 8–19
Special needs catered for: ASD,
ASP, AUT, CLD, DYS, DYSP, GLD, HA,
LD, MLD, MSI, PMLD, SCLD, SLD, SPLD
🏛 ✔

The Bridge@Barton School
Barrow Road, Barton-upon-
Humber, Lincolnshire DN18 6DA
Tel: 01652 631280
Head of School: Mr Mark Eames
Age range: 8–19
Special needs catered for:
🏛

North Lincolnshire

AALPS North
Winterton Road, Roxby,
Scunthorpe, North
Lincolnshire DN15 0BJ
Tel: 01724 733777
Centre Head: Mr Russell Leese
Age range: 16–30
Special needs catered for: ASD
16+ 🏛 16+

Demeter House
98-100 Oswald Road, Scunthorpe,
North Lincolnshire DN15 7PA
Tel: 01724 277877
Headteacher: Mrs L Wardlaw
Age range: B5–14
No. of pupils: 5
Special needs catered for:
ADD, EBD
🧍 🏛 ✔

South Yorkshire

FULLERTON HOUSE COLLEGE
For further details see p. 80
Tickhill Square, Denaby, Doncaster, South Yorkshire DN12 4AR
Tel: 01709 861663
Email: enquiries@ hesleygroup.co.uk
Website: www.hesleygroup.co.uk
Head: Jeff Cox
Age range: 18–25
No. of pupils: 9
Special needs catered for: ASD, ASP, AUT, CLD, DYS, DYSP, GLD, LD, MLD, SCLD, SLD, SPLD

FULLERTON HOUSE SCHOOL
For further details see p. 51
Tickill Square, Denaby, Doncaster, South Yorkshire DN12 4AR
Tel: 01709 861663
Email: enquiries@ hesleygroup.co.uk
Website: www.fullertonhouse school.co.uk
Head: Jeff Cox
Age range: 8–19
No. of pupils: 40
Special needs catered for: ASD, ASP, AUT, CLD, DYS, DYSP, GLD, LD, MLD, SCLD, SLD, SPLD

NAS Robert Ogden School
Clayton Lane, Thurnscoe, Rotherham, South Yorkshire S63 0BG
Tel: 01709 874443
Executive Principal: Dr Jacqui Ashton-Smith
Age range: 5–19
No. of pupils: 80
Special needs catered for: ASD, ASP, AUT

WILSIC HALL COLLEGE
For further details see p. 80
Wadworth, Doncaster, South Yorkshire DN11 9AG
Tel: 01302 856382
Head: Jeff Cox
Age range: 19–25
No. of pupils: 3
Special needs catered for: ASD, ASP, AUT, CLD, DYS, DYSP, GLD, LD, MLD, SCLD, SLD, SPLD

WILSIC HALL SCHOOL
For further details see p. 52
Wadworth, Doncaster, South Yorkshire DN11 9AG
Tel: 01302 856382
Email: enquiries@ hesleygroup.co.uk
Website: www.wilsichallschool.co.uk
Head: Geoff Turner
Age range: 11–19
No. of pupils: 33
Special needs catered for: ASD, ASP, AUT, CLD, DYS, DYSP, GLD, LD, MLD, SCLD, SLD, SPLD

Scotland

East Ayrshire

NAS Daldorch House School
Sorn Road, Catrine, East Ayrshire KA5 6NA
Tel: 01290 551666
Principal: Shona Pinkerton DCE, DPSE(SEN), MEdSEN
Age range: 5–21
No. of pupils: 64
Special needs catered for: ASD, ASP, AUT

Moray

Troup House School
Gamrie, Banff, Moray AB45 3JN
Tel: 01261 851 584
Principal: Mr David McNally
Age range: 8–16
No. of pupils: 12
Special needs catered for: AUT, BESD

South Lanarkshire

NAS Daldorch Satellite School
St Leonards, East Kilbride, South Lanarkshire G74
Tel: 01355 246242
Principal: Shona Pinkerton
Age range: 5–19
No. of pupils: 5
Special needs catered for: ASD, ASP, AUT

Wales

Carmarthenshire

Coleg Elidyr
Rhandirmwyn, Llandovery, Carmarthenshire SA20 ONL
Tel: 01550 760400
The College Manager: Contact
Age range: 18–25
No. of pupils: 43
Special needs catered for: ADD, ADHD, ASD, ASP, AUT, BESD, CLD, DEL, DYSP, EBD, EPI, GLD, LD, MLD, Phe, SCD, SLD

Flintshire

AALPS Cymru
Llanerch-y-mor, Holywell, Flintshire CH8 9DX
Tel: 01745 562570
Registered Manager: Shian Thomas
Age range: 18+
Special needs catered for: ASD

Kinsale School
Kinsale Hall, Llanerch-y-Mor, Holywell, Flintshire CH8 9DX
Tel: 01745 562500
Head of Service: Mr Mark Williams
Age range: 8–19
Special needs catered for: ASD, AUT, CLD, DYS, DYSP, EPI, GLD, LD, MLD, MSI, PH, PMLD, SCLD, SLD, SP&LD, SPLD

Torfaen

Priory Coleg Wales
Coleg Gwent, Pontypool Campus, Blaendare Road, Pontypool, Torfaen NP4 5YE
Tel: 01495 762609
Principal/Manager: Mr Simon Coles
Age range: 16–25
No. of pupils: 11
Special needs catered for: ASP, LD

Vale of Glamorgan

Beechwood College
Hayes Road, Penarth, Vale of Glamorgan CF64 5SE
Tel: 029 2053 2210
Principal: Mr Darren Jackson
Age range: 16+
No. of pupils: 66
Special needs catered for: ASD, ASP, SLD

Wrexham

Priory Coleg North Wales
67 King Street, Grove Park Road, Wrexham LL11 1HR
Tel: 01978 366 006
Principal/Manager: Mr Simon Coles
Age range: 16–25
No. of pupils: 5
Special needs catered for: ASP, LD

Schools and colleges specialising in emotional, behavioural and/or social difficulties (EBSD)

Abbreviations

ACLD	Autism, Communication and Associated Learning Difficulties
ADD	Attention Deficit Disorder
ADHD	Attention Deficit and Hyperactive Disorder (Hyperkinetic Disorder)
ASD	Autistic Spectrum Disorder
ASP	Asperger Syndrome
AUT	Autism
BESD	Behavioural, Emotional and Social Difficulties
CCD	Complex Communication Difficulties
CLD	Complex Learning Difficulties
CP	Cerebral Palsy
D	Deaf
DEL	Delicate
DYS	Dyslexia
DYSP	Dyspraxia
EBD	Emotional and Behavioural Difficulties
EBSD	Emotional, Behavioural and/or Social Difficulties
EPI	Epilepsy
GLD	General Learning Difficulties
HA	High Ability
HI	Hearing Impairment
HS	Hospital School
LD	Learning Difficulties
MLD	Moderate Learning Difficulties
MSI	Multi-sensory Impairment
OCD	Obsessive Compulsive Disorder
PD	Physical Difficulties
PH	Physical Impairment
Phe	Partially Hearing
PMLD	Profound and Multiple Learning Difficulties
PNI	Physical Neurological Impairment
PRU	Pupil Referral Unit
SCD	Social and Communication Difficulties
SCLD	Severe and Complex Learning Difficulties
SEBD	Severe Emotional and Behavioural Disorders
SEBN	Social, Emotional and Behavioural Needs
SLD	Severe Learning Difficulties
SLI	Specific Language Impairment
SPLD	Specific Learning Difficulties
SP&LD	Speech and Language Difficulties
SLCN	Speech Language & Communication Needs
VIS	Visually Impaired

Key to Symbols

Type of school:

(symbol)	Boys' school
(symbol)	Girls' school
(symbol)	International school

School offers:

(A)	A levels
(symbol)	Boarding accommodation
(16)	Entrance at 16+
(symbol)	Vocational qualifications
(symbol)	Learning support
(✓)	This is a DfE approved independent or non-maintained school under section 342 or 347(1) of the 1996 Education Act

Please note: Unless otherwise indicated, all schools are coeducational day schools. Single-sex and boarding schools will be indicated by the relevant icon.

Central & West

Buckinghamshire

Benjamin College
4 Wren Path, Fairford Leys,
Aylesbury, Buckinghamshire
HP19 7AR
Tel: 01296 483584
Principal: Mr Jeremy Yelland
Age range: 12–18
Special needs catered for: BESD
16+ ✔

Gloucestershire

Cotswold Chine School
Box, Stroud, Gloucestershire
GL6 9AG
Tel: 01453 837550
Headteacher: Maureen
Smith MA(Ed), PGCertSpLd,
PGCE, BA(Hons)
Age range: 9–19
No. of pupils: 48
Special needs catered for:
ADD, ADHD, ASP, AUT, DYS,
DYSP, EBD, EPI, MLD, SP&LD
♿ ♿ ✔

Oxfordshire

Action for Children Parklands Campus
Chardleigh House, Near Appleton,
Abingdon, Oxfordshire OX13 5QB
Tel: 01865 390436
Principal: Mr. Sean Cannon
Age range: 11–19
No. of pupils: 14 VIth6
Fees: Day £50,000 FB £192,000
Special needs catered for: ADHD,
ASD, ASP, AUT, BESD, LD, MLD, SPLD
♿ 16+ ✔

Chilworth House School
Thame Road, Wheatley, Oxford,
Oxfordshire OX33 1JP
Tel: 01844 339077
Head Teacher: Mr Dave
Willcox BEd (Hons)
Age range: 4–11
No. of pupils: 29
Special needs catered for: ADHD,
ASD, ASP, BESD, EBD, MLD, SCD, SLD
16+ ✔

Chilworth House Upper School
Grooms Farm, Thame Road,
Wheatley, Oxfordshire OX33 1JP
Tel: 01844 337720
Head Teacher: Mr Kevin
Larsen BEd(Hons), MA,
PGCE ED Management
Age range: 11–16
No. of pupils: 59
Special needs catered for: ADD,
ADHD, ASD, ASP, AUT, BESD,
DEL, GLD, HI, LD, MLD, Phe, SCD,
SCLD, SEBD, SP&LD, SPLD
✔

Hillcrest Park School
Southcombe, Chipping Norton,
Oxford, Oxfordshire OX7 5QH
Tel: 01608 644621
Headteacher: David
Davidson MA(Hons), PGCE
Age range: 7–18
Special needs catered for: ADD,
ADHD, ASD, ASP, BESD, DYS, DYSP,
EBD, GLD, MLD, SCD, SEBD
♿ ✔

Mulberry Bush School
Standlake, Witney,
Oxfordshire OX29 7RW
Tel: 01865 300202
Director: John Turberville BSc, MA
Age range: 5–12
No. of pupils: 36
Special needs catered for: EBD
♿ ✔

East

Bedfordshire

Advanced Education – Walnut Tree Lodge School
Avenue Farm, Renhold
Road, Wilden, Bedford,
Bedfordshire MK44 2PY
Tel: 01234 772081
Headteacher: Mr John Boslem
Age range: 11–16
Special needs catered for: EBD
✔

Cambridgeshire

Advanced Education – Wisbech School & Vocational Centre
Old Session House, 32 Somers Road,
Wisbech, Cambridgeshire PE13 1JF
Tel: 01945 427276
Headteacher: Mr Mick Coleman
Age range: 9–16
Special needs catered for:
EBD, SEBD
✔

Chartwell House School
Goodens Lane, Newton, Wisbech,
Cambridgeshire PE13 5HQ
Tel: 01945 870793
Head: Mrs D A Wright
No. of pupils: 8
Fees: FB £67,600
Special needs catered for: DYS, EBD
♿ ♿ ✔

The Old School House
March Road, Friday Bridge,
Wisbech, Cambridgeshire PE14 0HA
Tel: 01945 861114
Manager: Rick Ogle-Welbourn
Age range: B7–13
Special needs catered for: EBD
♿ ♿ ✔

Essex

Advanced Education – Essex School
Unit 7 Woodgates Farm, Broxted,
Dunmow, Essex CM6 2BN
Tel: 01279 850474
Headteacher: Julie Barnes
Age range: 11–16
Special needs catered for: BESD
✔

Continuum School Whitewebbs
Whitewebbs, Molehill Green,
Takely, Stansted, Essex CM22 6PQ
Tel: 01279 850474/07966 543931
Headteacher: Mr David Flack
Age range: 11–16
Special needs catered for: EBD
✔

Donyland Lodge School
Fingringhoe Road, Rowhedge,
Colchester, Essex CO5 7JL
Tel: 01206 728869
Director: Lesley Woodhouse
Age range: 11–18
Special needs catered for: EBD
✔

Hopewell School
Harmony House, Baden Powell
Close, Dagenham, Essex RM9 6XN
Tel: 020 8593 6610
Headteacher: Ms Sharina Klaasens
Age range: 5–18
Special needs catered for:
EBD, MLD, SEBD
16+ ✔

Jacques Hall
Harwich Road, Bradfield,
Manningtree, Essex CO11 2XW
Tel: 01255 870311
Principal: Mr Paul Emmerson
Age range: 11–18
No. of pupils: 21
Special needs catered for:
ADHD, BESD, EBD, MLD, SEBD
♿ 16+

The Ryes College & Community
New Road, Aldham,
Colchester, Essex CO6 3PN
Tel: 01206 243473
Headteacher: Miss Jackies Shanks
Age range: 7–24
Special needs catered for:
ADD, ADHD, ASD, ASP, AUT,
BESD, EBD, SCD, SEBD
♿ 16+ ✔

Norfolk

Avocet House
The Old Vicarage, School Lane,
Heckingham, Norfolk NR14 6QP
Tel: 01508 549320
Principal: Mr Jonathan Lees
Age range: B8–16
No. of pupils: 8
Special needs catered for:
EBD, SEBD, SPLD
♿ ♿ ✔

Copperfield School
22 Euston Road, Great
Yarmouth, Norfolk NR30 1DX
Tel: 07825130014
Age range: 11–16
Special needs catered for: BESD
✔

Future Education
168b Motum Road, Norwich,
Norfolk NR5 8EG
Tel: 01603 250505
Headteacher: Mr Dennis Freeman
Age range: 14–16
Special needs catered for: BESD
✔

Kadesh Education
DC3 Vinces Road, Diss,
Norfolk IP22 4HG
Tel: 01379 644223
Headteacher: Ms Andi Roy
Age range: 11–16
Special needs catered for: BESD
✔

Sheridan School
Thetford Road, Northwold,
Thetford, Norfolk IP26 5LQ
Tel: 01366 726040
Interim Principal: Mr John Steward
Age range: 8–18
No. of pupils: 40
Special needs catered for: ADD,
ADHD, ASD, ASP, BESD, EBD, SEBD

Suffolk

Bramfield House
Walpole Road, Bramfield,
Halesworth, Suffolk IP19 9AB
Tel: 01986 784235
Head: Mrs D Jennings
Age range: B10–18
No. of pupils: 51
Special needs catered for:
ADD, ADHD, BESD, DEL, EBD

Greenfield School
Four Elms, Norwich Road, Stonham
Parva, Stowmarket, Suffolk IP14 5LB
Tel: 01449 711105
Head: Raymond Saunders
Age range: B11–16
No. of pupils: 11
Special needs catered for:
EBD, MLD

**On Track Education
Centre (Mildenhall)**
82E & F Fred Dannatt Road,
Mildenhall, Suffolk IP28 7RD
Tel: 01638 715555
Headteacher: Mrs Ruth Durrant
Age range: 11–18
Special needs catered for: EBD

East Midlands

Derbyshire

Eastwood Grange School
Milken Lane, Ashover, Chesterfield,
Derbyshire S45 0BA
Tel: 01246 590255
Principal: Mr Ray Scales
Age range: B9–16+
No. of pupils: 34
Special needs catered for: ADD,
ADHD, BESD, DYS, EBD, HA, SCD

Ravenswood School
Ilkeston Road, Heanor,
Derbyshire DE75 7DT
Tel: 01733 719208
Head Teacher: Tree Price
Age range: 11–16
Special needs catered for: SEBD

**The Linnet Independent
Learning Centre**
107 Mount Pleasant Road,
Castle Gresley, Swadlincote,
Derbyshire DE11 9JE
Tel: 01283 213989
Head Teacher: Jan Sullivan
Age range: 5–16
No. of pupils: 13
Fees: Day £74,250
Special needs catered for: ADD,
ADHD, ASD, ASP, BESD, CLD,
DEL, DYS, DYSP, EBD, GLD, LD,
MLD, SCD, SEBD, SP&LD, SPLD

The Meadows
Beech Lane, Dove Holes,
Derbyshire SK17 8DJ
Tel: 01298 814000
Headteacher: Ms Rachel Dowle
Age range: 11–16
Special needs catered for: EBD

Leicestershire

Claybrook Cottage School
Frolesworth Lane, Claybrook
Magna, Lutterworth,
Leicestershire LE17 5DA
Tel: 01455 202049
Headteacher: Mrs
Jennifer Collighan
Age range: 8–16
Special needs catered for: BESD

Gryphon School
Slater Street Lodge, Abbey Park,
Leicester, Leicestershire LE1 3EJ
Tel: 07833 623420
Headteacher: Miss Christina Church
Age range: 11–17
Special needs catered for: EBD

Lewis Charlton School
North Street, Ashby-De-La-
Zouch, Leicestershire LE65 1HU
Tel: 01530 560775
Head: Ms Georgina Pearson
Age range: 11–16
No. of pupils: 20
Special needs catered for: EBD

**Meadow View
Farm School**
c/o Brookland Farm House, Kirby
Road, Barwell, Leicestershire LE9 8FT
Tel: 01455 840 825
Headteacher: Mr J Read
Age range: 6–11
Special needs catered for:
ASD, BESD, SCD

Oakwood School
20 Main Street, Glenfield,
Leicester, Leicestershire LE3 8DG
Tel: 0116 2876218
Headteacher: Mrs.
Jennifer Collighan
Age range: 8–18
No. of pupils: 18
Special needs catered for: EBD

The Cedars
33 Ashby Road, Stapleton,
Hinckley, Leicestershire LE9 8JF
Tel: 01455 844205
Principal Teacher: Mr
Troy Scrimshaw
Age range: B11–16
No. of pupils: 5
Special needs catered for: SEBD

Trinity College
Moor Lane, Loughborough,
Leicestershire LE11 1BA
Tel: 01509 218906
Headteacher: Mr Adam Brewster
Age range: 9–16
No. of pupils: 36
Fees: Day £36,075
Special needs catered for:
EBD, MLD

Lincolnshire

Broughton House
Brant Broughton,
Lincolnshire LN5 0SL
Tel: 0800 288 9779
Head of Service: Mr
Michael Semilore
Age range: 16–25
Special needs catered for: AUT,
BESD, LD, SCD, SCLD, SEBD, SLD

Northamptonshire

**Advanced Education –
Northampton School**
67 Queens Park Parade,
Kingsthorpe, Northampton,
Northamptonshire NN2 6LR
Tel: 01604 719711
Headteacher: Rob Bilbe
Age range: 11–16
Special needs catered for:
EBD, MLD

Ashmeads School
Buccleuch Farm, Haigham
Hill, Burton Latimer, Kettering,
Northamptonshire NN15 5PH
Tel: 01536 725998
Headteacher: Joyce Kuwazo
Age range: 11–16
No. of pupils: 12
Special needs catered for: EBD

Belview School
124b Midland Road,
Wellingborough,
Northamptonshire NN8 1NF
Tel: 01933 441877
Headteacher: Ms Candy Shaw
Age range: 11–17
No. of pupils: 4
Special needs catered for: BESD

Thornby Hall School
Thornby Hall, Thornby,
Northampton,
Northamptonshire NN6 8SW
Tel: 01604 740001
Director: Ms Rene Kennedy
CertEd, DipArt Therapy
Age range: 12–18
No. of pupils: 20
Fees: FB £106,177
Special needs catered for: EBD

Nottinghamshire

Freyburg School
The Poppies, Greenmile
Lane, Babworth,
Nottinghamshire DN22 8JW
Tel: 01777 709061
Headteacher: Mr David Carr
Age range: B11–16
Special needs catered for: BESD

Hope House School
Barnby Road, Newark,
Nottinghamshire NG24 3NE
Tel: 01636 700 380
Headteacher: Mrs Teri
Westmoreland
Age range: 4–19
No. of pupils: 3
Fees: Day £135,000–£155,000
FB £160,000–£180,000
Special needs catered for:
ADD, ADHD, ASD, ASP, AUT,
BESD, DEL, EBD, SCD, SEBD

**NoRSACA Whitegates
Further Education Unit**
The Dukeries Centre, Park Street,
Worksop, Nottinghamshire S80 1HH
Tel: 01909 509400
Principal: Ms Karen Bulmer
Special needs catered for: AUT, LD

Wings School, Nottinghamshire
Kirklington Hall, Kirklington, Newark, Nottinghamshire NG22 8NB
Tel: 01636 817430
Principal: Dr John Flint
Age range: 9–17
Special needs catered for:
ADD, ADHD, ASP, BESD, EBD

Rutland

The Grange Therapuetic School
Knossington, Oakham, Rutland LE15 8LY
Tel: 01664 454264
Director: Dr A J Smith MA, MEd, PhD, CPsychol, AFBPs
Age range: B8–16
No. of pupils: 75
Special needs catered for: EBD

Greater London

Essex

Barnardos
Tanners Lane, Barkingside, Ilford, Essex IG6 1QG
Tel: 020 8550 8822
Special needs catered for:
AUT, EBD, MLD, PH, PMLD, SLD, SP&LD, SPLD

Middlesex

Unity School
62 The Ride, Hounslow, Middlesex TW8 9LA
Age range: 11–16
No. of pupils: 4
Special needs catered for: EBD

West Middlesex College
Colne Lodge, Longbridge Way, Uxbridge, Middlesex UB8 2YG
Tel: 01895 619700
Principal: Ms Alison White
Special needs catered for: ASP, AUT

Surrey

Cressey College
Croydon, Surrey CR0 6XJ
Tel: 020 86545373
Headteacher: Ms Adrienne Barnes
Age range: 11–17
Special needs catered for:
BESD, EBD, SCD

Kingsdown Secondary School
112 Orchard Road, Sanderstead, Croydon, Surrey CR2 9LQ
Tel: 020 8657 1200
Headteacher: Ms Carole Nicholson
Age range: 11–16
No. of pupils: 12
Special needs catered for:
ASD, ASP, EBD, SPLD

London

London

East London

East London Independent School
Unit 7, Ibex House, 1c Maryland Park, Stratford, , London E15 1HB
Tel: 020 82211247
Headteacher: Mr David O'connor
Age range: 7–16
No. of pupils: 40
Special needs catered for:
ASD, BESD

Leaways School London
Theydon Road, Clapton, , London E5 9NZ
Tel: 020 8815 4030
Headmaster: Richard Gadd
Age range: 10–17
Special needs catered for: SEBD

North-West London

Gloucester House the Tavistock Children's Day Unit
33 Daleham Gardens, London NW3 5BU
Tel: 020 77943353
Headteacher: Ms Ellenore Nicholson
Age range: B5–12
Special needs catered for: BESD

South-East London

Cavendish School
58 Hawkstone Road, Southwark Park, London SE16 2PA
Tel: 020 73940088
Headteacher: Mrs Sara Craggs
Age range: 11–16
No. of pupils: 42
Special needs catered for: EBD

Trinity School
4 Recreation Road, Sydenham, , London SE26 4ST
Headteacher: Mr Philip Lee
Age range: 11–16
Special needs catered for: BESD

West London

Insights Independent School
3-5 Alexandria Road, Ealing, London W13 0NP
Tel: 020 8840 9099
Headteacher: Ms Barbara Quartey
Age range: 7–18
No. of pupils: 62
Special needs catered for: ADD, ADHD, ASD, ASP, BESD, DYS, EBD, GLD, MLD, SCD, SPLD

North West London Independent School
85 Old Oak Road, Ealing, , London W3 7DD
Tel: 020 87495403
CEO: Thomas Keaney
Age range: 7–17
No. of pupils: 40
Special needs catered for:
ASD, BESD

Emotional, behavioural and/or social difficulties (EBSD)

North-East

Durham

Highcroft School
The Green, Cockfield, Bishop Auckland, Durham DL13 5AG
Tel: 077 02916189
Headteacher: Mr David Laheney
Age range: 11–16
No. of pupils: 3
Special needs catered for: BESD
✔

Priory Pines House
Middleton St George, Darlington, Durham DL2 1TS
Tel: 01325 331177
Principal: Mr John Anderson
Age range: 7–16
No. of pupils: 16
Special needs catered for: EBD
🏛

East Riding of Yorkshire

Advanced Education – Beverley School
Units 19-20 Priory Road Industrial Estate, Beverley, East Riding of Yorkshire HU17 0EW
Tel: 01482 307830
School Manager: Melanie Jackson
Age range: 10–18
Special needs catered for: EBD, LD
16 ✔

Hartlepool

Advanced Education – Hartlepool School & Vocational Centre
Sovereign Park, Brenda Road, Hartlepool TS25 1NN
Tel: 01429 224965
Headteacher: Mr Paul Barnfather
Age range: 11–16
No. of pupils: 10
Special needs catered for: EBD
✔

Northumberland

Cambois House School
Cambois, Blyth, Northumberland NE24 1SF
Tel: 01670 857689
Headteacher: Mr David Smith
Age range: 11–16
No. of pupils: 8
Special needs catered for: BESD, EBD
✔

Tyne & Wear

Talbot House School
Hexham Road, Walbottle, Newcastle upon Tyne, Tyne & Wear NE15 8HW
Tel: 0191 229 0111
Director of Services: A P James DAES, BPhil, CRCCYP
Age range: 7–18
No. of pupils: 40
Special needs catered for: ADD, ADHD, ASD, BESD, EBD, MLD
✔

Thornbeck College
14 Thornhill Park, Sunderland, Tyne & Wear SR2 7LA
Tel: 0191 5102038
Principal: Ms Christine Dempster
Special needs catered for: ASP, AUT

West Yorkshire

Broadwood School
252 Moor End Road, Halifax, West Yorkshire HX2 0RU
Tel: 01422 355925
Headteacher: Mrs Deborah Nash
Age range: 11–18
No. of pupils: 38
Special needs catered for: EBD
✔

Meadowcroft School
145 Bolton Lane, Bradford, West Yorkshire BD2 4AT
Tel: 01274 634666
Headteacher: Mrs Susan Smith
Age range: 10–19
Special needs catered for: EBD
16 ✔

North-West

Cheshire

Advanced Education – Warrington School
2 Forrest Way, Gatewarth Industrial Estate, Warrington, Cheshire WA5 1DF
Tel: 01925 237580
Headteacher: Olufemi Onasanya
Age range: 11–18
No. of pupils: 10
Special needs catered for: BESD, EBD, SEBD
16 ✔

Halton School
33 Main Street, Halton Village, Runcorn, Cheshire WA7 2AN
Tel: 01928 589810
Headteacher: Emma McAllester
Age range: 7–14
No. of pupils: 14
Special needs catered for: EBD
✔

High Peak School
Mudhurst Lane, Higher Disley, Stockport, Cheshire SK12 2AP
Tel: 01663 721 731
Principal: David Glaves
Age range: 9–19
Special needs catered for: SEBD
🏛

Hope Corner Academy
70 Clifton Road, Runcorn, Cheshire WA7 4TD
Tel: 01928 897835
Head of School: Rev. D Tunningley
Age range: 14–16
Special needs catered for: ASD, BESD, MLD

Cumbria

APPLETREE SCHOOL
For further details see p. 54
Natland, Kendal, Cumbria LA9 7QS
Tel: 015395 60253
Email: admin@appletreeschool.co.uk
Website: www.appletreeschool.co.uk
Head of Education: Mr R Davies BEd, MSpEd
Age range: 6–12
Special needs catered for: ADD, ADHD, BESD, DEL, DYS, DYSP, EBD, GLD, HA, LD, MLD, SCD, SEBD
🏛 ✔

Eden Grove School
Bolton, Appleby, Cumbria CA16 6AJ
Tel: 01768 361346
Principal: Mr John McCaffrey
Age range: 8–19
No. of pupils: 65
Special needs catered for: ADHD, ASP, AUT, BESD, CP, DYS, EBD, EPI, MLD, PH, SP&LD
🏛 16 ✔

Fell House School
Grange Fell Road, Grange-Over-Sands, Cumbria LA11 6AS
Tel: 01539 535926
Headteacher: Mr Rob Davies
Age range: 7–12
No. of pupils: 8
Special needs catered for: EBD
🏛 ✔

Kirby Moor School
Longtown Road, Brampton, Cumbria CA8 2AB
Tel: 016977 42598
Headteacher: Mrs Catherine Garton
Age range: B10–18
Special needs catered for: BESD, CLD, EBD
🧍 🏛 16 ✔

Radical Education
119 Warwick Road, Carlisle, Cumbria CA1 1JZ
Tel: 01228 631770
Headteacher: Mr Jim Danson
Age range: 14–16
No. of pupils: 6
Special needs catered for: EBD

Underley Garden School
Kirkby Lonsdale, Carnforth, Cumbria LA6 2DZ
Tel: 01524 271569
Headteacher: Ellie Forrest
Age range: 9–19
No. of pupils: 43
Special needs catered for: ADD, ADHD, ASP, SLD, SP&LD
🏛 ✔

Whinfell School
110 Windermere Road, Kendal, Cumbria LA9 5EZ
Tel: 01539 723322
Headteacher: Mr R D Tyson
Age range: B11–19
No. of pupils: 5
Special needs catered for: AUT, EBD
🧍 🏛 16 ✔

Wings School, Cumbria
Whassett, Milnthorpe, Cumbria LA7 7DN
Tel: 01539 562006
Principal: Donagh McKillop
Age range: 11–17
Special needs catered for: ADD, ADHD, ASP, BESD, EBD
🏛 ✔

Witherslack Hall School
Witherslack, Grange-Over-Sands, Cumbria LA11 6SD
Tel: 01539 552397
Head Teacher: Mr. Robin Adams
Age range: B10–19
No. of pupils: 41
Special needs catered for: ADHD, ASD, ASP, AUT, BESD, EBD, MLD, SPLD
🧍 🏛 ✔

Greater Manchester

Acorns School
19b Hilbert Lane, Marple, Stockport, Greater Manchester SK6 7NN
Tel: 0161 449 5820
Headteacher: Naseem Akhtar
Age range: 5–17
No. of pupils: 40
Special needs catered for: EBD
✔

Ashcroft School (CYCES)
Schools Hill, Cheadle, Greater Manchester SK8 1JE
Tel: 0161 283 4832
Principal: Stephen Grimley MA, CertEd
Age range: 8–16
No. of pupils: 40
Special needs catered for: BESD
✔

Birch House School
98-100 Birch Lane, Longsight, Manchester, Greater Manchester M13 0WN
Tel: 0161 2247500
Headteacher: Mr Bilal Mahmud
Age range: 11–16
No. of pupils: 22
Special needs catered for: BESD, EBD, SEBD
✔

Lime Meadows
73 Taunton Road, Ashton-Under-Lyne, Greater Manchester OL7 9DU
Tel: 0161 3399412
Head of School: Mr W Baker
Age range: B14–19
No. of pupils: 5
Special needs catered for: EBD
✔ 🏢 16 ✔

Nugent House School
Carr Mill Road, Billinge, Wigan, Greater Manchester WN5 7TT
Tel: 01744 892551
Principal: Miss W Sparling BA(Hons), QTS, MA(SEN), PG Dip (Autism), NPQH
Age range: B7–19
No. of pupils: 65
Fees: Day £63,036–£84,048
Special needs catered for: EBD
✔ 🏢 16 ✔

St John Vianney School
Rye Bank Road, Firswood, Stretford, Greater Manchester M16 0EX
Tel: 0161 8817843
Age range: 4–19
No. of pupils: 80
Fees: Day £7,155
Special needs catered for: MLD
16 ✔

Lancashire

Belmont School
Haslingden Road, Rawtenstall, Rossendale, Lancashire BB4 6RX
Tel: 01706 221043
Headteacher: Mr M J Stobart
Age range: B10–16
No. of pupils: 70
Special needs catered for:
ADD, ADHD, ASD, ASP, AUT, BESD, DEL, EBD, SCD, SEBD
✔ ✔

Cedar House School
Bentham, Lancaster, Lancashire LA2 7DD
Tel: 015242 61149
Headteacher: Ms Kathryn Taylor BEd (Hons)
Age range: 7–18
No. of pupils: 63
Special needs catered for:
ADD, ADHD, ASD, ASP, BESD, DYSP, EBD, EPI, GLD, LD, MLD, SCD, SEBD, SP&LD, SPLD
🏢 ✔

Crookhey Hall School
Crookhey Hall, Garstang Road, Cockerham, Lancaster, Lancashire LA2 0HA
Tel: 01524 792618
Headteacher: Mr D P Martin
Age range: B11–16
No. of pupils: 64
Special needs catered for: ADD, ADHD, BESD, DEL, EBD, SCD, SEBD
✔ ✔

Cumberland School
Church Road, Bamber Bridge, Preston, Lancashire PR5 6EP
Tel: 01772 284435
Head Teacher: Mr Nigel Hunt BSc (Hons), PGCE (SEN), NPQH
Age range: 11–18
No. of pupils: 57
Special needs catered for:
ADHD, ASP, BESD, MLD, SP&LD
✔

Darwen School
3 Sudell Road, Darwen, Lancashire BB3 3HW
Tel: 01254 777154
Headteacher: Mr Sean Naylor
Age range: 7–16
No. of pupils: 10
Special needs catered for: EBD
✔

Egerton Street Independent School
48/50 Egerton Street, Heywood, Rochdale, Lancashire OL10 3BG
Tel: 01706 625982
Manager: Dave Edwards
Age range: 11–16
Special needs catered for: EBD
16 ✔

Elland House School
Unit 7, Roman Road, Royton, Lancashire OL2 5PJ
Tel: 0161 6283600
Headteacher: Mrs Jan Murray
Age range: 11–16
Special needs catered for: BESD
✔

Keyes Barn
Station Road, Salwick, Preston, Lancashire PR4 0YH
Tel: 01772 673672
Headteacher: Mr Gary Holliday
Age range: 5–12
Special needs catered for: EBD
✔

Learn 4 Life
Quarry Bank Community Centre, 364 Ormskirk Road, Tanhouse, Skelmersdale, Lancashire WN8 9AL
Tel: 01695 558698
Headteacher: Ms Elaine Booth
Age range: 11–16
No. of pupils: 4
Special needs catered for: BESD, EBD
✔

Moorlands View Children's Home and School
Manchester Road, Dunnockshaw, Burnley, Lancashire BB11 5PQ
Tel: 01282 431144
Head Teacher: Wayne Carradice
Age range: 11–16
No. of pupils: 12
Special needs catered for: EBD
✔

Pennsylvania House
1 Barclay Avenue, Blackpool, Lancashire FY4 4HH
Tel: 01253 313101
Head Teacher: Mr Bill Baker
Age range: B11–17
No. of pupils: 6
Special needs catered for: EBD
✔ 🏢 ✔

Piers House
334 St Anne's Road, Blackpool, Lancashire FY4 2QN
Tel: 01253 319651
Headteacher: Mr Keith Parker
Age range: B11–16
No. of pupils: 5
Special needs catered for: EBD
✔ 🏢 ✔

Primrose Cottage
c/o Northern Care, 214 Whitegate Drive, Blackpool, Lancashire FY3 9JL
Tel: 01253 316160
Head of Education: Valerie Gardener
Age range: G11–16
No. of pupils: 6
Special needs catered for: EBD, MLD
✔ 🏢 ✔

Roselyn House School
Moss Lane, Off Wigan Road, Leyland, Lancashire PR25 4SE
Tel: 01772 435948
Headteacher: Miss S Damerall
Age range: 11–16
No. of pupils: 21
Special needs catered for: AUT, EBD
✔

The Birches
106 Breck Road, Poulton-le-Fylde, Lancashire FY6 7HT
Tel: 01253 899102
Head Teacher: Mr Mike Simpkins
Age range: B11–17
No. of pupils: 6
Special needs catered for: EBD
✔ 🏢 ✔

The Brambles
159 Longmeanygate, Midge Hill, Leyland, Lancashire PR26 7BT
Tel: 01772 454826
Headteacher: Mr G Holiday
Age range: B11–16
Special needs catered for: EBD
✔ ✔

The Nook School
The Nook, Knotts Lane, Colne, Lancashire BB8 8HH
Tel: 01282 868840
Headteacher: Mr Paul Heaven
Age range: B8–16
Special needs catered for: EBD
✔ 🏢 ✔

The Willows at Oakfield House School
Station Road, Salwick, Preston, Lancashire PR4 0YH
Tel: 01772 672630
Headteacher: June Redhead
Age range: 5–11
No. of pupils: 23
Special needs catered for: EBD, SLD
✔

Waterloo Lodge School
Preston Road, Chorley, Lancashire PR6 7AX
Tel: 01257 230894
Headteacher: Mrs J Taylor
Age range: 11–16
No. of pupils: 45
Fees: Day £29,649
Special needs catered for: ADD, ADHD, BESD, DEL, EBD, SCD, SEBD
🏢 ✔

Merseyside

Balmoral Independent School
41 Balmoral Road, Newsham Park, Liverpool, Merseyside L6 8ND
Tel: 0151 2910787
Manager: Alison Morris
Age range: 10–16
Special needs catered for: EBD
✔

Emotional, behavioural and/or social difficulties (EBSD)

Clarence High School
West Lane, Freshfield,
Merseyside L37 7AS
Tel: 01704 872151
Head: Ms Carol Parkinson
Age range: 7–17
Special needs catered for: EBD
♿ ✓

Olsen House School
85-87 Liverpool Rd, GT. Crosby,
Liverpool, Merseyside L23 5TD
Tel: 0151 924 0234
Headteacher: Jeremy Keeble
Age range: 9–16
Special needs catered for: SEBD

Warrington

Chaigeley
Thelwall, Warrington WA4 2TE
Tel: 01925 752357
Principal: Mr Drew Crawshaw
Age range: B8–16
No. of pupils: 75
Fees: Day £27,780 WB £44,211
Special needs catered for:
ADD, ADHD, ASD, ASP, AUT,
BESD, DYS, EBD, GLD, HA,
LD, MLD, SCD, SEBD, SLD
♿ ♿ ✓

Cornerstones
2 Victoria Road, Grappenhall,
Warrington WA4 2EN
Tel: 01925 211056
Head: Ms Caron Bethell
Age range: B7–18
No. of pupils: 11
Special needs catered for: AUT, EBD
♿ ♿ 16 ✓

South-East

Berkshire

Cressex Lodge (SWAAY)
Terrace Road South, Binfield,
Bracknell, Berkshire RG42 4DE
Tel: 01344 862221
Headteacher: Ms Sarah Snape
Age range: B11–16
No. of pupils: 9
Special needs catered for: BESD
♿ ✓

High Close School
Wiltshire Road, Wokingham,
Berkshire RG40 1TT
Tel: 0118 9785767
Head: Mrs Zoe Lattimer
BSc(Hons), PGCE
Age range: 7–18
Special needs catered for: ADHD,
ASD, ASP, BESD, EBD, MLD
♿ 16 ✓

Buckinghamshire

Unity College
150 West Wycombe
Road, High Wycombe,
Buckinghamshire HP12 3AE
Tel: 077 02916189
Headteacher: Mrs Lois Hubbard
No. of pupils: 12
Special needs catered for:
BESD, MLD, SEBD
✓

East Sussex

Headstart School
Crouch Lane, Ninfield, Battle,
East Sussex TN33 9EG
Tel: 01424 893803
Headteacher: Ms Nicola Dann
Age range: 7–18
Special needs catered for: BESD
16 ✓

**Springboard
Education Junior**
39 Whippingham Road, St
Wilfred's Upper Hall, Brighton,
East Sussex BN2 3PS
Tel: 01273 885109
Headteacher: Elizabeth Freeman
Age range: 7–13
Special needs catered for:
ADHD, BESD
✓

The Lioncare School
87 Payne Avenue, Hove,
East Sussex BN3 5HD
Tel: 01273 734164
Headteacher: Mrs J Dance
Age range: 7–16
No. of pupils: 9
Special needs catered for: EBD
✓

**The Mount Camphill
Community**
Faircrouch Lane, Wadhurst,
East Sussex TN5 6PT
Tel: 01892 782025
Head of Education: Mr Julian Ritchie
Age range: 16–24
No. of pupils: 35
Special needs catered for: ADD,
ADHD, ASD, ASP, AUT, BESD, CLD,
CP, DEL, DYS, DYSP, EBD, EPI, GLD,
HI, LD, MLD, MSI, PD, Phe, PH,
PNI, SCD, SLD, SP&LD, SPLD, SLI
♿

Hampshire

Coxlease Abbeymead
Palace Lane, Beaulieu,
Hampshire SO42 7YG
Tel: 02380 283 633
Principal: Mr Rick Tracey
Age range: 9–16
No. of pupils: 5
Special needs catered for: EBD
♿

Coxlease School
Clay Hill, Lyndhurst,
Hampshire SO43 7DE
Tel: 023 8028 3633
Principal: Mr Rick Tracey
Age range: 9–18
No. of pupils: 55
Special needs catered for:
BESD, MLD
♿ 16 ✓

St Edward's School
Melchet Court, Sherfield English,
Romsey, Hampshire SO51 6ZR
Tel: 01794 885252
Head: L Bartel BEd(Hons)
Age range: B10–17
No. of pupils: 44
Special needs catered for:
BESD, DYS, EBD, MLD, SPLD
♿ ♿ ✓

The Serendipity Centre
399 Hinkler Road, Southampton,
Hampshire SO19 6DS
Tel: 023 8042 2255
Head Teacher: Dr. Michele Aldridge
Age range: G9–18
No. of pupils: 15
Special needs catered for: SEBD
♿ ✓

Kent

Brewood Middle School
146 Newington Road,
Ramsgate, Kent CT12 6PT
Tel: 01843 597088
Head of School: Mr Daniel Radlett
Age range: 5–13
No. of pupils: 8
Fees: Day £23,863
Special needs catered for: ADD,
ADHD, ASD, ASP, AUT, BESD, CLD,
DEL, EBD, EPI, GLD, HA, HI, LD,
MLD, PH, SCD, SLD, SP&LD, SLI

**Brewood Secondary
School**
86 London Road, Deal,
Kent CT14 9TR
Tel: 01304 363000
Head of School: Mr Daniel Radlett
Age range: 11–18
No. of pupils: 12
Fees: Day £23,863
Special needs catered for: ADD,
ADHD, ASD, ASP, AUT, BESD, CLD,
DEL, EBD, EPI, GLD, HA, HI, LD,
MLD, PH, SCD, SLD, SP&LD, SLI
✓

Browns School
Cannock House, Hawstead Lane,
Chelsfield, Orpington, Kent BR6 7PH
Tel: 01689 876816
Headteacher: Mr M F Brown
Age range: 7–12
No. of pupils: 32
Special needs catered for:
EBD, SPLD
✓

**Caldecott Foundation
School**
Hythe Road, Smeeth,
Ashford, Kent TN25 6PW
Tel: 01303 815678
Acting Head: Mrs Valerie Miller
Age range: 5–18
No. of pupils: 56
Special needs catered for: EBD
♿ 16 ✓

Greenfields School
Tenterden Road, Biddenden,
Kent TN27 8BS
Tel: 01580 292523
Director: Gary Yexley
Age range: 5–11
No. of pupils: 13
Fees: Day £29,004
Special needs catered for: EBD
✓

Heath Farm School
Egerton Road, Charing Heath,
Ashford, Kent TN27 0AX
Tel: 01233 712030
Head: Liz Cornish
Age range: 5–16
No. of pupils: 70
Special needs catered for: EBD
✓

Hope View School
Station Approach, Chilham,
Canterbury, Kent CT4 8EG
Tel: 01227 738000
Head of School: Ms Carla Kaushal
Age range: 11–17
No. of pupils: 16
Special needs catered for:
ADD, ADHD, ASD, ASP, BESD
✔

Hythe House Education
Power Station Road,
Sheerness, Kent ME12 3AB
Tel: 01795 581006
Headteacher: Mr Robert Duffy
Age range: 11–16
No. of pupils: 20
Special needs catered for: EBD
✔

ISP Sittingbourne School
Church Street, Sittingbourne,
Kent ME10 3EG
Tel: 01795 422 044
Headteacher: Craig Walter
Age range: 11–16
Special needs catered for:
BESD, SCD, SEBD
✔

Learning Opportunities Centre
Ringwould Road, Ringwould,
Deal, Kent CT14 8DN
Tel: 01304 381906
Headteacher: Mrs Diana Ward
Age range: 11–16
No. of pupils: 40
Special needs catered for: EBD
👤 ✔

Little Acorns School
London Beach Farm,
Ashford Road, St Michael's,
Tenterden, Kent TN30 6SR
Tel: 01233 850422
Headteacher: Miss Angela Flynn
Age range: 4–14
No. of pupils: 7
Special needs catered for: EBD
👤 ✔

Meadows School and Meadows 16+
London Road, Southborough,
Kent TN4 0RJ
Tel: 01892 529144
Principal: Mike Price
BEd(Hons), DipSEN, MA
Age range: 11–19
No. of pupils: 45
Special needs catered for: ADHD,
ASP, AUT, DYS, DYSP, EBD, MLD, SEBD
👤 16+ ✔

Ripplevale School
Chapel Lane, Ripple,
Deal, Kent CT14 8JG
Tel: 01304 373866
Principal: Mr Ted Schofield CRSW
Age range: B9–16
No. of pupils: 30
Special needs catered for: ADD,
ADHD, ASD, ASP, AUT, BESD, CLD,
DYS, DYSP, EBD, GLD, HA, LD, MLD,
PMLD, SCD, SCLD, SP&LD, SPLD
👤 👤 ✔

The Ashbrook Centre
8 Almond Close, Broadstairs,
Kent CT10 2NQ
Tel: 01843 482 043
Principal: Mr Nigel Troop
Age range: 5–18
No. of pupils: 5
Special needs catered for:
BESD, SEBD
16+ ✔

The Boulters Learning and Skills Centre
Units 12–13, Oare Gunpowder
Works, Off Bysingwood Road,
Faversham, Kent ME13 7UD
Tel: 01795 529184
Headteacher: Ms L Scott
Age range: 12–17
No. of pupils: 9
Special needs catered for: BESD
✔

The Davenport School
Princess Margaret Avenue,
Ramsgate, Kent CT12 6HX
Tel: 01843 589018
Headteacher: Mr Franklyn Brown
Age range: B7–12
Special needs catered for: EBD
👤 ✔

The New School at West Heath
Ashgrove Road, Sevenoaks,
Kent TN13 1SR
Tel: 01732 460553
Principal: Mrs Christina Wells
Age range: 10–19
No. of pupils: 120 B87 G33 VIth40
Fees: Day £46,583 WB £31,245
Special needs catered for:
ADD, ADHD, ASD, ASP, BESD,
DEL, EBD, SCD, SP&LD, SPLD
👤 16+ ✔

The Old Priory School
Priory Road, Ramsgate,
Kent CT11 9PG
Tel: 01843 599322
Head: Jack Banner
Age range: B10–15
Special needs catered for: EBD
👤 ✔

The Old School
Capel Street, Capel-le-Ferne,
Folkestone, Kent CT18 7EY
Tel: 01303 251116
Headteacher: Martyn Jordan
Age range: B9–17
No. of pupils: 24
Special needs catered for: EBD
👤 ✔

Surrey

Cornfield School
53 Hanworth Road, Redhill,
Surrey RH1 5HS
Tel: 01737 779578
Headteacher: Mrs Jayne Telfer
Age range: G11–18
No. of pupils: 25
Special needs catered for: EBD
👤 16+ ✔

Grafham Grange School
Nr Bramley, Guildford,
Surrey GU5 0LH
Tel: 01483 892214
Headteacher: Ms Debra Henderson
Special needs catered for:
ADHD, ASD, BESD, EBD, SP&LD
👤 👤 ✔

Tudor Lodge School
92 Foxley Lane, Woodcote,
Purley, Surrey CR8 3NA
Tel: 020 8763 8785
Headteacher: Ms Patricia Lines
Age range: 12–16
No. of pupils: 7
Special needs catered for: SEBD
👤 ✔

West Sussex

Brantridge School
Staplefield Place, Staplefield,
Haywards Heath, West
Sussex RH17 6EQ
Tel: 01444 400228
Headteacher: Gina Wagland
Age range: B6–13
No. of pupils: 27
Special needs catered for:
ADHD, ASD, ASP, BESD, EBD, LD
👤 👤 ✔

Farney Close School
Bolney Court, Bolney,
West Sussex RH17 5RD
Tel: 01444 881811
Head: Mr B Robinson MA, BEd(Hons)
Age range: 11–16
No. of pupils: 78
Fees: Day £55,222.10
Special needs catered for: ADHD,
ASP, DYS, EBD, MLD, SP&LD
👤 ✔

Hillcrest Slinfold School
Stane Street, Slinfold, Horsham,
West Sussex RH13 0QX
Tel: 01403 790939
Principal: Ms Sarah Olliver
Age range: B11–17
Special needs catered for: ADD,
ADHD, ASD, ASP, BESD, DYS, DYSP,
EBD, GLD, MLD, SCD, SEBD
👤 👤 ✔

Muntham House School Ltd
Barns Green, Muntham Drive,
Horsham, West Sussex RH13 0NJ
Tel: 01403 730302
Principal: Mr R Boyle
MEd, BEd, AdvDipSE
Age range: B8–18
No. of pupils: 51 VIth12
Special needs catered for:
ADD, ADHD, ASD, BESD, DYS,
EBD, MLD, SP&LD, SPLD
👤 👤 16+ ✔

PHILPOTS MANOR SCHOOL
For further details see p. 55
West Hoathly, East Grinstead,
West Sussex RH19 4PR
Tel: 01342 810268
Email: info@
philpotsmanorschool.co.uk
Website: www.philpotsmanor
school.co.uk
Education Co-ordinator: Ms
Linda Churnside BEd
Age range: 7–19
No. of pupils: 34
Fees: Day £65,000 WB £65,000
Special needs catered for:
ADD, ADHD, ASD, ASP, AUT,
BESD, DEL, DYS, EBD, EPI,
GLD, LD, MLD, SCD, SP&LD
👤 16+ ✔

Southways School
The Vale House, Findon Road,
Worthing, West Sussex BN14 0RA
Tel: 01903 877448
Headteacher: Gail Jay
Age range: 6–11
Special needs catered for: EBD
✔

Springboard Education Senior
55 South Street, Lancing,
West Sussex BN15 8HA
Tel: 01903 605980
Head Teacher: Mr Simon
Yorke-Johnson
Age range: 11–18
No. of pupils: 10
Special needs catered for: ADD,
ADHD, ASD, ASP, AUT, BESD, EBD
16+ ✔

South-West

Devon

Advanced Education – Devon School
Oaklands Park, Oaklands Road, Buckfastleigh, Devon TQ11 0BW
Tel: 01364 644 823
Headteacher: Swavek Nowakiewicz
Age range: 10–16
Special needs catered for: ASP, AUT, EBD, SEBD
✔

Chelfham Mill School
Chelfham, Barnstaple, Devon EX32 7LA
Tel: 01271 850448
Principal: Mrs K T Roberts BEd, BPhil(EBD)
Age range: B9–16
No. of pupils: 40
Special needs catered for: ADD, ADHD, ASP, DYS, DYSP, EBD, GLD, LD, MLD
🧒 🏠 ✔

Oakwood Court
7/9 Oak Park Villas, Dawlish, Devon EX7 0DE
Tel: 01626 864066
Principal: J F Loft BEd, BPhil(SEN), HNDHIM
Age range: 16–25
Special needs catered for: ADHD, ASP, DYS, DYSP, EBD, EPI, MLD, SLD
🏠 16+

The Libra School
Edgemoor Court, South Radworthy, South Molton, Devon EX36 3LN
Tel: 01598 740044
Headteacher: Ms J E Wilkes
Age range: 8–18
Special needs catered for: EBD
16+ ✔

Whitstone Head School
Whitstone, Holsworthy, Devon EX22 6TJ
Tel: 01288 341251
Principal: Mr D R McLean-Thorne
Age range: 10–16
No. of pupils: 37
Special needs catered for: ADD, ADHD, ASD, ASP, AUT, BESD, CLD, DEL, DYS, DYSP, EBD, GLD, MLD, SCD, SPLD
🏠 ✔

Dorset

Ivers College
Ivers, Hains Lane, Marnhull, Sturminster Newton, Dorset DT10 1JU
Tel: 01258 820164
Principal: Linda Matthews
Age range: 18+
No. of pupils: 23
Special needs catered for: EBD, LD, MLD, SCD
16+

Gloucestershire

Marlowe Education Unit
Hartpury Old School, Gloucester Road, Hartpury, Gloucestershire GL19 3BG
Tel: 01452 700855
Head Teacher: Diane McQueen
Age range: 8–16
No. of pupils: 8
Special needs catered for: EBD, MLD
✔

Somerset

Advanced Education – Somerset School
Westport House, Langport Road, Hambridge, Somerset TA10 0BH
Tel: 01460 281216
Headteacher: Mr Will Houghton
Age range: 10–16
Special needs catered for: AUT, EBD, HI, SEBD
✔

Aethelstan College
Newton Road, North Petherton, Somerset TA6 6NA
Tel: 01626 8663233
Headteacher: Mrs Ros Hagley
Age range: 11–16
Special needs catered for: EBD
✔

Inaura School
Moorview House, Burrowbridge, Bridgwater, Somerset TA7 0RB
Tel: 01823 690211
Headteacher: Dr Adam Abdelnoor
Age range: 8–18
No. of pupils: 24
Fees: Day £45,954
Special needs catered for: ADHD, ASD, BESD, CLD, EBD, LD, SCD
16+ ✔

Merryhay School
Merryhay House, Ilton Business Park, Ilminster, Somerset TA19 9DU
Tel: 01460 55524
Head of School: Mr Edward Underwood
Age range: 11–16
No. of pupils: 8
Special needs catered for: EBD, MLD

New Horizon Centre School
Bath House Farm, West Hatch, Taunton, Somerset TA3 5RH
Tel: 01823 481902
Headteacher: Jennie Meadows
Age range: 11–16
No. of pupils: 20
Special needs catered for: EBD
✔

Newbury Manor School
Nr Mells, Frome, Somerset BA11 3RG
Tel: 01373 814 980
Head of School: Mr. Andy Holder
Age range: 7–19

The Marchant-Holliday School
North Cheriton, Templecombe, Somerset BA8 0AH
Tel: 01963 33234
Head Teacher: Mr T J Kitts MEd, BEd(Hons), DPSE(SEN)
Age range: B5–13
No. of pupils: 38
Special needs catered for: ADD, ADHD, ASD, ASP, BESD, DYS, DYSP, EBD, SCD
🧒 🏠 ✔

Wiltshire

Wessex College
Wessex Lodge, Nunney Road, Frome, Wiltshire BA11 4LA
Tel: 01373 453414
Headteacher: Ms C Smith
Age range: 11–16
No. of pupils: 6
Special needs catered for: EBD
✔

West Midlands

Herefordshire

Queenswood School
Callows Hills Farm, Hereford Road, Ledbury, Herefordshire HR8 2PZ
Tel: 01531 670632
Principal: Mr James Imber
Age range: 11–19
No. of pupils: 15
Special needs catered for: BESD, SEBD
🏠 16+ ✔

The Larches School
Coningsby Road, Leominster, Herefordshire HR6 8LL
Tel: 01568 780094
Head: Nigel Kedword
Age range: 11–16
Special needs catered for: EBD
✔

Shropshire

Acorn School
Dale Acre Way, Hollinswood, Telford, Shropshire TF3 2EN
Tel: 01952 200410
Head: Ms Sarah Morgan
Age range: 11–16
No. of pupils: 16
Special needs catered for: EBD
✔

Care UK Children's Services
46 High Street, Church Stretton, Shropshire SY6 6BX
Tel: 01694 724488
Director: Simon W Rouse BA(Hons), CSS, DipPTh
Age range: 10–18
No. of pupils: 24
Special needs catered for: EBD
16+

Ditton Priors School
Station Road, Ditton Priors, Bridgnorth, Shropshire WV16 6SS
Tel: 01746 712985
Headteacher: Mr Stephen Piper
Age range: 11–16
No. of pupils: 10
Special needs catered for: BESD, EBD
✔

Smallbrook School
Smallbrook Lodge, Smallbrook Road, Whitchurch, Shropshire SY13 1BX
Tel: 01948 661110
Headteacher: Ms Sarah Morgan
Age range: 11–19
No. of pupils: 15
Special needs catered for: EBD
16+ ✔

Young Options College
Lamledge Lane, Shifnal, Shropshire TF11 8SD
Tel: 01952 468220
Head Teacher: Ms Julia Saint
Age range: 7–19
Special needs catered for: ADD, ADHD, ASP, BESD, DEL, EBD, SCD, SEBD
🏠 ✔

Staffordshire

Aidenswood
47 Liverpool Road East,
Kidsgrove, Stoke-on-Trent,
Staffordshire ST7 3AD
Tel: 01253 316160
Headteacher: Mr Paul Heaven
Age range: B13–17
No. of pupils: 6
Special needs catered for:
EBD, MLD

Bloomfield College
Bloomfield Road, Tipton,
Staffordshire DY4 9AH
Tel: 0121 5209408
Headteacher: Mr Andrew Harding
Age range: 11–16
Special needs catered for: EBD

Draycott Moor College
Draycott Old Road, Draycott-
in-the-Moors, Stoke-on-Trent,
Staffordshire ST11 9AH
Tel: 01782 399849
Headteacher: Mr David Rutter
Age range: 11–16
Special needs catered for: EBD

Hillcrest Oaklands College
Alrewas Road, Kings Bromley,
Staffordshire DE13 7HR
Tel: 01543 473772
Principal: Mr David Biddle
MAEd, BA (HONS), CertEd
Age range: G12–19
Special needs catered for: ADD,
ADHD, ASD, ASP, BESD, DYS, DYSP,
EBD, GLD, MLD, SCD, SEBD

Horizon School Staffordshire
Venture House, 12 Prospect
Park, Longford Road, Cannock,
Staffordshire WS11 0LG
Tel: 01543 572 143
Consultant Head Teacher: Mr
Stephen Ellis
Age range: 11–16
Special needs catered for: EBD

Longdon Hall School
Longdon Hall, Rugeley,
Staffordshire WS15 4PT
Tel: 01543 491051
Headteacher: Mr Matt Storey
Age range: 7–18
Special needs catered for:
BESD, EBD

The Roaches Independent School
Tunstall Road, Knypersley, Stoke-
on-Trent, Staffordshire ST8 7AB
Tel: 01782 523479
The Principal: Head of Education
Age range: 7–16
No. of pupils: 16
Fees: Day £30,780 FB £103,740
Special needs catered for: EBD

Young Options Pathway College Stoke
Phoenix House, Marlborough
Road, Longton, Stoke-on-
Trent, Staffordshire ST3 1EJ
Tel: 01782 320773
Headteacher: Mel Callaghan-Lewis
Age range: 11–19
No. of pupils: 11
Special needs catered for: ADD,
ADHD, ASP, AUT, BESD, CLD, DEL,
DYS, DYSP, EBD, GLD, HA, LD, MLD,
MSI, PMLD, SCD, SEBD, SLD, SPLD

Warwickshire

Arc School – Ansley
Ansley Lane, Ansley, Nuneaton,
Warwickshire CV10 9ND
Tel: 01676 543 810
Headteacher: Mr Christian Williams
Age range: 7–16
Special needs catered for:
ADHD, ASD, SEBD

Arc School – Church End
Church End, Ansley, Nuneaton,
Warwickshire CV10 0QR
Tel: 024 7639 4801
Headmistress: Pauline Garret
Age range: 7–11
No. of pupils: 30
Special needs catered for: BESD

Arc School – Napton
Vicarage Road, Napton-on-the-
Hill, Warwickshire CV47 8NA
Tel: 01926 817 547
Acting Head Teacher: Cathal Lynch
Age range: 7–16
Special needs catered for:
ADHD, ASD

Wathen Grange School
Church Walk, Mancetter,
Atherstone, Warwickshire CV9 1PZ
Tel: 01827 714454
**Head of Education
Service:** Mr Chris Nock
Age range: 11–16
No. of pupils: 15
Special needs catered for: EBD

West Midlands

Blue River Academy
36 Medley Road, Greet,
Birmingham, West Midlands B11 2NE
Tel: 0121 7667981
Age range: B14–16
Special needs catered for: BESD

Oaklands School
215 Barrows Lane, Yardley,
Birmingham, West
Midlands B26 1QS
Headteacher: Ms Rebecca Hill
Age range: 11–16
No. of pupils: 4
Special needs catered for: BESD

The Collegiate Centre for Values Education for Life
51-54 Hockley Hill, Hockley,
Birmingham, West
Midlands B18 5AQ
Tel: 0121 5230222
Headteacher: Mrs Val Russell
Age range: 11–17
No. of pupils: 25
Special needs catered for: BESD

Yorkshire & Humberside

East Riding of Yorkshire

Horton House School
Hilltop Farm, Sutton Road,
Wawne, Kingston upon Hull, East
Riding of Yorkshire HU7 5YY
Tel: 01482 875191
Head: Mr Matthew Stubbins
Age range: 8–23
Fees: Day £25,000–£50,000
WB £75,000–£150,000 FB £180,000
Special needs catered for: ADD,
ADHD, ASD, ASP, AUT, BESD, CLD,
DYS, DYSP, EBD, EPI, GLD, LD, MLD,
SCD, SCLD, SEBD, SLD, SPLD

North Yorkshire

Advanced Education – Scarborough School
Unit 11, Plaxton Park, Cayton Low
Road, Eastfield, Scarborough,
North Yorkshire YO11 1JR
Tel: 01723 581 475
Headteacher: Ms Anne Wood
Age range: 8–16
Special needs catered for: SEBD

Breckenbrough School
Sandhutton, Thirsk, North
Yorkshire YO7 4EN
Tel: 01845 587238
Headmaster: Geoffrey Brookes BEd
Age range: B9–19
No. of pupils: 49
Special needs catered for: ADD,
ADHD, ASP, BESD, DEL, DYS, EBD, HA

CLERVAUX
For further details see p. 57
Clow Beck Centre, Jolby
Lane, Croft-on-Tees, North
Yorkshire DL2 2TF
Tel: 01325 729860
Email: info@clervaux.org.uk
Website: www.clervaux.org.uk
Strategic Lead: Bonny
Etchell-Anderson
Age range: 16–25+
Special needs catered for:
ASD, ASP, AUT, BESD, CLD

Spring Hill School
Palace Road, Ripon, North
Yorkshire HG4 3HN
Tel: 01765 603320
Principal: Linda Nelson
Age range: 9–19
No. of pupils: 31
Special needs catered for:
ADHD, ASP, AUT, CP, DEL, DYS,
DYSP, EBD, EPI, MLD, SLD, SP&LD

South Yorkshire

BRANTWOOD SPECIALIST SCHOOL
For further details see p. 56
1 Kenwood Bank, Nether Edge,
Sheffield, South Yorkshire S7 1NU
Tel: 0114 258 9062
Email: enquiries@
brantwood.rmt.org
Website: www.rmt.org
Headteacher: Constantin Court
Age range: 7–19 years
Special needs catered for:
ADD, ADHD, ASD, ASP, BESD,
CLD, EBD, GLD, LD, MLD, PMLD,
SCD, SCLD, SEBD, SPLD

Emotional, behavioural and/or social difficulties (EBSD)

Chrysalis Therapeutic Educational Centre
48 Wostenholm Road, Nether Edge, South Yorkshire S7 1LL
Tel: 0114 2509455
Headteacher: Mrs Sarah Allkins
Age range: 8–14
No. of pupils: 4
Special needs catered for: BESD
✔

Dove School
194 New Road, Staincross, Barnsley, South Yorkshire S75 6PP
Tel: 01226 381380
Headteacher: Mrs Helen Mangham
Age range: 9–16
Special needs catered for: BESD
✔

West Yorkshire

Denby Grange School
Stocksmoor Road, Midgley, Wakefield, West Yorkshire WF4 4JQ
Tel: 01924 830096
Head: Miss Jennie Littleboy
Age range: 11–17
No. of pupils: 36
Special needs catered for: EBD, SCD
✔

New Gables School
2 New Close Road, Shipley, West Yorkshire BD18 4AB
Tel: 01274 584705
Teacher-in-charge: Caroline Matson
Age range: 11–16
Special needs catered for: SEBD

The Grange School
2 Milner Way, Ossett, Wakefield, West Yorkshire WF5 9JE
Tel: 01924 378957
Headteacher: Phil Bennett
Age range: 7–14
No. of pupils: 12
Special needs catered for: BESD
✔

William Henry Smith School
Boothroyd, Brighouse, West Yorkshire HD6 3JW
Tel: 01484 710123
Principal: B J Heneghan BA, PGCE, DipSpEd
Age range: B8–16
Fees: Day £57,810 FB £70,435
Special needs catered for: ADD, ADHD, BESD, SCD, SEBD
♦ ♦ ✎ ✔

Northern Ireland

County Down

Camphill Community Glencraig
Craigavad, Holywood, County Down BT18 0DB
Tel: 028 9042 3396
School Co-ordinator: Vincent Reynolds
Age range: 7–19
No. of pupils: 32
Fees: FB £66,500
Special needs catered for: ADHD, ASP, AUT, CP, DYSP, EBD, EPI, HI, MLD, PH, PMLD, SLD, SP&LD, SPLD, VIS
16+ ♦ 16+

Scotland

Edinburgh

Harmeny Education Trust Ltd
Harmeny School, Balerno, Edinburgh EH14 7JY
Tel: 0131 449 3938
Chief Executive: Peter Doran BA(Hons)Econ, CQSW, MA Social Work, AdvCert SW
Age range: 6–13
No. of pupils: 36
Special needs catered for: ADD, ADHD, ASP, DYS, EBD, SPLD
♦

Fife

Falkland House School
Falkland Estate, Cupar, Fife KY15 7AE
Tel: 01337 857268
Head: Mr Stuart Jacob
Age range: B5–18
No. of pupils: 30
Fees: FB £70,000
Special needs catered for: ADD, ADHD, ASP, BESD, DYS, EBD, EPI, SCD, SPLD
♦ ♦ ✎ 16+

Hillside School
Hillside, Aberdour, Fife KY3 0RH
Tel: 01383 860731
Principal: Mrs Anne Smith
Age range: B10–16
No. of pupils: 39
Fees: Day £10,830 FB £26,594–£58,959
Special needs catered for: DYS, EBD, SPLD
♦ ♦

Starley Hall School
Aberdour Road, Burntisland, Fife KY3 0AG
Tel: 01383 860314
Head: Philip Barton BA
Age range: 10–16
No. of pupils: 48
Special needs catered for: EBD, MLD
♦

North Ayrshire

Geilsland School
Beith, North Ayrshire KA15 1HD
Tel: 01505 504044
Head of School: Mr Paul Gilroy
Age range: B14–18
No. of pupils: 26
Special needs catered for: EBD, MLD, SEBD
♦ ♦

Seafield School
86 Eglinton Road, Ardrossan, North Ayrshire KA22 8NL
Tel: 01294 470355
Head: Mrs Elaine McIntosh
Age range: B5–16
Special needs catered for: EBD
♦ ♦

North Lanarkshire

St Philip's School
10 Main Street, Plains, Airdrie, North Lanarkshire ML6 7SF
Tel: 01236 765407
Head: Mr P Hanrahan
Age range: B12–16
No. of pupils: 61
Special needs catered for: EBD
♦ ♦

Perth & Kinross

Balnacraig School
Fairmount Terrace, Perth, Perth & Kinross PH2 7AR
Tel: 01738 636456
Head: Charles Kiddie
Age range: 12–16
No. of pupils: 24
Special needs catered for: BESD, EBD

Seamab House School
Rumbling Bridge, Kinross,
Perth & Kinross KY13 0PT
Tel: 01577 840307
Chief Executive: Ms
Joanna McCreadie
Age range: 5–12
No. of pupils: 15
Special needs catered for: EBD
♿

Renfrewshire

**Kibble Education
and Care Centre**
Goudie Street, Paisley,
Renfrewshire PA3 2LG
Tel: 0141 889 0044
Head: Graham Bell
Age range: 12–16
No. of pupils: 93
Special needs catered for:
EBD, MLD, SCD, SLD, SPLD
♿

Spark of Genius
Trojan House, Phoenix Business
Park, Paisley, Renfrewshire PA1 2BH
Tel: 0141 587 2710
Director: Mr Tom McGhee
Age range: 5–18
No. of pupils: 106
Special needs catered for:
ASD, EBD
♿

**The Good Shepherd
Secure/Close Support Unit**
Greenock Road, Bishopton,
Renfrewshire PA7 5PW
Tel: 01505 864500
Head: Mr Sand Cunningham
Age range: G12–17
Special needs catered for:
EBD, MLD
♿ ♿

Stirling

**Ballikinrain
Residential School**
Fintry Road, Balfron, Stirling G63 0LL
Tel: 01360 440244
Manager: Mr Paul Gilroy
Age range: B8–14
No. of pupils: 40
Special needs catered for: BESD
♿ ♿

Snowdon School
31 Spittal Street, Stirling FK8 1DU
Tel: 01786 464746
Headteacher: Annette P Davison
Age range: G13–17
Special needs catered for: BESD
♿ ♿

West Lothian

Moore House School
21 Edinburgh Road, Bathgate,
West Lothian EH48 1EX
Tel: 01506 652312
Age range: 8–16
No. of pupils: 37
Special needs catered for:
ADHD, EBD
♿

Wales

Denbighshire

The Branas School
Branas Isaf, Llandrillo, Corwen,
Denbighshire LL21 0TA
Tel: 01490 440545
Age range: B12–17
No. of pupils: 12
Special needs catered for: EBD
♿

Monmouthshire

Talocher School
Talocher Farm, Wonastow
Road, Monmouth,
Monmouthshire NP25 4DN
Tel: 01600 740777
Principal: Mr Mike Borland
Age range: 11–18
No. of pupils: 25
Special needs catered for:
BESD, SEBD
♿ 16⁺

Neath Port Talbot

Blackwood School
Ferryboat House, Ellwood
Jersey Marine, Neath, Neath
Port Talbot SA10 6NG
Headteacher: Nicky Jones
Age range: B11–18
No. of pupils: 4
Special needs catered for:
EBD, SPLD
♿ ♿

Pembrokeshire

St David's Education Unit
Pembroke House, Brawdy
Business Park, Haverfordwest,
Pembrokeshire SA62 6NP
Tel: 01437 721234
Head: Mrs Alison Wilkinson
Age range: 8–17
No. of pupils: 7
Special needs catered for: EBD

Wrexham

**Woodlands Children's
Development Centre**
27 Pentrefelyn Road,
Wrexham LL13 7NB
Tel: 01978 262777
Head: Ms Vivien Devereaux
Age range: B11–18
No. of pupils: 8
Special needs catered for:
BESD, EBD
♿

Schools and colleges specialising in learning difficulties (including dyslexia/SPLD)

Abbreviations

ACLD	Autism, Communication and Associated Learning Difficulties
ADD	Attention Deficit Disorder
ADHD	Attention Deficit and Hyperactive Disorder (Hyperkinetic Disorder)
ASD	Autistic Spectrum Disorder
ASP	Asperger Syndrome
AUT	Autism
BESD	Behavioural, Emotional and Social Difficulties
CCD	Complex Communication Difficulties
CLD	Complex Learning Difficulties
CP	Cerebral Palsy
D	Deaf
DEL	Delicate
DYS	Dyslexia
DYSP	Dyspraxia
EBD	Emotional and Behavioural Difficulties
EBSD	Emotional, Behavioural and/or Social Difficulties
EPI	Epilepsy
GLD	General Learning Difficulties
HA	High Ability
HI	Hearing Impairment
HS	Hospital School
LD	Learning Difficulties
MLD	Moderate Learning Difficulties
MSI	Multi-sensory Impairment
OCD	Obsessive Compulsive Disorder
PD	Physical Difficulties
PH	Physical Impairment
Phe	Partially Hearing
PMLD	Profound and Multiple Learning Difficulties
PNI	Physical Neurological Impairment
PRU	Pupil Referral Unit
SCD	Social and Communication Difficulties
SCLD	Severe and Complex Learning Difficulties
SEBD	Severe Emotional and Behavioural Disorders
SEBN	Social, Emotional and Behavioural Needs
SLD	Severe Learning Difficulties
SLI	Specific Language Impairment
SPLD	Specific Learning Difficulties
SP&LD	Speech and Language Difficulties
SLCN	Speech Language & Communication Needs
VIS	Visually Impaired

Key to Symbols

Type of school:

♂	Boys' school
♀	Girls' school
🌐	International school

School offers:

Ⓐ	A levels
🏫	Boarding accommodation
⑯⁺	Entrance at 16+
☣	Vocational qualifications
✐	Learning support
✓	This is a DfE approved independent or non-maintained school under section 342 or 347(1) of the 1996 Education Act

Please note: Unless otherwise indicated, all schools are coeducational day schools. Single-sex and boarding schools will be indicated by the relevant icon.

Central & West

Bristol

Belgrave School
10 Upper Belgrave Road,
Clifton, Bristol BS8 2XH
Tel: 0117 974 3133
Head Teacher: Pat Jones
Age range: 5–13
Fees: Day £6,000
Special needs catered for:
ADD, ASD, ASP, DEL, DYS, DYSP,
HA, MLD, SP&LD, SPLD, SLI
✓

Bristol Dyslexia Centre
10 Upper Belgrave Road,
Clifton, Bristol BS8 2XH
Tel: 0117 973 9405
Headmistress: Mrs Pat
Jones BEd(Hons), SEN, SpLD,
CertEd, IrSc, CMBDA
Special needs catered for:
DYS, DYSP, SLD

Sheiling School, Thornbury
Thornbury Park, Thornbury,
Bristol BS35 1HP
Tel: 01454 412194
Age range: 6–19
No. of pupils: 22
Fees: Day £66,419–£83,428
WB £125,931–£172,096
FB £140,578–£197,157
Special needs catered for: ADD,
ADHD, ASD, ASP, AUT, BESD, CLD,
CP, DEL, DYS, DYSP, EBD, EPI, GLD,
HA, HI, LD, MLD, MSI, PD, Phe, SCD,
SCLD, SEBD, SLD, SP&LD, SPLD, SLI
🏛 16 ✓

ST CHRISTOPHER'S SCHOOL
For further details see p. 61
Carisbrooke Lodge, Westbury
Park, Bristol BS6 7JE
Tel: 0117 973 6875
Email: info@st-christophers.
bristol.co.uk
Website: www.st-christophers.
bristol.sch.uk
Principal: Ms Orna Matz
BEd, MEd(Autism)
Age range: 5–19
No. of pupils: 42
Special needs catered for:
ASD, AUT, CLD, CP, EPI, PD,
PH, PMLD, SCLD, SLD, SP&LD
🏛 16 ✓

Buckinghamshire

MacIntyre Wingrave School
Leighton Road, Wingrave,
Buckinghamshire HP22 4PA
Tel: 01296 681274
Principal: Ms Annemari Ottridge
Age range: 10–19
No. of pupils: 38
Fees: FB £182,000
Special needs catered for:
ASD, SCD, SLD
🏛 16 ✓

Gloucestershire

Cambian Southwick Park School
Gloucester Road, Tewkesbury,
Gloucestershire GL20 7DG
Tel: 0800 288 9779
Head: Mr Jason Goddard
Age range: 11–19
Special needs catered for: AUT,
LD, SCD, SCLD, SEBD, SLD
🏛 16

RUSKIN MILL COLLEGE
For further details see p. 60
The Fisheries, Horsley,
Gloucestershire GL6 0PL
Tel: 01453 837500
Email: enquiries@rmc.rmt.org
Website: www.rmt.org
Principal: Dan Alipaz
Age range: 16–25
Special needs catered for:
ADHD, ASD, ASP, BESD, CLD,
EBD, GLD, LD, MLD, PMLD,
SCD, SCLD, SEBD, SPLD
16 🏛

William Morris House
William Morris Camphill
Community, Eastington,
Stonehouse, Gloucestershire
GL10 3SH
Tel: 01453 824025
Contact: Admissions Group
Age range: 16–25
No. of pupils: 30
Special needs catered for:
ASP, AUT, DYSP, EBD, EPI, MLD
🏛

Oxfordshire

Action for Children Penhurst School
New Street, Chipping Norton,
Oxfordshire OX7 5LN
Tel: 01608 642559
Principal: Derek Lyseight-Jones
Age range: 5–19
No. of pupils: 21
Special needs catered for: CP,
EPI, HI, PH, PMLD, SLD, SP&LD, VIS
🏛 16

Bruern Abbey School
Chesterton, Bicester,
Oxfordshire OX26 1UY
Tel: 01869 242448
Principal: Mr P Fawkes MBA, CertEd
Age range: B7–13
No. of pupils: 44
Fees: Day £5,703 WB £7,791
Special needs catered for:
DYS, DYSP
🏃 🧩 🏛

THE UNICORN SCHOOL
For further details see p. 62
20 Marcham Road, Abingdon,
Oxfordshire OX14 1AA
Tel: 01235 530222
Email: info@unicornoxford.co.uk
Website:
www.unicornoxford.co.uk
Headteacher: Mr. Andrew
Day BEd (Hons)University
of Wales (Cardiff)
Age range: 6–14
No. of pupils: 68
Special needs catered for:
DYS, DYSP
✏ ✓

Wiltshire

Appleford School
Shrewton, Salisbury,
Wiltshire SP3 4HL
Tel: 01980 621020
Headmaster: Mr. David King
Age range: 7–18
No. of pupils: 105
Fees: Day £16,608 FB £25,491
Special needs catered for:
ADD, ADHD, ASP, DYS, DYSP,
HA, MLD, SP&LD, SPLD
🧩 🏛 16 ✓

Calder House School
Thickwood Lane, Colerne,
Wiltshire SN14 8BN
Tel: 01225 742329
Head: Mr Andrew Day BEd(Hons)
Age range: 6–13
No. of pupils: 48
Fees: Day £13,800
Special needs catered for: DEL,
DYS, DYSP, SP&LD, SPLD, SLI
✓

Fairfield Farm College
Dilton Marsh, Westbury,
Wiltshire BA13 4DL
Tel: 01373 866066
Principal: Ms Janet Kenward
Age range: 16–25
Special needs catered for: MLD
16 🏛

Tumblewood Project School
The Laurels, 4 Hawkeridge
Road, Heywood, Westbury,
Wiltshire BA13 4LF
Tel: 01373 824 466
Head: Mr Philip Madden
Age range: G11–18
No. of pupils: 12
Special needs catered for:
ADHD, DYS, DYSP, LD
🏃 🏛 16 ✓

East

Bedfordshire

Holme Court School
Great North Road, Biggleswade,
Bedfordshire SG18 9ST
Tel: 01767 312766
Headteacher: Mrs Julia Hewerdine
Age range: 5–16
No. of pupils: 27
Special needs catered for: ADD,
ADHD, ASP, CLD, DYS, DYSP, GLD,
HA, LD, MLD, SCD, SP&LD, SPLD, VIS
✓

Essex

Doucecroft School
Abbots Lane, Eight Ash Green,
Colchester, Essex CO6 3QL
Tel: 01206 771234
Head Teacher: Miss
Kathy Cranmer BEd
Age range: 3–19
No. of pupils: 46
Fees: Day £52,779–£54,291
WB £86,211–£88,211
Special needs catered for:
ASD, ASP, AUT
(金) (16+) ✓

Woodcroft School
Whitakers Way, Loughton,
Essex IG10 1SQ
Tel: 020 8508 1369
Headteacher: Mrs
Margaret Newton
Age range: 2–11
No. of pupils: 36
Special needs catered for:
ADD, ADHD, ASD, ASP, AUT,
CLD, CP, DEL, DYSP, EBD, EPI,
LD, MLD, MSI, PH, PMLD, SCLD,
SLD, SP&LD, SPLD, SLI, VIS
✓

Hertfordshire

EGERTON ROTHESAY SCHOOL
For further details see p. 63
Durrants Lane, Berkhamsted,
Hertfordshire HP4 3UJ
Tel: 01442 877060
Email: admin.dl@eger-roth.co.uk
Website: www.eger-roth.co.uk
Headteacher: Mr Colin Parker
BSc(Hons), Dip.Ed (Oxon),
PGCE, C.Math MIMA
Age range: 6–19
No. of pupils: 143
Fees: Day £14,310–£20,370
Special needs catered for:
DYS, DYSP, MLD, SP&LD
🔵 ⚫

Lincolnshire

Kisimul Upper School
Acacia Hall, Shortwood
Lane, Friesthorpe, Lincoln,
Lincolnshire LN3 5AL
Tel: 01673 880022
Head of School: Paul Routledge
Special needs catered for:
(金)

Norfolk

The Beehive
Stubbs House, Stubbs Green,
Loddon, Norfolk NR14 6EA
Tel: 01508 521190
Headteacher: Mrs Valerie Freear
Age range: 5–14
No. of pupils: 4
Special needs catered for:
ASD, BESD, MLD, SPLD
✓

Suffolk

Centre Academy East Anglia
Church Road, Brettenham,
Ipswich, Suffolk IP7 7QR
Tel: 01449 736404
Principal: Duncan Rollo
BA, MA, PhD
Age range: 4–19
No. of pupils: 45
Fees: Day £16,500–£25,000
WB £33,000–£37,500
Special needs catered for:
ADHD, ASP, CLD, DYS, DYSP,
GLD, HA, LD, SP&LD, SPLD
(金) (£) ✓

East Midlands

Derbyshire

Alderwasley Hall School & Sixth Form Centre
Alderwasley, Belper,
Derbyshire DE56 2SR
Tel: 01629 822586
Head Teacher: Ms Angela
Findlay MEd, NPQH, CertEd
Age range: 5–19
Special needs catered for:
ASD, ASP, AUT, DYSP, GLD, HA,
LD, SCD, SP&LD, SPLD, SLI
(金) (16+) ✓

Pegasus School
Caldwell Hall, Main Street,
Caldwell, Derbyshire DE12 6RS
Tel: 01283 761352
Head Teacher: Ms
Suzanne Pennington
Age range: 8–19
Special needs catered for: ADHD,
ASD, AUT, CLD, EPI, HI, LD, PMLD,
SCLD, SLD, SP&LD, SPLD, SLI, VIS
(金) (16+) ✓

Lincolnshire

KISIMUL SCHOOL
For further details see p. 64
The Old Vicarage, 61 High
Street, Swinderby, Lincoln,
Lincolnshire LN6 9LU
Tel: 01522 868279
Email: admissions@kisimul.co.uk
Website: www.kisimul.co.uk
Director of Education: Mr Danny
Carter BA(Hons), MA, MEd
Age range: 8–19
No. of pupils: 60
Special needs catered for:
ASD, AUT, CLD, EPI, LD, MSI,
PMLD, SCLD, SLD, SP&LD, SPLD
(金) (16+) ✓

Linkage College – Toynton Campus
Toynton All Saints, Spilsby,
Lincolnshire PE23 5AE
Tel: 01790 752499
Age range: 16–25
Special needs catered for:
ADD, ADHD, ASD, ASP, AUT, CLD,
CP, D, DEL, DYS, DYSP, EPI, GLD,
HI, LD, MLD, PD, Phe, PH, SCD,
SCLD, SLD, SP&LD, SPLD, VIS
(16+) (金)

Nottinghamshire

I CAN'S DAWN HOUSE SCHOOL
For further details see p. 66
Helmsley Road, Rainworth,
Mansfield, Nottinghamshire
NG21 0DQ
Tel: 01623 795361
Email: dawnhouse@
ican.notts.sch.uk
Website:
www.dawnhouseschool.org.uk
or www.ican.org.uk
Principal: Angela Child
Age range: 5–19
No. of pupils: 75
Special needs catered for: CLD,
DYS, DYSP, SCD, SLD, SP&LD, SPLD
(金) (16+) ✓

Landmarks
Upper Mill Farm Sheffield
Road, Creswell, Worksop,
Nottinghamshire S80 4HP
Tel: 01909 724724
Principal: Mr Vic Hartwell
Special needs catered for: LD

Sutherland House – Continuing Education Centre
8 Clinton Avenue, Nottingham,
Nottinghamshire NG5 1AW
Tel: 0115 9693373
Principal: Maria Allen
Age range: 11–19
Special needs catered for: ASD, AUT
(16+)

Sutherland House School
Sutherland Road, Nottingham,
Nottinghamshire NG3 7AP
Tel: 0115 9873375
Executive Principal: Ian
Thorsteinsson
Age range: 3–19
No. of pupils: 84
Fees: Day £41,525–£45,473
Special needs catered for:
ASD, ASP, AUT
(16+) ✓

Greater London

Essex

St John's RC Special School
Turpins Lane, Woodford
Bridge, Essex IG8 8AX
Tel: 020 8504 1818
Principal: Mrs Susan Burnside
Age range: 5–19
Special needs catered for:
MLD, SLD
✔

Middlesex

Hillingdon Manor School
Moorcroft Complex,
Harlington Road, Hillingdon,
Middlesex UB8 3HD
Tel: 01895 813679
Principal: Ms Angela Austin
Age range: 3–19
No. of pupils: 70
Fees: Day £32,646
Special needs catered for:
ASD, CLD
16+ ✔

PIELD HEATH HOUSE SCHOOL
For further details see p. 67
Pield Heath Road, Uxbridge,
Middlesex UB8 3NW
Tel: 01895 258507
Email: admin@
pieldheathschool.org.uk
Website:
pieldheathschool.org.uk
Principal: Sister Julie Rose
Age range: 7–19
No. of pupils: 78
Special needs catered for:
MLD, SLD, SP&LD
♿ 16+ ✔

Surrey

Link Primary Day School
138 Croydon Road, Beddington,
Croydon, Surrey CR0 4PG
Tel: 020 8688 5239
Head Teacher: Mrs Beverley
Dixon CertEd, ASE, NPQH
Age range: 5–12
No. of pupils: 40
Fees: Day £24,508
Special needs catered for:
ASD, ASP, DYSP, GLD, LD,
MLD, SCD, SP&LD, SLI
✔

Link Secondary Day School
82-86 Croydon Road, Beddington,
Croydon, Surrey CR0 4PD
Tel: 020 8688 7691
Headteacher: Mr J Pearson
CertEd, BEd, AdvDipSEN, NPQH
Age range: 11–19
No. of pupils: 48
Special needs catered for: ASD,
ASP, DYS, SCD, SP&LD, SPLD, SLI
✔

Rutherford School
1A Melville Avenue, South
Croydon, Surrey CR2 7HZ
Tel: 0208 406 8222
Head of School: Sylvia Kerambrum
Age range: 3–19
No. of pupils: 26
Fees: Day £50,400
Special needs catered for:
CP, D, EPI, HI, MSI, PD, Phe, PH,
PMLD, PNI, SLD, SP&LD, VIS
16+ ✔

The Anchor School
Sutton Junior Tennis Centre, Rose
Hill, Sutton, Surrey SM1 3HH
Tel: 077 34110054
Headteacher: Mrs Wendy Holmes
Age range: 4–11
Special needs catered for: SPLD
✔

London

London

East London

Side by Side Kids School
9 Big Hill, London E5 9HH
Tel: 020 88808300
Headteacher: Ms R Atkins
Age range: 2–16
No. of pupils: 60
Special needs catered for:
MLD, SLD, SP&LD
✔

North London

Limespring School
Park House, 16 High Road, East
Finchley, , London N2 9PJ
Tel: 020 8444 1387
Principal: Denise Drinkwater
Age range: 7–11
Special needs catered for:
DYS, DYSP
✔

North-West London

Kisharon School
1011 Finchley Road,
London NW11 7HB
Tel: 020 8455 7483
Age range: 4–19
No. of pupils: 35
Fees: Day £27,000–£42,000
Special needs catered for: ADD,
ADHD, ASD, ASP, AUT, BESD, CLD,
CP, D, DEL, DYS, DYSP, EBD, EPI,
GLD, HA, HI, LD, MLD, MSI, PD,
Phe, PH, PMLD, PNI, SCD, SCLD,
SEBD, SLD, SP&LD, SPLD, SLI, VIS
✔

South-West London

Blossom Lower School and Upper House
Station Road, Motspur Park,
New Malden, London KT3 6JJ
Tel: 020 8946 7348
Principal: Joanna Burgess DipCST,
MRCSLT, DipRSA SpLD, PGCE
Age range: 3–19
No. of pupils: 202
Fees: Day £26,244–£35,889
Special needs catered for:
ADD, ADHD, ASP, DYS,
DYSP, SCD, SP&LD, SPLD
16+ ✔

Centre Academy London
92 St John's Hill, Battersea,
London SW11 1SH
Tel: 020 7738 2344
Principal: Duncan Rollo
BA, MA, PhD
Age range: 9–19
No. of pupils: 60
Fees: Day £28,000–£39,000
Special needs catered for:
ADD, ADHD, ASD, ASP, AUT,
CLD, DYS, DYSP, HA, SP&LD
£ ✏ 16+ ✔

Fairley House School
30 Causton Street,
London SW1P 4AU
Tel: 020 7976 5456
**Principal & Educational
Psychologist:** Jacqueline
Murray BA(Hons), MEd, MSc,
DipPsychol, DipRSA(SpLD)
Age range: 5–14
Fees: Day £27,975
Special needs catered for:
DYS, DYSP, HA, SPLD
🌐 ✔

Frederick Hugh House
48 Old Church Street,
London SW3 5BY
Tel: 020 73498833
Headteacher: Miss Tanya Jamil
Age range: 4–16
Special needs catered for:
MLD, PD, SP&LD
✔

Parayhouse School
New Kings School Annex,
New Kings Road, Fulham,
London SW6 4LY
Tel: 020 7751 0914
Head: Mrs Sarah Jackson
CertEd, DipEd(Complex
Learning Handicap)
Age range: 7–16
No. of pupils: 46
Fees: Day £25,494
Special needs catered for: ADD,
BESD, CLD, CP, DEL, EBD, EPI, MLD,
Phe, SCD, SCLD, SLD, SP&LD
✔

The Dominie
55 Warriner Gardens,
Battersea, London SW11 4DX
Tel: 020 7720 8783
Principal: Miss Anne O'Doherty
Age range: 6–13
No. of pupils: 30
Special needs catered for:
DYS, DYSP, SP&LD
✔

THE MOAT SCHOOL
For further details see p. 68
Bishops Avenue, Fulham,
London SW6 6EG
Tel: 020 7610 9018
Email: office@
moatschool.org.uk
Website:
www.moatschool.org.uk
Head: Ms Clare King
Age range: 11–16
Fees: Day £26,349
Special needs catered for: SPLD
🌐 ✏ ✔

West London

Abingdon House School
Broadley Terrace, London NW1 6LG
Tel: 0845 2300426
Head: Ms Julie Fardell
Age range: 5–13
No. of pupils: 55
Fees: Day £26,665
Special needs catered for: ADD,
ADHD, ASP, DYS, DYSP, SP&LD, SPLD
🌐 ✏ ✔

North-East

Northumberland

Cambian Dilston College
Dilston Hall, Corbridge,
Northumberland NE45 5RJ
Tel: 0800 288 9779
Vice Principal: Nicola Moxon
Age range: 16–25
Special needs catered for: ASP, AUT,
CP, EPI, HI, MLD, SCD, SLD, SPLD, VIS
⊛

Nunnykirk Centre for Dyslexia
Netherwitton, Morpeth,
Northumberland NE61 4PB
Tel: 01670 772685
Headteacher: C Hodgson
BA(Hons), PGCE, NPQH,
ACFPS (SpLD/Dys)
Age range: 9–18
No. of pupils: 39
Fees: Day £12,960–£13,935
WB £21,555–£23,520
Special needs catered for:
DYS, DYSP, SPLD
⊛ 16+ ✔

North-West

Cheshire

The David Lewis School
Mill Lane, Warford, Alderley
Edge, Cheshire SK9 7UD
Tel: 01565 640066
Headteacher: Mrs Pauline
Greenall BA, MEd
Age range: 14–19
No. of pupils: 20
Special needs catered for:
AUT, CP, EPI, HI, PD, PMLD,
SCD, SLD, SP&LD, SPLD, VIS
⊛ 16+ ✔

Greater Manchester

Birtenshaw Hall School
Bromley Cross, Bolton, Greater
Manchester BL7 9AB
Tel: 01204 306043
Head Teacher: Mrs Julie Barnes
Age range: 3–19
No. of pupils: 12
Fees: Day £49,757–£67,330
Special needs catered for: ADD,
ADHD, ASD, ASP, AUT, CLD, CP,
DEL, EPI, GLD, HI, LD, MLD, MSI,
PD, Phe, PH, PMLD, PNI, SCD,
SCLD, SLD, SP&LD, SLI, VIS
⊛ 16+ ✔

Bridge College
Curzon Road, Offerton, Stockport,
Greater Manchester SK2 5DG
Tel: 0161 487 4293
Principal: Maggie Thompson
Age range: 16–23
No. of pupils: 75
Special needs catered for:
AUT, CLD, PH

Inscape Centre for Autism (INCA)
Schools Hill, Cheadle, Greater
Manchester SK8 1JE
Tel: 0161 283 4761
Head: Susan Allison
Special needs catered for: AUT

Inscape House Salford
Walkden Road, Worsley,
Manchester, Greater
Manchester M28 7FG
Tel: 0161 975 2340
Headteacher: Keith Cox
Age range: 5–19
No. of pupils: 65
Special needs catered for: AUT
16+

Langdon College
9 Leicester Avenue, Salford,
Greater Manchester M7 4HA
Tel: 0161 740 5900
Principal: Mr Christopher Mayho
Age range: 16–25
Special needs catered for:
ASD, ASP, AUT, BESD, DYS, DYSP,
EBD, GLD, HI, LD, MLD, Phe, PH,
SCD, SP&LD, SPLD, SLI, VIS

Lancashire

Pontville
Black Moss Lane, Ormskirk,
Lancashire L39 4TW
Tel: 01695 578734
Head Teacher: Ms Elaine Riley
Age range: 5–19
No. of pupils: 59
Special needs catered for:
ASD, ASP, CLD, MLD, SCD,
SP&LD, SPLD, SLI
⊛ 16+ ✔

Progress School
Gough Lane, Bamber Bridge,
Preston, Lancashire PR26 7TZ
Tel: 01772 334832
Principal: Mrs Lyn Lewis
Age range: 7–19
No. of pupils: 17
Fees: WB £3,269 FB £170,000
Special needs catered for:
AUT, PMLD, SCLD, SLD
⊛ 16+ ✔

Springvale Independent School
Springfield House, 71 Todmorden
Road, Burnley, Lancashire BB11 3ES
Tel: 01282 458891
Head Teacher: Mrs Elaine Kruse
Age range: 7–16
No. of pupils: 6
Special needs catered for:
ADHD, DYS, DYSP

Merseyside

Walton Progressive School
Progressive Lifestyles Education
Services, Rice Lane, Liverpool,
Merseyside L9 1NR
Tel: 0151 5254004
Headteacher: Ms Diane Jones
Age range: 8–19
No. of pupils: 20
Special needs catered for: SP&LD
16+ ✔

Wargrave House School
449 Wargrave Road, Newton-le-
Willows, Merseyside WA12 8RS
Tel: 01925 224899
Principal: Mrs Wendy Mann
BSc, PGCE, DipSpLD, NPQH
Age range: 5–19
No. of pupils: 70
Special needs catered for: ASP, AUT
⊛ 16+ ✔

South-East

East Sussex

Frewen College
Brickwall, Rye Road, Northiam,
Rye, East Sussex TN31 6NL
Tel: 01797 252494
Principal: Mrs Linda Smith
BA(Hons), PGCE
Age range: 7–19
No. of pupils: 103
Fees: Day £13,686–£21,801
WB £21,078–£30,264
FB £21,078–£30,264
Special needs catered for:
DYS, DYSP, SP&LD, SPLD
🎭 ⊛ £ ✎ ✔

Northease Manor School
Rodmell, Lewes, East Sussex BN7 3EY
Tel: 01273 472915
Headteacher: Carmen Harvey-
Browne BA(Hons), PGCE, NPQH
Age range: 10–17
No. of pupils: 95
Special needs catered for:
ADD, ADHD, ASD, ASP, DYS,
DYSP, SCD, SP&LD, SPLD
🎭 ⊛ ✔

Owlswick School
Newhaven Road, Kingston,
Lewes, East Sussex BN7 3NF
Tel: 01273 473078
Headteacher: Michael Mayne
Age range: 10–17
Special needs catered for: ADD,
ADHD, ASD, ASP, BESD, DYS,
DYSP, EBD, GLD, LD, MLD, SCD
⊛ 16+ ✔

ST JOHN'S SCHOOL & COLLEGE
For further details see p. 73
Business Centre, 17
Walpole Road, Brighton,
East Sussex BN2 0AF
Tel: 01273 244000
Email: admissions@st-johns.co.uk
Website: www.st-johns.co.uk
Principal & Chief Executive: Mr Mark Hughes
Age range: 7–25
No. of pupils: 97
Fees: Day £50,000 FB £95,000
Special needs catered for: ADD, ADHD, ASD, ASP, AUT, BESD, CLD, CP, D, DEL, DYS, DYSP, EBD, EPI, SCLD, SEBD, SLD, SP&LD, SPLD, SLI
🏛 16⁺

Hampshire

Chiltern Tutorial School
Otterbourne New Hall,
Cranbourne Drive, Otterbourne,
Winchester, Hampshire SO21 2ET
Tel: 01962 717696
Headmistress: Mrs Jane Gaudie BA, CertEd, AMBDA
Age range: 7–12
No. of pupils: 10
Fees: Day £8,850
Special needs catered for: DYS, DYSP
✔

Clay Hill School
Clay Hill, Lyndhurst,
Hampshire SO43 7DE
Tel: 023 8028 3633
Head of School: Mrs. Helen Sharpe
Age range: 5–19
Special needs catered for: ASD, LD

Minstead Training Project
Minstead Lodge, Minstead,
Lyndhurst, Hampshire SO43 7FT
Tel: 023 80812254
Principal: Mr Martin Lenaerts
Age range: 18+
No. of pupils: 14
Special needs catered for: GLD, LD, MLD
16⁺

The Loddon School
Wildmoor Lane, Sherfield-
on-Loddon, Hook,
Hampshire RG27 0JD
Tel: 01256 884600
Principal: Lynn Young BEd, MEd(SLD)
Age range: 8–19
No. of pupils: 29
Fees: FB £197,000
Special needs catered for: ADD, ADHD, ASD, AUT, CLD, EPI, SCLD, SLD, SP&LD
🏛 16⁺ ✔

The Sheiling Ringwood
Horton Road, Ashley, Ringwood,
Hampshire BH24 2EB
Tel: 01425 477488
Principal: Ms Corine van Barneveld
Age range: 6–19
No. of pupils: 38
Fees: Day £28,121
WB £62,165 FB £62,165
Special needs catered for: ASD, AUT, CLD, EBD, EPI, GLD, LD, MLD, SCD, SCLD, SLD, SP&LD, SPLD
16⁺ 🏛 16⁺ ✔

Isle of Wight

ST CATHERINE'S SCHOOL
For further details see p. 72
Grove Road, Ventnor,
Isle of Wight PO38 1TT
Tel: 01983 852722
Email: general@stcatherines.org.uk
Website: www.stcatherines.org.uk
Principal: Dr B Carleton
Age range: 7–19
No. of pupils: 46 VIth28
Special needs catered for: ADD, ADHD, ASD, ASP, AUT, DYS, DYSP, SCD, SLD, SP&LD, SLI
🏛 16⁺ ✔

Kent

Great Oaks Small School
Ebbsfleet Farmhouse,
Ebbsfleet Lane, Minster,
Ramsgate, Kent CT12 5DL
Tel: 01843 822 022
Head of School: Mrs Liz Baker
Age range: 10–18
No. of pupils: 18 VIth3
Special needs catered for: SPLD
Ⓐ ✔

Trinity School
13 New Road, Rochester,
Medway, Kent ME1 1BG
Tel: 01634 812233
Principal: Mrs C Dunn BA(Hons),
RSA(Dip), SpLD(NHCSS)
Age range: 6–16
No. of pupils: 43
Fees: Day £9,270–£9,750
Special needs catered for: ASD, ASP, DYS, DYSP, SLD, SP&LD
✔

Surrey

I CAN'S MEATH SCHOOL
For further details see p. 69
Brox Road, Ottershaw,
Surrey KT16 0LF
Tel: 01932 872302
Email: meath@meath-ican.org.uk
Website: www.meathschool.org.uk
or www.ican.org.uk
Headteacher: Janet Dunn
OBE, MA, AdvDipSpecEduc
No. of pupils: 54
Special needs catered for: SP&LD
🏛 ✔

KISIMUL SCHOOL – WOODSTOCK HOUSE
For further details see p. 70
Woodstock Lane North, Long
Ditton, Surbiton, Surrey KT6 5HN
Tel: 020 8335 2570
Email: admissions@kisimul.co.uk
Website: www.kisimul.co.uk
Director of Education: Mr Danny
Carter BA(Hons), MA, MEd
Age range: 8–19
No. of pupils: 40
Special needs catered for: ASD, AUT, CLD, EPI, LD, MSI, PMLD, SCLD, SLD, SP&LD, SPLD
🏛 16⁺ ✔

Moon Hall College
Burys Court, Flanchford Road,
Leigh, Reigate, Surrey RH2 8RE
Tel: 01306 611372
Principal: Mrs Berry Baker
BA(Hons)Hist,PGCE,BSc(Hons)
Psych,BDA Diploma,AMBDA
Age range: 3–16
Fees: Day £6,630–£17,220
Special needs catered for: DYS, LD, SPLD

Moon Hall School
Pasturewood Road, Holmbury St
Mary, Dorking, Surrey RH5 6LQ
Tel: 01306 731464
Head: Mrs Pamela Lore
BA(Hons) (Psych), MA(Ed),
Dip RSA SpLD, PGCE
Age range: 7–13
Fees: Day £14,400–£16,470
WB £16,015–£18,085
Special needs catered for: DYS, SPLD
🎨 🏛 ✔

More House School
Moons Hill, Frensham,
Farnham, Surrey GU10 3AP
Tel: 01252 792303
Headmaster: Barry Huggett
BA(Hons), QTS, MIBiol
Age range: B8–18
No. of pupils: 330
Fees: Day £11,055–£15,498
WB £17,805–£22,260
FB £19,650–£24,105
Special needs catered for: SPLD
♿ 🎨 🏛 16⁺ ✔

Orchard Hill College of Further Education
6 Elm Avenue, Foutain Drive,
Carshalton, Surrey SM5 4NR
Tel: 020 8770 8126
Principal: Ms Caroline Allen
OBE, BEd(Hons), MBA(Ed)
Age range: 16+
Special needs catered for: ADD, ADHD, ASD, ASP, AUT, BESD, CLD, CP, DEL, DYS, DYSP, EBD, EPI, GLD, HA, HI, LD, MLD, MSI, PD, Phe, PH, PMLD, PNI, SCD, SCLD, SEBD, SLD, SP&LD, SPLD, SLI, VIS

St Dominic's School
Hambledon, Godalming,
Surrey GU8 4DX
Tel: 01428 684693/682741
Principal: Mrs Angela Drayton
Age range: 7–19
No. of pupils: 77 VIth19
Special needs catered for: ADD, ADHD, ASD, ASP, BESD, CLD, DEL, DYS, DYSP, EPI, HA, SCD, SP&LD, SPLD
🏛 🎨 ✔

ST JOSEPH'S SPECIALIST SCHOOL & COLLEGE
For further details see p. 74
Amlets Lane, Cranleigh,
Surrey GU6 7DH
Tel: 01483 272449
Email: admissions@st-josephscranleigh.surrey.sch.uk
Website: www.st-josephscranleigh.surrey.sch.uk
Principal: Mrs Mary Fawcett
Age range: 5–19
No. of pupils: 73
Fees: Day £57,905 FB £83,898
Special needs catered for: ADHD, ASD, CLD, DYS, DYSP, EPI, LD, MLD, SCLD, SLD, SP&LD
🏛 🎨 16⁺ ✔

The Knowl Hill School
School Lane, Pirbright,
Woking, Surrey GU24 0JN
Tel: 01483 797032
Principal: Dr. Ruth Bailey D.
Ed,MA,MSc,MSc(FPC),BA(Hons),MBPSS,PGCE,NPQH
Age range: 7–16
No. of pupils: 57
Fees: Day £15,606
Special needs catered for: DYS, DYSP, SPLD
£ 🎨 ✔

South-West

Devon

Kingsley School
Northdown Road, Bideford,
Devon EX39 3LY
Tel: 01237 426200
Headmaster: Mr Simon
Woolcott BSc ARCS
Age range: 0–18
No. of pupils: 395
Fees: Day £1,840–£3,310
WB £5,330 FB £6,770
Special needs catered for:
DYS, DYSP
🌍 Ⓐ 🏛 £ ✏ 16+

Dorset

Boveridge House School (formerly Philip Green Memorial School)
Boveridge House, Cranborne,
Wimborne, Dorset BH21 5RU
Tel: 01725 517218
Headmistress: Mrs L Water
Age range: 8–19
No. of pupils: 38
Special needs catered for:
MLD, SCD, SLD
🏛 16+ ✓

Somerset

Cambian Lufton College
Lufton, Yeovil, Somerset BA22 8ST
Tel: 0800 288 9779
Principal: Jonathan James
Age range: 16–25
No. of pupils: 72
Special needs catered for:
HI, MLD, PH, PMLD, SLD
🏛

Foxes Academy
The Esplanade, Minehead,
Somerset TA24 5QP
Tel: 01643 708529
Principal: Sharon Bowden
Age range: 18–25
No. of pupils: 80
Special needs catered for: ASD,
ASP, AUT, MLD, Phe, SCD, SP&LD
🏛

Foxes Fields
Foxes Academy, The Esplanade,
Minehead, Somerset TA24 5QP
Tel: 01643 708529
Principal: Sharon Bowden
Age range: 11–19
No. of pupils: 20
Special needs catered for:
ADD, ADHD, ASD, ASP, AUT,
BESD, CLD, DEL, DYS, DYSP, EBD,
GLD, HA, HI, LD, MLD, MSI, PD,
Phe, SCD, SCLD, SLD, SPLD
🏛

Mark College
Mark, Highbridge,
Somerset TA9 4NP
Tel: 01278 641632
Principal: Ms Michelle
Whitham-Jones
Age range: 10–19
No. of pupils: 88
Special needs catered for:
DYS, DYSP, SLD, SPLD
🌍 🏛 16+ ✓

Shapwick Prep
Mark Road, Burtle, Bridgwater,
Somerset TA7 8NJ
Tel: 01278 722012
Headmaster: Mr M Lee
BA (Hons); PGCE
Age range: 8–18
No. of pupils: 142
Fees: Day £11,220–£13,533
WB £16,995 FB £16,473–£19,515
Special needs catered for: DYS
🌍 🏛 ✓

West Midlands

Herefordshire

Rowden House School
Rowden, Bromyard,
Herefordshire HR7 4LS
Tel: 01885 488096
Principal: Mr Martin Carter
NPQH, BEd(Hons), Adv Diploma
(Behaviour Support)
Age range: 11–19
Special needs catered for: ADD,
ADHD, ASD, AUT, CLD, EPI, GLD,
LD, MLD, PMLD, SCLD, SLD, SPLD
🏛 16+ ✓

Shropshire

Access School
Holbrook Villa Farm, Harmer
Hill, Broughton, Shrewsbury,
Shropshire SY4 3EW
Tel: 01939 220797
Headteacher: Miss Verity White
Age range: 5–16
No. of pupils: 10
Special needs catered for:
EBD, GLD, MLD
✓

Jigsaw School
Queensway, Hadley, Telford,
Shropshire TF1 6AJ
Tel: 01952 388555
Headteacher: Nigel Griffiths
Age range: 11–16
Special needs catered for:
EBD, SPLD
✓

Staffordshire

Bladon House School
Newton Solney, Burton upon
Trent, Staffordshire DE15 0TA
Tel: 01283 563787
Head Teacher: Mrs Kate Britt
CEd, MA(Educ Management)
Age range: 5–19
Special needs catered for: ADD,
ADHD, ASD, AUT, CLD, EPI, HI, LD,
MLD, SLD, SP&LD, SPLD, SLI, VIS
🏛 16+ ✓

Maple Hayes Dyslexia School
Abnalls Lane, Lichfield,
Staffordshire WS13 8BL
Tel: 01543 264387
Principal: Dr E N Brown MSc,
BA, MINS, MSCMe, AFBPsS,
CPsychol, FRSA, CSci
Age range: 7–17
No. of pupils: 118
Fees: Day £14,190–£18,975
Special needs catered for:
DYS, DYSP, SPLD
🌍 £ ✓

Regent College
77 Shelton New Road, Shelton,
Stoke-on-Trent, Staffordshire ST4 7AA
Tel: 01782 263326
Principal: Ms Wendy Williams
Age range: 16–25
No. of pupils: 30
Special needs catered for:
CLD, EPI, PD, SLD, SP&LD

West Midlands

GLASSHOUSE COLLEGE
For further details see p. 76
Wollaston Road,
Amblecote, Stourbridge,
West Midlands DY8 4HF
Tel: 01384 399400
Email: enquiries@ghc.rmt.org
Website: www.rmt.org
Principal: Paul Gawdan
Age range: 16–25
Special needs catered for:
ADHD, ASD, ASP, BESD, CLD,
EBD, GLD, LD, PMLD, SCD,
SCLD, SEBD, SLD, SPLD
16+ 🏛

OVERLEY HALL SCHOOL
For further details see p. 77
Overley, Wellington, Telford,
West Midlands TF6 5HE
Tel: 01952 740262
Email: info@overleyhall.com
Website: www.overleyhall.com
Headteacher: Mrs
Beverley Doran
Age range: 8–19
No. of pupils: 20
Special needs catered for:
ADD, ADHD, ASD, ASP, AUT,
CLD, DYSP, EPI, GLD, LD, PMLD,
SCD, SCLD, SLD, SP&LD
🏛 16+ ✓

SUNFIELD SCHOOL
For further details see p. 78
Clent Grove, Woodman
Lane, Stourbridge, West
Midlands DY9 9PB
Tel: 01562 882253
Email: referrals@sunfield.org.uk
Website: www.sunfield.org.uk
Principal: Caroline Bell
Age range: 6–19
Special needs catered for: ADD,
ADHD, ASD, AUT, BESD, CLD, DYS,
EPI, GLD, LD, MLD, MSI, PMLD,
SCD, SCLD, SEBD, SLD, SP&LD, SLI
🏛 16+ ✓

Worcestershire

Our Place School
The Orchard, Bransford,
Worcestershire WR6 5JE
Tel: 01886 833378
Director: David French
Special needs catered for:
ASD, PMLD, SLD

Yorkshire & Humberside

North-East Lincolnshire

Linkage College – Weelsby Campus
Weelsby Road, Grimsby, North-East Lincolnshire DN32 9RU
Tel: 01472 241044
Director of Education: Hugh Williams
Age range: 16–25
No. of pupils: 220
Special needs catered for:
ADD, ADHD, ASD, ASP, AUT, CLD, CP, D, DEL, DYS, DYSP, EPI, GLD, HI, LD, MLD, Phe, PH, SCD, SCLD, SLD, SP&LD, SPLD, VIS
16· ⬆

South Yorkshire

FREEMAN COLLEGE
For further details see p. 79
Sterling Works, 88 Arundel Street, Sheffield, South Yorkshire S1 2NG
Tel: 0114 252 5940
Email: enquiries@fmc.rmt.org
Website: www.rmt.org
Principal: Bonny Etchell-Anderson
Age range: 16–25
Special needs catered for:
ADHD, ASD, ASP, BESD, CLD, EBD, GLD, LD, MLD, PMLD, SCD, SCLD, SEBD, SLD
16· ⬆

FULLERTON HOUSE COLLEGE
For further details see p. 80
Tickhill Square, Denaby, Doncaster, South Yorkshire DN12 4AR
Tel: 01709 861663
Email: enquiries@ hesleygroup.co.uk
Website: www.hesleygroup.co.uk
Head: Jeff Cox
Age range: 18–25
No. of pupils: 9
Special needs catered for:
ASD, ASP, AUT, CLD, DYS, DYSP, GLD, LD, MLD, SCLD, SLD, SPLD
⬆

FULLERTON HOUSE SCHOOL
For further details see p. 51
Tickill Square, Denaby, Doncaster, South Yorkshire DN12 4AR
Tel: 01709 861663
Email: enquiries@ hesleygroup.co.uk
Website: www.fullertonhouse school.co.uk
Head: Jeff Cox
Age range: 8–19
No. of pupils: 40
Special needs catered for:
ASD, ASP, AUT, CLD, DYS, DYSP, GLD, LD, MLD, SCLD, SLD, SPLD
⬆ 16· ✓

WILSIC HALL COLLEGE
For further details see p. 80
Wadworth, Doncaster, South Yorkshire DN11 9AG
Tel: 01302 856382
Head: Jeff Cox
Age range: 19–25
No. of pupils: 3
Special needs catered for:
ASD, ASP, AUT, CLD, DYS, DYSP, GLD, LD, MLD, SCLD, SLD, SPLD
⬆

WILSIC HALL SCHOOL
For further details see p. 52
Wadworth, Doncaster, South Yorkshire DN11 9AG
Tel: 01302 856382
Email: enquiries@ hesleygroup.co.uk
Website: www.wilsichallschool.co.uk
Head: Geoff Turner
Age range: 11–19
No. of pupils: 33
Special needs catered for:
ASD, ASP, AUT, CLD, DYS, DYSP, GLD, LD, MLD, SCLD, SLD, SPLD
⬆ 16· ✓

West Yorkshire

Hall Cliffe School
Dovecote Lane, Horbury, Wakefield, West Yorkshire WF4 6BB
Tel: 01924 663 420
Head of School: Dr. Chris Lingard
Age range: 8–16
Special needs catered for:
ADHD, AUT, BESD, MLD, SLD
16·

Pennine Camphill Community
Wood Lane, Chapelthorpe, Wakefield, West Yorkshire WF4 3JL
Tel: 01924 255281
Principal: S Hopewell
Age range: 16–25
No. of pupils: 46
Fees: Day £14,000–£45,000
FB £26,000–£69,000
Special needs catered for: ADHD, ASD, ASP, AUT, CLD, DYSP, EBD, EPI, LD, MLD, SCLD, SLD, SPLD
⬆ ✎

Northern Ireland

County Tyrone

Parkanaur College
57 Parkanaur Road, Dungannon, County Tyrone BT70 3AA
Tel: 028 87761272
Principal: Mr Wilfred Mitchell
Age range: 18–65
Special needs catered for: ADD, ADHD, ASP, AUT, BESD, CLD, CP, DYS, DYSP, EBD, EPI, GLD, HA, HI, LD, MLD, PD, Phe, PH, PMLD, PNI, SCD, SCLD, SLD, SPLD, VIS

Scotland

Aberdeen

VSA Linn Moor Campus
Peterculter, Aberdeen AB14 0PJ
Tel: 01224 732246
Head Teacher: Victoria Oumarou
Age range: 5–18
No. of pupils: 25
Fees: Day £38,326
FB £76,650–£239,114
Special needs catered for:
ASD, AUT, CLD, GLD, LD, MLD, SCD, SCLD, SPLD
⬆ 16·

Clackmannanshire

Struan House
Bradbury Campus, 100 Smithfield Loan, Alloa, Clackmannanshire FK10 1NP
Tel: 01259 222000
Director of Education & Support Services: Jim Taylor
Age range: 5–17
Special needs catered for: ASD, AUT
⬆

Glasgow

East Park
1092 Maryhill Road, Glasgow G20 9TD
Tel: 0141 946 2050
Principal: Mrs L Gray
Age range: 0–25
Fees: Day £12,298 FB £22,958
Special needs catered for:
AUT, CP, DEL, EPI, HI, MLD, PH, PMLD, SLD, SP&LD, VIS
⬆ 16·

Springboig St John's
1190 Edinburgh Road, Glasgow G32 4EH
Tel: 0141 774 9791
Principal: Mr W Fitzgerald
Age range: B14–17
No. of pupils: 37
Special needs catered for:
DYS, EBD, MLD, SPLD
♂ ⬆

Perth & Kinross

Ochil Tower
140 High Street, Auchterarder,
Perth, Perth & Kinross PH3 1AD
Tel: 01764 662416
Co-ordinators: Mr Ueli Ruprecht
& Ms Hilary Ruprecht
Age range: 5–18
No. of pupils: 35
Fees: Day £23,500 FB £41,100
Special needs catered for: ADD,
ADHD, ASD, BESD, CLD, EBD, EPI, LD,
MLD, MSI, PMLD, SCD, SCLD, SP&LD
(£) (16+)

THE NEW SCHOOL
For further details see p. 83
Butterstone, Dunkeld,
Perth & Kinross PH8 0HA
Tel: 01350 724216
Email: info@thenewschool.co.uk
Website:
www.thenewschool.co.uk
Head of School: Mr Scott Gordon
Age range: 11–19
No. of pupils: 26
Fees: Day £40,085 WB £51,571
Special needs catered for: ADD,
ADHD, ASD, ASP, AUT, BESD,
CLD, DEL, DYS, DYSP, EBD, GLD,
HA, LD, MLD, SCD, SEBD, SPLD
(£) (£) (✎) (16+)

Wales

Denbighshire

Cambian Pengwern College
Sarn Lane, Rhuddlan, Rhyl,
Denbighshire LL18 5UH
Tel: 0800 288 9779
Principal: Tina Ruane
Age range: 16–25
Special needs catered for: ADD,
ADHD, ASD, ASP, AUT, BESD, CLD,
CP, DYSP, EBD, EPI, GLD, HI, LD,
MLD, MSI, PD, Phe, PH, PMLD, SCD,
SCLD, SEBD, SLD, SP&LD, SLI, VIS
(£) (✎)

Gwynedd

Aran Hall School
Rhydymain, Dolgellau,
Gwynedd LL40 2AR
Tel: 01341 450641
Head Teacher: Mr Duncan
Pritchard CertEd, DipAppSS,
BSc(Hons), MSc(psych)
Age range: 11–19
Special needs catered for:
ADHD, ASD, ASP, AUT, CLD,
EPI, GLD, LD, MLD, PMLD, SCD,
SCLD, SLD, SP&LD, SPLD, SLI
(£) (16+)

Pembrokeshire

COLEG PLAS DWBL
For further details see p. 84
Mynachlog-ddu, Clunderwen,
Pembrokeshire SA66 7SE
Tel: 01994 419420
Email: info@plasdwbl.rmt.org
Website: www.rmt.org
Principal: Dan Alipaz
Age range: 16–25
Special needs catered for:
ASD, ASP, CLD, EBD

Vale of Glamorgan

Action for Children Headlands School
2 St Augustine's Road, Penarth,
Vale of Glamorgan CF64 1YY
Tel: 02920 709771
Principal: Matthew Burns
Age range: 8–19
Special needs catered for: ADD,
ADHD, ASD, ASP, AUT, BESD,
DYS, EBD, MLD, SP&LD, SPLD
(£) (16+)

Wrexham

Prospects for Young People
12 Grosvenor Road,
Wrexham LL11 1BU
Tel: 01978 313777
Head Teacher: Tony Clifford
Age range: 11–16
No. of pupils: 21
Special needs catered for:
MLD, SPLD
(£)

Schools and colleges specialising in sensory or physical impairment

Abbreviations

ACLD	Autism, Communication and Associated Learning Difficulties
ADD	Attention Deficit Disorder
ADHD	Attention Deficit and Hyperactive Disorder (Hyperkinetic Disorder)
ASD	Autistic Spectrum Disorder
ASP	Asperger Syndrome
AUT	Autism
BESD	Behavioural, Emotional and Social Difficulties
CCD	Complex Communication Difficulties
CLD	Complex Learning Difficulties
CP	Cerebral Palsy
D	Deaf
DEL	Delicate
DYS	Dyslexia
DYSP	Dyspraxia
EBD	Emotional and Behavioural Difficulties
EBSD	Emotional, Behavioural and/ or Social Difficulties
EPI	Epilepsy
GLD	General Learning Difficulties
HA	High Ability
HI	Hearing Impairment
HS	Hospital School
LD	Learning Difficulties
MLD	Moderate Learning Difficulties
MSI	Multi-sensory Impairment
OCD	Obsessive Compulsive Disorder
PD	Physical Difficulties
PH	Physical Impairment
Phe	Partially Hearing
PMLD	Profound and Multiple Learning Difficulties
PNI	Physical Neurological Impairment
PRU	Pupil Referral Unit
SCD	Social and Communication Difficulties
SCLD	Severe and Complex Learning Difficulties
SEBD	Severe Emotional and Behavioural Disorders
SEBN	Social, Emotional and Behavioural Needs
SLD	Severe Learning Difficulties
SLI	Specific Language Impairment
SPLD	Specific Learning Difficulties
SP&LD	Speech and Language Difficulties
SLCN	Speech Language & Communication Needs
VIS	Visually Impaired

Key to Symbols

Type of school:

⚢	Boys' school
⚣	Girls' school
🌍	International school

School offers:

Ⓐ	A levels
⬗	Boarding accommodation
⑯	Entrance at 16+
⬗	Vocational qualifications
✎	Learning support
✔	This is a DfE approved independent or non-maintained school under section 342 or 347(1) of the 1996 Education Act

Please note: Unless otherwise indicated, all schools are coeducational day schools. Single-sex and boarding schools will be indicated by the relevant icon.

Central & West

Buckinghamshire

PENN SCHOOL
For further details see p. 86
Church Road, Penn,
High Wycombe,
Buckinghamshire HP10 8LZ
Tel: 01494 812139
Email: office@pennschool.
bucks.sch.uk
Website:
www.pennschool.bucks.sch.uk
Headteacher: Mary-
Nest Richardson
Age range: 11–18
No. of pupils: 29
Special needs catered for:
HI, SP&LD

The PACE Centre
Philip Green House,
Coventon Road, Aylesbury,
Buckinghamshire HP19 9JL
Tel: 01296 392739
Head Teacher: Mr D O'Connor
Age range: 0–12
Special needs catered for: CLD,
CP, DYSP, HI, LD, MLD, MSI, PD,
PNI, SCLD, SLD, SP&LD, VIS

Gloucestershire

National Star College
Ullenwood, Cheltenham,
Gloucestershire GL53 9QU
Tel: 01242 527631
**Principal & Chief Executive
Officer:** Ms Kathryn Rudd OBE
Age range: 16–25
No. of pupils: 178
Special needs catered for:
ASD, ASP, AUT, CLD, CP, DYS,
DYSP, EPI, GLD, HI, LD, MLD, MSI,
PD, Phe, PH, PMLD, PNI, SCD,
SCLD, SLD, SP&LD, SPLD, VIS

St Rose's School
Stratford Lawn, Stroud,
Gloucestershire GL5 4AP
Tel: 01453 763793
Headteacher: Mr Jan Daines
Age range: 2–25
No. of pupils: 54
Special needs catered for: CLD,
CP, D, DEL, DYS, DYSP, EPI, GLD, HI,
LD, MLD, MSI, PD, Phe, PH, PMLD,
PNI, SCD, SCLD, SLD, SP&LD, SLI, VIS

West Berkshire

Mary Hare Primary School for the Deaf
Mill Hall, Pigeons Farm Road,
Thatcham, Newbury, West
Berkshire RG19 8XA
Tel: 01635 573800
Head of Centre: Mrs K D Smith
Age range: 5–12
Fees: Day £26,681 FB £33,186
Special needs catered for: HI

Mary Hare School
Arlington Manor, Snelsmore
Common, Newbury, West
Berkshire RG14 3BQ
Tel: 01635 244200
Principal: Mr D A J Shaw
BTech, MEd(Aud), NPQH
Age range: 11–19
No. of pupils: 205 VIth68
Fees: Day £28,372 FB £31,676
Special needs catered for: D, HI

East

Hertfordshire

Meldreth Manor School
Fenny Lane, Meldreth, Royston,
Hertfordshire SG8 6LG
Tel: 01763 268000
Principal: Roger Gale MSc(Ed)
Age range: 9–19+
No. of pupils: 30
Special needs catered for: CP,
D, EPI, GLD, HI, LD, MLD, MSI,
PD, Phe, PH, PMLD, SP&LD, VIS

St Elizabeth's School
South End, Much Hadham,
Hertfordshire SG10 6EW
Tel: 01279 844270
Principal: Ms. Sharon Wallin
Age range: 5–19
Special needs catered for:
AUT, CP, DYS, DYSP, EBD, EPI,
MLD, SLD, SP&LD, SPLD

East Midlands

Derbyshire

Royal School for the Deaf Derby
Ashbourne Road, Derby,
Derbyshire DE22 3BH
Tel: 01332 362512
Principal: Cheryll Ford
BA, BPhil, NPQH
Age range: 3–19
No. of pupils: 140
Fees: Day £21,696 FB £33,474
Special needs catered for: D

Leicestershire

Homefield College
42 St Mary's Road,
Sileby, Loughborough,
Leicestershire LE12 7TL
Tel: 01509 815696
Principal: Mr Gerry Short
Age range: 16–25
No. of pupils: 54 VIth54
Special needs catered for:
ASD, BESD, LD, SCD

RNIB COLLEGE LOUGHBOROUGH
For further details see p. 87
Radmoor Road, Loughborough,
Leicestershire LE11 3BS
Tel: 01509 611077
Email: hannah.wharton@
rnib.org.uk
Website:
www.rnib.org.uk/rnibcollege
Principal: June Murray
Age range: 16–65
No. of pupils: 109
Special needs catered for:
ASP, AUT, MLD, VIS

Northamptonshire

Hinwick Hall College of Further Education
Hinwick, Wellingborough,
Northamptonshire NN29 7JD
Tel: 01933 312470
Principal: Mr Martyn Hays
Age range: 19–25
No. of pupils: 58
Special needs catered for: CP,
DYSP, EPI, PH, SCD, SLD, SP&LD

Nottinghamshire

Portland College
Nottingham Road,
Mansfield, Nottingham,
Nottinghamshire NG18 4TJ
Tel: 01623 499111
Principal: Dr Mark Dale
Age range: 16–59
No. of pupils: 230
Special needs catered for: CP, DYS,
DYSP, EPI, HI, MLD, PH, SP&LD, SPLD

Rutland

The Shires School
Great North Road, Stretton,
Rutland LE15 7QT
Tel: 01780 411944
Director of Care &
Education: Gail Pilling
Age range: 11–19
Special needs catered for: AUT, SLD

Greater London

Kent

Nash College
Croydon Road, Bromley,
Kent BR2 7AG
Tel: 020 8315 4844
Principal: Ms Claire Howley-
Mummery BEd (Hons)
Age range: 18–25
Special needs catered for: AUT,
CP, EPI, MLD, PH, PMLD, PNI, SCD,
SCLD, SLD, SP&LD, SPLD, VIS

Middlesex

RNIB SUNSHINE HOUSE
SCHOOL AND RESIDENCE
For further details see p. 88
33 Dene Road, Northwood,
Middlesex HA6 2DD
Tel: 01923 822538
Email: shsadmin@rnib.org.uk
Website:
www.rnib.org.uk/sunshinehouse
Head: John Ayres
Age range: 2–14
Special needs catered for: VIS

London

London
North London

The London School
for Children with
Cerebral Palsy
54 Muswell Hill, London N10 3ST
Tel: 020 84447242
Headteacher: Ms. Gabriella Czifra
Age range: 3–11
Special needs catered for: CP, PD

North-East

Tyne & Wear

Percy Hedley College
Station Road, Forest Hall, Newcastle
upon Tyne, Tyne & Wear NE12 8YY
Tel: 0191 266 5491
Headteacher: Mr N O
Stromsoy MA, DipSE
Age range: 14–19
No. of pupils: 170
Fees: Day £19,944 FB £42,134
Special needs catered for: HI

Percy Hedley School
– Newcastle
Great North Road, Newcastle
upon Tyne, Tyne & Wear NE2 3BB
Tel: 0191 281 5821
Headteacher: Mrs Frances Taylor
Age range: 3–19
Fees: Day £13,767–£29,772
FB £19,134–£33,162
Special needs catered for:
AUT, HI, PMLD, SLD, VIS

Percy Hedley School
– North Tyneside
Forest Hall, Newcastle upon
Tyne, Tyne & Wear NE12 8YY
Head Teacher: Ms Lynn Watson
Age range: 3–14
Special needs catered for: CP, SCD

North-West

Greater Manchester

Seashell Trust
Stanley Road, Cheadle Hulme, Cheadle, Greater Manchester SK8 6RQ
Tel: 0161 610 0100
Age range: 2–22
No. of pupils: 83
Fees: Day £37,280–£59,354 FB £61,866–£178,658
Special needs catered for: ASD, AUT, CLD, CP, D, HI, MSI, PD, PH, PMLD, PNI, SCD, SCLD, SLD, SP&LD, VIS
⊞ 16· ✔

Lancashire

Beaumont College
Slyne Road, Lancaster, Lancashire LA2 6AP
Tel: 01524 541400
Principal: Mr Graeme Pyle
Age range: 16–25
No. of pupils: 77
Special needs catered for: ASD, AUT, BESD, CLD, CP, DYS, DYSP, EBD, EPI, GLD, HI, MSI, PD, PH, PMLD, PNI, SCD, SCLD, SEBD, SLD, SP&LD, SLI, VIS
16· ⊞

Merseyside

Royal School for the Blind
Church Road North, Wavertree, Liverpool, Merseyside L15 6TQ
Tel: 0151 733 1012
Principal: J Byrne
Age range: 2–19
Fees: Day £35,721–£40,418 FB £47,185–£55,649
Special needs catered for: BESD, CLD, CP, EBD, EPI, HI, MLD, MSI, PD, PH, PMLD, PNI, SCLD, SLD, SPLD, SLI, VIS
⊞ 16· ✔

St Vincent's School for the Visually Handicapped
Yew Tree Lane, West Derby, Liverpool, Merseyside L12 9HN
Tel: 0151 228 9968
Headmaster: Mr A Macquarrie
Age range: 3–17
Fees: Day £19,566 FB £27,363
Special needs catered for: MLD, VIS
⊞ ✔

South-East

East Sussex

CHAILEY HERITAGE SCHOOL
For further details see p. 89
Haywards Heath Road, North Chailey, Lewes, East Sussex BN8 4EF
Tel: 01825 724444
Email: office@chf.org.uk
Website: www.chf.org.uk
Charity Chief Executive: Helen Hewitt
Age range: 3–19
No. of pupils: 73
Special needs catered for: ASD, AUT, CLD, CP, D, EBD, EPI, HI, MLD, MSI, PD, PH, PMLD, PNI, SCLD, SLD, SP&LD, VIS
⊞ 16· ✔

Hamilton Lodge School
9 Walpole Road, Brighton, East Sussex BN2 0LS
Tel: 01273 682362
Principal: Mrs A K Duffy MEd
Age range: 5–18
No. of pupils: 72
Fees: Day £23,008–£24,846 FB £30,766–£32,799
Special needs catered for: HI
⊞ 16· ✔

ST MARY'S SCHOOL & 6TH FORM COLLEGE
For further details see p. 92
Wrestwood Road, Bexhill-on-Sea, East Sussex TN40 2LU
Tel: 01424 730740
Email: admin@stmarysbexhill.org
Website: www.stmarysbexhill.org
CEO & Principal: Dr Sharon Menghini Doctorate, PGCE, SpID Diploma, M.Ed (SEN), Cert.Ed
Age range: 7–19
No. of pupils: 104
Special needs catered for: ASD, ASP, AUT, CLD, CP, D, DEL, DYS, DYSP, EPI, GLD, HI, SCD, SP&LD, SPLD, SLI, VIS
⊞ 16· ✔

Hampshire

TRELOAR SCHOOL
For further details see p. 94
Holybourne, Alton, Hampshire GU34 4GL
Tel: 01420 547400
Email: admissions@treloar.org.uk
Website: www.treloar.org.uk
Head: Jo McSherrie
Age range: 2–19 yrs
No. of pupils: 95 VIth31
Special needs catered for: CLD, CP, DEL, DYSP, EPI, HA, HI, MLD, MSI, PD, Phe, PH, PNI, SCLD, SP&LD, SPLD, SLI, VIS
⊞ ✔

Kent

Dorton College of Further Education
Seal Drive, Seal, Sevenoaks, Kent TN15 0AH
Tel: 01732 592600
Director of Education: Dorothea Hackman
Age range: 16–19
No. of pupils: 60
Special needs catered for: VIS
16· ⊞

Royal London Society for the Blind, Dorton House School
Seal, Sevenoaks, Kent TN15 0ED
Tel: 01732 592650
Headteacher: Ms Jude Thompson
Age range: 5–16
No. of pupils: 78
Fees: Day £18,536 FB £25,090
Special needs catered for: ADHD, ASP, AUT, CP, DYS, EBD, EPI, HI, PH, SLD, SP&LD, VIS
⊞ ✔

The Royal School for Deaf Children Margate and Westgate College
Victoria Road, Margate, Kent CT9 1NB
Tel: 01843 227561
Headteacher: Mr C Owen BA(Hons), MA(Ed), ToD
Age range: 4–16
No. of pupils: 82
Special needs catered for: ADD, ADHD, ASD, ASP, AUT, BESD, CP, D, DEL, EBD, EPI, HI, LD, MLD, PMLD, SCD, SCLD, SLD, SPLD, VIS
⊞ 16· ✔

Surrey

MOOR HOUSE SCHOOL & COLLEGE
For further details see p. 90
Mill Lane, Hurst Green, Oxted, Surrey RH8 9AQ
Tel: 01883 712271
Email: admissionsteam@moorhouseschool.co.uk; info@moorhouseschool.co.uk
Website: www.moorhouseschool.co.uk
Principal: Mrs H A Middleton
Age range: 7–19
No. of pupils: 107
Special needs catered for: ASP, DYS, DYSP, SLD, SP&LD, SLI
Ⓐ ⊞ ✔

QEF Neuro Rehabilitation Services Brain Injury Centre
Banstead Place, Park Road, Banstead, Surrey SM7 3EE
Tel: 01737 356222
Principal: Eileen Jackman MA, BSc
Age range: 16–35
No. of pupils: 28
Special needs catered for: EBD, SP&LD
⊞

Queen Elizabeth's Training College
Leatherhead Court, Leatherhead, Surrey KT22 0BN
Tel: 01372 841100
Principal: Garry Billing
Age range: 18–63
No. of pupils: 171
Special needs catered for: ADD, ADHD, ASD, ASP, AUT, CP, DYS, DYSP, EPI, GLD, LD, MLD, PD, PH
16· ⊞

St Piers School and College
St Piers Lane, Lingfield,
Surrey RH7 6PW
Tel: 01342 832243
Chief Executive: Mr D Ford BSc,
MSc(Econ), MBA, CQSW
Age range: 5–25
No. of pupils: 181
Special needs catered for: ADD,
ADHD, ASP, AUT, CP, EPI, MLD,
PMLD, PNI, SCD, SCLD, SLD, SP&LD
🏛 16+ ✔

Stepping Stones School
Tower Road, Hindhead,
Surrey GU26 6SU
Tel: 01428 609083
Headteacher: Melissa Farnham
NPQH,BAQTS(Hon)
Age range: 8–19
No. of pupils: 40
Fees: Day £11,000–£14,800
Special needs catered for: ASD,
ASP, AUT, MLD, PD, SP&LD
✔

THE CHILDREN'S TRUST SCHOOL
For further details see p. 93
Tadworth Court, Tadworth,
Surrey KT20 5RU
Tel: 01737 365810
Email: school@
thechildrenstrust.org.uk
Website:
www.thechildrenstrust.org.uk
/school
Interim Head: Pam Walden
Age range: 3–19
Special needs catered for:
CLD, CP, EPI, HI, MSI, PD, PH,
PMLD, PNI, SLD, SP&LD, VIS
🏛 16+ ✔

West Sussex

Ingfield Manor School
Five Oaks, Billingshurst,
West Sussex RH14 9AX
Tel: 01403 782294/784241
Age range: 3–16
Special needs catered for: CP
🏛 ✔

South-West

Devon

Dame Hannah Rogers School
Woodland Road, Ivybridge,
Devon PL21 9HQ
Tel: 01752 892461
Head: Mr Brian Carlyon
Age range: 5–19
Special needs catered for:
CP, PH, PMLD
🏛 16+ ✔

Exeter Royal Academy for Deaf Education
50 Topsham Road, Exeter,
Devon EX2 4NF
Tel: 01392 267023
Chief Executive: Jonathan Farnhill
Age range: 5–25
No. of pupils: VIth68
Fees: Day £23,007–£39,195
WB £31,779–£46,800
FB £36,360–£48,990
Special needs catered for: AUT, CP,
D, EPI, HI, MLD, MSI, Phe, SP&LD, VIS
🏛 16+ ✔

On Track Training Centre
Unit 8, Paragon Buildings, Ford
Road, Totnes, Devon TQ9 5LQ
Tel: 01803 866462
Head Teacher: Mrs J Cox
Age range: 11–18
No. of pupils: 24
Special needs catered for:
ASP, EBD, MSI, SPLD
16+ ✔

Vranch House
Pinhoe Road, Exeter,
Devon EX4 8AD
Tel: 01392 468333
Head Teacher: Miss Viktoria
Pavlics MEd(SEN)
Age range: 2–12
Fees: Day £19,425
Special needs catered for: CP,
EPI, MLD, PD, PH, PMLD, SP&LD
✔

WESC FOUNDATION – THE SPECIALIST COLLEGE FOR VISUAL IMPAIRMENT
For further details see p. 95
Countess Wear, Exeter,
Devon EX2 6HA
Tel: 01392 454200
Email: info@
wescfoundation.ac.uk
Website:
www.wescfoundation.ac.uk
Principal: Mrs Tracy de
Bernhardt-Dunkin
Age range: 16+
Special needs catered for:
EPI, PH, PMLD, VIS
16+ 🏛 ✔

WESC FOUNDATION – THE SPECIALIST SCHOOL FOR VISUAL IMPAIRMENT
For further details see p. 96
Countess Wear, Exeter,
Devon EX2 6HA
Tel: 01392 454200
Email: info@
wescfoundation.ac.uk
Website:
www.wescfoundation.ac.uk
Chief Executive: Mrs Tracy
de Bernhardt-Dunkin
Age range: 5–16
Special needs catered for:
EPI, PH, PMLD, VIS
🏛 ✔

Dorset

Langside School
Langside Avenue, Parkstone,
Poole, Dorset BH12 5BN
Tel: 01202 518635
Principal: J. Seaward BEd
(Hons) Oxon NPQH
Age range: 2–19
No. of pupils: 24
Special needs catered for: CLD, CP,
EPI, MSI, PD, PMLD, SCD, SCLD, SLD
16+ ✔

The Fortune Centre of Riding Therapy
Avon Tyrrell, Bransgore,
Christchurch, Dorset BH23 8EE
Tel: 01425 673297
Director: Mrs J Dixon-Clegg SRN
Age range: 16–25
No. of pupils: 47
Special needs catered for: AUT,
CP, DEL, DYS, EBD, EPI, HI, MLD,
PH, PMLD, SLD, SP&LD, SPLD, VIS
🏛

Victoria Education Centre
12 Lindsay Road, Branksome
Park, Poole, Dorset BH13 6AS
Tel: 01202 763697
Head: Mrs Christina Davies
Age range: 3–19
No. of pupils: 90
Special needs catered for:
DEL, EPI, PH, SP&LD
🏛 16+ ✔

West Midlands

Herefordshire

THE ROYAL NATIONAL COLLEGE FOR THE BLIND (RNC)
For further details see p. 98
Venns Lane, Hereford,
Herefordshire HR1 1DT
Tel: 01432 265725
Email: info@rnc.ac.uk
Website: www.rnc.ac.uk
Principal: Ms Sheila Tallon
Age range: 16–65
Special needs catered for: ASP, AUT, DYS, HA, MLD, PD, Phe, VIS
16+ ♿

Shropshire

Derwen College
Oswestry, Shropshire SY11 3JA
Tel: 01691 661234
Director: D J Kendall
BEng, FCA, MEd
Age range: 16–25
No. of pupils: 160
Fees: FB £17,928
Special needs catered for:
CP, DEL, DYS, EPI, HI, MLD, PH, PMLD, SLD, SP&LD, SPLD, VIS
♿

West Midlands

Hereward College of Further Education
Bramston Crescent, Tile Hill Lane,
Coventry, West Midlands CV4 9SW
Tel: 024 7646 1231
Headmistress: Mrs Cath
Cole BA, RGN, CertEd
Age range: 16+
No. of pupils: 400
Special needs catered for: ASP, AUT, CP, DEL, DYS, DYSP, EBD, EPI, HA, HI, MLD, PH, SPLD, VIS
♿

National Institute for Conductive Education
Cannon Hill House, Russell
Road, Moseley, Birmingham,
West Midlands B13 8RD
Tel: 0121 449 1569
Director of Services: Dr
Melanie R Brown
Age range: 0–11
No. of pupils: 18
Fees: Day £25,000
Special needs catered for:
CP, DYSP, PNI
✓

Queen Alexandra College (QAC)
Court Oak Road, Harborne,
Birmingham, West Midlands B17 9TG
Tel: 0121 428 5050
Principal: Hugh J Williams
Age range: 16–25
No. of pupils: 170
Special needs catered for: ADD, ADHD, ASD, ASP, AUT, BESD, CP, D, DEL, DYS, DYSP, EBD, EPI, GLD, HI, LD, MLD, MSI, PD, Phe, PH, PMLD, PNI, SCD, SP&LD, SPLD, SLI, VIS
♿ £

RNIB PEARS CENTRE FOR SPECIALIST LEARNING
For further details see p. 97
Wheelwright Lane, Ash
Green, Coventry, West
Midlands CV7 9RA
Tel: 024 7636 9500
Email: pearscentre@rnib.org.uk
Website:
www.rnib.org.uk/pearscentre
Executive Headteacher: Andy
Moran
Age range: 2–19
No. of pupils: 29
Special needs catered for:
ASD, AUT, CLD, CP, D, EPI, HI, LD, MSI, PD, PH, PMLD, SCLD, SLD, SPLD, VIS
♿ 16+ ✓

Worcestershire

New College Worcester
Whittington Road, Worcester,
Worcestershire WR5 2JX
Tel: 01905 763933
Principal: Mardy Smith
Age range: usually 11–19
No. of pupils: 88
Fees: Day £30,049–£32,485
WB £40,076–£42,268
FB £44,366–£46,813
Special needs catered for: VIS
♿ 16+ ✓

Yorkshire & Humberside

North Yorkshire

Henshaws College
Bogs Lane, Harrogate,
North Yorkshire HG1 4ED
Tel: 01423 886451
Head of Education: Mr Robert Jones
Age range: 16–25
Special needs catered for: CLD, CP, D, EPI, HI, LD, MLD, MSI, PD, Phe, SCD, SLD, SP&LD, VIS
16+ ♿

South Yorkshire

Doncaster College for the Deaf
Leger Way, Doncaster,
South Yorkshire DN2 6AY
Tel: 01302 386720
Executive Principal: Alan
W Robinson
Age range: 16–59
No. of pupils: 185
Special needs catered for: HI
♿

DONCASTER SCHOOL FOR THE DEAF
For further details see p. 99
Leger Way, Doncaster,
South Yorkshire DN2 6AY
Tel: 01302 386733
Email: principal@ddt-deaf.org.
uk or secretary@ddt-deaf.org.uk
Website: www.deaf-trust.co.uk
Executive Principal: Mr
Alan W Robinson
Age range: 3–19
No. of pupils: 27
Special needs catered for: BESD, CP, D, DYS, GLD, HI, MLD, PH, PMLD, SLD, SP&LD, SPLD, VIS
♿ ✓

Paces High Green School for Conductive Education
Paces High Green Centre, Pack
Horse Lane, High Green, Sheffield,
South Yorkshire S35 3HY
Tel: 0114 284 5298
Headteacher: Gabor Fellner
Age range: 0–18
No. of pupils: 30
Fees: Day £27,452
Special needs catered for: CP, PD
16+ ✓

West Yorkshire

Holly Bank School
Roe Head, Far Common Road,
Mirfield, West Yorkshire WF14 0DQ
Tel: 01924 490833
Headteacher: Ms Lyn Pollard
Age range: 5–19
No. of pupils: 20 VIth10
Fees: Day £35,000–£45,000
WB £70,000–£75,000
FB £99,000–£105,000
Special needs catered for: CLD, CP, MSI, PD, PH, PMLD, PNI, SCLD, SLD
♿ 16+

ST JOHN'S CATHOLIC SCHOOL FOR THE DEAF
For further details see p. 100
Church Street, Boston
Spa, Wetherby, West
Yorkshire LS23 6DF
Tel: 01937 842144
Email: info@stjohns.org.uk
Website: www.stjohns.org.uk
Headteacher: Mrs A Bradbury
BA(Hons), MSc, NPQH
Age range: 4–19
No. of pupils: 68
Special needs catered for: ADD, ADHD, ASD, ASP, AUT, BESD, CP, D, DEL, DYS, DYSP, EBD, EPI, PMLD, SCD, SLD, SP&LD, SLI, VIS
♿ 16+ ✓

Sensory or physical impairment

Northern Ireland

County Antrim

Jordanstown Schools
85 Jordanstown Road,
Newtownabbey, County
Antrim BT37 0QE
Tel: 028 9086 3541
Principal: Mrs A P Magee
MEd, DipSpEd(VI), PQH(NI)
Age range: 4–19
No. of pupils: 67
Special needs catered for: ASD, D,
EBD, GLD, HI, LD, MSI, PD, SP&LD, VIS

County Tyrone

**Buddy Bear Trust
Conductive
Education School**
Killyman Road, Dungannon,
County Tyrone BT71 6DE
Tel: 02887 752 025
Special needs catered for: CP

Scotland

Aberdeen

Camphill School Aberdeen
Murtle House, Bieldside,
Aberdeen AB15 9EP
Tel: 01224 867935
Administrator: Mr Piet Hogenboom
Age range: 3–19
Fees: Day £25,198–£50,397
FB £50,397–£100,794
Special needs catered for: ADD,
ADHD, ASD, ASP, AUT, BESD, CLD,
CP, D, DEL, DYS, DYSP, EBD, EPI,
GLD, HA, HI, LD, MLD, MSI, PD,
Phe, PH, PMLD, PNI, SCD, SCLD,
SEBD, SLD, SP&LD, SPLD, SLI, VIS

Edinburgh

**THE ROYAL BLIND
SCHOOL**
For further details see p. 102
43-45 Canaan Lane,
Edinburgh EH10 4SG
Tel: 0131 446 3120
Email: office@
royalblindschool.org.uk
Website:
www.royalblind.org/education
Head Teacher: Elaine
Brackenridge (BEd)
Age range: 5–19
No. of pupils: 44
Special needs catered for:
AUT, CP, DEL, EPI, MLD, PH,
PMLD, SLD, SP&LD, SPLD, VIS

Renfrewshire

Corseford School
Milliken Park, Johnstone,
Renfrewshire PA10 2NT
Tel: 01505 702141
Headteacher: Mrs M Boyle
Age range: 3–18
No. of pupils: 50
Special needs catered for:
CP, DEL, DYSP, EPI, HI, MLD,
PH, SP&LD, SPLD, VIS

South Lanarkshire

Stanmore House School
Lanark, South Lanarkshire ML11 7RR
Tel: 01555 665041
Head Teacher: Hazel Aitken
Age range: 0–18
No. of pupils: 47
Special needs catered for:
CP, PH, SCLD, SP&LD, VIS

West Lothian

Donaldson's School
Preston Road, Linlithgow,
West Lothian EH49 6HZ
Tel: 01506 841900
Principal: Ms Laura Battles
Age range: 2–19
No. of pupils: 43
Special needs catered for:
ASP, AUT, D, HI, Phe, PMLD,
SCD, SLD, SP&LD, SLI

Wales

Glamorgan

Craig-y-Parc School
Pentyrch, Cardiff,
Glamorgan CF15 9NB
Tel: 029 2089 0397/2089 0361
Principal: Anthony Mulcamy
Age range: 3–19
Special needs catered for: CP,
EPI, HI, LD, MLD, MSI, PD, Phe, PH,
PMLD, SCLD, SLD, SP&LD, VIS

Special Educational Needs and the independent and non-maintained schools and colleges that cater for them

Attention Deficit Disorder (ADD)

Abingdon House School, London..D131
Action for Children Headlands School, Vale of Glamorgan..............D136
Appleford School, Wiltshire...D129
Appletree School, Cumbria...54, D118
Avon Park School, Warwickshire...D111
Belgrave School, Bristol...D129
Belmont School, Lancashire..D119
Birtenshaw Hall School, Greater Manchester.........................D132
Bladon House School, Staffordshire..D134
Blossom Lower School and Upper House, London......................D131
Bramfield House, Suffolk..D116
Brantwood Specialist School, South Yorkshire...................56, D123
Breckenbrough School, North Yorkshire..................................D123
Brewood Middle School, Kent..D120
Brewood Secondary School, Kent..D120
Cambian Pengwern College, Denbighshire.............................D136
Camphill School Aberdeen, Aberdeen...................................D144
Cedar House School, Lancashire...D119
Centre Academy London, London...D131
Chaigeley, Warrington...D120
Chelfham Mill School, Devon...D122
Chilworth House Upper School, Oxfordshire............................D115
Coleg Elidyr, Carmarthenshire...D112
Cotswold Chine School, Gloucestershire.................................D115
Crookhey Hall School, Lancashire...D119
Cruckton Hall, Shropshire...48, D111
Demeter House, North Lincolnshire..D111
Eastwood Grange School, Derbyshire.....................................D116
Falkland House School, Fife...D124
Farleigh College Mells, Somerset...D111
Foxes Fields, Somerset..D134
Harmeny Education Trust Ltd, Edinburgh.................................D124
Hillcrest Oaklands College, Staffordshire................................D123
Hillcrest Park School, Oxfordshire..D115
Hillcrest Slinfold School, West Sussex....................................D121
Holme Court School, Bedfordshire...D130
Hope House School, Nottinghamshire....................................D116
Hope View School, Kent..D121
Horton House School, East Riding of Yorkshire........................D123
Insights Independent School, London......................................D117
Kisharon School, London...D131
Lakeside School, Merseyside...D109
Linkage College - Toynton Campus, Lincolnshire.....................D130
Linkage College - Weelsby Campus, North-East Lincolnshire..........D135
Muntham House School Ltd, West Sussex................................D121
North Hill House, Somerset..D111
Northease Manor School, East Sussex....................................D132
Ochil Tower, Perth & Kinross...D136
Orchard Hill College of Further Education, Surrey....................D133
Overley Hall School, West Midlands.................................77, D134
Owlswick School, East Sussex..D132
Parayhouse School, London...D131
Parkanaur College, County Tyrone..D135
Philpots Manor School, West Sussex.................................55, D121
Potterspury Lodge School, Northamptonshire....................40, D108
Queen Alexandra College (QAC), West Midlands....................D143
Queen Elizabeth's Training College, Surrey.............................D141
Ripplevale School, Kent...D121
Rossendale School, Lancashire..D109
Rowden House School, Herefordshire.....................................D134
Sheiling School, Thornbury, Bristol...D129
Sheridan School, Norfolk...D116
Springboard Education Senior, West Sussex............................D121
St Andrews School, Norfolk...D107
St Catherine's School, Isle of Wight..................................72, D133
St Dominic's School, Surrey...D133
St John's Catholic School for the Deaf, West Yorkshire..........100, D143
St John's School & College, East Sussex...........................73, D133
St Piers School and College, Surrey.......................................D142
Sunfield School, West Midlands.......................................78, D134
Talbot House School, Tyne & Wear..D118
The Linnet Independent Learning Centre, Derbyshire................D116
The Loddon School, Hampshire..D133
The Marchant-Holliday School, Somerset................................D122
The Mount Camphill Community, East Sussex..........................D120
The New School, Perth & Kinross......................................83, D136
The New School at West Heath, Kent.....................................D121
The Royal School for Deaf Children Margate and
    Westgate College, Kent..D141
The Ryes College & Community, Essex...................................D115
Underley Garden School, Cumbria...D118
Waterloo Lodge School, Lancashire.......................................D119
West Kirby Residential School, Merseyside........................47, D109
Whitstone Head School, Devon..D122
William Henry Smith School, West Yorkshire...........................D124
Wings School, Cumbria, Cumbria..D118
Wings School, Nottinghamshire, Nottinghamshire....................D117
Woodcroft School, Essex...D130
Young Options College, Shropshire...D122
Young Options Pathway College Stoke, Staffordshire................D123

Attention Deficit and Hyperactive Disorder (ADHD)

3 Dimensions, Somerset..D111
Abingdon House School, London..D131
Action for Children Headlands School, Vale of Glamorgan..............D136
Action for Children Parklands Campus, Oxfordshire..................D115
Appleford School, Wiltshire...D129
Appletree School, Cumbria...54, D118
Aran Hall School, Gwynedd..D136
Arc School - Ansley, Warwickshire...D123
Arc School - Napton, Warwickshire.......................................D123
Avon Park School, Warwickshire...D111
Belmont School, Lancashire...D119
Birtenshaw Hall School, Greater Manchester.........................D132
Bladon House School, Staffordshire..D134
Blossom Lower School and Upper House, London......................D131
Bracken School, Lancashire...D109
Bramfield House, Suffolk..D116
Brantridge School, West Sussex...D121
Brantwood Specialist School, South Yorkshire...................56, D123
Breckenbrough School, North Yorkshire..................................D123
Brewood Middle School, Kent..D120
Brewood Secondary School, Kent..D120
Cambian Pengwern College, Denbighshire.............................D136
Camphill Community Glencraig, County Down.........................D124
Camphill School Aberdeen, Aberdeen...................................D144
Cedar House School, Lancashire...D119
Centre Academy East Anglia, Suffolk.....................................D130
Centre Academy London, London...D131
Chaigeley, Warrington...D120
Chelfham Mill School, Devon...D122
Chelfham Senior School, Devon...D110
Chilworth House School, Oxfordshire.....................................D115
Chilworth House Upper School, Oxfordshire............................D115
Coleg Elidyr, Carmarthenshire...D112
Cotswold Chine School, Gloucestershire.................................D115
Crookhey Hall School, Lancashire...D119
Cruckton Hall, Shropshire...48, D111
Cumberland School, Lancashire...D119
Eastwood Grange School, Derbyshire.....................................D116
Eden Grove School, Cumbria...D118
Falkland House School, Fife...D124
Farleigh College Mells, Somerset...D111
Farney Close School, West Sussex..D121
Foxes Fields, Somerset..D134
Freeman College, South Yorkshire.....................................79, D135
Glasshouse College, West Midlands..................................76, D134
Grafham Grange School, Surrey...D121
Hall Cliffe School, West Yorkshire..D135
Harmeny Education Trust Ltd, Edinburgh.................................D124
High Close School, Berkshire..D120
Hill Farm College, Northamptonshire......................................D107
Hillcrest Oaklands College, Staffordshire................................D123
Hillcrest Park School, Oxfordshire..D115
Hillcrest Slinfold School, West Sussex....................................D121
Holme Court School, Bedfordshire...D130

Autistic Spectrum Disorder(s) (ASD)

Asperger Syndrome (ASP)

Autism (AUT)

Schools and colleges by category

Behaviour, Emotional and Social Difficulties (BESD) – see also EBSD and SEBD

Complex Learning Difficulties (CLD)

Cerebral Palsy (CP)

Deaf (D) – see also Hearing Impairment (HI)

Delicate (DEL)

Dyslexia (DYSL) – see also SPLD

Dyspraxia (DYSP)

Emotional, Behavioural Difficulties (EBD) – see also BESD and SEBD

Schools and colleges by category

Epilepsy (EPI)

General Learning Difficulties (GLD)

High Ability (HA)

Hearing Impairment (HI)

Learning Difficulties (LD)

Moderate Learning Difficulties (MLD)

Schools and colleges by category

Multi-sensory Impairment (MSI)

Barton School, Lincolnshire...D111
Beaumont College, Lancashire D141
Birtenshaw Hall School, Greater Manchester D132
Cambian Pengwern College, Denbighshire D136
Camphill School Aberdeen, Aberdeen D144
Chailey Heritage School, East Sussex.......................89, D141
Craig-y-Parc School, Glamorgan D144
Exeter Royal Academy for Deaf Education, Devon D142
Foxes Fields, Somerset D134
Henshaws College, North Yorkshire D143
Higford School, Shropshire D111
Holly Bank School, West Yorkshire D143
Jordanstown Schools, County Antrim D144
Kinsale School, Flintshire D112
Kisharon School, London D131
Kisimul School, Lincolnshire 64, D130
Kisimul School - Woodstock House, Surrey 70, D133
Langside School, Dorset D142
Meldreth Manor School, Hertfordshire D139
National Star College, Gloucestershire D139
Ochil Tower, Perth & Kinross D136

On Track Training Centre, Devon D142
Orchard Hill College of Further Education, Surrey D133
Queen Alexandra College (QAC), West Midlands D143
RNIB Pears Centre for Specialist Learning, West Midlands............97, D143
Royal College Manchester, Cheshire 45, D109
Royal School for the Blind, Merseyside D141
Royal School Manchester, Cheshire 46, D109
Rutherford School, Surrey D131
Seashell Trust, Greater Manchester D141
Sheiling School, Thornbury, Bristol D129
St John's Catholic School for the Deaf, West Yorkshire.............. 100, D143
St Mary's School & 6th Form College, East Sussex.......... 92, D141
St Rose's School, Gloucestershire D139
Sunfield School, West Midlands 78, D134
The Children's Trust School, Surrey 93, D142
The Mount Camphill Community, East Sussex D120
The PACE Centre, Buckinghamshire D139
Treloar School, Hampshire 94, D141
Woodcroft School, Essex D130
Young Options Pathway College Stoke, Staffordshire D123

Partially Hearing (Phe)

Birtenshaw Hall School, Greater Manchester D132
Cambian Pengwern College, Denbighshire D136
Camphill School Aberdeen, Aberdeen D144
Chilworth House Upper School, Oxfordshire D115
Coleg Elidyr, Carmarthenshire D112
Craig-y-Parc School, Glamorgan D144
Donaldson's School, West Lothian D142
Exeter Royal Academy for Deaf Education, Devon D142
Foxes Academy, Somerset D134
Foxes Fields, Somerset D134
Henshaws College, North Yorkshire D143
Kisharon School, London D131
Langdon College, Greater Manchester D132
Linkage College - Toynton Campus, Lincolnshire.............. D130
Linkage College - Weelsby Campus, North-East Lincolnshire D135

Meldreth Manor School, Hertfordshire D139
National Star College, Gloucestershire D139
Orchard Hill College of Further Education, Surrey D133
Parayhouse School, London D131
Parkanaur College, County Tyrone D135
Queen Alexandra College (QAC), West Midlands D143
Rutherford School, Surrey D131
Sheiling School, Thornbury, Bristol D129
St John's Catholic School for the Deaf, West Yorkshire.............. 100, D143
St Mary's School & 6th Form College, East Sussex.......... 92, D141
St Rose's School, Gloucestershire D139
The Mount Camphill Community, East Sussex D120
The Royal National College for the Blind (RNC),
     Herefordshire 98, D143
Treloar School, Hampshire 94, D141

Physical Difficulties (PD)

Beaumont College, Lancashire D141
Birtenshaw Hall School, Greater Manchester D132
Cambian Pengwern College, Denbighshire D136
Camphill School Aberdeen, Aberdeen D144
Chailey Heritage School, East Sussex.......................89, D141
Craig-y-Parc School, Glamorgan D144
Foxes Fields, Somerset D134
Frederick Hugh House, London D131
Henshaws College, North Yorkshire D143
Holly Bank School, West Yorkshire D143
Jordanstown Schools, County Antrim D144
Kisharon School, London D131
Langside School, Dorset D142
Linkage College - Toynton Campus, Lincolnshire.............. D130
Meldreth Manor School, Hertfordshire D139
National Star College, Gloucestershire D139
Orchard Hill College of Further Education, Surrey D133
Paces High Green School for Conductive Education,
     South Yorkshire D143
Parkanaur College, County Tyrone D135
Queen Alexandra College (QAC), West Midlands D143
Queen Elizabeth's Training College, Surrey D141

Regent College, Staffordshire D134
RNIB Pears Centre for Specialist Learning, West Midlands............97, D143
Royal College Manchester, Cheshire 45, D109
Royal School for the Blind, Merseyside D141
Rutherford School, Surrey D131
Seashell Trust, Greater Manchester D141
Sheiling School, Thornbury, Bristol D129
St Christopher's School, Bristol 61, D129
St John's Catholic School for the Deaf, West Yorkshire.............. 100, D143
St John's School & College, East Sussex 73, D133
St Mary's School & 6th Form College, East Sussex.......... 92, D141
St Rose's School, Gloucestershire D139
Stepping Stones School, Surrey D142
The Children's Trust School, Surrey 93, D142
The David Lewis School, Cheshire D132
The London School for Children with Cerebral Palsy, London...........D140
The Mount Camphill Community, East Sussex D120
The PACE Centre, Buckinghamshire D139
The Royal National College for the Blind (RNC), Herefordshire...98, D143
Treloar School, Hampshire 94, D141
Vranch House, Devon D142

Physical Impairment (PH)

Action for Children Penhurst School, Oxfordshire.............................. D129
Barnardos, Essex D117
Beaumont College, Lancashire D141

Birtenshaw Hall School, Greater Manchester D132
Brewood Middle School, Kent D120
Brewood Secondary School, Kent D120

Profound and Multiple Learning Difficulties (PMLD)

Physical Neurological Impairment (PNI)

Social and Communication Difficulties (SCD)

Severe and Complex Learning Difficulties (SCLD)

Severe Emotional and Behavioural Difficulties (SEBD) – see also BESD and EBD

Severe Learning Difficulties (SLD)

Speech and Language Difficulties (SP&LD)

Specific Learning Difficulties (SPLD)

Specific Language Impairment (SLI)

Visually Impaired (VIS)

Useful associations and websites

Action for Blind People

14-16 Verney Road
London SE16 3DZ
Tel: 020 7635 4800
Helpline: 0303 123 9999
Email: helpline@rnib.org.uk
Website: www.actionforblindpeople.org.uk

A UK based charity (nos. 205913, SCO40050) that works to inspire change and create opportunities to enable blind and partially sighted people to have an equal voice and equal choice. They enable visually impaired people to transform their lives through work, housing, leisure and support. Part of the RNIB.

Action for Sick Children

32b Buxton Road
High Lane
Stockport SK6 8BH
Tel: 01663 763 004
Helpline: 0800 0744 519
Website: www.actionforsickchildren.org

Healthcare charity (no. 296295) formed in the 1960s to help parents whose children have to spend extended stays in hospital.

Action on Hearing Loss

19-23 Featherstone Street
London EC1Y 8SL
Tel: 020 7296 8000
Textphone: 020 7296 8001
Fax: 020 7296 8199
Email: informationline@hearingloss.org.uk
Website: www.actiononhearingloss.org.uk

Action on Hearing Loss, formerly the Royal National Institute for Deaf People, is the largest national charity (nos. 207720, SCO38926) representing the nine million deaf and hard of hearing people in the UK. As a membership charity we aim to achieve a radically better quality of life for deaf and hard of hearing people. We do this by campaigning and lobbying vigorously, by raising awareness of deafness and hearing loss, by providing services and through social medical and technical research.

Follow us on Twitter.

Action on Hearing Loss Cymru

16 Cathedral Road
Cardiff CF11 9LJ
Tel: 02920 333 034
Text: 02920 333 036
Fax: 02920 333 035
Email: informationline@hearingloss.org.uk

See main entry above.

Action on Hearing Loss Northern Ireland

4-8 Adelaide Street
Belfast
BT2 8GA
Tel: 028 9023 9619
Fax: 028 9031 2032
Textphone: 028 9024 9462
Email: information.nireland@hearingloss.org.uk

See main entry above.

Action on Hearing Loss Scotland

Empire House
131 West Nile Street
Glasgow
G1 2RXJ
Tel: 0141 341 5330
Text: 0141 341 5347
Fax: 0161 354 0176
Email: scotland@hearingloss.org.uk

See main entry above.

ADDISS – National Attention Deficit Disorder Information & Support Service

Premier House
112 Station Road
Edgware, Middlesex HA8 7BJ
Tel: 020 8952 2800
Fax: 020 8952 2909
Email: info@addiss.co.uk
Website: www.addiss.co.uk

ADDISS provides information and assistance for those affected by ADHD. Registered charity no. 1070827.

Advisory Centre for Education – (ACE)

36 Nicholay Road
London N19 3EZ
Tel: 020 8407
Email: enquiries@ace-ed.org.uk
Website: www.ace-ed.org.uk

ACE is an independent national advice centre for parents/carers of children aged 5 to 16. Advice booklets can be downloaded or ordered from the website. Training courses and seminars for LA officers, schools and governors are available. As well as a training package for community groups advising parents on education matters. Has Facebook page and you can follow them on Twitter.

AFASIC – Unlocking Speech and Language

20 Bowling Green Lane
London EC1R 0BD
Tel: 020 7490 9410
Fax: 020 7251 2834
Helpline: 0845 3 55 55 77
Website: www.afasicengland.org.uk

Helps children and young people with speech and language impairments. Provides: training/conferences for parents and professionals; a range of publications; support through local groups; and expertise in developing good practice. Registered charity nos. 1045617, SCO39170. Has a Facebook page.

AFASIC – Cymru

Titan House
Cardiff Bay Business Centre
Lewis Road
Ocean Park
Cardiff CF24 5BS
Tel: 029 2046 5854
Website: www.afasiccymru.org.uk
Fax: 029 2046 5854

See main entry above.

AFASIC – Northern Ireland

Cranogue House
19 Derry Courtney Road
Caledon
County Tyrone BT68 4UF
Tel: 028 3756 9611 (M-F 10.30am-2.30pm)
Email: mary@afasicnorthernireland.org.uk
Website: www.afasicnorthernireland.org.uk

See main entry above.

AFASIC – Scotland

The Vine
43 Magdalen Yard Road
Dundee DD1 4NE
Tel: 01382 250060
Fax: 01382 568391
Email: info@afasicscotland.org.uk

Registered charity no. SCO39170.

See main entry above.

Association of Blind and Partially-Sighted Teachers and Students (ABAPTAS)

BM Box 6727
London
WC1N 3XX
Tel: 0117 966 4839
Website: www.abapstas.org.uk

National organisation of visually impaired people that focuses on education and employment issues. Registered charity no. 266056.

Association of Sign Language Interpreters (ASLI)

51 Derngate St
Northampton NN1 1UE
Tel: 0871 474 0522
Textphone: 18001 0871 474 0522
Fax: 01908 325259
Email: office@asli.org.uk
Website: www.asli.org.uk

Has a useful online directory of sign language interpreters.

Asthma UK

18 Mansell St
London E1 8AA
Tel: 0800 121 6255
UK Advice Line: 0800 121 6244 (Mon-Fri 9am-5pm)
Fax: 020 7256 6075
Twitter: @AsthmaUK
Email: info@asthma.org.uk
Website: www.asthma.org.uk

Charity dedicated to helping the 5.2 million people in the UK who are affected by asthma. Registered charity nos. 802364, SCO39322.

Ataxia (UK)

Lincoln House, Kennington Park
1-3 Brixton Road
London SW9 6DE
Tel: 020 7582 1444
Helpline: 0845 644 0606
Twitter: @AtaxiaUK
Email: office@ataxia.org.uk
Website: www.ataxia.org.uk

Aims to support all people affected by ataxia. Registered charity nos. 1102391 and SCO406047. Has a Facebook page and you can follow them on Twitter.

AVM Support UK

Suite G03, Blyth CEC
Ridley Street
Blyth
Northumberland NE24 3AG
Email: info@avmsupport.co.uk
Website: www.avmsupport.co.uk

Offers support and information for those affected by Arteriovenous Malformation (AVM).

BCS – IT Can Help

c/o Information Technologists
39a Bartholomew Close
London EC1A 7JN
Freephone & text phone helpline: 0800 269 545
Email: enquiries@abilitynet.org.uk
Website: www.itcanhelp.org.uk

Provides onsite volunteers to help individuals with disabilities who have computer problems Registered charity no. 292786.

BIBIC (British Institute for Brain Injured Children)

Old Kelways
Somerton Road
Langport
Somerset TA10 9SJ
Tel: 01458 253344
Fax: 01278 685573
Email: info@bibic.org.uk
Twitter: @bibic_charity
Website: www.bibic.org.uk

As a registered charity (no. 1057635) BIBIC helps children with a disability or learning difficulty caused by conditions such as cerebral palsy, Down's syndrome and other genetic disorders; acquired brain injury caused by trauma or illness; and developmental disorders such as autism, ADHD, Asperger syndrome and dyspraxia.

All children are assessed by a multi-professional team who put together a report and a therapy plan that is taught to the family by the child's key worker. This provides support for the family to learn about their child and how they can make a positive difference to their development. Sections of the plan are designed to be shared with the child's school and social groups to ensure a consistent approach in areas such as communication, behaviour and learning. Families return on a regular basis for reassessments and updated therapy programmes.

Blind Children UK

Hillfields
Reading Road
Burghfield Common
Reading
Berkshire RG7 3YG
Tel: 0800 781 1444
Email: services@blindchildrenuk.org
Website: www.blindchildrenuk.org
Twitter: @BlindChildrenUK

Formerly the National Blind Children's Society, Blind Children UK offers advice and support for blind and partially sighted children and their families and carers. Registered charity no. 1051607. Has a Facebook page.

Brain and Spine Foundation

3.36 Canterbury Court
Kennington Park
1-3 Brixton Road
London SW9 6DE
Tel: 020 7793 5900
Helpline: 0808 808 1000
Fax: 020 7793 5939
Fax helpline: 020 7793 5939
Email: info@brainandspine.org.uk
Twitter: @brainspine
Website: www.brainandspine.org.uk

Registered charity (no. 1098528), which was founded in 1992 to help those people affected by brain and spine conditions.

British Blind Sport (BBS)

Pure Offices
Plato Close
Tachbrook Park
Leamington Spa
Warwickshire CV34 6WE
Tel: 01926 424247
Fax: 01926 427775
Email: info@britishblindsport.org.uk
Twitter: @BritBlindSport
Website: www.britishblindsport.org.uk

A registered charity (no. 271500) providing sport and recreation for blind and partially sighted people.

British Deaf Association England

356 Holloway Road
London N7 6PA
Tel: 020 7405 0090
Textphone: 05603 115295
Fax: 01772 561610
Email: bda@bda.org.uk
Website: www.bda.org.uk
Twitter: @BritishDeafNews

The BDA is a democratic, membership-led national charity (no. 1031687) campaigning on behalf of deaf sign language users in the UK. It exists to advance and protect the interests of the deaf community, to increase deaf people's access to facilities and lifestyles that most hearing people take for granted and to ensure greater awareness of their rights and responsibilities as members of society. The association has several main service areas, with teams covering education and youth, information, health promotions, video production and community services, offering advice and help. There is a national helpline that provides information and advice on a range of subjects such as welfare rights, the Disability Discrimination Act (DDA) and education.

British Deaf Association of Northern Ireland

Unit 5c, Weavers Court
Linfield Road
Belfast BT12 5GH
Tel: 02890 437486
Textphone: 02890 437480
Fax: 02890 437487
Email: northernireland@bda.org
Website: www.bda.org.uk

See main entry under British Deaf Association England.

British Deaf Association Scotland

1st Floor Central Chambers, Suite 58
93 Hope Street
Glasgow G2 6LD
Tel: 0141 248 5554
Fax: 0141 248 5565
Email: scotland@bda.org.uk
Website: www.bda.org.uk

See main entry under British Deaf Association England.

British Dyslexia Association

Unit 8, Bracknell Beeches
Old Bracknell Lane
Bracknell RG12 7BW
Tel: 0845 251 9002 (Helpline) or
0845 251 9003 (Admin)
Fax: 0845 251 9005
Email: helpline@bdadyslexia.org.uk
Website: www.bdadyslexia.org.uk

Helpline/information service open between 10am and 4.00pm (M-F) also open late on Wednesdays 5-7pm. Has a Facebook page. Registered charity no. 289243.

British Institute of Learning Disabilities (BILD)

Birmingham Research Park
97 Vincent Drive
Edgbaston
Birmingham B15 2SQ
Tel: 01562 723010
Fax: 01562 723029
Email: enquiries@bild.org.uk
Website: www.bild.org.uk

Registered charity (no. 1019663) committed to improving the quality of life of people with learning disabilities. They do this by advancing education, research and practice and by promoting better ways of working with children and adults with learning disabilities. BILD provides education, training, information, publications, journals, membership services, research and consultancy. Has a Facebook page and you can follow them on Twitter.

British Psychological Society

St Andrews House
48 Princess Road East
Leicester LE1 7DR
Tel: 0116 254 9568
Fax: 0116 227 1314
Email: enquiries@bps.org.uk
Website: www.bps.org.uk
Twitter: @BPSofficial

The representative body for psychology and psychologists in the UK. Has search facility for details on psychologists. Registered charity nos. 229642 & SCO39452.

Brunel Able Children's Education (BACE) Centre

Brunel University
School of Sport & Education,
Kingston Lane
Uxbridge, Middlesex UB8 3PH
Tel: 01895 267152
Fax: 01895 269806
Email: catherina.emery@brunel.ac.uk
Website: www.brunel.ac.uk/sse/education/research/bace

Conducts research into all aspects of identification and provision for able and exceptionally able children. The centre has been involved in supporting the education of able children in inner city schools for a number of years. A number of courses are run for teachers to train them to make effective provision for able pupils.

CALL Scotland

University of Edinburgh
Paterson's Land
Holyrood Road
Edinburgh
Midlothian EH8 8AQ
Tel: 0131 651 6235
Fax: 0131 651 6234
Email: info@callcentrescotland.org.uk
Website: www.callcentrescotland.org.uk
Twitter: @CallScotland

CALL Scotland provides services and carries out research and development projects across Scotland for people, particularly children with severe communication disabilities, their families and people who work with them in augmentative communication techniques and technology, and specialised computer use.

Capability Scotland (ASCS)

Head Office, Westerlea
11 Ellersly Road
Edinburgh
Midlothian EH12 6HY
Tel: 0131 337 9876
Textphone: 0131 346 2529
Twitter: @capability_scot
Fax: 0131 346 7864
Website: www.capability-scotland.org.uk

ASCS is a national disability advice and information service, which provides free confidential advice and information on a range of disability issues including advice on cerebral palsy. Registered charity no. SCO11330.

Carers UK

20 Great Dover Street
London SE1 4LX
Tel: 020 7378 4999
Fax: 020 7378 9781
Adviceline: 0808 808 7777 (W & Th 10-12 and 2-4pm) or Email: adviceline@carersuk.org
Email: info@carersuk.org
Website: www.carersuk.org
Twitter: @CarersUK

For carers run by carers. Registered charity nos. 246329 & SCO39307.

Carers Northern Ireland

58 Howard Street
Belfast BT1 6PJ
Tel: 028 9043 9843
Twitter: @CarersNI
Email: info@carersni.org
Website: www.carersuk.org/northern-ireland

See main entry under Carers UK.

Carers Scotland

The Cottage
21 Pearce Street
Glasgow G51 3UT
Tel: 0141 445 3070
Twitter: @CarersScotland
Email: info@carersscotland.org
Website: www.carersuk.org/scotland

See main entry under Carers UK.

Carers Wales

River House
Gwaelod-y-Garth
Cardiff CF15 9SS
Tel: 029 2081 1370
Twitter: @carerswales
Email: info@carerswales.org
Website: www.carersuk.org/wales

See main entry under Carers UK.

Centre for Studies on Inclusive Education (CSIE)

The Park
Daventry Road
Knowle
Bristol BS4 1DQ
Tel: 0117 353 3150
Fax: 0117 353 3151
Email: admin@csie.org.uk
Website: www.csie.org.uk
Twitter: @CSIE_UK

Promoting inclusion for all children in restructured mainstream schools. Registered charity no. 327805.

Challenging Behaviour Foundation

c/o The Old Courthouse
New Road Avenue
Chatham
Kent ME4 6BE
Tel: 01634 838739
Family support line: 0845 602 7885
Email: info@thecbf.org.uk
Website: www.challengingbehaviour.org.uk
Twitter: @CBFdn

Supports families, professionals and stakeholders who live/work with people with severe learning disabilities who have challenging behaviour. Registered charity no. 1060714.

Child Brain Injury Trust (CBIT)

Unit 1, The Great Barn
Baynards Green Farm
Bicester
Oxfordshire OX27 7SG
Tel: 01869 341075
Twitter: @CBITUK
Email: info@cbituk.org
Website: www.childbraininjurytrust.org.uk

Formerly known as the Children's Head Injury Trust (CHIT) this organisation was originally set up in 1991. It offers support to children and families affected by brain injuries that happen after birth. Registered charity nos. 1113326 & SCO39703. Has Facebook page and you can follow them on Twitter.

Communication Matters

Catchpell House
Carpet Lane
Edinburgh EH6 6SP
Tel/Fax: 0845 456 8211
Email: admin@communications.org.uk
Website: www.communicationmatters.org.uk

Support for people who find communication difficult.

Contact a Family

209-211 City Road
London EC1V 1JN
Tel: 020 7608 8700
Helpline: 0808 808 3555 Textphone: 0808 808 3556
Fax: 020 7608 8701
Email: helpline@cafamily.org.uk
Website: www.cafamily.org.uk
Twitter: @ContactAFamily

Registered charity (nos. 284912, SCO39169) that provides support, advice and information to families with disabled children. Has a Facebook page and you can follow them on Twitter.

Coram Children's Legal Centre

Riverside Office Centre
Century House North, North Station Road
Colchester,
Essex CO1 1RE
Tel: 01206 877 910
Fax: 01206 877 963
Email: clc@essex.ac.uk
Website: www.childrenslegalcentre.com

The Children's Legal Centre is an independent national charity (no. 281222) concerned with law and policy affecting children and young people. The centre runs a free and confidential legal advice and information service covering all aspects of law and the service is open to children, young people and anyone with concerns about them. The Education Legal Advocacy unit provides advice and representation to children and/or parents involved in education disputes with a school or a local education authority.

Council for Disabled Children

National Children's Bureau
8 Wakley Street
London EC1V 7QE
Tel: 020 7843 1900
Fax: 020 7843 6313
Email: cdc@ncb.org.uk
Website: www.councilfordisabledchildren.org.uk
Twitter: @CDC_tweets

The council promotes collaborative work and partnership between voluntary and non-voluntary agencies, parents and children and provides a national forum for the discussion, development and dissemination of a wide range of policy and practice issues relating to service provision and support for children and young people with disabilities and special educational needs. Has a particular interest in inclusive education, special education needs, parent partnership services, play and leisure and transition. Registered charity no. 258825.

Council for the Registration of Schools Teaching Dyslexic Pupils (CReSTeD)

Old Post House
Castle Street
Whittington
Shropshire SY11 4DF
Tel: 01691 665783
Email: admin@crested.org.uk
Website: www.crested.org.uk

CReSTeD's aim is to help parents and also those who advise them choose an educational establishment for children with Specific Learning Difficulties (SpLD). It maintains a register of schools and teaching centres which meets its criteria for the teaching of pupils with Specific Learning Difficulties.

All schools and centres included in the Register are visited regularly to ensure they continue to meet the criteria set by CReSTeD. CReSTeD acts as a source of names for educational establishments which parents can use as their first step towards making a placement decision which will be critical to their child's educational future.

Cystic Fibrosis Trust

11 London Road
Bromley
Kent BR1 1BY
Tel: 020 8464 7211
Helpline: 0300 373 1000
Fax: 020 8313 0472
Email: enquiries@cftrust.org.uk
Website: www.cftrust.org.uk
Twitter: @CFtrust

The Cystic Fibrosis Trust is a national registered charity (nos. 1079049, SCO40196) established in 1964. It offers information and support to people with cystic fibrosis, their families, their carers and anyone affected by cystic fibrosis. It funds research, offers some financial support to people with cystic fibrosis and campaigns for improved services. It provides a wide range of information including fact sheets, publications and expert concensus documents on treatment and care for people with cystic fibrosis.

Disabled Living Foundation

Ground Floor, Landmark House
Hammersmith Bridge Road
London W6 9EJ
Tel: 020 7289 6111
Helpline: 0845 130 9177
Twitter: @DLFUK
Email: info@dlf.org.uk
Website: www.dlf.org.uk

This foundation provides free, impartial advice about products for disabled people. Registered charity no. 290069.

Down's Syndrome Education International

6 Underley Business Centre
Kirkby, Lonsdale
Cumbria LA6 2DY
Tel: 023 9285 5330
Fax: 023 9285 5320
Email: enquiries@downsed.org
Website: www.downsed.org
Twitter: @dseint

Down's Syndrome Education International works around the world to improve the development, education and social achievements of many thousands of people living with Down's syndrome. We undertake and support scientific research and disseminate quality information and advice widely through our websites, books, films and training courses.

Our education services support families and professionals to help people with Down's syndrome achieve sustained gains in all areas of their development.

For 30 years, we have disseminated the latest research findings in practical and accessible formats to the widest audiences, from birth to adulthood. Please visit our website for more information. Registered charity no. 1062823. We have a Facebook page and you can follow us on Twitter.

Down's Syndrome Association

Langdon Down Centre
2a Langdon Park
Teddington TW11 9PS
Tel: 020 8614 5100
Fax: 0845 230 0373
Email: info@downs-syndrome.org.uk
Website: www.downs-syndrome.org.uk
Twitter: @DSAInfo

We provide information and support for people with Down's syndrome, their families and carers, and the professionals who work with them. We strive to improve knowledge of the condition. We champion the rights of people with Down's syndrome. Registered charity no. 1061474.

Down's Syndrome Association Northern Ireland

Unit 2, Marlborough House
348 Lisburn Road
Belfast BT9 6GH
Tel: 028 90666 5260
Fax: 028 9066 7674
Email: enquiriesni@downs-syndrome.org.uk

See main entry above.

Down's Syndrome Association Wales

Suite 1, 206 Whitchurch Road
Heath
Cardiff CF14 3NB
Tel: 029 2052 2511
Email: wales@downs-syndrome.org.uk

See main entry above.

Dyslexia Action

Park House
Wick Road
Egham
Surrey TW20 0HH
Tel: 01784 222300
Fax: 01784 222333
Email: info@dyslexiaaction.org.uk
Website: www.dyslexiaaction.org.uk
Twitter: @DyslexiaAction

Registered charity (nos. 268502, SCO39177) and the UK's leading provider of services and support for people with dyslexia and literacy difficulties. We specialise in assessment, teaching and training. We also develop and distribute teaching materials and undertake research.

Dyslexia Action is the largest supplier of specialist training in this field and is committed to improving public policy and practice. We partner with schools, LAs, colleges, universities, employers, voluntary sector organisations and government to improve the quality and quantity of help for people with dyslexia and specific learning difficulties.

Our services are available through our 26 centres around the UK.

Dyslexia Scotland

2nd floor – East Suite
Wallace House
17-21 Maxwell Place
Stirling FK8 1JU
Tel: 01786 446 650
Fax: 01786 471235
Email: info@dyslexiascotland.org.uk
Website: www.dyslexiascotland.org.uk
Twitter: @DyslexiaScotlan

Scottish association set up to support and campaign on behalf of people affected by dyslexia. They have a useful and easy to use website. Registered charity no. SCO00951.

Dyspraxia Foundation

8 West Alley
Hitchin
Hertfordshire SG5 1EG
Tel: 01462 455016
Helpline: 01462 454 986 (M-F 10am-1pm)
Fax: 01462 455052
Email: dyspraxia@dyspraxiafoundation.org.uk
Website: www.dyspraxiafoundation.org.uk
Twitter: @DyspraxiaFdtn

The foundation exists to support individuals and families affected by dyspraxia; to promote better diagnostic and treatment facilities for those who have dyspraxia; to help professionals in health and education to assist those with dyspraxia; and to promote awareness and understanding of dyspraxia. As well as various publications, the Dyspraxia Foundation organises conferences and talks and supports a network of local groups across the United Kingdom.

Registered charity no. 1058352.

Education Scotland

Denholm House
Almondvale Business Park
Almondvale Way
Livingston EH54 6GA
Tel: 0141 282 5000
Textphone: 01506 600236
Email: enquiries@educationscotland.org.uk
Website: www.educationscotland.gov.uk
Twitter: @EducationScot

Education Scotland is an executive non-departmental public body sponsored by the Scottish government. It is the main organisation for the development and support of the Scottish curriculum and is at the heart of all major developments in Scottish education, moving education forward with its partners.

ENABLE Scotland

Inspire House
3 Renshaw Place
Eurocentral
Lanarkshire ML1 4UF
Tel: 0141 226 4541
Fax: 0141 204 4398
Email: enabledirect@enable.org.uk
Website: www.enable.org.uk
Twitter: @ENABLEScotland

Contact the ENABLE Scotland Information Service about any aspect of learning disability. They offer jobs, training, respite breaks, day services, supported living, housing and support for people with learning disabilities in different parts of Scotland. Its legal service can assist families with wills and trusts. Registered charity no. SCO09024.

English Federation of Disability Sport

Sport Park, Loughborough University
3 Oakwood Drive
Loughborough
Leicestershire LE11 3QF
Tel: 01509 227750
Fax: 0509 227777
Email: info@efds.org.uk
Website: www.efds.co.uk
Twitter: @Eng_Dis_Sport

Charity (no. 1075180) that creates opportunities for disabled people to participate in sporting activities.

Epilepsy Action

New Anstey House
Gate Way Drive,
Yeadon
Leeds LS19 7XY
Tel: 0113 210 880
Fax: 0113 391 0300
Email: helpline@epilepsy.org.uk
Website: www.epilepsy.org.uk
Twitter: @epilepsyaction

Epilepsy Action is the UK's leading epilepsy organisation and exists to improve the lives of everyone affected by the condition. As a member-led association, it is led by and represent people with epilepsy, their friends, families and healthcare professionals.

GIFT

24 Martingale Road
Billericay
Essex CM11 1SG
Tel: 01277 654228
Email: enquiries@giftltd.co.uk
Website: www.giftltd.co.uk

GIFT aims to offer a value-for-money education consultancy of quality, which meets the needs of gifted and talented children and those working to support them in the excitement and challenge of achieving their full potential as human beings. Residential and non-residential courses are organised for exceptionally able children aged five to 18 throughout the year (see our website). INSET courses for schools on provision, identification and school policy are provided with a special emphasis on workshops for practical activities.

Haringey Association for Independent Living (HAIL)

Tottenham Town Hall
Town Hall Approach Road
Tottenham
London N15 4RY
Tel: 020 8275 6550
Fax: 020 8275 6559
Email: admin@hailltd.org
Website: www.hailltd.org

Haringey Association for Independent Living is a support service for adults with learning difficulties moving towards independent living. You can follow them on Twitter.

Headway

Bradbury House
190 Bagnall Road
Old Basford
Nottingham NG6 8SF
Tel: 0115 924 0800
Helpline: 0808 800 2244
Fax: 0115 958 4446
Email: enquiries@headway.org.uk
Website: www.headway.org.uk
Twitter: @HeadwayUK

Registered charity no.1025852 supporting people with brain injuries and their carers.

Helen Arkell Dyslexia Centre

Arkell Lane
Frensham
Farnham
Surrey GU10 3BL
Tel: 01252 792400
Twitter: @ArkellDyslexia
Email: enquiries@arkellcentre.org.uk
Website: www.arkellcentre.org.uk

A registered charity (no. 1064646) providing comprehensive help and care for children with specific learning difficulties, including assessment, specialist tuition, speech and language therapy, summer schools and short courses. Initial consultations can be arranged in order to give advice on options for support. Professional teacher-training programmes and schools' support. Financial help available in cases of need.

Huntington's Disease Association

Head Office
Suite 24
Liverpool Science Park
Innovation Centre 1
131 Mount Pleasant
Liverpool L3 5TF
Tel: 0151 331 5444
Fax: 0151 331 5441
Email: info@hda.org.uk
Website: www.hda.org.uk
Twitter: @HDA_tweeting

Registered charity (no. 296453) offering support to people affected by Huntington's Disease (HD); which is sometimes referred to as Huntington's Chorea. Has a Facebook page.

Independent Panel for Special Education Advice (IPSEA)

Hunters Court
Debden Road
Saffron Walden CB11 4AA
Tel: 01799 582030
Adviceline: 0800 018 4016
Twitter: @IPSEAcharity
Email: info@ipsea.org.uk
Website: www.ipsea.org.uk

IPSEA offers free and independent advice and support to parents of children with special educational needs including: free advice on LAs' legal duties towards children with free accompanied visits where necessary, free support and possible representation for those parents appealing to the Special Educational Needs Tribunal, free second opinions on a child's needs and the provision required to meet those needs. Registered charity no. 327691.

Institute for Neuro-Physiological Psychology (INPP)

1 Stanley Street
Chester
Cheshire CH1 2LR
Tel: 01244 311414
Fax: 01244 311414
Website: www.inpp.org.uk

Established in 1975 to research into the effect central nervous system (CNS) dysfunctions have on children with learning difficulties, to develop appropriate CNS remedial and rehabilitation programmes, and to correct underlying physical dysfunctions in dyslexia, dyspraxia and attention deficit disorder (ADD).

Ivemark Syndrome Association

18 French Road
Poole
Dorset BH17 7HB
Tel: 01202 699824

Support group for families with children affected by Ivemark Syndrome (also know as right atrial isomerism).

Jeans for Genes

199 Victoria Street
London SW1E 5NE
Tel: 0800 980 4800
Twitter: @JeansforGenes
Email: hello@jeanforgenes.com
Website: www.jeansforgenes.com

The first Friday of every October is Jeans for Genes Day. Their aim is to raise money to fund research into genetic disorders and their target figure is £3million each year. Registered charity no.1062206.

KIDS

49 Mecklenburgh Square
London
WC1N 2NY
Tel: 020 7520 0405
Website: www.kids.org.uk

KIDS was established in 1970 to help disabled children in their development and communication skills. Registered charity no. 275936. Has a Facebook page and you can follow them on Twitter.

Leonard Cheshire Disability England

66 South Lambeth Road
London SW8 1RL
Tel: 020 3242 0200
Fax: 020 3242 0250
Email: info@lcdisability.org
Website: www.lcdisability.org
Twitter: @LeonardCheshire

Leonard Cheshire – the UK's largest voluntary-sector provider of support services for disabled people. They also support disabled people in 52 countries around the world. Registered charity nos. 218186 and SCO05117.

Leonard Cheshire Disability Northern Ireland

Unit 5, Boucher Plaza
Boucher Road
Belfast BT12 6HR
Tel: 028 9024 6247
Fax: 028 9024 6395
Email: northernirelandoffice@lcdisability.org

See main entry – Leonard Cheshire Disability England.

Leonard Cheshire Disability Scotland

Murrayburgh House
17 Corstorphine Road
Edinburgh EH12 6DD
Tel: 0131 346 9040
Fax: 0131 346 9050
Email: scotlandoffice@lcdisability.org

See main entry – Leonard Cheshire Disability England.

Leonard Cheshire Disability Wales

Centre for Business
Office 3
12 Devon Place
Newport
Gwent NP20 4NN
Tel: 01633 263807

See main entry – Leonard Cheshire Disability England.

Leukaemia Care UK

1 Birch Court
Blackpole East
Worcester WR3 8SG
Tel: 01905 755977 Careline: 08088 010 444
Fax: 01905 755 166
Email: care@leukaemiacare.org.uk
Website: www.leukaemiacare.org.uk
Twitter: @LeukaemiaCareUK

Registered charity (nos. 259483, SCO39207) that exists to provide care and support to anyone affected by leukaemia.

Leukaemia Care Scotland

Regus Management
Maxim 1, Maxim Office Park
2 Parklands Way, Eurocentral
Motherwell ML1 4WR
Tel: 01698 209073
Email: scotland@leukaemiacare.org.uk

See main entry above.

Listening Books

12 Lant Street
London SE1 1QH
Tel: 020 7407 9417
Fax: 020 7403 1377
Email: info@listening-books.org.uk
Website: www.listening-books.org.uk
Twitter: @ListeningBooks

Registered charity (no. 264221) that provides a postal and internet based audio library service to anyone who is unable to read in the usual way due to an illness, disability or learning difficulty such as dyslexia.

Has a range of educational audio material to support all aspects of the National Curriculum, as well as thousands of general fiction and non-fiction titles for all ages. There is no limit to the number of titles you may borrow during the year.

Manx Dyslexia Asociation

Coan Aalin
Greeba Bridge
Greba
Isle of Man IM4 3LD
Tel: 07624 315724
Email: manxdyslexia@gmail.com
Website: www.manxdyslexia.org

Charity (no. IM706) founded in 1993 to help raise the awareness of dyslexia on the Isle of Man.

MENCAP England

123 Golden Lane
London EC1Y 0RT
Tel: 020 7454 0454
Helpline: 0808 808 1111
Fax: 020 7608 3254
Email: information@mencap.org.uk
Website: www.mencap.org.uk
Twitter: @mencap_charity

The Royal MENCAP Society is a registered charity (nos. 222377, SCO41079) that offers services to adults and children with learning disabilities. We offer help and advice in benefits, housing and employment via our helpline.

Helplines are open from Monday to Friday 9.30am-4.30pm; Wednesday – subject to change: (open am-closed pm). Language line is also used. Our office is open Monday-Friday 9-5pm.

We also offer help and advice to anyone who has any other issues or we can signpost them in the right direction. We can also provide information and support for leisure, recreational services (Gateway Clubs) residential services and holidays.

MENCAP Northern Ireland

Segal House
4 Annandale Avenue
Belfast BT7 3JH
Tel: 028 9069 1351
Email: helpline.ni@mencap.org.uk

See main entry – MENCAP England.

MENCAP Cymru

31 Lambourne Crescent
Cardiff Business Park
Llanishen, Cardiff CF14 5GF
Helpline: 02920 747588
Email: helpline.wales@mencap.org.uk

See main entry – MENCAP England.

MENSA

British Mensa Ltd
St John's House
St John's Square
Wolverhampton WV2 4AH
Tel: 01902 772771
Fax: 01902 392500
Email: enquiries@mensa.org.uk
Website: www.mensa.org.uk
Twitter: @BritishMensa

MENSA aims to bring about awareness that giftedness in a child is frequently a specific learning difficulty and should be recognised and treated as such, train teachers to recognise giftedness in a child, train teachers to teach gifted children, establish mutually beneficial relationships with other organisations having similar aims to our own and to devise and implement strategies aimed, at ministerial and senior civil servant levels, at bringing about recognition of the importance of catering for the needs of gifted children.

Mind, the National Association for Mental Health

15-19 Broadway
Stratford
London E15 4BQ
Tel: 020 8519 2122
Fax: 020 8522 1725
Email: contact@mind.org.uk
Website: www.mind.org.uk
Twitter: @MindCharity

Mind (the National Association for Mental Health) is the leading mental health charity (no. 219830) in England and Wales. Mind works for a better life for everyone with experience of mental or emotional stress. It does this by: advancing the views, needs and ambitions of people experiencing mental distress; promoting inclusion and challenging discrimination; influencing policy through effective campaigning and education; providing quality services that meet the expressed needs of people experiencing mental distress and which reflect the requirements of a diverse community; achieving equal legal and civil rights through campaigning and education.

With over 60 years of experience, Mind is a major national network consisting of over 200 local Mind associations, which cover most major towns and rural areas in England and Wales. These are separately registered charities operating under the Mind brand. The Mind network is the largest charitable provider of mental health services in the community. The work of the local associations is strengthened and supported by staff and activities through its many offices in England and Wales. This ensures that, as a national charity, Mind keeps a distinct local perspective to their work.

Mind believes in the individual and equipping them to make informed choices about options open to them. Mind's mental health telephone information service (Mindinfoline) deals with thousands of calls each year. We offer a vital lifeline to people in distress, their relatives and carers, as well as providing mental health information to members of the public, professionals and students.

Mind Cymru

3rd Floor, Quebec House
Castlebridge
5-19 Cowbridge Road East
Cardiff CF11 9AB
Tel: 029 2039 5123
Fax: 029 2034 6585
Email: contactwales@mind.org.uk

See main entry above.

Motability

Warwick House
Roydon Road
Harlow
Essex CM19 5PX
Tel: 0300 4564566 Minicom/textphone: 01279 632213 Fax: 01279 632000
Website: www.motability.co.uk

Registered charity no. 299745. Motability helps disabled people to use their mobility allowance to obtain new transport.

MS Society

MS National Centre
372 Edgware Road
London NW2 6ND
Tel: 020 8438 0700
Fax: 020 8438 0701
Website: www.mssociety.org.uk
Twitter: @MSSocietyUK

Multiple Sclerosis Society. Registered charity nos. 207495 and SCO16433.

MS Society Cymru

Temple Court
Cathedral Road
Cardiff CF11 9HA
Tel: 029 2078 6676
Fax: 029 2078 6677

See main entry above.

MS Society Northern Ireland

The Resource Centre
34 Annadale Avenue
Belfast BT7 3JJ
Tel: 02890 802 802

See main entry above.

MS Society Scotland

National Office, Ratho Park
88 Glasgow Road
Ratho Station
Newbridge EH28 8PP
Tel: 0131 335 4050
Fax: 0131 335 4051

See main entry above.

Muscular Dystrophy Campaign

61 Southwark Street
London SE1 0HL
Tel: 020 7803 4800
Email: info@muscular-dystrophy.org
Website: www.muscular-dystrophy.org
Twitter: @TargetMD

Registered charity (nos. 205395, SCO39445). Provides information and advice for families affected by muscular dystrophy and other neuromuscular conditions.

NAS – The National Autistic Society – England

393 City Road
London EC1V 1NG
Tel: 020 7833 2299
Autism Helpline: 0800 800 4104 (M-F 10-4)
Fax: 020 7833 9666
Email: nas@nas.org.uk
Website: www.autism.org.uk

The National Autistic Society is the UK's leading charity (nos. 269425, SCO39427) for people affected by autism. For more than 50 years we have worked to support children and young people with autism (including Asperger syndrome) to reach their goals. A well-rounded education, tailored to the needs of the individual, can help people to reach their full potential.

NAS Cymru

6/7 Village Way,
Greenmeadow Springs Business Park
Tongwynlais
Cardiff CF15 7NE
Tel: 02920 629 312
Fax: 02920 629 317
Email: wales@nas.org.uk

See main entry NAS – England.

NAS Northern Ireland

59 Malone Road
Belfast BT9 6SA
Tel: 02890 687 066
Fax: 02890 688 518
Email: northern.ireland@nas.org.uk

See main entry NAS – England.

NAS Scotland

Central Chambers
1st Floor
109 Hope Street
Glasgow G2 6LL
Tel: 0141 221 8090
Fax: 0141 221 8118
Email: scotland@nas.org.uk

See main entry NAS – England.

nasen

4/5 Amber Business Village
Amber Close
Amington
Tamworth
Staffordshire B77 4RP
Tel: 01827 311500
Fax: 01827 313005
Email: welcome@nasen.org.uk
Website: www.nasen.org.uk

nasen promotes the interests of children and young people with exceptional learning needs and influences the quality of provision through strong and cohesive policies and strategies for parents and professionals.

Membership offers a number of journals, professional development and publications at a reduced cost, and provides a forum for members to share concerns and disseminate expertise and knowledge.

National Association for Able Children in Education (NAACE)

NACE National Office
The Core Business Centre
Milton Hill
Abingdon
Oxfordshire OX13 6AB
Tel: 01235 828280
Fax: 01235 828281
Email: info@nace.co.uk
Website: www.nace.co.uk

NAACE works with teachers to support able children in schools. The organisation also provides, publications, journals, booklets, courses and conferences. Registered charity no. 327230.

National Association of Independent Schools and Non-Maintained Special Schools (NASS)

PO Box 705
York YO30 6WW
Tel: 01904 624446
Email: krippon@nasschools.org.uk
Website: www.nasschools.org.uk

NASS is a voluntary organisation that represents the interests of those special schools outside the maintained sector of the education system.

Our commitment is to achieve excellence and to attain the highest professional standards in working with unique children and young people who have physical, sensory and intellectual difficulties. We exist to promote, develop and maintain the highest professional standards for non-maintained and independent special schools. We offer free information and advice on our member schools to families and professionals. Registered charity no. 1083632.

National Federation of the Blind of the UK

Sir John Wilson House
215 Kirkgate
Wakefield
Yorkshire WF1 1JG
Tel: 01924 291313
Fax: 01924 200244
Email: nfbuk@nfbuk.org
Website: www.nfbuk.org

Registered charity no. 236629 set up to better the understanding between blind and sighted people.

Epilepsy Society

Chesham Lane
Chalfont St Peter
Gerrards Cross,
Buckinghamshire SL9 0RJ
Tel: 01494 601300
Helpline 01494 601400 (Mon-Fri 10am-4pm)
Fax: 01494 871927
Website: www.epilepsysociety.org.uk
Twitter: @EpilepsySociety

The Epilepsy Society provides information and support to those affected by epilepsy. Registered charity no. 206186.

NDCS – The National Deaf Children's Society

Head Office
15 Dufferin Street
London EC1Y 8UR
Tel: 020 7490 8656
Minicom: 020 7490 8656
Fax: 020 7251 5020
Email: ndcs@ndcs.org.uk
Website: www.ndcs.org.uk
Twitter: @NDCS_UK

Leading provider of information, advice, advocacy and support for deaf children, their parents and professionals on all aspects of childhood deafness. This includes advice and information on education, including further and higher education, and support at Special Educational Needs Tribunals.

NDCS also provides advice on equipment and technology for deaf children at home and at school. Registered charity nos. 1016532 and SCO40779.

NDCS Cmyru

4 Cathedral Road
Cardiff CF11 9LJ
Tel: 029 2037 3474
Minicom: 029 2023 2739
Fax: 029 2037 9800
Email: ndcswales@ndcs.org.uk

See main entry above.

NDCS Northern Ireland

38-42 Hill Street
Belfast BT1 2LB
Tel: 028 9031 3170 Minicom: 028 9027 8177
Fax: 028 9027 8205
Email: nioffice@ndcs.org.uk

See main entry above.

NDCS Scotland

Second Floor, Empire House
131 West Nile Street
Glasgow G1 2RX
Tel: 0141 354 7850 Textphone: 0141 332 6133
Fax: 0141 331 2780
Email: ndcs.scotland@ndcs.org.uk

See main entry above.

Network 81

10 Boleyn Way
West Clacton
Essex CO15 2NJ
Tel: 0845 077 4056 (Admin)
Helpline: 0845 077 4055
Fax: 0845 077 4057
Email: Network81@hotmail.co.uk
Website: www.network81.org

Network 81 offers practical help and support to parents throughout all stages of assessment and statementing as outlined in the Education Act 1996. Their national helpline offers an individual service to parents linked to a national network of local contacts.

NIACE

Chetwynd House
21 DeMontfort Street
Leicester LE1 7GE
Tel: 0116 204 4200
Minicom: 0116 255 6049
Fax: 0116 204 6988
Email: enquiries@niace.org.uk
Website: www.niace.org.uk

Works across sectors and age groups to raise national standards and encourage adults in achieving literacy, numeracy and language skills. Registered charity no. 1002775. You can follow them on Twitter.

NOFAS – UK

165 Beaufort Park
London NW11 6DA
Tel: 0208 458 5951
Email: info@nofas-uk.org
Website: www.nofas-uk.org

Offers advice, support and information about Foetal Alcohol Spectrum Disorder. Registered charity no. 1101935.

Cambian Group

Helpline: 0800 138 1418
Email: education@cambiangroup.com
Website: www.cambiangroup.com

Cambian Group is one of the UK's leading providers of specialist services in education, care, mental health and learning disabilities. Works with 140 public authorities.

Paget Gorman Signed Speech

PGS Administrative Secretary
43 Westover Road
Fleet GU51 3DB
Tel: 01252 621 183
Website: www.pagetgorman.org

Advice and information for parents and professionals concerned with speech and language-impaired children.

Parents for Inclusion (PI)

336 Brixton Road
London SW9 7AA
Tel: 020 7738 3888
Helpline: 0800 652 3145
Email: info@parentsforinclusion.org
Website: www.parentsforinclusion.org

A network of parents of disabled children and children with special needs. Registered charity no.1070675.

Physically Disabled and Able Bodied (PHAB Ltd)

Summit House
50 Wandle Road
Croydon
CR0 1DF
Tel: 020 8667 9443
Fax: 020 8681 1399
Email: info@phab.org.uk
Website: www.phab.org.uk

Registered charity (no. 283931) that works to promote and encourage people with and without physical disabilities to work together to achieve inclusion for all in the wider community.

Potential Plus UK

Suite 1-2
Challenge House
Sherwood Drive
Bletchley
Milton Keynes MK3 6DP
Tel: 01908 646433
Fax: 0870 770 3219
Email: amazingchildren@nagcbritain.org.uk
Website: www.potentialplusuk.org

Registered charity (no. 313182). It is a mutually supportive self-help organisation offering services both through local branches and nationally. Membership is open to individuals, families, education professionals and schools.

Royal National Institute of Blind People (RNIB)

105 Judd Street
London WC1H 9NE
Tel: 020 7388 1266
Fax: 020 7388 2034
Helpline: 0303 123 9999
Twitter: @RNIB
Email: helpline@rnib.org.uk
Website: www.rnib.org.uk

Every day another 100 people start to lose their sight – there are around two million people in the UK with sight problems, blindness being one of the major causes of disability in the UK. RNIB's pioneering work helps anyone with a sight problem – not just with Braille, Talking Books and computer training, but with imaginative and practical solutions to everyday challenges. They fight for equal rights for people with sight problems; fund pioneering research into preventing and treating eye disease; and campaign to change society's attitudes, actions and assumptions so that people with sight problems can enjoy the same rights, freedoms and responsibilties as fully-sighted people.

RNIB promotes eye health by running public health awareness campaigns and their schools and colleges help educate hundreds of children and students with sight problems. They run campaigns on a wide variety of issues, from community care to the design of banknotes and coins, from legislation about broadcasting to accessible information. They lobby national and local government, hold public meetings, organise letter-writing campaigns and work in coalitions to achieve their aims. Registered charity no. 226227.

Scope

6 Market Road
London N7 9PW
Tel: 0808 800 3333 (Scope response)
Switchboard: 020 7619 7100
Text SCOPE plus message to 80039
Twitter: @Scope
Email: response@scope.org.uk
Website: www.scope.org.uk

Scope is a national disability organisation whose focus is people with cerebral palsy. We provide a range of support, information and campaigning services both locally and nationally in addition to providing opportunities in early years, education, employment and daily living. For more information about cerebral palsy and Scope services, contact Scope Response, which provides free information, advice and initial counselling. Open 9am-7pm weekdays and 10am-2pm Saturdays. Registered charity no. 208231.

Scope Cymru

4 Ty Nant Court
Morganstown
Cardiff CF15 8LW
Tel: 029 20 815 450
Email: response@scope.org.uk

See main entry above.

Scottish Society for Autism

Hilton House,
Alloa Business Park
Whins Road
Alloa FK10 3SA
Tel: 01259 720044
Twitter: @scottishautism
Email: autism@scottishautism.org
Website: www.scottishautism.org

The Scottish Society for Autism is a registered charity (no. SC009068) established in 1968. They aim to work with individuals of all ages with autism spectrum disorder (ASD), their families and carers, to provide and promote exemplary services and training in education, care, support and life opportunities.

Sense – The National Deafblind Charity

101 Pentonville Road
London N1 9LG
Tel/Textphone: 0845 127 0066
Fax: 0845 127 0061
Email: info@sense.org.uk
Website: www.sense.org.uk
Twitter: @Sensetweets

Sense is the leading national charity that supports and campaigns for children and adults who are deafblind. We provide expert advice and information as well as specialist services to deafblind people, their families, carers and the professionals who work with them. We also support people who have sensory impairments with additional disabilities.

Our services include on-going support for deafblind people and families. These range from day services where deafblind people have the opportunity to learn new skills and Sense-run houses in the community – where people are supported to live as independently as possible. We also provide leading specialist advice, for example on education options and assistive technology. Registered charity no. 289868.

Shine

42 Park Road
Peterborough PE1 2UQ
Tel: 01733 421309
Fax: 01733 555985
Email: info@shinecharity.org.uk
Website: www.shinecharity.org.uk
Twitter: @SHINEUKCharity

The new name for the Association for Spina Bifida and Hydrocephalus (ASBAH). Europe's largest organisation dedicated to supporting individuals and families as they face the challenges arising from spina bifida and hydrocephalus.

Advisers are available to explain the problems associated with spina bifida and or hydrocephalus and may be able to arrange visits to schools and colleges to discuss difficulties. Registered charity no. 249338. Has a Facebook page and you can follow them on Twitter.

Signature

Mersey House
Mandale Business Park
Belmont
Country Durham DH1 1TH
Tel: 0191 383 1155 Text: 07974 121594
Fax: 0191 3837914
Email: enquiries@signature.org.uk
Website: www.signature.org.uk
Twitter: @SignatureDeaf

Association promoting communication with deaf and deafblind people.

SNAP-CYMRU

Head Office
10 Coopers Yard
Curran Road
Cardiff CF10 5NB
Tel: 029 2038 4868
Helpline: 0845 120 3730
Fax: 029 2034 8998
Email: headoffice@snapcymru.org
Website: www.snapcymru.org
Twitter: @SNAPCymru

An all-Wales service for children and families, which provides: accurate information and impartial advice and support for parents, carers, and young people in relation to special educational needs and disability; disagreement resolution service; casework service; independent parental support service; advocacy for children and young people in receipt of services; training for parents, carers, young people; training for professionals in relation to SEN/disability. Has a Facebook page.

Spinal Injuries Association

SIA House
2 Trueman Place
Oldbrook
Milton Keynes MK6 2HH
Tel: 0845 678 6633
Adviceline: 0800 980 0501
Fax: 0845 070 6911
Email: sia@spinal.co.uk
Website: www.spinal.co.uk
Twitter: @spinalinjuries

Registered charity no.1054097 set up to provide services for people with spinal cord injuries.

The ACE Centre

Hollinwood Business Centre,
Albert Street
Hollinwood
Oldham OL8 3QL
Tel: 0161 358 0151
Fax: 0161 358 6152
Email: enquiries@ace-north.org.uk
Website: www.ace-north.org.uk
Twitter: @ACECentre

The centre offers independent advice and information, assessments and training in the use of assistive technology for individuals with physical and communication disabilities across the north of England. Registered charity no. 1089313.

The Alliance for Inclusive Education

336 Brixton Road
London SW9 7AA
Tel: 020 7737 6030
Email: info@allfie.org.uk
Website: www.allfie.org.uk

National network campaigning for the rights of disabled children in education.

The Association of National Specialist Colleges (NATSPEC)

c/o Derwen College
Oswestry
Shropshire SY11 3JA
Tel: 0117 923 2830
Email: chiefexecutive@natspec.org.uk
Website: www.natspec.org.uk

NATSPEC represents independent specialist colleges across England, Wales and Northern Ireland, providing for over 3000 learners with learning difficulties and/or disabilities, often with complex or additional needs. Most colleges offer residential provision. Member colleges support learners in their transition to adult life, participation in the community and where possible, employment. NATSPEC acts as a national voice for its member colleges and works in partnership with a range of other providers, agencies and organisations. You can contact colleges directly, via the website, or through your connexions/careers service.

The Brittle Bone Society

Grant-Paterson House
30 Guthrie Street
Dundee DD1 5BS
Tel: 01382 204446
Fax: 01382 206771
Email: contact@brittlebone.org
Website: www.brittlebone.org
Twitter: @BrittleBoneUK

A UK registered charity (nos. 272100, SCO10951) providing support for people affected by Osteogenesis Imperfecta (OI).

The Disability Law Service

39-45 Cavell Street
London E1 2BP
Tel: 020 7791 9800
Minicom: 020 7791 9801
Fax: 020 7791 9802
Email: advice@dls.org.uk
Website: www.dls.org.uk
Twitter: @DLS_law

The Disability Law Service (DLS) offers free, confidential legal advice to disabled people in the following areas: benefits; children; community care; consumer/contract; discrimination; further and higher education; and employment. In some cases they are able to offer legal representation. The Disability Law Service is made up of solicitors, advisers and trained volunteers who provide up-to-date, informed legal advice for disabled people, their families, enablers and carers. The advice they give is free, and the service offers complete confidentiality. They aim to offer a service that enables disabled people to access relevant information and clarify their rights. Registered charity no. 280805.

The Fragile X Society

Rood End House
6 Stortford Road
Great Dunmow,
Essex CM6 1DA
Tel: 01371 875 100
Fax: 01371 859 915
Email: info@fragilex.org.uk
Website: www.fragilex.org.uk

The aims of The Fragile X Society are to provide support and comprehensive information to families whose children and adult relatives have fragile X syndrome, to raise awareness of fragile X and to encourage research. There is a link network of family contacts, national helplines for statementing, benefits and family support for epilepsy. They publish information booklets, leaflets, a publications list, video and three newsletters a year. There are also national conferences four times a year. Family membership (UK) is free. Welcomes associate membership from interested professionals. Registered charity no. 1127861.

The Guide Dogs for the Blind Association

Burghfield Common
Reading
Berkshire RG7 3YG
Tel: 0118 983 5555
Fax: 0118 983 5433
Email: guidedogs@guidedogs.org.uk
Website: www.guidedogs.org.uk
Twitter: @guidedogs

The Guide Dogs for the Blind Association provides guide dogs, mobility and other rehabilitation services to blind and partially sighted people. Registered charity nos. 209617 and SCO38979.

The Haemophilia Society

First Floor
Petersham House
57a Hatton Garden
London EC1N 8JG
Tel: 020 7381 1020
Fax: 020 7405 4824
Helpline: 0800 018 6068
Email: info@haemophilia.org.uk
Website: www.haemophilia.org.uk
Twitter: @HaemoSocUK

Founded in 1950, this registered charity (nos. 288260, SCO39732) has over 4000 members and a network throughout the UK providing information, advice and support services to sufferers of haemophilia, von Willebrand's and related bleeding disorders. You can follow them on Twitter.

The Hyperactive Children's Support Group (HACSG)

71 Whyke Lane
Chichester
Sussex PO19 7PD
Tel: 01243 539966
Email: hacsg@hacsg.org.uk
Website: www.hacsg.org.uk

Support group. Will send information pack if you send a large SAE. Registered charity no. 277643.

The London Centre for Children with Cerebral Palsy

54 Muswell Hill
London N10 3ST
Tel: 020 8444 7242
Fax: 020 8444 7241
Email: info@cplondon.org.uk
Website: www.cplondon.org.uk
Twitter: @lcccp

Provides education for young children with cerebral palsy using the system of Conductive Education. Registered charity no. 1124524.

The Makaton Charity

Westmead House
Farnborough
Hampshire GU14 7LP
Tel: 01276 606760
Fax: 01276 36725
Email: info@makaton.org
Website: www.makaton.org
Twitter: @MakatonCharity

Makaton vocabulary is a language programme using speech, signs and symbols to provide basic means of communication and encourage language and literacy skills to develop in children and adults with communication and learning difficulties. Training workshops, courses and a variety of resource materials are available and there is a family support helpline too. Registered charity no. 1119819.

The Planned Environment Therapy Trust (PETT)

Archive and Study Centre
Church Lane
Toddington
Cheltenham
Gloucestershire GL54 5DQ
Tel: 01242 620125
Fax: 01242 620125
Website: www.pettrust.org.uk
Twitter: @pettconnect

Founded to promote effective treatment for those with emotional and psychological disorders. Registered charity no. 248633.

The Social, Emotional and Behavioural Difficulties Association (SEBDA)

c/o Goldwyn School
Godinton Lane
Great Chart
Ashford
Kent TN23 3BT
Tel: 01233 622958
Twitter: @SebdaOrg
Email: admin@sebda.org
Website: www.sebda.org

SEBDA exists to campaign on behalf of and to provide information, training and a support service to professionals who work with children and young people with social, emotional and behavioural difficulties. Registered charity no. 258730.

Please note: they do not provide any services to parents.

The Stroke Association

Stroke House
240 City Road
London EC1V 2PR
Tel: 020 7566 0300
Textphone: 020 7251 9096
Fax: 020 7490 2686
Email: info@stroke.org.uk
Website: www.stroke.org.uk
Twitter: @thestrokeassoc

More than 250,000 people in the UK live with the disabilities caused by a stroke. The association's website provides information and advice for free. Registered charity nos. 211015, SCO37789, IOM945, NP0369 (Jersey).

The Thalidomide Society

Tel: 020 7252 0972
Email: info@thalsoc.demon.co.uk
Website: www.thalidomidesociety.co.uk

Registered charity no. 231708 created in 1962. Support group for impaired adults whose disabilities are a result of the drug Thalidomide.

Together for Short Lives

4th Floor
Bridge House
48-52 Baldwin Street
Bristol BS1 1QB
Tel: 0117 989 7820
Helpline: 0808 8088 100
Email: info@togetherforshortlives.org
Website: www.togetherforshortlives.org.uk
Twitter: @Tog4ShortLives

The new name for the Association for Children's Palliative Care (ACT). Helps families with children who have life-limiting or life threatening conditions.

Tourette's Action

Kings Court
91-93 High Street
Camberley
Surrey GU15 3RN
Tel: 01276 482903
Email: admin@tourettes-action.org.uk
Website: www.tourettes-action.org.uk
Twitter: @tourettesaction

Registered charity no. 1003317 offering support and information about Tourette's.

U Can Do IT

1 Taylors Yard
67 Alderbrook Road
London SW12 8AD
Tel: 020 8673 3300
Fax: 020 8675 9571
Website: www.ucandoit.org.uk

U CAN DO IT is a London charity (no. 1070571) providing blind, deaf and physically disabled children and adults with the skills they need to utilise the internet. Tuition is one to one at home, by highly skilled police-vetted tutors (CRB level 2), with costs starting from £1 per lesson.

WheelPower – British Wheelchair Sport

Stoke Mandeville Stadium
Guttman Road
Stoke Mandeville
Buckinghamshire HP21 9PP
Tel: 01296 395995
Fax: 01296 424171
Email: info@wheelpower.org.uk
Website: www.wheelpower.org.uk
Twitter: @wheelpower

The British Wheelchair Sports Foundation is the national organisation for wheelchair sport in the UK and exists to provide, promote and develop opportunities for men, women and children with disabilities to participate in recreational and competitive wheelchair sport. Registered charity no. 265498.

Young Minds

Suite 11
Baden Place
Crosby Row
London SE1 1YW
Tel: 020 7089 5050
Fax: 020 7407 8887
Website: www.youngminds.org.uk
Email: ymenquiries@youngminds.org.uk
Twitter: @youngmindsuk

National charity (nos. 1016968, SCO39700) committed to improving the mental health of young people and children in the UK. Their website has advice, information and details of how you can help.

WEBSITES

www.abilitynet.org.uk

Ability Net is a charity (no. 1067673) that provides impartial, expert advice about computer technology for disabled people. You can follow them on Twitter.

www.abilityonline.net

Disability information and news and views online. Registered charity no. 1089117.

www.apparelyzed.com

Spinal cord injury peer support – has a forum with useful links.

www.ukdpc.net

United Kingdom's Disabled People's Council – a national umbrella organisation set up by disabled people to represent their interests at a national level. Registered charity no. 1067873.

www.cae.org.uk

Centre for Accessible Environments – a registered charity (no. 1050820), which is the leading authority on providing a built enviroment that is accessible for everyone, including disabled people.

www.choicesandrights.org.uk

CRDC – Choices and Rights Disability Coalition. Run for and by disabled people in the Kingston upon Hull and East Riding of Yorkshire area. Registered charity no. 1106462.

www.amyandfriends.org

Website set up to support those families affected by Cockayne Syndrome in the UK. Registered charity no. 1119746.

www.deafcouncil.org.uk

UK Council on Deafness. Has interesting list of member websites.

www.disabilitynow.org.uk

Disability Now – award winning online newspaper for everyone with an interest in disability.

www.focusondisability.org.uk

Focus on Disability – resource of general information regarding disability in the UK.

www.direct.gov.uk/disabledpeople

The UK government's web page for disabled people..

www.actionondisability.org.uk

Formerly HAFAD – Hammersmith and Fuham Action for Disability. Campaigning for rights of disabled people, the site is managed and controlled by disabled people.

www.heartnsoul.co.uk

Heart 'n' Soul Music Theatre – a leading disability arts group. Has a Facebook page.

www.mugsy.org

National Autistic Society – Surrey branch. Website has pages dedicated to all areas of the UK as well as international pages.

www.ncil.org.uk

National Centre for Independent Living. A resource on independent living and direct payments for disabled people and others working in the field. Registered charity no. 1113427.

www.qefd.org

Queen Elizabeth's Foundation – a national charity (no. 251051) supporting over 20,000 physically disabled people annually.

www.ssc.education.ed.ac.uk

Scottish Sensory Centre – for everyone who is involved in the education of children and young people with sensory impairment.

www.theark.org.uk

A registered charity (no. 1098204) set up to enhance the lives of people with multi-sensory impairment, learning difficulties and physical disabilities.

www.tuberous-sclerosis.org

Tuberous Sclerosis Association of Great Britain. Registered charity no. 1039549. Website provides information and support for people and families affected by TSC.

www.vitalise.org.uk

Vitalise (formerly The Winged Fellowship Trust) provides respite care for disabled children, adults and their carers. Registered charity no. 295072.

www.westminster.gov.uk/weldis

WELDIS – an online information resource of services in and around Westminster for older people, adults and children with disabilities and their carers.

www.youreable.com

Information, products and services for the disabled community including news, shopping, pen pals and discussion forums.

Maintained special schools and colleges

ENGLAND – BATH & NORTH EAST SOMERSET

Children's Services

Special Educational Needs Team, Lewis House, Manvers Street, Bath, BA1 1JG
Tel: 01225 394306 Fax: 01225 394251 Email: special_educationalneeds@bathnes.gov.uk Website: www.bathnes.gov.uk

BATH

Aspire Academy
Frome Road, Odd Down,
BATH BA2 5RF
Tel: 01225 832212
Head: Mr Colin Cattanach
Category: EBD (Coed 4-16)

Fosse Way School
Longfellow Road, Midsomer
Norton, BATH BA3 3AL
Tel: 01761 412198
Head: Mr Justin Philcox
Category: PH SLD SPLD ASD
MLD MSI CLD (Coed 3-19)

Three Ways School
180 Frome Road, Odd
Down, BATH BA2 5RF
Tel: 01225 838070
Head: Mrs Julie Dyer
Category: PH SLD SPLD ASD
MLD MSI CLD (Coed 2-19)

BEDFORD BOROUGH COUNCIL

Education Authority

SEND Team, 5th Floor, Borough Hall, Cauldwell Street, Bedford, MK42 9AP
Tel: 01234 267422 Email: statass@bedford.gov.uk Website: www.bedscc.gov.uk

BEDFORD

Grange School
Halsey Road, Kempston, BEDFORD,
Bedfordshire MK42 8AU
Tel: 01234 407100
Head: Mr I Davidson
Category: MLD with provision
for ASD (Coed 5-16)

Ridgeway Special School
Hill Rise, Kempston,
BEDFORD MK42 7EB
Tel: 01234 402402
Head: Mr G Allard
Category: PD (Coed 2-19)

**St Johns Special
School & College**
Austin Cannons, Kempston,
BEDFORD MK42 8AA
Tel: 01234 345565
Head: Mr R Babbage
Category: SLD PMLD (Coed 2-19)

CENTRAL BEDFORDSHIRE COUNCIL

Children & Young People Service

SEND Team, Priory House, Monks Walk, Chicksands Shefford, SG17 5TQ
Tel: 03003 008301 Email: send.feedback@centralbedfordshire.gov.uk Website: www.centralbedfordshire.gov.uk

BIGGLESWADE

Ivel Valley Primary School
The Baulk, BIGGLESWADE,
Bedfordshire SG18 0PT
Tel: 01767 601010
Head: Miss Julie Mudd
Category: SLD PMLD (Coed 3-10)

**Ivel Valley Secondary
School**
Hitchmead Road, BIGGLESWADE,
Bedfordshire SG18 0NL
Tel: 01767 601010
Head: Miss Julie Mudd
Category: SLD PMLD (Coed 11-19)

DUNSTABLE

**The Chiltern
Primary School**
Beech Road, DUNSTABLE,
Bedfordshire LU6 3LY
Tel: 01582 667106
Head: Mrs Shirley Crosbie
Category: SLD PMLD (Coed 3-10)

Weatherfield Academy
Brewers Hill Road, DUNSTABLE,
Bedfordshire LU6 1AF
Tel: 01582 605632
Head: Mr Joe Selmes
Category: MLD (7-18)

HOUGHTON REGIS

**The Chiltern
Secondary School**
Parkside Drive, HOUGHTON
REGIS, Bedfordshire LU5 5PX
Tel: 01582 667106
Head: Mrs Shirley Crosbie
Category: SLD PMLD (Coed 11-19)

LEIGHTON BUZZARD

Oak Bank School
Sandy Lane, LEIGHTON BUZZARD,
Bedfordshire LU7 3BE
Tel: 01525 374550
Head: Mr Peter Cohen
Category: BESD (Coed 9-16)

WEST BERKSHIRE
Council

SEN Team, West Street House, West Street, Newbury, Berkshire, RG14 1BZ
Tel: 01635 503100 Email: fis@westberks.gov.uk Website: www.westberks.gov.uk

NEWBURY

The Castle School
Love Lane, Donnington,
NEWBURY, Berkshire RG14 2JG
Tel: 01635 42976
Heads: Mr Jon Hewitt
Category: ASD SLD SPLD
GLD PH (Coed 2-19)

READING

Brookfields Special School
Sage Road, Tilehurst, READING,
Berkshire RG31 6SW
Tel: 01189 421382
Head: Mrs Jane Headland
Category: AUT MSI Complex Needs

BLACKBURN WITH DARWEN
Borough Council

Children's Services Department, 10 Duke Street, Blackburn, Lancashire, BB2 1DH
Tel: 01254 666605 Fax: 01254 666884 Email: childrensservices@blackburn.gov.uk Website: www.blackburn.gov.uk

BLACKBURN

Crosshill School
Haslingden Road, BLACKBURN,
Lancashire BB2 3HJ
Tel: 01254 667713
Head: Mr Ian Maddison
Category: MLD (Coed Day 11-16)

Newfield School
Old Bank Lane, Off Shadsworth
Road, BLACKBURN,
Lancashire BB1 2PW
Tel: 01254 588600
Head: Mr Geoff Fitzpatrick
Category: Complex
(Coed Day 2-19)

St. Thomas' Centre
Lambeth Street, BLACKBURN,
Lancashire BB1 1NA
Tel: 01254 680523
Head: Ms Joanne Siddle
Category: Pupil Referral
Unit (Coed Day 5-16)

DARWEN

Sunnyhurst Centre
Salisbury Road, DARWEN,
Lancashire BB3 1HZ
Tel: 01254 702317
Head: Mrs Shazia Sarwar
Category: Pupil Referral
Unit (Coed Day 5-11)

BLACKPOOL
Children and Young People's Department

Children's services, Progress House, Clifton Road, Blackpool, FY4 4US
Tel: 01253 476553 Email: sen@blackpool.gov.uk Website: www.blackpool.gov.uk

BLACKPOOL

Highfurlong School
Blackpool Old Road, BLACKPOOL,
Lancashire FY3 7LR
Tel: 01253 392188
Acting Head: Ms Rosie Sycamore
Category: PH

**Park Community
Academy**
158 Whitegate Drive, BLACKPOOL,
Lancashire FY3 9HF
Tel: 01253 764130
Head: Mr Keith Berry
Category: MLD CLD
SEBD (Coed 4-16)

Woodlands School
Whitegate Drive, BLACKPOOL,
Lancashire FY3 9HF
Tel: 01253 316722
Head: Mr Cole Andrew
Category: SLD PMLD
MSI (Coed 2-19)

BOURNEMOUTH

Children and Families Services

St Stephen's Road, Bournemouth, Dorset, BH2 6DY
Tel: 01202 451451 Email: cs@bournemouth.gov.uk Website: www.bournemouth.gov.uk

BOURNEMOUTH

Linwood School
Alma Road, BOURNEMOUTH,
Dorset BH9 1AJ
Tel: 01202 525107
Head: Mr S Brown
Category: ASD MLD SLD
PMLD (Coed 3-19)

Tregonwell Special Academy
Petersfield Road, BOURNEMOUTH,
Dorset BH7 6QP
Tel: 01202 424361
Associate Principal: Mr
Adam Coshan
Category: BESD (Coed 7-16)

BRACKNELL FOREST

Children, Young People and Learning

Time Square, Market Street, Bracknell, Berkshire, RG12 1JD
Tel: 01344 352000 Email: cypl@bracknell-forest.gov.uk Website: www.bracknell-forest.gov.uk

BRACKNELL

Kennel Lane School
Kennel Lane, BRACKNELL,
Berkshire RG42 2EX
Tel: 01344 483872
Head: Ms Andrea de Bunsen
Category: MLD SLD AUT PMLD

BRADFORD

Department of Children's Services

Future House, Bolling Road, Bradford, West Yorkshire, BD4 7EB

Tel: 01274 385500 Email: sen@ bradford.gov.uk

BRADFORD

Chellow Heights School
Thorn Lane, Bingley Road,
BRADFORD, West Yorkshire BD9 6AL
Tel: 01274 484242
Head: Ms S Haithwaite
Category: SLD PMLD ADS (Primary)

Delius School
Barkerend Road, BRADFORD,
West Yorkshire BD3 8QX
Tel: 01274 666472
Head: Ms S Joy
Category: SLD PMLD ASD (Primary)

Hazelbeck School
Wagon Lane, Bingley, BRADFORD,
West Yorkshire BD16 1EE
Tel: 01274 777107
Head: Ms S Pierce
Category: SLD PMLD
ASD (Secondary)

High Park School
Thorn lane, BRADFORD,
West Yorkshire BD9 6RY
Tel: 01274 696740
Head: Mrs A Andrew
Category: ASD (Primary
& Secondary)

Oastler's School
Flockton Road, BRADFORD,
West Yorkshire BD4 7RH
Tel: 01274 307456
Head: Mrs L Brown
Category: (Coed Day 11-19)

Southfield School
Haycliffe Lane, BRADFORD,
West Yorkshire BD5 9ET
Tel: 01274 779662
Head: Mr D Wall
Category: SLD PMLD
ASD (Secondary)

KEIGHLEY

Beechcliffe School
Green Head Road, KEIGHLEY,
West Yorkshire BD20 6ED
Tel: 01535 603041
Head: Mrs P Pearson
Category: SLD PMLD
ASD (Secondary)

Phoenix School
Braithwaite Avenue, KEIGHLEY,
West Yorkshire BD22 6HZ
Tel: 01535 607038
Head: Mrs R Stirland
Category: SLD PMLD ASD (Primary)

BRIGHTON & HOVE
City Council

SEN Team, Kings House, Grand Avenue, Hove, East Sussex, BN3 2LS
Tel: 01273 293552 Fax: 01273 293547 Email: sen.team@brighton-hove.gov.uk Website: www.brighton-hove.gov.uk

BRIGHTON

Cedar Centre
Lynchet Close, Hollingdean,
BRIGHTON, East Sussex BN1 7FP
Tel: 01273 558622
Head: Ms Chris Coleby
Category: MLD

Downs Park School
Foredown Road, Portslade,
BRIGHTON, East Sussex BN41 2FU
Tel: 01273 417448
Head: Ms Jackie Brooks
Category: ASD (Coed 5-16)

Downs View School
Warren Road, BRIGHTON,
East Sussex BN2 6BB
Tel: 01273 601680
Head: Mr Adrian Carver
Category: SLD ASD HI VIS (4-19)

Hillside Special School
Foredown Road, Portslade,
BRIGHTON, East Sussex BN41 2FU
Tel: 01273 416979
Head: Ms Rachel Burstow
Category: SLD

Homewood College
Queensdown School Road,
off Lewes Road, BRIGHTON,
East Sussex BN1 7LA
Tel: 01273 604472
Head: Mr Simon Charleton
Category: SEBD (Coed 5-16)

Patcham House School
Old London Road, Patcham,
BRIGHTON, East Sussex BN1 8XR
Tel: 01273 551028
Head: Ms Gayle Adam
Category: PD Del ASP
MLD SPLD (11-16)

BRISTOL
Children and Young People's Services

Special Educational Needs Team, PO Box 3176, Bristol, BS3 9FS
Tel: 01179 223700 Website: www.bristol.gov.uk

BRISTOL

Briarwood School
Briar Way, Fishponds,
BRISTOL BS16 4EA
Tel: 01173 532651
Head: Mr David Hussey
Category: SLD PMLD
AUT (Coed 3-19)

Bristol Gateway School
Long Cross, Lawrence
Weston, BRISTOL BS11 0QA
Tel: 01173 772275
Head: Ms Kaye Palmer-Green
Category: SEBD (Coed 10-16)

Claremont School
Henleaze Park, Westbury-
on-Trym, BRISTOL BS9 4LR
Tel: 01173 533622
Head: Ms Alison Ewins
Category: PD SLD PMLD (Coed 3-19)

**Elmfield School for
Deaf Children**
Greystoke Avenue, Westbury-
on-Trym, BRISTOL BS10 6AY
Tel: 01179 030366
(Text:07891 898188)
Acting Head: Ms Kate Murray
Category: D HI (Coed 5-16)

Kingsweston School
Napier Miles Road, Kingsweston,
BRISTOL BS11 0UT
Tel: 01179 030400
Head: Mr Neil Galloway
Category: MLD SLD AUT (Coed 3-19)

Knowle DGE
Leinster Avenue, Knowle,
BRISTOL BS4 1NN
Tel: 01173 532011
Head: Mr Peter Evans
Category: CLD SEBD MLD
Complex Needs (Coed 5-16)

New Fosseway School
Bridge Learning Campus, Teyfant
Road, Hartcliffe, BRISTOL BS13 0RG
Tel: 01179 030220
Head: Mrs Shan Wynne-Jones
Category: SLD PMLD
AUT (Coed 6-19)

Notton House School
28 Notton, Lacock,
BRISTOL SN15 2NF
Tel: 01249 730407
Head: Mr Jon Houston
Category: SEBD (Boys 9-16)

Woodstock School
Rectory Gardens, Henbury,
BRISTOL BS10 7AH
Tel: 01173 772175
Head: Hilary Harris
Category: SEBD (Primary)

BUCKINGHAMSHIRE

SEND Information, Advice & Support Service

County Hall, Walton Street, Aylesbury, Buckinghamshire, HP20 1UA
Tel: 01296 383754 Email: sendias@buckscc.gov.uk Website: www.buckscc.gov.uk

AMERSHAM

Stony Dean School
Orchard End Avenue, Off
Pineapple Road, AMERSHAM,
Buckinghamshire HP7 9JW
Tel: 01494 762538
Head: Mrs Pauline Dichler
Category: MLD Language &
Communication (Coed 11-18)

AYLESBURY

Booker Park School
Stoke Leys Close, AYLESBURY,
Buckinghamshire HP21 9ET
Tel: 01296 427221
Head: Ms Marianne Murphy
Category: MLD SLD
ASD (Coed 3-11)

**Chiltern Way Federation -
Wendover House School**
Church Lane, Wendover,
AYLESBURY, Buckinghamshire
HP22 6NL
Tel: 01296 622157
Head: Mr Nigel Morris
Category: BESD (Boys
Day/boarding 11-16)

Pebble Brook School
Churchill Avenue, AYLESBURY,
Buckinghamshire HP21 8LZ
Tel: 01296 415761/2
Head: Mr David Miller
Category: MLD SLC (Coed
Day/boarding 11-19)

**Stocklake Park
Community School**
Stocklake, AYLESBURY,
Buckinghamshire HP20 1DP
Tel: 01296 423507
Head: Ms Gill Mullis
Category: SLD (Coed 11-19)

BEACONSFIELD

Alfriston School
Penn Road, Knotty
Green, BEACONSFIELD,
Buckinghamshire HP9 2TS
Tel: 01494 673740
Head: Mrs Jinna Male
Category: MLD (Girls Day/
boarding 11-19)

CHESHAM

Heritage House School
Cameron Road, CHESHAM,
Buckinghamshire HP5 3BP
Tel: 01494 771445
Head: Mr James Boylan
Category: SLD (Coed 2-19)

GREAT MISSENDEN

**Chiltern Way Federation
- Prestwood Campus**
Nairdwood Lane, Prestwood,
GREAT MISSENDEN,
Buckinghamshire HP16 0QQ
Tel: 01494 863514
Head: Mr Ian McCaul
Category: BESD (Boys
Day/boarding 11-16)

HIGH WYCOMBE

Chiltern Gate School
Verney Avenue, HIGH WYCOMBE,
Buckinghamshire HP12 3NE
Tel: 01494 532621/2
Head: Mr Bradley Taylor
Category: MLD EBD ASD SLD
Communication difficulties
(Coed Day/boarding 4-11)

Maplewood School
Faulkner Way, Downley,
HIGH WYCOMBE,
Buckinghamshire HP13 5HB
Tel: 01494 525728
Head: Mr Bradley Taylor
Category: SLD (Coed 2-19)

Westfield School
Highfield Road, Bourne
End, HIGH WYCOMBE,
Buckinghamshire SL8 5BE
Tel: 01628 533125
Head: Mr Geoff Allen
Category: BESD (Coed 4-11)

WINSLOW

Furze Down School
Verney Road, WINSLOW,
Buckinghamshire MK18 3BL
Tel: 01296 713385
Head: Mrs Sue Collins
Category: A Range Of
Needs (Coed 5-19)

CAMBRIDGESHIRE

SEND Information, Advice & Support Service

Box No. CC1101, Castle Court, Cambridge, CB3 0AP
Tel: 01223 699214 Email: pps@cambridgeshire.gov.uk Website: www.cambridgeshire.gov.uk

CAMBRIDGE

Castle School
Courtney Way,
CAMBRIDGE CB4 2EE
Tel: 01223 442400
Head: Ms Carol McCarthy
Category: PMLD SLD
MLD (Coed 2-19)

Granta School
Cambridge Road, Linton,
CAMBRIDGE CB21 4NN
Tel: 01223 896890
Head: Mrs Lucie-Claire Calow
Category: ASD PMLD SLD
MLD (Coed 2-19)

Trinity School
8 Station Road, Foxton,
CAMBRIDGE, Cambridgeshire
CB22 6SA
Tel: 01223 712995
Head: Ms Diane Stygal

COTTENHAM

The Centre School
Cottenham Village College,
High Street, COTTENHAM,
Cambridgeshire CB24 8UA
Tel: 01954 288789
Head: Mrs Susan Raven
Category: (Coed 11-16)

ELY

Highfield Special School
Downham Road, ELY,
Cambridgeshire CB6 1BD
Tel: 01353 662085
Head: Mr Simon Bainbridge
Category: PMLD SLD MLD
ASD PD VIS (Coed 2-19)

The Harbour School
Station Road, Wilburton, ELY,
Cambridgeshire CB6 3RR
Tel: 01353 740229
Head: Ms Julie Potter
Category: ADD EBD MLD
SEBN (Coed 5-17)

EYNESBURY

Samuel Pepys School
Cromwell Road, EYNESBURY,
Cambridgeshire PE19 2EZ
Tel: 01480 375012
Head: Ms Joanne Hardwick
Category: ASD PMLD SLD
Complex needs (Coed 2-19)

HUNTINGDON

Spring Common School
American Lane, HUNTINGDON,
Cambridgeshire PE29 1TQ
Tel: 01480 377403
Head: Mrs Kim Taylor
Category: PMLD SLD MLD
ASD EBD (Coed 2-19)

WISBECH

Meadowgate School
Meadowgate Lane, WISBECH,
Cambridgeshire PE13 2JH
Tel: 01945 461836
Head: Mrs Jackie McPherson
Category: SLD MLD (Coed 2-19)

CHESHIRE EAST

Borough Council

Children, Families and Adults, Westfields, Middlewich Road, Sandbach, CW11 1HZ
Tel: 03001 235500 Email: senteam@cheshireeast.gov.uk Website: www.cheshireeast.gov.uk

CREWE

Adelaide School
Adelaide Street, CREWE,
Cheshire CW1 3DT
Tel: 01270 685151
Head: Mr L Willday
Category: BESD (Coed 11-16)

Springfield School
Crewe Green Road, CREWE,
Cheshire CW1 5HS
Tel: 01270 685446
Head: Mr M Swaine
Category: SLD (Coed 2-19)

KNUTSFORD

**St John's Wood
Community School**
Longridge, KNUTSFORD,
Cheshire WA16 8PA
Tel: 01625 383045
Executive Head: Mr L Willday
Category: BESD (Coed Day 11-16)

MACCLESFIELD

Park Lane School
Park Lane, MACCLESFIELD,
Cheshire SK11 8JR
Tel: 01625 384040
Head: Mrs Lorraine Warmer
Category: SLD (Coed Day 2-19)

CHESHIRE WEST & CHESTER

Council

SEN Assessment, Monitoring & Support Team, 4 Civic Way, Ellesmere Port, CH65 0BE
Tel: 03001 238123 Email: senteam@cheshirewestandchester.gov.uk Website: www.cheshirewestandchester.gov.uk

CHESTER

Dee Banks School
Dee Banks, CHESTER,
Cheshire CH3 5UX
Tel: 01244 981031
Head: Rev Raymond Elliott
Category: ASD SLD PMLD
(Coed Day 2-19)

**Dorin Park School &
Specialist SEN College**
Wealstone Lane, Upton,
CHESTER, Cheshire CH2 1HD
Tel: 01244 981191
Head: Ms Annie Hinchcliffe
Category: PD Complex
needs (Coed Day 2-19)

ELLESMERE PORT

**Capenhurst
Grange School**
Chester Road, Great
Sutton, ELLESMERE PORT,
Cheshire CH66 2NA
Tel: 01513 382141
Head: Mr Graham Stothard
Category: BESD (Coed 11-16)

Hinderton School
Capenhurst Lane,
Whitby, ELLESMERE PORT,
Cheshire CH65 7AQ
Tel: 01513 382200
Head: Mr Liam Dowling
Category: ASD with complex
learning needs (Coed Day 3-11)

NORTHWICH

Greenbank School
Greenbank Lane, Hartford,
NORTHWICH, Cheshire CW8 1LD
Tel: 01606 76521
Head: Mrs Chris Brennan
Category: ASD MLD
(Coed Day 6-18)

Rosebank School
Townfield Lane, Barnton,
NORTHWICH, Cheshire CW8 4QP
Tel: 01606 74975
Head: Mrs Judith McGuiness
Category: ASD with complex
learning needs (Coed Day 3-11)

The Russett School
Middlehurst Avenue, Weaverham,
NORTHWICH, Cheshire CW8 3BW
Tel: 01606 853005
Head: Mrs Catherine Lewis
Category: SLD PMLD MSI
(Coed Day 2-19)

WINSFORD

**Hebden Green
Community School**
Woodford Lane West,
WINSFORD, Cheshire CW7 4EJ
Tel: 01606 594221
Head: Mr Andrew Farren
Category: PD Complex needs
(Coed Day/Residential 2-19)

Oaklands School
Montgomery Way, WINSFORD,
Cheshire CW7 1NU
Tel: 01606 551048
Head: Mr Kevin Boyle
Category: HI MLD SP&LD
(Coed Day 11-16)

CORNWALL
Children, Schools and Families

County Hall, Treyew Road, Truro, Cornwall, TR1 3AY
Tel: 03001 234101 Email: children@cornwall.gov.uk Website: www.cornwall.gov.uk

PENZANCE

Nancealverne School
Madron Road, PENZANCE,
Cornwall TR20 8TP
Tel: 01736 365039
Head: Miss Sarah Moseley
Category: SLD PMLD (Coed 2-19)

REDRUTH

Curnow School
Drump Road, REDRUTH,
Cornwall TR15 1LU
Tel: 01209 215432
Head: Ms Gina Briggs
Category: PMLD SLD (Coed 2-19)

ST AUSTELL

Doubletrees School
St Blazey Gate, St Blazey, Par, ST
AUSTELL, Cornwall PL24 2DS
Tel: 01726 812757
Head: Ms Kim Robertson
Category: SLD PMLD (Coed 2-19)

TRURO

Pencalenick School
St Clement, TRURO, Cornwall TR1 1TE
Tel: 01872 520385
Head: Mr A Barnett
Category: SCLD (Coed 11-16)

CUMBRIA
Children's Services

The Courts, Lower Gaol Yard, Carlisle, Cumbria, CA3 8NA
Tel: 07824 541499 Email: localoffer@cumbria.gov.uk Website: www.cumbria.gov.uk

BARROW IN FURNESS

George Hastwell School
Moor Tarn Lane, Walney, BARROW
IN FURNESS, Cumbria LA14 3LW
Tel: 01229 475253
Head: Mr Bernard Gummett
Category: SLD PMLD

KENDAL

Sandgate School
Sandylands Road, KENDAL,
Cumbria LA9 6JG
Tel: 01539 792100
Head: Ms Joyce Fletcher
Category: SLD PMLD

WHITEHAVEN

Mayfield School
Moresby Road, Hensingham,
WHITEHAVEN, Cumbria CA28 8TU
Tel: 01946 691253
Head: Ms Gillian Temple
Category: SLD PMLD

CARLISLE

James Rennie School
California Road, Kingstown,
CARLISLE, Cumbria CA3 0BX
Tel: 01228 554280
Head: Kris Williams
Category: SLD PMLD

ULVERSTON

Sandside Lodge School
Sandside Road, ULVERSTON,
Cumbria LA12 9EF
Tel: 01229 588825
Head: Ms Susan Gill
Category: SLD PMLD

DERBYSHIRE
Children & Younger Adults

Special Needs Section, County Hall, Matlock, Derbyshire, DE4 3AG
Tel: 01629 536539 Email: sen.admin@derbyshire.gov.uk Website: www.derbyshire.gov.uk

ALFRETON

Alfreton Park Community Special School
Alfreton Park, ALFRETON,
Derbyshire DE55 7AL
Tel: 01773 832019
Head: Mrs Cheryl Smart
Category: SLD (2-19)

Swanwick School and Sports College
Hayes Lane, Swanwick,
ALFRETON, Derbyshire DE55 1AR
Tel: 01773 602198
Head: Mr Christopher Greenhough
Category: MLD (5-16)

BELPER

Holbrook School for Autism
Port Way, Holbrook, BELPER,
Derbyshire DE56 0TE
Tel: 01332 880208
Head: Mr Julian Scholefield
Category: AUT (5-19)

BUXTON

Peak School
Buxton Road, Chinley, High Peak,
BUXTON, Derbyshire SK23 6ES
Tel: 01663 750324
Head: Mr John McPherson
Category: SLD (2-19)

CHESTERFIELD

Ashgate Croft School
Ashgate Road, CHESTERFIELD,
Derbyshire S40 4BN
Tel: 01246 275111
Head: Mrs Claire Jones
Category: MLD SLD (2-19)

Holly House School
Church Street North, Old
Whittington, CHESTERFIELD,
Derbyshire S41 9QR
Tel: 01246 450530
Head: Mr Peter Brandt
Category: EBD (7-14)

ILKESTON

**Bennerley Fields
Specialist Speech and
Language College**
Stratford Street, ILKESTON,
Derbyshire DE7 8QZ
Tel: 01159 326374
Head: Ms Debbie Gerring
Category: MLD (2-16)

LONG EATON

Brackenfield School
Bracken Road, LONG
EATON NG10 4DA
Tel: 01159 733710
Head: Mrs Sarah Gilraine
Category: MLD (5-16)

**Stanton Vale
Special School**
Thoresby Road, LONG
EATON NG10 3NP
Tel: 01159 72 9769
Head: Mr Christopher White
Category: PMLD SLD (2-19)

SHIREBROOK

Stubbin Wood School
Common Lane, SHIREBROOK,
Derbyshire NG20 8QF
Tel: 01623 742795
Head: Mr Lee Floyd
Category: MLD SLD (2-19)

DERBY CITY
Education & Learning

Families Information Service, The Council House, Corporation Street, Derby, Derbyshire, DE1 2FS
Tel: 01332 642610 Fax: 01332 643299 Email: fis@derby.gov.uk Website: www.derby.gov.uk

DERBY

Ivy House School
Moorway Lane, Littleover,
DERBY DE23 7FS
Tel: 01332 777920
Head: Ms Susan Allen
Category: SLD PMLD (Coed 2-19)

Kingsmead School
Bridge Street, DERBY DE1 3LB
Tel: 01332 715970
Head: Ms Yvonne Barry
Category: EBD (Coed 11-16)

St Andrew's School
St Andrew's View, Breadsall
Hilltop, DERBY DE21 4EW
Tel: 01332 832746
Head: Ms Heather Flockton
Category: SLD (Coed 11-19)

St Clare's School
Rough Heanor Road,
Mickleover, DERBY DE3 9AZ
Tel: 01332 511757
Head: Ms Carmel McKenna
Category: MLD SP&LD AUT
PD SLD (Coed 11-16)

St Giles' School
Hampshire Road, Chaddesden,
DERBY DE21 6BT
Tel: 01332 343039
Head: Ms Pamela Thomas
Category: SLD AUT (Coed 4-11)

St Martin's School
Bracknell Drive, Alvaston,
DERBY DE24 0BR
Tel: 01332 571151
Head: Mr Gary Dodds
Category: MLD AUT EBD
SLD (Coed 11-16)

DEVON
Children & Young People's Services

0-25 SEN Team, County Hall, Topsham Road, Exeter, Devon, EX2 4QD
Tel: 01392 383913 Email: specialeducation0-25-mailbox@devon.gov.uk Website: www.devon.gov.uk

BARNSTAPLE

Marland Day School
Springfield Court, Brannam
Crescent, Roundswell Business Park,
BARNSTAPLE, Devon EX31 3TD
Tel: 01271 384100
Head: Mr Keith Bennett
Category: SEBD (10-16)

Pathfield School
Abbey Road, Pilton,
BARNSTAPLE, Devon EX31 1JU
Tel: 01271 342423
Head: Mrs Claire May
Category: SLD PMLD (3-19)

**The Lampard
Community School**
St John's Lane, BARNSTAPLE,
Devon EX32 9DD
Tel: 01271 345416
Head: Mrs Karen Rogers
Category: Complex and
difficulties with communication
and interaction (including
SLCN and/or ASC) (7-16)

BUDLEIGH SALTERTON

**Mill Water Community
School**
Bicton, East Budleigh, BUDLEIGH
SALTERTON, Devon EX9 7BJ
Tel: 01395 568890
Head: Mrs Sarah Pickering
Category: SLD PMLD (3-19)

DAWLISH

Oaklands Park School
John Nash Drive, DAWLISH,
Devon EX7 9SF
Tel: 01626 862363
Acting Head: Mrs Cherie White
Category: SLD ASC PMLD
(Day/boarding 3-19)

Ratcliffe School
John Nash Drive, DAWLISH,
Devon EX7 9RZ
Tel: 01626 862939
Head: Mrs Cherie White
Category: ASC and Associated
Social Development Needs (5-16)

EXETER

Barley Lane School
Barley Lane, St Thomas,
EXETER, Devon EX4 1TA
Tel: 01392 430774
Head: Mr Michael MacCourt
Category: BESD (7-16)

Ellen Tinkham School
Hollow Lane, EXETER,
Devon EX1 3RW
Tel: 01392 467168
Head: Mrs Jacqueline Warne
Category: SLD PMLD (3-19)

Southbrook School
Bishop Westall Road,
EXETER, Devon EX2 6JB
Tel: 01392 258373
Head: Mrs Bronwen Caschere
Category: MLD ASC (11-16)

TORRINGTON

Marland Residential School
Petersmarland, TORRINGTON,
Devon EX38 8QQ
Tel: 01805 601324
Head: Mr Keith Bennett
Category: SEBD (10-16)

TOTNES

Bidwell Brook School
Shinner's Bridge, Dartington,
TOTNES, Devon TQ9 6JU
Tel: 01803 864120
Head: Mrs Jacqueline Warne
Category: SLD PMLD (3-19)

DORSET
County Council

Children's Services, County Hall, Dorchester, DT1 1XJ
Tel: 01305 224888 Fax: 01305 224547 Email: dorsetdirect@dorsetcc.gov.uk Website: www.dorsetcc.gov.uk

BEAMINSTER

Mountjoy School
Tunnel Road, BEAMINSTER,
Dorset DT8 3HB
Tel: 01308 861155
Acting Head: Ms Jackie Shanks
Category: ASD SLD PMLD
Complex (2-19)

STURMINSTER NEWTON

Yewstock School
Honeymead Lane, STURMINSTER
NEWTON, Dorset DT10 1EW
Tel: 01258 472796
Head: Mr S Kretz
Category: ASD MLD/
Comlex PMLD SLD (2-19)

WEYMOUTH

Westfield Arts College
Littlemoor Road, Preston,
WEYMOUTH, Dorset DT3 6AA
Tel: 01305 833518
Head: Mr A Penman
Category: MLD/Complex ASD (3-16)

Wyvern School
Dorchester Road, WEYMOUTH,
Dorset DT3 5AL
Tel: 01305 817917
Head: Mrs S Hoxey
Category: ASD PMLD
SLD Complex (2-19)

WIMBORNE

Beaucroft Foundation School
Wimborne Road, Colehill,
WIMBORNE, Dorset BH21 2SS
Tel: 01202 886083
Head: Mr P McGill
Category: MLD/Complex ASD (4-16)

DURHAM
County Council

Children and Adult Services, Broom Cottages Primary & Nursery School, Ferryhill, County Durham, DL17 8AN
Tel: 03000 267800 Website: www.durham.gov.uk

BISHOP AUCKLAND

Evergreen School
Warwick Road, BISHOP
AUCKLAND, Durham DL14 6LS
Tel: 01388 459721
Head: Mrs Andrea E English
Category: MLD SLD PMLD AUT (2-11)

DURHAM

Durham Trinity School and Sports College
Aykley Heads, DURHAM DH1 5TS
Tel: 01913 864612
Head: Mrs Julie Anne Rutherford
Category: MLD SLD PMLD AUT (2-19)

NEWTON AYCLIFFE

Walworth School
Bluebell Way, NEWTON
AYCLIFFE, Durham DL5 7LP
Tel: 01325 300194
Head: Mr Peter Wallbanks
Category: SEBD (4-11)

SHERBURN

Elemore Hall School
Littletown, SHERBURN,
Durham DH6 1QD
Tel: 01913 720275
Head: Mr Richard J Royle
Category: SEBD (11-16)

CONSETT

Villa Real School
Villa Real Road, CONSETT,
Durham DH8 6BH
Tel: 01207 503651
Head: Mrs Sharon Common
Category: SLD PMLD AUT (2-19)

FERRYHILL

Windlestone School
Chilton, FERRYHILL,
Durham DL17 0HP
Tel: 01388 720337
Head: Mr Tim Bennett
Category: SEBD (11-16)

PETERLEE

Glendene Arts Academy
Crawlaw Road, Easington Colliery,
PETERLEE, Durham SR8 3LP
Tel: 01915 691420
Head: Mr Eric W Baker
Category: MLD SLD PMLD AUT (2-19)

SPENNYMOOR

The Meadows School
Whitworth Lane, SPENNYMOOR,
Durham DL16 7QW
Tel: 01388 811178
Head: Mrs Susan M Cook
Category: SEBD (11-16)

The Oaks School
Rock Road, SPENNYMOOR,
Durham DL16 7DB
Tel: 01388 827380
Head: Mrs Andrea E English
Category: MLD SLD
PMLD AUT (11-19)

STANLEY

Hare Law School
Hare Law, STANLEY,
Durham DH9 8DT
Tel: 01207 234547
Head: Mrs Margaret Collins
Category: MLD SLD AUT (5-16)

ESSEX

Essex Parent Partnership Service

SEND Information, Advice & Support Service, County Hall, Market Road, Chelmsford, Essex, CM1 1QH
Tel: 03330 138913 Email: send.iass@essex.gov.uk Website: www.essex.gov.uk

BASILDON

Castledon School
Bromfords Drive, Wickford,
BASILDON, Essex SS12 0PW
Tel: 01268 761252
Head: Mrs Philippa Holliday
Category: ASD MLD (5-16)

BENFLEET

Cedar Hall School
Hart Road, Thundersley,
BENFLEET, Essex SS7 3UQ
Tel: 01268 774723
Head: Mr Peter Whelan
Category: MLD (4-16)

Glenwood School
Rushbottom Lane, New
Thundersley, BENFLEET,
Essex SS7 4LW
Tel: 01268 792575
Head: Mrs Judith Salter
Category: SLD (3-19)

BRAINTREE

The Edith Borthwick School
Fennes Road, Church Street,
BRAINTREE, Essex CM7 5LA
Tel: 01376 529300
Head: Mr Ian Boatman
Category: ASD MLD SLD (3-19)

BRENTWOOD

The Endeavour School
Hogarth Avenue, BRENTWOOD,
Essex CM15 8BE
Tel: 01277 217330
Head: Mr John Chadwick
Category: MLD (5-16)

CHIGWELL

Wells Park School
School Lane, Lambourne Road,
CHIGWELL, Essex IG7 6NN
Tel: 02085 026442
Head: Miss Sue Wraw
Category: BESD (5-12)

CLACTON ON SEA

Shorefields School
114 Holland Road, CLACTON
ON SEA, Essex CO15 6HF
Tel: 01255 424412
Head: Mrs Jo Hodges
Category: ASD MLD SLD (3-19)

COLCHESTER

Kingswode Hoe School
Sussex Road, COLCHESTER,
Essex CO3 3QJ
Tel: 01206 576408
Head: Mrs Elizabeth Drake
Category: MLD (5-16)

Lexden Springs School
Halstead Road, Lexden,
COLCHESTER, Essex CO3 9AB
Tel: 01206 563321
Head: Mr Simon Wall
Category: SLD (3-19)

Market Field School
Paxman Avenue, COLCHESTER,
Essex CO2 9DQ
Tel: 01206 825195
Head: Mr Gary Smith
Category: ASD MLD SLD (4-16)

HARLOW

**Harlow Fields School
& College**
Tendring Road, HARLOW,
Essex CM18 6RN
Tel: 01279 423670
Acting Head: Mrs Kathleen Wall
Category: ASD MLD SLD (3-19)

LOUGHTON

Oak View School
Whitehills Road, LOUGHTON,
Essex IG10 1TS
Tel: 02085 084293
Head: Ms Dianne Ryan
Category: MLD SLD (3-19)

WITHAM

Southview School
Conrad Road, WITHAM,
Essex CM8 2TA
Tel: 01376 503505
Head: Mr Julian Cochrane
Category: PD (3-19)

GLOUCESTERSHIRE

Children & Young People's Services

SEN Team, Shire Hall, Westgate Street, Gloucester, GL1 2TG
Tel: 01452 425000 Email: sendprogramme@gloucestershire.gov.uk Website: www.gloucestershire.gov.uk/learning

CHELTENHAM

Battledown Centre for Children and Families
Harp Hill, Battledown,
CHELTENHAM,
Gloucestershire GL52 6PZ
Tel: 01242 525472
Head: Ms Jane Cummins
Category: VI SLCN ASD
SEMH PD MLD SLD (2-7)

Belmont School
Warden Hill Road, CHELTENHAM,
Gloucestershire GL51 3AT
Tel: 01242 216180
Head: Mr Kevin Day
Category: MLD (Coed 4-16)

Bettridge School
Warden Hill Road, CHELTENHAM,
Gloucestershire GL51 3AT
Tel: 01242 514934
Head: Mrs Amanda Roberts
Category: VI SLCN ASD SLD (2-19)

CIRENCESTER

Paternoster School
Watermoor Road, CIRENCESTER,
Gloucestershire GL7 1JR
Tel: 01285 652480
Head: Ms Julie Mantell
Category: SLD (2-17)

COLEFORD

Heart of the Forest Community School
Speech House, Coalway,
COLEFORD, Gloucestershire
GL16 7EJ
Tel: 01594 822175
Head: Mrs Melissa Bradshaw
Category: SLD PMLD (Coed 3-19)

FAIRFORD

Coln House School
Horcott Road, FAIRFORD,
Gloucestershire GL7 4DB
Tel: 01285 712308
Head: Mr C Clarke
Category: SEMH (Coed
Day/boarding 9-16)

GLOUCESTER

The Milestone School
Longford Lane, GLOUCESTER,
Gloucestershire GL2 9EU
Tel: 01452 500499
Head: Mrs Lyn Dance
Category: VI SLCN ASD SEMH
PD MLD SLD (Coed 2-16)

STONEHOUSE

The Shrubberies School
Oldends Lane, STONEHOUSE,
Gloucestershire GL10 2DG
Tel: 01453 822155
Head: Ms Jane Jones
Category: SLD (Coed 2-19)

TEWKESBURY

Alderman Knight School
Ashchurch Road, TEWKESBURY,
Gloucestershire GL20 8JJ
Tel: 01684 295639
Head: Mrs Clare Steel
Category: MLD (4-16)

SOUTH GLOUCESTERSHIRE

Council

0-25 Service, Department for Children, Adults & Health, PO Box 298, Civic
Centre, High Street Bristol, South Gloucestershire, BS15 0DQ
Tel: 01454 863301 or 01454 863173 Website: www.southglos.gov.uk

KINGSWOOD

New Horizons Learning Centre
Mulberry Drive, KINGSWOOD,
South Gloucestershire BS15 4ED
Tel: 01454 865340
Head: Mrs T Craig
Category: BESD

THORNBURY

New Siblands School
Easton Hill Road, THORNBURY,
South Gloucestershire BS35 2JU
Tel: 01454 866754
Head: Mr A Buckton
Category: SLD

WARMLEY

Warmley Park School
Tower Road North, WARMLEY,
South Gloucestershire BS30 8XL
Tel: 01454 867272
Head: Miss L Parker
Category: SLD (Day 3 -19)

YATE

Culverhill School
Kelston Close, YATE, South
Gloucestershire BS37 8SZ
Tel: 01454 866930
Head: Ms N Jones
Category: CLD (Day 7 - 16)

HALTON
Borough Council

Halton SEND Partnership, Rutland House, Halton Lea, Runcorn, Cheshire, WA7 2GW
Tel: 01515 117733 Email: sendpartnership@halton.gov.uk Website: www3.halton.gov.uk

RUNCORN

Cavendish Academy
Lincoln Close, RUNCORN,
Cheshire WA7 4YX
Tel: 01928 561706
Head: Mrs C Dickinson
Category: SLD (11-19)

WIDNES

Ashley School
Cawfield Avenue, WIDNES,
Cheshire WA8 7HG
Tel: 01514 244892
Head: Mrs Linda King
Category: MLD Complex
emotional needs (11-16)

Brookfields School
Moorfield Road, WIDNES,
Cheshire WA8 0JA
Tel: 01514 244329
Head: Mrs S Ainsworth
Category: SLD (2-11)

**Chesnut Lodge School &
Specialist SEN College**
Green Lane, WIDNES,
Cheshire WA8 7HF
Tel: 01514 240679
Head: Mrs Heather Austin
Category: PH (2-16)

HAMPSHIRE
County Council

Children's Services Department, Elizabeth II Court, The Castle, Winchester, Hampshire, SO23 8UG
Tel: 03005 551384 Email: childrens.services@hants.gov.uk Website: www.hants.gov.uk

ANDOVER

Icknield School
River Way, ANDOVER,
Hampshire SP11 6LT
Tel: 01264 365297
Head: Sharon Salmon
Category: SLD (Coed 2-19)

Norman Gate School
Vigo Road, ANDOVER,
Hampshire SP10 1JZ
Tel: 01264 323423
Head: Christine Gayler
Category: MLD ASD (Coed 2-11)

The Mark Way School
Batchelors Barn Road, ANDOVER,
Hampshire SP10 1HR
Tel: 01264 351835
Head: Sonia Longstaff-Bishop
Category: MLD ASD (Coed 11-16)

**Wolverdene
Special School**
22 Love Lane, ANDOVER,
Hampshire SP10 2AF
Tel: 01264 362350
Head: Paul Van Walwyk
Category: BESD (Coed 5-11)

BASINGSTOKE

Coppice Spring School
Pack Lane, BASINGSTOKE,
Hampshire RG22 5TH
Tel: 01256 336601
Head: Sarah Mascall
Category: BESD (Coed 11-16)

Dove House School
Sutton Road, BASINGSTOKE,
Hampshire RG21 5SU
Tel: 01256 351555
Head: Colin House
Category: MLD ASD (Coed 11-16)

Limington House School
St Andrews Road, BASINGSTOKE,
Hampshire RG22 6PS
Tel: 01256 322148
Head: Justin Innes
Category: SLD (Coed 2-19)

Maple Ridge School
Maple Crescent, BASINGSTOKE,
Hampshire RG21 5SX
Tel: 01256 323639
Head: Deborah Gooderham
Category: MLD ASD (Coed 4-11)

Saxon Wood School
Rooksdown, Barron
Place, BASINGSTOKE,
Hampshire RG24 9NH
Tel: 01256 356635
Head: Richard Parratt
Category: PD (Coed 2-11)

BORDON

Hollywater School
Mill Chase Road, BORDON,
Hampshire GU35 0HA
Tel: 01420 474396
Head: Steph Clancy
Category: LD (Coed 2-19)

CHANDLERS FORD

Lakeside School
Winchester Road, CHANDLERS
FORD, Hampshire SO53 2DW
Tel: 02380 266633
Head: Gareth Evans
Category: BESD (Boys 11-16)

FAREHAM

Baycroft School
Gosport Road, Stubbington,
FAREHAM, Hampshire PO14 2AE
Tel: 01329 664151
Head: Chris Toner
Category: MLD ASD (Coed 11-16)

Heathfield School
Oldbury Way, FAREHAM,
Hampshire PO14 3BN
Tel: 01329 845150
Head: Nicky Cunningham
Category: MLD ASD PD (Coed 2-11)

St Francis Special School
Patchway Drive, Oldbury Way,
FAREHAM, Hampshire PO14 3BN
Tel: 01329 845730
Head: Steve Hollinghurst
Category: SLD (Coed 2-19)

FARNBOROUGH

Henry Tyndale School
Ship Lane, FARNBOROUGH,
Hampshire GU14 8BX
Tel: 01252 544577
Head: Rob Thompson
Category: LD ASD (Coed 2-19)

**The Samuel Cody
Specialist Sports College**
Ballantyne Rode,
Cove, FARNBOROUGH,
Hampshire GU14 6SS
Tel: 01252 514194
Head: Anna Dawson
Category: MLD ASD (Coed 11-16)

HAVANT

Prospect School
Freeley Road, HAVANT,
Hampshire PO9 4AQ
Tel: 02392 485150
Head: Marijke Miles
Category: BESD (Boys 11-16)

PORTSMOUTH

Glenwood School
Washington Road,
Emsworth, PORTSMOUTH,
Hampshire PO10 7NN
Tel: 01243 373120
Head: Ruth Witton
Category: MLD ASD (Coed 11-16)

SOUTHAMPTON

Forest Park Primary School
Ringwood Road,
Totton, SOUTHAMPTON,
Hampshire SO40 8EB
Tel: 02380 864949
Acting Head: Jill Pike
Category: LD (Coed 2-11)

Forest Park Secondary School
Commercial Road,
Totton, SOUTHAMPTON,
Hampshire SO40 3AF
Tel: 02380 864211
Acting Head: Jill Pike
Category: LD (Coed 11-19)

Lord Wilson School
Montiefiore Drive, Sarisbury
Green, SOUTHAMPTON,
Hampshire SO31 7NL
Tel: 01489 582684
Head: Stuart Parker-Tyreman
Category: BESD (Male 11-16)

Oak Lodge School
Roman Road, Dibden
Purlieu, SOUTHAMPTON,
Hampshire SO45 4RQ
Tel: 02380 847213
Head: Beverley Hawker
Category: MLD ASD (Coed 11-16)

WATERLOOVILLE

Rachel Madocks School
Eagle Avenue, Cowplain,
WATERLOOVILLE,
Hampshire PO8 9XP
Tel: 02392 241818
Head: Jacqueline Sumner
Category: SLD (Coed 2-19)

Riverside Community Special School
Scratchface Lane,
Purbrook, WATERLOOVILLE,
Hampshire PO7 5QD
Tel: 02392 250138
Head: Catherine Marsh
Category: MLD ASD (Coed 3-11)

The Waterloo School
Warfield Avenue, WATERLOOVILLE,
Hampshire PO7 7JJ
Tel: 02392 255956
Acting Head: Kirsty Roman
Category: BESD (Boys 4-11)

WINCHESTER

Osborne School
Athelstan Road, WINCHESTER,
Hampshire SO23 7GA
Tel: 01962 854537
Head: Sonia O'Donnell
Category: LD ASD (Coed 11-19)

Shepherds Down Special School
Shepherds Lane, Compton,
WINCHESTER, Hampshire SO21 2AJ
Tel: 01962 713445
Head: Jane Sansome
Category: LD ASD (Coed 4-11)

HARTLEPOOL

Borough Council

Child and Adult Services Department, Civic Centre, Victoria Road, Hartlepool, TS24 8AY
Tel: 01429 266522 Email: customer.service@hartlepool.gov.uk Website: www.hartlepool.gov.uk

HARTLEPOOL

Catcote School
Catcote Road,
HARTLEPOOL TS25 4EZ
Tel: 01429 264036
Head: Mr A Chapman
Category: MLD SLD PMLD ASD BESD

Springwell School
Wiltshire Way, HARTLEPOOL TS26 0IB
Tel: 01429 280600
Head: Mr K Telfer
Category: MLD SLD PMLD ASD BESD

HEREFORDSHIRE

The Children, Young People and Families Directorate

Special Educational Needs Team, Blackfriars, Blackfriars Street, Hereford, Herefordshire, HR4 9ZR
Tel: 01432 260869 Email: senteam@herefordshire.gov.uk Website: www.herefordshire.gov.uk

HEREFORD

Barrs Court School
Barrs Court Road,
HEREFORD HR1 1EQ
Tel: 01432 265035
Head: Ms Lisa Appleton
Category: CLD PMLD MSI PD ADHD
ASD OCD SP&LD SLD (Coed 11-19)

Blackmarston School
Honddu Close, HEREFORD HR2 7NX
Tel: 01432 272376
Head: Mrs S Bailey
Category: SLD ASD
PMLD(Coed 3-11)

The Brookfield School & Specialist College
Grandstand Road,
HEREFORD HR4 9NG
Tel: 01432 265153
Head: Mrs O Evans
Category: BESD MLD ASD
ADHD (Coed 7-16)

LEOMINSTER

Westfield School
Westfield Walk,
LEOMINSTER HR6 8HD
Tel: 01568 613147
Head: Ms N Gilbert
Category: SLD ASD
PMLD (Coed 2-19)

HERTFORDSHIRE
Children's Services

County Hall, Pegs Lane, Hertford, SG13 8DQ
Tel: 03001 234043 Email: hertsdirect@hertscc.gov.uk Website: www.hertsdirect.org

BALDOCK

Brandles School
Weston Way, BALDOCK,
Hertfordshire SG7 6EY
Tel: 01462 892189
Head: Mr David Vickery
Category: EBD (Boys 11-16)

BUSHEY

Meadow Wood School
Cold Harbour Lane, BUSHEY,
Hertfordshire WD23 4NN
Tel: 02084 204720
Head: Mr Nathan Taylor
Category: PI (Coed Day 3-12)

HATFIELD

Southfield School
Woods Avenue, HATFIELD,
Hertfordshire AL10 8NN
Tel: 01707 276504
Head: Ms Libby Duggan
Category: MLD (Coed Day 3-11)

HEMEL HEMPSTEAD

Haywood Grove School
St Agnells Lane, HEMEL HEMPSTEAD,
Hertfordshire HP2 7BG
Tel: 01442 250077
Head Teacher: C Smith
Category: EBD (Coed Day 5-11)

The Collett School
Lockers Park Lane, HEMEL
HEMPSTEAD, Hertfordshire HP1 1TQ
Tel: 01442 398988
Head: Mr Stephen Hoult-Allen
Category: MLD AUT (Coed 4-16)

Woodfield School
Malmes Croft, Leverstock
Green, HEMEL HEMPSTEAD,
Hertfordshire HP3 8RL
Tel: 01442 253476
Head: Mrs Gill Waceba
Category: SLD AUT (Coed Day 3-19)

HERTFORD

Hailey Hall School
Hailey Lane, HERTFORD,
Hertfordshire SG13 7PB
Tel: 01992 465208
Head: Ms Heather Boardman
Category: EBD (Boys 11-16)

LETCHWORTH GARDEN CITY

**Woolgrove School Special
Needs Academy**
Pryor Way, LETCHWORTH GARDEN
CITY, Hertfordshire SG6 2PT
Tel: 01462 622422
Head: Mrs Susan Selley
Category: MLD AUT
(Coed Day 5-11)

REDBOURN

St Luke's School
Crouch Hall Lane, REDBOURN,
Hertfordshire AL3 7ET
Tel: 01582 626727
Head: Mr P Johnson
Category: MLD (Coed Day 9-16)

ST ALBANS

Batchwood School
Townsend Drive, ST ALBANS,
Hertfordshire AL3 5RP
Tel: 01727 868021
Acting Head: Mrs Anne Spencer
Category: EBD (Coed 11-16)

Heathlands School
Heathlands Drive, ST ALBANS,
Hertfordshire AL3 5AY
Tel: 01727 754060
Head: Ms Deborah Jones-Stevens
Category: HI (Coed Day
& boarding 3-16)

Watling View School
Watling View, ST ALBANS,
Hertfordshire AL1 2NU
Tel: 01727 850560
Head: Ms Pauline Atkins
Category: SLD (Coed Day 2-19)

STEVENAGE

Greenside School
Shephall Green, STEVENAGE,
Hertfordshire SG2 9XS
Tel: 01438 315356
Head: Mr David Victor
Category: SLD AUT (Coed Day 2-19)

Larwood School
Webb Rise, STEVENAGE,
Hertfordshire SG1 5QU
Tel: 01438 236333
Head: Mr Sean Trimble
Category: EBD (Coed
Day & boarding 5-11)

Lonsdale School
Brittain Way, STEVENAGE,
Hertfordshire SG2 8BL
Tel: 01438 726999
Head Teacher: Ms
Annemarie Ottridge
Category: PH (Coed Day
& boarding 5-19)

The Valley School
Valley Way, STEVENAGE,
Hertfordshire SG2 9AB
Tel: 01438 747274
Head: Mr David Harrison
Category: MLD (Coed Day 11-19)

WARE

**Amwell View School &
Specialist Sports College**
Stanstead Abbotts, WARE,
Hertfordshire SG12 8EH
Tel: 01920 870027
Head: Mrs Janet Liversage
Category: SLD AUT (Coed Day 2-19)

Middleton School
Walnut Tree Walk, WARE,
Hertfordshire SG12 9PD
Tel: 01920 485152
Head: Ms Donna Jolly
Category: MLD AUT
(Coed Day 5-11)

Pinewood School
Hoe Lane, WARE,
Hertfordshire SG12 9PB
Tel: 01920 412211
Head: Mr Adrian Lloyd
Category: MLD (Coed
Residential 11-16)

WATFORD

Breakspeare School
Gallows Hill Lane, Abbots Langley,
WATFORD, Hertfordshire WD5 0BU
Tel: 01923 263645
Head Teacher: M Paakkonen
Category: SLD (Coed Day 3-19)

Colnbrook School
Hayling Road, WATFORD,
Hertfordshire WD19 7UY
Tel: 02084 281281
Head: Mr Richard Hill
Category: MLD AUT
(Coed Day 4-11)

Falconer School
Falconer Road, Bushey, WATFORD,
Hertfordshire WD23 3AT
Tel: 02089 502505
Head Teacher: Mr Jonathan Kemp
Category: EBD (Boys Day/
boarding 10-19)

Garston Manor School
Horseshoe Lane, Garston,
WATFORD, Hertfordshire WD25 7HR
Tel: 01923 673757
Head: Ms Julie Lowman
Category: MLD (Coed Day 11-16)

WELWYN GARDEN CITY

Knightsfield School
Knightsfield, WELWYN GARDEN
CITY, Hertfordshire AL8 7LW
Tel: 01707 376874
Head: Mrs Lucy Leith
Category: HI (Coed Day
& boarding 10-19)

Lakeside School
Stanfield, Lemsford Lane,
WELWYN GARDEN CITY,
Hertfordshire AL8 6YN
Tel: 01707 327410
Head: Mrs Judith Chamberlain
Category: SLD PD (Coed Day 2-19)

FORTROSE

**Black Isle Education
Centre**
Raddery, FORTROSE IV10 8SN
Tel: 01381 621600
Head: Mr Ross Waldie
Category: BESD (Boys Day 9-16)

ISLE OF WIGHT

Children's Services Directorate

Special Needs Support Services, Thompson House, Sandy Lane, Newport, Isle of Wight, PO30 3NA
Tel: 01983 533 523 Website: www.eduwight.iow.gov.uk

NEWPORT

**Medina House
Special School**
School Lane, NEWPORT,
Isle of Wight PO30 2HS
Tel: 01983 522917
Head: Ms Julie Stewart
Category: Severe & complex
needs (Coed 2-11)

St Georges School
Watergate Road, NEWPORT,
Isle of Wight PO30 1XW
Tel: 01983 524634
Head: Mrs S Holman
Category: Severe complex
needs (Coed 11-19)

KENT

Education, Learning and Skills Directorate

Information, Advice and Support Team (SEN), Shepway Centre, Oxford Road, Maidstone, Kent, ME15 8AW
Tel: 03000 412412 Fax: 01622 671198 Email: iask@kent.gov.uk Website: www.kent.gov.uk

ASHFORD

**Goldwyn Community
Special School**
Godinton Lane, Great Chart,
ASHFORD, Kent TN23 3BT
Tel: 01233 622958
Head: Mr Robert Law
Category: BESD (Coed 11-16)

The Wyvern School
Great Chart Bypass,
ASHFORD, Kent TN23 4ER
Tel: 01233 621468
Head: Mr David Spencer
Category: PMLD SLD
CLD PD (Coed 3-19)

BROADSTAIRS

Stone Bay School
70 Stone Road, BROADSTAIRS,
Kent CT10 1EB
Tel: 01843 863421
Head: Mr Billy McInally
Category: SLD AUT SLCN MLD C&I
(Coed Day & residential 11-19)

The Foreland School
Lanthorne Road, BROADSTAIRS,
Kent CT10 3NX
Tel: 01843 863891
Head: Mr Nick Howard
Category: ASD PMLD SLD
PSCN (Coed 2-19)

CANTERBURY

St Nicholas' School
Holme Oak Close, Nunnery Fields,
CANTERBURY, Kent CT1 3JJ
Tel: 01227 464316
Head: Mr Daniel Lewis
Category: PMLD SLD CLD
PSCN (Coed 3-19)

The Orchard School
Cambridge Road,
CANTERBURY, Kent CT1 3QQ
Tel: 01227 769220
Head: Ms Pauline Baines
Category: MLD CLD
B&L (Coed 11-16)

DARTFORD

Milestone School
Ash Road, New Ash Green,
DARTFORD, Kent DA3 8JZ
Tel: 01474 709420
Head: Mrs Margaret Fisher
Category: PMLD SLD AUT
MLD PSCN (Coed 2-19)

Rowhill School
Main Road, Longfield,
DARTFORD, Kent DA3 7PW
Tel: 01474 705377
Head: Mr Timothy South
Category: B&L AUT LD
Complex needs Behavioural
difficulties (Coed Day 4-16)

DOVER

Harbour School
Elms Vale Road, DOVER,
Kent CT17 9PS
Tel: 01304 201964
Acting Head: Mr W Deane
Category: BESD ASD MLD
B&L (Coed 4-16)

Portal House School
Sea Street, St Margarets-at-
Cliffe, DOVER, Kent CT15 6SS
Tel: 01304 853033
Head: Mrs Rose Bradley
Category: BESD (Coed 11-16)

FOLKESTONE

Highview School
Moat Farm Road, FOLKESTONE,
Kent CT19 5DJ
Tel: 01303 258755
Head: Mr Neil Birch
Category: MLD CLD Complex
needs (Coed 4-17)

GRAVESEND

The Ifield School
Cedar Avenue, GRAVESEND,
Kent DA12 5JT
Tel: 01474 365485
Head: Mrs Pamela Jones
Category: CLD PMLD SLD
MLD PSCN (Coed 4-18)

HYTHE

Foxwood School
Seabrook Road, HYTHE,
Kent CT21 5QJ
Tel: 01303 261155
Head: Mr Neil Birch
Category: AUT SLD (Coed 2-19)

MAIDSTONE

Bower Grove School
Fant Lane, MAIDSTONE,
Kent ME16 8NL
Tel: 01622 726773
Head: Mr Trevor Phipps
Category: BESD MLD ASD
B&L (Coed Day 5-16)

Five Acre Wood School
Boughton Lane, Loose Valley,
MAIDSTONE, Kent ME15 9QF
Tel: 01622 743925
Head: Ms Peggy Murphy
Category: ASD PMLD SLD PD
CLD PSCN (Coed 4-19)

MARGATE

Laleham Gap School
Northdown Park Road,
MARGATE, Kent CT9 2TP
Tel: 01843 221946
Head: Mr Keith Mileham
Category: AUT ABD PD
SLCN C&I (Coed 3-16)

St Anthony's School
St Anthony's Way, MARGATE,
Kent CT9 3RA
Tel: 01843 292015
Head: Mr Neil Rees-Davies
Category: MLD ASD LD SEBD
SLCN B&L (Coed 3-11)

SEVENOAKS

Grange Park School
Borough Green Road, Wrotham,
SEVENOAKS, Kent TN15 7RD
Tel: 01732 882111
Head: Mr Robert Wyatt
Category: AUT C&I (Coed 11-19)

SITTINGBOURNE

Meadowfield School
Swanstree Avenue,
SITTINGBOURNE, Kent ME10 4NL
Tel: 01795 477788
Head: Ms Jill Palmer
Category: CLD PMLD SLD ASD
SP&LD PSCN (Coed 4-19)

SWANLEY

Furness School
Rowhill Road, Hextable,
SWANLEY, Kent BR8 7RP
Tel: 01322 662937
Head: Ms Jill Howson
Category: BESD (Coed
Day/boarding 10-16)

TONBRIDGE

Ridge View School
Cage Green Road,
TONBRIDGE, Kent TN10 4PT
Tel: 01732 771384
Head: Ms Jacqui Tovey
Category: PMLD SLD CLD
PSCN (Coed 2-19)

TUNBRIDGE WELLS

Broomhill Bank School
Broomhill Road, Rusthall,
TUNBRIDGE WELLS, Kent TN3 0TB
Tel: 01892 510440
Head: Ms Emma Leitch
Category: MLD SP&LD CLD AUT
C&I (Girls Boarding & day 8-19)

Oakley School
Pembury Road, TUNBRIDGE
WELLS, Kent TN2 4NE
Tel: 01892 823096
Head: Mr Gordon Tillman
Category: PMLD ASD MLD
PSCN (Coed 3-19)

WESTERHAM

Valence School
Westerham Road, WESTERHAM,
Kent TN16 1QN
Tel: 01959 562156
Head: Mr Roland Gooding
Category: PD Sensory Medical
(Coed Day/boarding 4-19)

KINGSTON UPON HULL

City Council

0-25 Integrated SEN Team, The Helmsley Centre, 64 Helmsley Grove, Hull, HU5 5ED
Tel: 01482 300300 Email: send@hullcc.gov.uk Website: www.hullcc.gov.uk

KINGSTON UPON HULL

Bridgeview School
262a Pickering Road, KINGSTON
UPON HULL HU4 7AB
Tel: 01482 303300
Head: Mrs C Patton
Category: BESD

Frederick Holmes School
Inglemire Lane, KINGSTON
UPON HULL HU6 8JJ
Tel: 01482 804766
Head: Mrs B Ribey
Category: PH

Ganton School
294 Anlaby Park Road South,
KINGSTON UPON HULL HU4 7JB
Tel: 01482 564646
Head: Mrs S Jones
Category: SLD

Northcott School
Dulverton Close, Bransholme,
KINGSTON UPON HULL HU7 4EL
Tel: 01482 822253
Head: Mrs K Coxall
Category: Vulnerable ASD

Oakfield School
Hopewell Road, KINGSTON
UPON HULL HU9 4HD
Tel: 01482 854589
Head: Mrs R Davies
Category: BESD

Tweendykes School
Midmere Avenue, Leads Road,
KINGSTON UPON HULL HU7 4PW
Tel: 01482 826508
Head: Mrs B Dobson
Category: SLD

LANCASHIRE

Children & Young People Directorate

PO Box 78, County Hall, Fishergate, Preston, Lancashire, PR1 8XJ
Tel: 03001 236706 Email: information.lineteam@lancashire.gov.uk Website: www.lancashire.gov.uk

ACCRINGTON

**Broadfield Specialist
School for SEN**
Fielding Lane, Oswaldtwistle,
ACCRINGTON, Lancashire BB5 3BE
Tel: 01254 381782
Head: Mrs Angela Banner
Category: MLD SLD
ASD (Coed 4-16)

White Ash School
Thwaites Road, Oswaldtwistle,
ACCRINGTON, Lancashire BB5 4QG
Tel: 01254 235772
Head: Mrs Phillipa Conti
Category: SLD ASD
PMLD (Coed 3-19)

BURNLEY

Holly Grove School
Burnley Campus, Barden Lane,
BURNLEY, Lancashire BB10 1JD
Tel: 01282 682278
Head: Ms Sue Kitto
Category: SLD MLD PMLD ASD
Medical needs (Coed 2-11)

**Ridgewood Community
High School**
Eastern Avenue, BURNLEY,
Lancashire BB10 2AT
Tel: 01282 682316
Head: Mrs Frances Entwistle
Category: MSI PD LD (Coed 11-16)

The Rose School
Greenock Street, BURNLEY,
Lancashire BB11 4DT
Tel: 01282 683050
Head: Mr Russell Bridge
Category: BESD (Coed 11-16)

CARNFORTH

Bleasdale House School
27 Emesgate Lane, Silverdale,
CARNFORTH, Lancashire LA5 0RG
Tel: 01524 701217
Head: Ms Kairen Dexter
Category: PMLD PH (Coed 2-19)

CHORLEY

Astley Park School
Harrington Road, CHORLEY,
Lancashire PR7 1JZ
Tel: 01257 262227
Head: Mr Kieran Welsh
Category: MLD SLD ASD
EBD(Coed 4-17)

Mayfield Specialist School
Gloucester Road, CHORLEY,
Lancashire PR7 3HN
Tel: 01257 263063
Head: Ms Rachel Kay
Category: CLD ASD
EBD (Coed 2-19)

COLNE

Pendle View Primary School
Gibfield Road, COLNE,
Lancashire BB8 8JT
Tel: 01282 865011
Head: Ms Debbie Morris
Category: LD PD SLD PMLD
ASD MSI (Coed 2-11)

HASLINGDEN

Tor View Community Special School
Clod Lane, HASLINGDEN,
Lancashire BB4 6LR
Tel: 01706 214640
Head: Mr Andrew Squire
Category: AUT MLD SLD
PMLD MSI (Coed 4-19)

KIRKHAM

Pear Tree School
29 Station Road, KIRKHAM,
Lancashire PR4 2HA
Tel: 01772 683609
Head: Ms Lesley Sullivan
Category: SLD PMLD
ASD (Coed 2-19)

LANCASTER

The Loyne Specialist School
Sefton Drive, LANCASTER,
Lancashire LA1 2PZ
Tel: 01524 64543
Head: Mrs Carol Murphy
Category: MSI LD CLD
PD AUT EPI (2-19)

Wennington Hall School
Lodge Lane, Wennington,
LANCASTER, Lancashire LA2 8NS
Tel: 01524 221333
Head: Mr Joseph Prendergast
Category: SEBD (Boys
Day or resident 11-16)

MORECAMBE

Morecambe Road School
Morecambe Road, MORECAMBE,
Lancashire LA3 3AB
Tel: 01524 414384
Head: Mr Paul Edmondson
Category: LD ASD BESD (Coed 3-16)

NELSON

Pendle Community High School and College
Oxford Road, NELSON,
Lancashire BB9 8LF
Tel: 01282 682240
Head: Mr Paul Wright
Category: MLD BESD
ASD (Coed 11-19)

POULTON-LE-FYLDE

Brookfield School
Fouldrey Avenue, POULTON-
LE-FYLDE, Lancashire FY6 7HE
Tel: 01253 886895
Head: Mrs Jane Fallon
Category: SEBD ADHD
ASD SPLD (Coed 11-16)

PRESTON

Acorns Primary School
Blackpool Road, Moor Park,
PRESTON, Lancashire PR1 6AU
Tel: 01772 792681
Head: Ms Gail Beaton
Category: AUT SLD
PMLD (Coed 2-19)

Hillside Specialist School and College
Ribchester Road, Longridge,
PRESTON, Lancashire PR3 3XB
Tel: 01772 782205
Head: Mrs Alison Foster
Category: ASD (Coed 2-16)

Moor Hey School
Far Croft, off Leyland Road, Lostock
Hall, PRESTON, Lancashire PR5 5SS
Tel: 01772 336976
Head: Mrs Helen-Ruth McLenahan
Category: MLD CLD EBD (4-16)

Moorbrook School
Ainslie Road, Fulwood, PRESTON,
Lancashire PR2 3DB
Tel: 01772 774752
Head: Mr Mick Ironmonger
Category: SEBN (11-16)

Royal Cross Primary School
Elswick Road, Ashton-on-Ribble,
PRESTON, Lancashire PR2 1NT
Tel: 01772 729705
Head: Ms Ruth Bonney
Category: SLCN D ASD (Coed 4-11)

Sir Tom Finney Community High School
Blackpool Road, Moor Park,
PRESTON, Lancashire PR1 6AA
Tel: 01772 795749
Head: Mr Shaun Jukes
Category: PD PMLD BESD
MLD (Coed 2-19)

The Coppice School
Ash Grove, Bamber Bridge,
PRESTON, Lancashire PR5 6GY
Tel: 01772 336342
Head: Mrs Liz Davies
Category: SLD PMLD CLD
Medical needs (Coed 2-19)

RAWTENSTALL

Cribden House Community Special School
Haslingden Road, RAWTENSTALL,
Lancashire BB4 6RX
Tel: 01706 213048
Head: Siobhan Halligan
Category: SEBD (Coed 5-11)

SKELMERSDALE

Elm Tree Community Primary School
Elmers Wood Road, SKELMERSDALE,
Lancashire WN8 6SA
Tel: 01695 50924
Head: Mr David Lamb
Category: BESD (Coed)

Hope High School
Clay Brow, SKELMERSDALE,
Lancashire WN8 9DP
Tel: 01695 721066
Head: Ms Helen Dunbavin
Category: EBD (Coed 11-16)

Kingsbury Primary School
School Lane, Chapel
House, SKELMERSDALE,
Lancashire WN8 8EH
Tel: 01695 722991
Head: Ms Fiona Grieveson
Category: SLD PMLD LD
ASD MLD (Coed 2-11)

West Lancashire Community High School
School Lane, Chapel
House, SKELMERSDALE,
Lancashire WN8 8EH
Tel: 01695 721487
Head: Mrs Austin
Category: MLD SLD PMLD
AUT (Coed 11-19)

THORNTON-CLEVELEYS

Great Arley School
Holly Road, THORNTON-
CLEVELEYS, Lancashire FY5 4HH
Tel: 01253 821072
Head: Mrs Anne Marshfield
Category: MLD ASD SLD
BESD (Coed Day 4-16)

Red Marsh School
Holly Road, THORNTON-
CLEVELEYS, Lancashire FY5 4HH
Tel: 01253 868451
Head: Ms Catherine Dellow
Category: SLD PMLD
CLD (Coed 2-19)

LEICESTER CITY COUNCIL
Education Authority

City Hall, 115 Charles Street, Leicester, LE1 1F2
Tel: 01164 541000 Website: www.leicester.gov.uk

LEICESTER

Children's Hospital School
University Hospitals of Leicester
NHS Trust, Infirmary Square,
LEICESTER LE1 5WW
Tel: 01162 585330
Head: Mr George Sfougaras
Category: HS

Ellesmere College
40 Braunstone Lane East,
LEICESTER LE3 2FD
Tel: 01162 894242
Heads: Lisa Pittwood &
Linda Richardson

Keyham Lodge School
Keyham Lane, LEICESTER LE5 1FG
Tel: 01162 41 6852
Head: Mr Chris Bruce
Category: EBD (Boys Secondary)

Millgate School
18A Scott Street, LEICESTER LE2 6DW
Tel: 01162 704922
Head: Mr Chris Bruce

Nether Hall School
Keyham Lane West,
LEICESTER LE5 1RT
Tel: 01162 417258
Head: Ms Erica Dennies

Oaklands School
Whitehall Road, LEICESTER LE5 6GJ
Tel: 01162 415921
Head: Mrs E Shaw
Category: MLD (Primary)

On-Trak Inclusion Service (linked to PRU)
495 Welford Road,
LEICESTER LE2 6BN
Tel: 01162 706016
Head: Mr Shaun Whittingham
Category: PRU

Phoenix (PRU)
c/o Thurnby Lodge Primary School,
Dudley Avenue, LEICESTER LE5 2EG
Tel: 01162 419538
Team Leader: Allison Benson
Category: Primary PRU

The ARC (PRU)
c/o Holy Cross Primary School,
Stonesby Avenue, LEICESTER LE2 6TY
Tel: 01162 832185
Team Leader: Mrs C H Pay
Category: Primary PRU

West Gate School
Glenfield Road, LEICESTER LE3 6DN
Tel: 01162 856181
Head: Ms Jan Hesketh
Category: SLD MLD

Wigston Lane Educational Unit (PRU)
126 Wigston Lane, Aylestone,
LEICESTER LE2 8TN
Tel: 01162 836139
Head: Mr Shaun Whittingham
Category: Children Centre, PRU

LEICESTERSHIRE
County Council

SEND Information Advice & Support Service, Abington House, 85 Station Road, Wigston, Leicestershire, LE18 2DP
Tel: 01163 055614/01163 056545 Email: sendqueries@leics.gov.uk Website: www.leics.gov.uk

COALVILLE

Forest Way School
Warren Hills Road, COALVILLE,
Leicestershire LE67 4UU
Tel: 01530 831899
Head: Mrs Lynn Slinger
Category: SLD PMLD (2-18)

HINCKLEY

Dorothy Goodman School Hinckley
Stoke Road, HINCKLEY,
Leicestershire LE10 0EA
Tel: 01455 634582
Head: Ms Janet Thompson
Category: (2-18)

Sketchley Hill Menphys Nursery
Sketchley Road, Burbage,
HINCKLEY, Leicestershire LE10 2DY
Tel: 01455 890684
Head: Mrs Helen Johnston

LOUGHBOROUGH

Ashmount School
Thorpe Hill, LOUGHBOROUGH,
Leicestershire LE11 4SQ
Tel: 01509 268506
Head: Mr Dave Thomas
Category: SLD PMLD (2-18)

Maplewell Hall School
Maplewell Road, Woodhouse
Eaves, LOUGHBOROUGH,
Leicestershire LE12 8QY
Tel: 01509 890237
Head: Mr Jason Brooks
Category: MLD AUT (10-15)

MELTON MOWBRAY

Birch Wood (Melton Area Special School)
Grange Drive, MELTON MOWBRAY,
Leicestershire LE13 1HA
Tel: 01664 483340
Head: Ms Nina Watts
Category: MLD SLD AUT (5-19)

WIGSTON

Birkett House Community Special School
Launceston Road, WIGSTON,
Leicestershire LE18 2FZ
Tel: 01162 885802
Head: Mrs Susan Horn
Category: SLD PMLD (2-18)

Wigston Menphys Centre
Launceston Road, WIGSTON,
Leicestershire LE18 2FZ
Tel: 01162 889977
Head: Mrs Helen Johnston

LINCOLNSHIRE
County Council

SEN Team, County Offices, Newland, Lincoln, Lincolnshire, LN1 1YL
Tel: 01522 553332 Website: www.lincolnshire.gov.uk

BOSTON

John Fielding School
Ashlawn Drive, BOSTON,
Lincolnshire PE21 9PX
Tel: 01205 363395
Acting Head: Mr Daran Bland
Category: SLD (2-19)

The Pilgrim School
Pilgrim Hospital, Sibsey Road,
BOSTON, Lincolnshire PE21 9QS
Tel: 01205 445641
Head: Mrs C M Seymour
Category: HS (4-16)

BOURNE

Willoughby School
South Road, BOURNE,
Lincolnshire PE10 9JE
Tel: 01778 425203
Head: Mr Adam Booker
Category: SLD (2-19)

GAINSBOROUGH

**The Aegir Community
School**
Gainsborough Educational Village,
Sweyn Lane, GAINSBOROUGH,
Lincolnshire DN21 1PB
Tel: 01427 619360
Executive Principal: Mr Gary Nixon
Category: MLD SLD (11-19)

**Warren Wood
Community School**
Middlefield Lane, GAINSBOROUGH,
Lincolnshire DN21 1PU
Tel: 01427 615498
Executive Principal: Mr Gary Nixon
Category: MLD SLD (3-11)

GOSBERTON

Gosberton House School
Westhorpe Road, GOSBERTON,
Lincolnshire PE11 4EW
Tel: 01775 840250
Head: Ms L Stanton
Category: MLD (3-11)

GRANTHAM

Sandon School
Sandon Close, GRANTHAM,
Lincolnshire NG31 9AX
Tel: 01476 564994
Principal: Ms Ann White
Category: SLD (2-19)

**The Ambergate Sports
College Specialist
Education Centre**
Dysart Road, GRANTHAM,
Lincolnshire NG31 7LP
Tel: 01476 564957
Principal: Ms Ann White
Category: MLD (5-16)

The Phoenix School
Great North Road, GRANTHAM,
Lincolnshire NG31 7US
Tel: 01476 574112
Acting Principals: Mr Stan
Kilroy & Mrs Diana Bush
Category: EBD (11-16)

HORNCASTLE

St Lawrence School
Bowl Alley Lane, HORNCASTLE,
Lincolnshire LN9 5EJ
Tel: 01507 522563
Head: Ms Michelle Hockham
Category: MLD (5-16)

LINCOLN

St Christopher's School
Hykeham Road, LINCOLN,
Lincolnshire LN6 8AR
Tel: 01522 528378
Head: Mr Allan Lacey
Category: MLD (3-16)

St Francis School
Wickenby Crescent, Ermine Estate,
LINCOLN, Lincolnshire LN1 3TJ
Tel: 01522 526498
Head: Mrs Ann Hoffmann
Category: PD Sensory (2-19)

The Fortuna Primary School
Kingsdown Road, Doddington
Park, LINCOLN, Lincolnshire LN6 0FB
Tel: 01522 705561
Head: Miss B Robson
Category: EBD (4-11)

The Sincil Sports College
South Park, LINCOLN,
Lincolnshire LN5 8EL
Tel: 01522 534559
Head: Mr Rob Parkin
Category: EBD (11-16)

LOUTH

St Bernard's School
Wood Lane, LOUTH,
Lincolnshire LN11 8RS
Tel: 01507 603776
Head: Ms Ann Stebbings
Category: SLD (2-19)

SLEAFORD

The Ash Villa School
Willoughby Road, Greylees,
SLEAFORD, Lincolnshire NG34 8QA
Tel: 01529 488066
Head: Mr Leigh Bentley
Category: HS (8-16)

SPALDING

The Garth School
Pinchbeck Road, SPALDING,
Lincolnshire PE11 1QF
Tel: 01775 725566
Head: Mr Daran Bland
Category: SLD (2-19)

The Priory School
Neville Avenue, SPALDING,
Lincolnshire PE11 2EH
Tel: 01775 724080
Head: Mr Daran Bland
Category: MLD (11-16)

SPILSBY

The Eresby School
Eresby Avenue, SPILSBY,
Lincolnshire PE23 5HU
Tel: 01790 752441
Head: Ms Michele Holiday
Category: SLD (2-19)

**The Lady Jane
Franklin School**
Partney Road, SPILSBY,
Lincolnshire PE23 5EJ
Tel: 01790 753902
Head: Mr Chris Armond
Category: EBD (11-16)

NORTH LINCOLNSHIRE
People Directorate

SEND Team, Hewson House, PO Box 35, Station Road Brigg, North Lincolnshire, DN20 8XJ
Tel: 01724 297148 Email: special.needssection@northlincs.gov.uk Website: www.northlincs.gov.uk

SCUNTHORPE

**St Hugh's Communication
& Interaction
Specialist College**
Bushfield Road, SCUNTHORPE,
North Lincolnshire DN16 1NB
Tel: 01724 842960
Head: Mrs Tracy Millard
Category: MLD SLD
PMLD (Coed 11-19)

St Luke's Primary School
Grange Lane North, SCUNTHORPE,
North Lincolnshire DN16 1BN
Tel: 01724 844560
Head: Mr Alastair Sutherland
Category: PMLD SLD
MLD (Coed 3-11)

NORTH EAST LINCOLNSHIRE
Directorate of Learning & Children

SEN Team, Riverside Children's Centre, Central Parade, Grimsby, DN34 4HE
Tel: 01472 326293 Email: fis@nelincs.gov.uk Website: www.nelincs.gov.uk

GRIMSBY

**Humberston Park
Special School**
St Thomas Close, Humberston,
GRIMSBY, N E Lincolnshire DN36 4HS
Tel: 01472 590645
Head: Mr Andrew Zielinski
Category: SLD PMLD PD
CLD MSI (Coed 3-19)

**The Cambridge
Park Academy**
Cambridge Road, GRIMSBY,
N E Lincolnshire DN34 5EB
Tel: 01472 230110
Head: Mr Mark Eames
Category: ASD SLCN MLD
SLD (Coed 3-19)

London
BARKING AND DAGENHAM
Education, Health and Care Team

Roycraft House, 5th Floor, 15 Linton Road, Barking, Essex, IG11 8HE
Tel: 02082 272400 Fax: 02082 273104 Email: joseph.wilson@lbbd.gov.uk

DAGENHAM

Trinity School
Heathway, DAGENHAM,
Essex RM10 7SJ
Tel: 02082 701601
Head: Mr Peter McPartland
Category: SLD ASD
PMLD (Coed 3-19)

London
BARNET
Council

SEN Referral & Assessment Team, North London Business Park, Oakleigh Road South, London, N11 1NP
Tel: 02083 597007 Email: senadmin@barnet.gov.uk Website: www.barnet.gov.uk

LONDON

Mapledown School
Claremont Road, Golders
Green, LONDON NW2 1TR
Tel: 02084 554111
Head: Mr S Caroll
Category: SLD CLD (Mixed 11-19)

Northway School
The Fairway, Mill Hill,
LONDON NW7 3HS
Tel: 02083 595450
Head: Ms L Burgess
Category: CLD AUT (Mixed 5-11)

Oak Lodge School
Heath View, Off East End
Road, LONDON N2 0QY
Tel: 02084 446711
Head: Mrs L Walker
Category: MLD ASD SCLN
EBD (Mixed 11-19)

Oakleigh School
Oakleigh Road North,
Whetstone, LONDON N20 0DH
Tel: 02083 685336
Head: Ms J Gridley
Category: SLD AUT
PMLD (Mixed 3-11)

London
LONDON BOROUGH OF BEXLEY
Directorate of Education and Social Care

SEN Team, Civic Offices, 2 Watling Street, Bexleyheath, Kent, DA6 7AT
Tel: 02083 037777 Email: specialneeds.els@bexley.gov.uk Website: www.bexley.gov.uk

BELVEDERE

Woodside School
Halt Robin Road, BELVEDERE,
Kent DA17 6DW
Tel: 01322 433494
Head: Ms Madelaine Caplin
Category: MLD (Primary/
Secondary)

BEXLEY HEATH

Oakwood School
Woodside Road, BEXLEY
HEATH, Kent DA7 6LB
Tel: 01322 553787
Head: Ms Beverley Evans
Category: BESD (Coed 11-16)

CRAYFORD

Shenstone School
94 Old Road, CRAYFORD,
Kent DA1 4DZ
Tel: 01322 524145
Head: Ms Lori Mackey
Category: SLD (2-11)

SIDCUP

Marlborough School
Marlborough Park Avenue,
SIDCUP, Kent DA15 9DP
Tel: 02083 006896
Head: Ms Linda Lee
Category: SLD (11-19)

WELLING

Westbrooke School
Gipsy Road South, WELLING,
Kent DA16 1JB
Tel: 02083 041320
Head: Mr Phill Collins
Category: BESD (5-11)

London
BRENT
Children & Families Department

SENDIASS, Brent Civic Centre, Engineers Way, Wembley, Middlesex, HA9 0FJ
Tel: 02089 373434 Email: brentsendias@brent.gov.uk Website: www.brent.gov.uk

KENSALE RISE

Manor School
Chamberlayne Road, KENSALE
RISE, London NW10 3NT
Tel: 02089 683160
Head: Ms Jayne Jardine
Category: MLD SLD CLD
ASD (Coed 4-11)

KINGSBURY

The Village School
Grove Park, KINGSBURY,
London NW9 0JY
Tel: 02082 045396
Head: Ms Kay Johnson
Category: LD DD VIS Medical
needs (Coed 2-19)

Woodfield School
Glenwood Avenue, KINGSBURY,
London NW9 7LY
Tel: 02082 051977
Head: Ms Desi Lodge-Patch
Category: MLD BESD
ASD (Coed 11-16)

NEASDEN

Phoenix Arch School
Drury Way, NEASDEN,
London NW10 0NQ
Tel: 02084 516961
Head: Ms Jude Towell
Category: BESD LD ADHD
ASD (Coed 5-11)

London
BROMLEY
Council

Information, Advice and Support Service (IASS), Blenheim Children & Family Centre, Blenheim Road, Orpington, Kent, BR6 9BH
Tel: 01689 881024 Email: iass@bromley.gov.uk Website: www.bromley.gov.uk

BECKENHAM

Riverside School (Beckenham ASD Centre)
2 Hayne Road, BECKENHAM, Kent BR3 4HY
Tel: 02086 390079
Head: Mr Steve Solomons
Category: ASD (Coed 4-19)

CHISLEHURST

Marjorie McClure School
Hawkwood Lane, CHISLEHURST, Kent BR7 5PS
Tel: 02084 670174
Head: Mrs Denise James-Mason
Category: PD SLD Medical needs (Coed 3-18)

ORPINGTON

Burwood School
Avalon Road, ORPINGTON, Kent BR6 9BD
Tel: 01689 821205
Head: Mr Gareth McCullough
Category: EBD (Boys 7-16)

Riverside School
Main Road, St Paul's Cray, ORPINGTON, Kent BR5 3HS
Tel: 01689 870519
Head: Mr Steve Solomons
Category: (Coed 4-19)

WEST WICKHAM

Glebe School
Hawes Lane, WEST WICKHAM, Kent BR4 9AE
Tel: 02087 774540
Head: Mr K Seed
Category: Complex needs SCD ASD SLD (Coed 11-19)

London Borough
CAMDEN
Children, Schools & Families Directorate

Special Educational Needs Team, 10th Floor, 5 Pancras Square, c/o Town Hall, Judd Street London, WC1H 9JE
Tel: 02079 746500 Fax: 02079 746501 Website: www.camden.gov.uk

LONDON

Chalcot School
Harmood Street, LONDON NW1 8DP
Tel: 02074 852147
Head: Ms Jeanette Lowe
Category: BESD (Coed 11-16)

Frank Barnes Primary School for Deaf Children
Jubilee Waterside Centre, 105 Camley Street, LONDON N1C 4PF
Tel: 02073 917040
Head: Ms Karen Simpson
Category: HI (Coed 2-11)

Great Ormond Street Hospital School
(Grant Maintained), Great Ormond Street, LONDON WC1N 3JH
Tel: 02078 138269
Head: Ms Jayne Franklin
Category: HS (Coed 0-19)

Royal Free Hospital School
Royal Free Hospital, Pond Street, LONDON NW3 2QG
Tel: 02074 726298
Head: Mr Alex Yates
Category: HS (5-16)

Swiss Cottage School Development and Research Centre
80 Avenue Road, LONDON NW8 6HX
Tel: 02076 818080
Head: Ms Kay Bedford
Category: LD (2-16)

London
CROYDON

Children, Young People & Learners

SEN Team, Taberner House, Park Lane, Croydon, Surrey, CR9 3JS
Tel: 02087 266000 ext 62394 Email: senss@croydon.gov.uk Website: www.croydon.gov.uk

BECKENHAM

Beckmead School
Monks Orchard Road,
BECKENHAM, Kent BR3 3BZ
Tel: 02087 779311
Heads: Mr Sean Campbell
& Mr Dean Monfries
Category: BESD (Boys 5-16)

CROYDON

Chaffinch Brook School
32 Moorland Road, CROYDON,
Surrey CR0 6NA
Tel: 02083 254612
Head: Ms Judith Azzopardi
Category: BESD ASD (Boys 5-16)

Red Gates School
Farnborough Avenue,
CROYDON, Surrey CR2 8HD
Tel: 02086 516540
Head: Mrs Susan Beaman
Category: SLD PMLD
ASD (Coed 4-12)

St Giles School
207 Pampisford Road,
CROYDON, Surrey CR2 6DF
Tel: 02086 802141
Head: Ms Ginny Marshall
Category: PH Complex
medical needs (Coed 4-19)

Victoria House School
Southbridge Place, CROYDON,
Surrey CR0 4HA
Tel: 02086 860393
Head: Ms Alison Page
Category: BESD (Boys 5-16)

PURLEY

St Nicholas School
Old Lodge Lane, PURLEY,
Surrey CR8 4DN
Tel: 02086 604861
Head: Mr Nick Dry
Category: MLD ASD SLCN
AUT (Coed 4-11)

THORNTON HEATH

Bensham Manor School
Ecclesbourne Road, THORNTON
HEATH, Surrey CR7 7BN
Tel: 02086 840116
Head: Mr Philip Poulton
Category: MLD BESD SLD
ASD (Coed 11-16)

UPPER NORWOOD

Priory School
Hermitage Road, UPPER
NORWOOD, Surrey SE19 3QN
Tel: 02086 538222
Head: Mr Simon Vines
Category: PMLD CLD (Coed 11-19)

London
EALING

Education Department

SEN Team, 2nd Floor NE, Perceval House, 14-16 Uxbridge Road London, W5 2HL
Tel: 02088 255533 Email: education@ealing.gov.uk Website: www.ealing.gov.uk

EALING

Castlebar School
Hathaway Gardens, EALING,
London W13 0DH
Tel: 02089 983135
Head: Mr Paul Adair
Category: MLD SLD ASD
(Coed Day 4-11)

GREENFORD

Mandeville School
Horsenden Lane North,
GREENFORD, Middlesex UB6 0PA
Tel: 02088 644921/0911
Head: Ms Denise Feasey
Category: SLD ASD PMLD
(Coed Day 2-12)

Springhallow School
William Perkin C of E High
School, Oldfield Lane North,
GREENFORD, London UB6 8PR
Tel: 02088 328979
Head: Mr Andy Balmer
Category: ASD (Coed Day 4-16/17)

HANWELL

St Ann's School
Springfield Road, HANWELL,
London W7 3JP
Tel: 02085 676291
Head: Ms Gillian Carver
Category: SLD MSI PNLD
SLCN Complex medical
conditions (Coed Day 12-19)

NORTHOLT

Belvue School
Rowdell Road, NORTHOLT,
London UB5 6AG
Tel: 02088 455766
Head: Mrs Shelagh O'Shea
Category: MLD SLD ASD
(Coed Day 11-18)

John Chilton School
Compton Crescent, NORTHOLT,
London UB5 5LD
Tel: 02088 421329
Head: Mr Simon Rosenberg
Category: PH/Medical
(Coed Day 2-18)

London
ENFIELD

Education & Learning

Education Office, Civic Centre, Silver Street, Enfield, Middlesex, EN1 3XY
Tel: 02083 791000 Email: enfield.council@enfield.gov.uk Website: www.enfield.gov.uk

EDMONTON

West Lea School
Haselbury Road, EDMONTON,
London N9 9TU
Tel: 02088 072656
Head: Mrs Susan Tripp
Category: HA ASD PD
LD (Coed 4-18)

ENFIELD

Aylands School
Keswick Drive, ENFIELD,
London EN3 6NY
Tel: 01992 761229
Head: Ms Sashi Sivaloganathan
Category: EBD (Coed 7-16)

Durants School
4 Pitfield Way, ENFIELD,
London EN3 5BY
Tel: 02088 041980
Head: Mr Peter De Rosa
Category: CLD ASD (Coed 4-19)

Russet House School
11 Autumn Close, ENFIELD,
London EN1 4JA
Tel: 02083 500650
Head: Mrs Julie Foster
Category: AUT (Coed 3-11)

Waverley School
105 The Ride, ENFIELD,
London EN2 7DL
Tel: 02088 051858
Head: Ms Gail Weir
Category: PMLD SLD (Coed 3-19)

SOUTHGATE

Oaktree School
Chase Side, SOUTHGATE,
London N14 4HN
Tel: 02084 403100
Head: Mr Richard Yarwood
Category: Complex
needs (Coed 7-19)

London
ROYAL BOROUGH OF GREENWICH

Children's Services

1st Floor, The Woolwich Centre, 35 Wellington Street, Woolwich London, SE18 6HQ
Tel: 02089 218945 Website: www.royalgreenwich.gov.uk

LONDON

Charlton Park Academy
Charlton Park Road,
LONDON SE7 8HX
Tel: 02082 496844
Head: Mark Dale-Emberton
Category: SCLD SCD PMLD
PD ASD (Coed 11-19)

Moatbridge School
Eltham Palace Road,
LONDON SE9 5LX
Tel: 02088 508081
Head: Mike Byron
Category: BESD (Boys 11-16)

Waterside School
Robert Street, Plumstead,
LONDON SE18 7NB
Tel: 02083 177659
Head: Meic Griffiths
Category: BESD (Coed 5-11)

Willow Dene School
Swingate Lane, Plumstead,
LONDON SE18 2JD
Tel: 02088 549841
Executive Head: John Camp
Category: SCLD CLD PMLD
PD ASD (Coed 5-16)

London
HACKNEY

Hackney Learning Trust

Technology & Learning Centre, 1 Reading Lane, London, E8 1GQ
Tel: 02088 207000 Fax: 02088 207001 Email: info@learningtrust.co.uk Website: www.hackney.gov.uk

LONDON

Ickburgh School
Kenworthy Road, LONDON E9 5RB
Tel: 02088 064638
Head: Ms Sue Davis
Category: SLD PMLD (2-19)

New Regents College
Ickburgh Road, LONDON E5 8AD
Tel: 02089 856833
Head: Mr Shane Foley

Stormont House School
Downs Park Road, LONDON E5 8NP
Tel: 02089 854245
Head: Mr Kevin McDonnell
Category: Complex
needs (Secondary)

The Garden School
Wordsworth Road,
LONDON N16 8BZ
Tel: 02072 548096
Heads: Ms Kt Khan & Ms Pat Quigley
Category: MLD ASD (Secondary)

London
HAMMERSMITH & FULHAM
Council

SEN Team, Town Hall, King Street, Hammersmith London, W6 9JU
Tel: 02073 613311 Email: localoffer@rbkc.gov.uk Website: www.lbhf.gov.uk

LONDON

Cambridge School
61 Bryony Road, Hammersmith,
LONDON W12 0SP
Tel: 02087 350980
Head: Mr Anthony Rawdin
Category: MLD (11-16)

Jack Tizard School
South Africa Road,
LONDON W12 7PA
Tel: 02087 353590
Head: Ms Cathy Welsh
Category: SLD PMLD
(Coed Day 3-19)

Queensmill School
1 Askham Road, Shepherds
Bush, LONDON W12 0NW
Tel: 02073 842330
Head: Ms Jude Ragan
Category: ASD (Coed 3-19)

**The Courtyard at
Langford Primary**
The Courtyard, Langford Primary,
Gilstead Road, LONDON SW6 2LG
Tel: 02076 108075
Head: Ms Janet Packer
Category: BESD (5-11)

Woodlane High School
Du Cane Road, LONDON W12 0TN
Tel: 02087 435668
Head: Mr Peter Harwood
Category: SCLN SPLD SEBD MSI
Medical difficulties (Coed 11-16)

London
HARINGEY
Children & Young People's Service

Additional Needs and Disabilities, 40 Cumberland Road, London, N22 7SG
Tel: 02084 893668 Email: sen@haringey.gov.uk Website: www.haringey.gov.uk

MUSWELL HILL

**Blanche Nevile
Secondary School**
Burlington Road, MUSWELL
HILL, London N10 1NJ
Tel: 02084 422750
Head: Ms Veronica Held
Category: HI (Coed Day 11-18)

NORTH HILL

**Blanche Nevile
Primary School**
Storey Road, NORTH HILL,
London N6 4ED
Tel: 02083 473760
Head: Ms Veronica Held
Category: HI (Coed Day 3-10)

TOTTENHAM

Riverside School
Wood Green Inclusive Learning
Campus, White Hart Lane,
TOTTENHAM, London N22 5QJ
Tel: 02088 897814
Head: Mr Martin Doyle

The Brook on Broadwaters
Adams Road, TOTTENHAM,
London N17 6HW
Tel: 02088 087120
Head: Ms Margaret Sumner
Category: (Coed Day 4-11)

WEST GREEN

The Vale School
Northumberland Park Community
School, Trulock Road, WEST
GREEN, London N17 0PG
Tel: 02088 016111
Head: Ms Sarah McLay
Category: PD (Coed Day 2-16)

London
BOROUGH OF HARROW
Childrens Service

Children with Disabilities Service, Alexandra Avenue Health & Social Care Centre,
275 Alexandra Avenue, South Harrow, Middlesex, HA2 9DX
Tel: 02089 666481 Fax: 02089 666489 Email: childrenwithdisabilities@harrow.gov.uk Website: www.harrow.gov.uk

EDGWARE

Woodlands School
Bransgrove Road, EDGWARE,
Middlesex HA8 6JP
Tel: 02083 812188
Head: Mr John Feltham
Category: SLD PMLD ASD (Coed 3-11)

HARROW

Alexandra School
Alexandra Avenue, HARROW,
Middlesex HA2 9DX
Tel: 02088 642739
Head: Ms Perdy Buchanan-Barrow
Category: MLD EBD ASD (Coed 4-11)

Kingsley High School
Whittlesea Road, HARROW,
Middlesex HA3 6ND
Tel: 02084 213676
Head: Mrs Hazel Paterson
Category: SLD PMLD (Coed 11-19)

Shaftesbury High School
Headstone Lane, HARROW,
Middlesex HA3 6LE
Tel: 02084 282482
Head: Mr Paul Williams
Category: MLD EBD
ASD (Coed 11-19)

London Borough of
HAVERING
Education Authority

Children's Services, Mercury House, Mercury Gardens, Romford, Essex, RM1 3SL
Tel: 01708 434343 Website: www.havering.gov.uk

ROMFORD

Dycorts School
Settle Road, Harold Hill,
ROMFORD, Essex RM3 9YA
Tel: 01708 343649
Head: Mr G Wroe
Category: MLD

Ravensbourne School
Neave Cres, Faringdon Ave, Harold
Hill, ROMFORD, Essex RM3 8HN
Tel: 01708 341800
Head: Mrs M Cameron
Category: SLD PMLD

UPMINSTER

Corbets Tey School
Harwood Hall Lane, Corbets Tey,
UPMINSTER, Essex RM14 2YQ
Tel: 01708 225888
Head: Mrs Emma Allen
Category: MLD/SLD/
Complex Needs

London
HILLINGDON
Education

SEN Team, 4E/05, Civic Centre, High Street, Uxbridge, Middlesex, UB8 1UW
Tel: 01895 250489 Email: swynn@hillingdon.gov.uk Website: www.hillingdon.gov.uk

HAYES

**Hedgewood
Special School**
Weymouth Road, HAYES,
Middlesex UB4 8NF
Tel: 02088 456756
Head: Mr John Goddard
Category: MLD ASD
Complex moderate learning
needs (Coed 5-11)

The Willows School
Stipularis Drive, HAYES,
Middlesex UB4 9QB
Tel: 02088 417176
Head: Mr Malcolm Shaw
Category: SEBD ASD ADHD
Challenging behaviour (Coed 3-11)

PINNER

Grangewood School
Fore Street, Eastcote, PINNER,
Middlesex HA5 2JQ
Tel: 01895 676401
Head: Ms Hillary McDermott
Category: SLD PMLD
AUT (Coed 3-11)

UXBRIDGE

Meadow High School
Royal Lane, Hillingdon,
UXBRIDGE, Middlesex UB8 3QU
Tel: 01895 443310
Head: Mr Ross McDonald
Category: CLD ASD
Complex moderate learning
needs (Coed 11-19)

Moorcroft Special School
Bramble Close, Hillingdon,
UXBRIDGE, Middlesex UB8 3BF
Tel: 01895 437799
Head: Mr Andrew Sanders
Category: SLD PMLD
AUT (Coed 11-19)

WEST DRAYTON

Chantry Special School
Falling Lane, Yiewsley, WEST
DRAYTON, Middlesex UB7 8AB
Tel: 01895 446747
Head: Mr Mark Pearson
Category: BESD AUT
ADHD (Coed 11-16)

London
HOUNSLOW
Children's Services and Lifelong Learning

Special Educational Needs Team, Civic Centre, Lampton Road, Hounslow, TW3 4DN
Tel: 02085 832672 Email: sen@hounslow.gov.uk Website: www.hounslow.gov.uk

BEDFONT

Marjory Kinnon School
Hatton Road, BEDFONT,
London TW14 9QZ
Tel: 02088 902032
Head: Ms Denise Morton
Category: MLD AUT (5-16)

CRANFORD

The Cedars Primary School
High Street, CRANFORD,
London TW5 9RU
Tel: 02082 300015
Head: Mrs Lesley Julian
Category: EBD (Primary)

HANWORTH

The Lindon Bennett School
Main Street, HANWORTH,
London TW13 6ST
Tel: 02088 980479
Head: Ms Clare Longhurst
Category: SLD (Primary)

ISLEWORTH

Oaklands School
Woodlands Road, ISLEWORTH,
London TW7 6JZ
Tel: 02085 603569
Head: Ms Anne Clinton
Category: SLD (Secondary)

London
ISLINGTON

Special Educational Needs team

First Floor, 222 Upper Street, London, N1 1XR
Tel: 02075 275518/4860 Email: sen.camb-ed@islington.gov.uk Website: www.islington.gov.uk

LONDON

Richard Cloudesley School
Golden Lane Campus,
101 Whitecross Street,
LONDON EC1Y 8JA
Tel: 02077 864800
Head: Ms Anne Corbett
Category: PD (Coed 2-19)

Samuel Rhodes Primary School
Montem Community Campus,
Hornsey Road, LONDON N7 7QT
Tel: 02072 815114
Head: Ms Julie Keylock
Category: MLD ASD
BESD (Coed 5-11)

Samuel Rhodes Secondary School
11 Highbury New Park,
LONDON N5 2EG
Tel: 02077 047490
Head: Ms Julie Keylock
Category: MLD ASD
BESD (Coed 12-18)

The Bridge Primary School
251 Hungerford Road,
LONDON N7 9LD
Tel: 02076 191000
Head: Ms Penny Barratt
Category: ASD SLD
PMLD (Coed 2-11)

The Bridge Secondary School
28 Carleton Road, LONDON N7 0EQ
Tel: 02077 150320
Head: Ms Penny Barratt
Category: ASD SLD
PMLD (Coed 12-18)

London
ROYAL BOROUGH OF KINGSTON UPON THAMES

Education Authority

Learning & Children's Services, Guildhall 2, Kingston upon Thames, Surrey, KT1 1EU
Tel: 02085 474615 Website: www.kingston.gov.uk

CHESSINGTON

St Philip's School & Post 16
Harrow Close, Leatherhead Road,
CHESSINGTON, Surrey KT9 2HR
Tel: 02083 972672
Head: Mrs Jude Bowen
Category: MLD SLD ASD (11-19)

KINGSTON UPON THAMES

Bedelsford School
Grange Road, KINGSTON UPON
THAMES, Surrey KT1 2QZ
Tel: 02085 469838
Head: Ms Julia James
Category: PD PMLD (3-16)

SURBITON

Dysart School
190 Ewell Road, SURBITON,
Surrey KT6 6HL
Tel: 02084 122600
Head: Ms Leigh Edser
Category: SLD ASD (5-19)

London
LAMBETH

Children & Young People's Service

SEN Team, Olive Morris House, 18 Brixton Hill, London, SW2 1RD
Email: sendsupport@lambeth.gov.uk Website: www.lambeth.gov.uk

RUSKIN PARK

The Michael Tippet School
Heron Road, RUSKIN PARK,
London SE24 0HZ
Tel: 02073 265898
Head: Ms Jan Stogden
Category: CLD AUT PD
SLD PMLD (Coed 11-19)

STOCKWELL

Lansdowne School
Argyll Close, Dalyell Road,
STOCKWELL, London SW9 9QL
Tel: 02077 373713
Head: Ms Linda Adams
Category: MLD SEBD ASD
CLD SLD (Coed 11-16)

STREATHAM

Livity School
Adare walk, STREATHAM,
London SW16 2PW
Tel: 02087 691009
Head: Ms Carol Argent
Category: SLD PMLD
ASD (Coed 2-11)

WEST DULWICH

Turney School
Turney Road, WEST DULWICH,
London SE21 8LX
Tel: 02086 707220
Head: Ms Linda Adams
Category: MLD SLD CLD
ASD (Coed 5-16)

WEST NORWOOD

Elm Court School
96 Elm Park, WEST NORWOOD,
London SW2 2EF
Tel: 02086 743412
Head: Ms Joanna Tarrant
Category: SEBN SLCN (Coed 11-16)

London
LEWISHAM

Children & Young People

Special Educational Needs, Kaleidoscope Child Development Centre, 32 Rushey Green, London, SE6 4JF
Tel: 02030 491475 Email: sen@lewisham.gov.uk Website: www.lewisham.gov.uk

BROMLEY

Drumbeat School
Roundtable Road, Downham,
BROMLEY, Kent BR1 5LE
Tel: 02086 989738
Head: Dr Vivan Hinchcliffe
Category: ASD (5-19)

DOWNHAM

New Woodlands School
49 Shroffold Road,
DOWNHAM, Kent BR1 5PD
Tel: 02086 952380
Head: Mr Duncan Harper
Category: BESD (Coed 5-14)

LONDON

Abbey Manor College
40 Falmouth Close, Lee,
LONDON SE12 8PJ
Tel: 02082 977060
Head: Dr Liz Jones
Category: BESD (Coed 11-19)

Brent Knoll School
Mayow Road, Forest Hill,
LONDON SE23 2XH
Tel: 02086 991047
Head: Mr Jonathan Sharpe
Category: AUT ASP SLCN
Emotionally Vulnerable (Coed 4-16)

Greenvale School
Waters Road, LONDON SE6 1UF
Tel: 02084 650740
Head: Ms Lynne Haines
Category: SLD PMLD (Coed 11-19)

Watergate School
Lushington Road, Bellingham,
LONDON SE6 3WG
Tel: 02086 956555
Head: jine Nĺ Ruairc
Category: SLD PMLD (Coed 3-11)

London
MERTON

Department of Children, Schools and Families

SENDIS, 1st Floor Civic Centre, London Road, Morden, Surrey, SM4 5DX
Tel: 02085 454810 Email: sen@merton.gov.uk Website: www.merton.gov.uk

MITCHAM

Cricket Green School
Lower Green West, MITCHAM,
Surrey CR4 3AF
Tel: 02086 401177
Head: Mrs Celia Dawson
Category: CLD (Coed 5-19)

Melrose School
Church Road, MITCHAM,
Surrey CR4 3BE
Tel: 02086 462620
Head: Mr Steve Childs
Category: SEBD (Coed 11-16)

MORDEN

Perseid School
Bordesley Road, MORDEN,
Surrey SM4 5LT
Tel: 02086 489737
Head: Mrs Tina Harvey
Category: PMLD (Coed 3-19)

London
NEWHAM
Local Authority

Special Educational Needs (SEN), Newham Dockside, 1st Floor, East Wing, 1000 Dockside Road London, E16 2QU
Tel: 02084 302000 Website: www.newham.gov.uk

PLAISTOW

Eleanor Smith School
North Street, PLAISTOW,
London E13 9HN
Tel: 02084 710018
Head Teacher: Mr Graham Smith
Category: SEBD (5-16)

STRATFORD

John F Kennedy School
Pitchford Street, STRATFORD,
London E15 4RZ
Tel: 02085 348544
Heads: Ms Diane Rochford
& Mr Bob Hewis
Category: SLD PMLD ASD Complex
medical needs (Coed 2-19)

London
REDBRIDGE
Education Authority

Lynton House, 255-259 High Road, Ilford, Essex, IG1 1NN
Tel: 02085 545000 Email: customer.cc@redbridge.gov.uk Website: www.redbridge.gov.uk

GOODMAYES

**Newbridge School -
Barley Lane Campus**
258 Barley Lane, GOODMAYES,
Essex IG3 8XS
Tel: 02085 991768
Head: Mrs L Parr
Category: SLD PMLD ASD
Complex medical needs (11-19)

HAINAULT

New Rush Hall School
Fencepiece Road,
HAINAULT, Essex IG6 2LJ
Tel: 02085 013951
Head: Mr J V d'Abbro OBE
Category: SEBD (6-16)

ROMFORD

**Little Heath
Foundation School**
Hainault Road, Little Heath,
ROMFORD, Essex RM6 5RX
Tel: 02085 994864
Head: Mr J Brownlie
Category: MLD Learning difficulties
& complex needs (11-16)

Newbridge School -
Gresham Drive Campus
161 Gresham Drive, Chadwell
Heath, ROMFORD, Essex RM6 4TR
Tel: 02085 907272
Head: Mrs L Parr
Category: SLD PMLD ASD
Complex medical needs (2-11)

WOODFORD GREEN

Hatton School
Roding Lane South, WOODFORD
GREEN, Essex IG8 8EU
Tel: 02085 514131
Head: Mrs Sue Blows
Category: AUT SP&LD (3-11)

London
RICHMOND UPON THAMES
Education Authority

Education, Children's and Cultural Services, Civic Centre, 44 York Street, Twickenham, Middlesex, TW1 3BZ
Tel: 02088 911411 Website: www.richmond.gov.uk

HAMPTON

Clarendon School
Hanworth Road, HAMPTON,
Surrey TW12 3DH
Tel: 02089 791165
Head: Mr John Kipps
Category: MLD (7-16) (offsite EBD 7-11)

RICHMOND

Strathmore School
Meadlands Drive, Petersham,
RICHMOND, Surrey TW10 7ED
Tel: 02089 480047
Head: Mr Ivan Pryce
Category: SLD PMLD (7-19)

London
SOUTHWARK
Council

SEN Team, PO Box 64529, London, SE1P 5LX
Tel: 02075 254278 Email: sen@southwark.gov.uk Website: www.southwark.gov.uk

BERMONDSEY

Beormund Primary School
Crosby Row, Long Lane,
BERMONDSEY SE1 3PS
Tel: 02075 259027
Head: Mr Andrew Henderson
Category: EBD (Boys 5-11)

Cherry Garden School
Macks Road, BERMONDSEY
SE16 3XU
Tel: 02072 374050
Head: Ms Teresa Neary
Category: SCLD (Coed 2-11)

Spa School
Monnow Road,
BERMONDSEY SE1 5RN
Tel: 02072 373714
Head: Mr Simon Eccles
Category: MLD AUT ASP
SLD SCD (Coed 11-19)

PECKHAM

Highshore Secondary School
Bellenden Road,
PECKHAM SE15 5BB
Tel: 02076 397211
Head: Ms Christine Wood
Category: DYS PD SLCN EBD
Complex needs (Coed 11-16)

Newlands School
Stuart Road, PECKHAM SE15 3AZ
Tel: 02076 392541
Head: Ms Debbie Lipkin
Category: SEBD (Boys 11-16)

Tuke Secondary School
Daniels Gardens,
PECKHAM SE15 6ER
Tel: 02076 395584
Head: Ms Heidi Tully
Category: SLD PMLD
ASD (Coed 11-19)

London
SUTTON
Local Offer

SEN Team, Civic Offices, St Nicholas Way, Sutton, Surrey, SM5 3AL
Tel: 02087 706000 Email: familyinfo@sutton.gov.uk Website: www.sutton.gov.uk

CARSHALTON

Wandle Valley School
Welbeck Road, CARSHALTON,
Surrey SM5 1LW
Tel: 02086 481365
Head: Mal Fjord-Roberts
Category: SEBD (Coed 5-16)

WALLINGTON

Carew Academy
Church Road, WALLINGTON,
Surrey SM6 7NH
Tel: 02086 478349
Acting Head: Mr John Prior
Category: MLD ASD (Coed 7-16)

Sherwood Park School
Streeters Lane, WALLINGTON,
Surrey SM6 7NP
Tel: 02087 739930
Head: Mrs Ann Nanasi
Category: SLD PMLD (Coed 2-19)

London
TOWER HAMLETS
Education Authority

SEN Team, 5th Floor, Mulberry Place, 5 Clove Crescent, London, E14 2BG
Tel: 02073 644880 Email: sen@towerhamlets.gov.uk Website: www.towerhamlets.gov.uk

BOW

Cherry Trees School
68 Campbell Road, BOW,
London E3 4EA
Tel: 02089 834344
Head: Mr Stuart Walker
Category: SEBD (Boys Day 5-11)

Phoenix School
49 Bow Road, BOW, London E3 2AD
Tel: 02089 804740
Head: Mr Stewart Harris
Category: ASD (Coed Day 3-19)

BROMLEY-BY-BOW

Ian Mikardo High School
60 William Guy Gardens,
Talwin Street, BROMLEY-BY-
BOW, London E3 3LF
Tel: 02089 812413
Head: Ms Claire Lillis
Category: SEBD (Boys Day 11-16)

LIMEHOUSE

Stephen Hawking School
2 Brunton Place, LIMEHOUSE,
London E14 7LL
Tel: 02074 239848
Head: Dr Matthew Rayner
Category: PMLD (Coed Day 2-11)

MILE END

Beatrice Tate School
41 Southern Grove, MILE
END, London E3 4PX
Tel: 02089 833760
Head: Mr Alan Black
Category: PMLD SLD
(Coed Day 11-19)

SEAFORD (East Sussex)

Bowden House School
Firle Road, SEAFORD (East
Sussex) BN25 2JB
Tel: 01323 893138
Head: Mr Gerry Crook
Category: BESD (Boys
Boarding 9-16)

London
WALTHAM FOREST

Children and Young People Services

SEN Team, Wood Street Health Centre, 6 Linford Road, Walthamstow London, E17 3LA
Tel: 02084 966505 Email: senteam@walthamforest.gov.uk Website: www.walthamforest.gov.uk

HALE END

Joseph Clarke School
Vincent Road, Highams Park,
HALE END, London E4 9PP
Tel: 02085 234833
Head: Ms Maureen Duncan
Category: VIS Complex
needs (Coed 2-18)

WALTHAM FOREST

Whitefield School & Centre
Macdonald Road, WALTHAM
FOREST, London E17 4AZ
Tel: 02085 313426
Head: Ms Elaine Colquhoun
Category: LD MSI SP&LD
(Coed 2-19)

WOODFORD GREEN

Brookfield House School
Alders Avenue, WOODFORD
GREEN, Essex IG8 9PY
Tel: 02085 272464
Executive Principal: Mr
Gary Pocock
Category: HI PD Complex
medical needs (Coed 2-16)

LEYTON

Belmont Park School
101 Leyton Green Road,
LEYTON, London E10 6DB
Tel: 02085 560006
Interim Head: Ms Maddy Reina
Category: Challenging
behaviour (Coed 11-16)

WALTHAMSTOW

William Morris School
Folly Lane, WALTHAMSTOW,
London E17 5NT
Tel: 02085 032225
Head: Mr Alan Campbell
Category: MLD SLD
PMLD (Coed 11-16)

London
WANDSWORTH

Children's Services

Special Needs Assessment Section, The Town Hall, High Street, Wandsworth London, SW18 3LL
Tel: 02088 718061 Email: cssnas@wandsworth.gov.uk Website: www.wandsworth.gov.uk

BALHAM

Oak Lodge School
101 Nightingale Lane, BALHAM,
London SW12 8NA
Tel: 02086 733453
Head: Ms Shanee Buxton
Category: D (Coed, Day/
boarding 11-19)

BROADSTAIRS

Bradstow School
Dumpton Park Drive,
BROADSTAIRS, Kent CT10 1BY
Tel: 01843 862123
Head: Ms Sarah Dunn
Category: PD AUT Challenging
behaviour (Coed 5-19)

EARLSFIELD

Garratt Park School
Waldron Road, EARLSFIELD,
London SW18 3BT
Tel: 02089 465769
Head: Mrs Irene Parks
Category: MLD SP&LD (Coed 11-18)

PUTNEY

Paddock Primary School
St Margaret's Crescent,
PUTNEY, London SW15 6HL
Tel: 02087 885648
Head: Ms Sarah Santos
Category: ASD MLD
SLD (Coed 3-11)

ROEHAMPTON

Greenmead School
St Margaret's Crescent,
ROEHAMPTON, London SW15 6HL
Tel: 02087 891466
Head: Mrs Lucy Wijsveld
Category: PD PMLD (Coed 3-11)

**Paddock Secondary
School**
Priory Lane, ROEHAMPTON,
London SW15 5RT
Tel: 02088 781521
Head: Ms Peggy Walpole
Category: SCLD ASD with
SLD (Coed 11-19)

SOUTHFIELDS

Linden Lodge School
61 Princes Way, SOUTHFIELDS,
London SW19 6JB
Tel: 02087 880107
Head: Mr Roger Legate
Category: VIS PMLD MSI (Coed 3-11)

TOOTING

Nightingale School
Beechcroft Road, TOOTING,
London SW17 7DF
Tel: 02088 749096
Head: Ms Alina Page
Category: BESD (Boys 11-19)

London
CITY OF WESTMINSTER

Children's Service Authority

SEN Team, 2nd Floor, The Town Hall, Green Zone, Hornton Street London, W8 7NX
Tel: 02073 613311 Website: www.westminster.gov.uk

LONDON

College Park School
Garway Road, LONDON W2 4PH
Tel: 02072 213454
Head: Ms Jackie Brathwaite
Category: MLD (Coed 5-19)

Queen Elizabeth II Jubilee School
Kennet Road, LONDON W9 3LG
Tel: 02076 415825
Head: Mr Scott Pickard
Category: SLD (Coed 5-19)

LUTON

Borough Council

SEN Team, Futures House, The Moakes, Luton, LU3 3QB
Tel: 01582 548132 Email: senat@luton.gov.uk Website: www.luton.gov.uk

LUTON

Lady Zia Werner School
Ashcroft Road, LUTON,
Bedfordshire LU2 9AY
Tel: 01582 728705
Head: Mrs D May
Category: SLD PMLD (Yr 1-6 & Early Years)

Richmond Hill School
Sunridge Avenue, LUTON,
Bedfordshire LU2 7JL
Tel: 01582 721019
Head: Mrs J Miller
Category: SLD PMLD (Primary Yr 1-6)

Woodlands Secondary School
Northwell Drive, LUTON,
Bedfordshire LU3 3SP
Tel: 01582 572880
Head: Mr D Foolkes
Category: SLD PMLD (11-19)

Greater Manchester
BOLTON

Children's Services Offices

Inclusion & Statutory Assessment, Paderborn House, 16 Howell Croft North, Bolton, BL1 1AU
Tel: 01204 338612 Email: ea.sen@bolton.gov.uk Website: www.bolton.gov.uk

BOLTON

Firwood School
Crompton Way, BOLTON BL2 3AF
Tel: 01204 333044
Head: Ms Karen Walker
Category: SLD PMLD
ASD (Coed 11-19)

Ladywood School
Masefield Road, Little
Lever, BOLTON BL3 1NG
Tel: 01204 333400
Head: Mrs Sally McFarlane
Category: MLD with Complex
needs incl ASD PD MSI (Coed 4-11)

Rumworth School
Armadale Road, Ladybridge,
BOLTON BL3 4TP
Tel: 01204 333600
Head: Mr Gary Johnson
Category: MLD with Complex
needs incl ASD PD MSI (Coed 11-19)

Thomasson Memorial School
Devonshire Road, BOLTON BL1 4PJ
Tel: 01204 333118
Head: Mr Bill Wilson
Category: D HI (Coed 4-11)

FARNWORTH

Green Fold School
Highfield Road,
FARNWORTH BL4 0RA
Tel: 01204 335883
Head: Mr Andrew Feeley
Category: SLD ASD
PMLD (Coed 4-11)

HORWICH

Lever Park School
Stocks Park Drive,
HORWICH BL6 6DE
Tel: 01204 332666
Head: Mr Colin Roscoe
Category: SEBD (Coed 11-16)

Greater Manchester
BURY

Children's Services

SEN Team, Seedfield Centre, Parkinson Street, Bury, Lancashire, BL9 6NY
Tel: 01612 535969 Email: senteam@bury.gov.uk Website: www.bury.gov.uk

BURY

Elms Bank Specialist Arts College
Ripon Avenue, Whitefield,
BURY M45 8PJ
Tel: 01617 661597
Head: Mrs E J Parkinson
Category: LD (Coed 11-19)

Millwood Primary School
School Street, Radcliffe,
BURY M26 3BW
Tel: 01617 242266
Head: Ms H Chadwick
Category: SLD PMLD ASD AUT
Complex needs (Coed 2-11)

Primary PRU - The Ark
Albert Road, Whitefield,
BURY M25 8HN
Tel: 01617 963259
Head: Ms J Hart

PRESTWICH

**Cloughside College
(Hospital Special School)**
Bury New Road,
PRESTWICH M25 3BL
Tel: 01617 724625
Head: Ms F Shah
Category: HS (Coed 14-19)

RAMSBOTTOM

Secondary PRU ñ Pupil Learning Centre (PLC)
New Summerseat House,
Summerseat Lane,
RAMSBOTTOM BL0 9UD
Tel: 01204 885275
Acting Head: Mrs M Brettell

Greater Manchester
MANCHESTER

City Council

Children's Services, 1st Floor, Universal Square, Devonshire Street North Manchester, Lancashire, M12 6JH
Tel: 01612 457459 Fax: 01612 747084 Email: sen@manchester.gov.uk Website: www.manchester.gov.uk

CONGLETON

Buglawton Hall
Buxton Road, CONGLETON,
Cheshire CW12 3PQ
Tel: 01260 274492
Head of Centre: Mr Jonathan Gillie
Category: SEBD
(Residential Boys 8-16)

MANCHESTER

Ashgate School
Crossacres Road, Peel
Hall, Wythenshawe,
MANCHESTER M22 5DR
Tel: 01612 196642
Headteacher: Ms Dianne
Wolstenholme
Category: SLD (5-11)

Camberwell Park
Bank House Road, Blackley,
MANCHESTER M9 8LT
Tel: 01617 401897
Headteacher: Mrs Mary Isherwood
Category: SLD (5-11)

Grange School
Matthews Lane, Longsight,
MANCHESTER M12 4GR
Tel: 01612 312590
Headteacher: Mr Keith Cox
Category: ASD CLD (4-19)

Lancasterian School
Elizabeth Springer Road, West
Didsbury, MANCHESTER M20 2XA
Tel: 01614 450123
Headteacher: Mrs Katie Cass
Category: PD (2-16)

Meade Hill School
Chain Road, Higher Blackley,
MANCHESTER M9 6GN
Tel: 01612 343925
Head of Centre: Mr
George Campbell
Category: SEBD (11-16)

Melland High School
Gorton Education Village,
50 Wembley Road, Gorton,
MANCHESTER M18 7DT
Tel: 01612 239915
Headteacher: Ms Sue Warner
Category: SLD (11-19)

North Ridge High School
Higher Blackley Education
Village, Alworth Road,
MANCHESTER M9 0RP
Tel: 01612 343588
Headteacher: Mrs Bernice Kostick
Category: MLD (11-19)

Piper Hill High School
Firbank Road, Newall Green,
MANCHESTER M23 2YS
Tel: 01614 363009
Headteacher: Ms Linda Jones
Category: SLD (11-19)

Rodney House School
Barrass Street, Openshaw,
MANCHESTER M11 1WT
Tel: 01612 237197
Headteacher: Ms Nuala Finegan
Category: ASD (2-7)

Royal Manchester Children's Hospital
Oxford Road, MANCHESTER
M13 9WL
Tel: 01617 010684
Head of Centre: Mrs Sandra Hibbert
Category: HS

Southern Cross School
Barlow Hall Road, Chorlton,
MANCHESTER M21 7JJ
Tel: 01618 812695
Head of Centre: Ms Kate Scott
Category: SEBD (11-16)

The Birches
Newholme Road, West Didsbury,
MANCHESTER M20 2XZ
Tel: 01614 488895
Headteacher: Mr Andrew Pitts
Category: SLD (5-11)

Greater Manchester
OLDHAM
Parent Partnership Service

SEND Information Advice and Support (IAS) Service, Italia House, Pass Street, Oldham, Greater Manchester, OL9 6HZ
Tel: 01616 672055 Email: iass@pointoldham.co.uk Website: www.oldham.gov.uk

CHADDERTON

The Kingfisher Community Special School
Foxdenton Lane,
CHADDERTON OL9 9QR
Tel: 01617 705910
Head: Mrs Anne Redmond
Category: PMLD SLD
ASD (Coed 4-11)

OLDHAM

New Bridge Learning Centre
St Martin's Road, Fitton
Hill, OLDHAM OL8 2PZ
Tel: 01618 832402
Head: Mrs Jean Warner
Category: (Coed 16-19)

New Bridge School
Roman Road, Hollinwood,
OLDHAM, Greater
Manchester OL8 3PH
Tel: 01618 832401
Head: Mrs Jane Hilldrup
Category: PMLD SLD MLD
ASD PD (Coed 11-19)

Spring Brook School
Heron Street, OLDHAM, Greater
Manchester OL8 4JD
Tel: 01617 705007
Head: Ms Rebeckah Hollingsworth
Category: BESD (Coed 4-16)

Greater Manchester
ROCHDALE
Metropolitan Borough Council

SEN Assessment Team, Number One Riverside, Smith Street, Rochdale, OL16 1XU
Tel: 01706 925981 Email: sen@rochdale.gov.uk Website: www.rochdale.gov.uk

MIDDLETON

Newlands School
Waverley Road,
MIDDLETON M24 6JG
Tel: 01616 550220
Head: Mrs Deborah Rogers
Category: Generic Primary
Special School (Coed 3-11)

ROCHDALE

Brownhill School
Heights Lane, ROCHDALE OL12 0PZ
Tel: 03003 038384
Head: Mrs Kate Connolly
Category: EBD (Coed 7-16)

Redwood School
Hudson's Walk, ROCHDALE OL11 5EF
Tel: 01706 750815
Head: Mr Stuart Pidgeon
Category: Generic Secondary
Special School (Coed 11-19)

Springside School
Albert Royds Street,
ROCHDALE OL16 2SU
Tel: 01706 764451
Head: Mrs Jane Herring
Category: Generic Primary
Special School (Coed 3-11)

Greater Manchester
SALFORD
Children's Services Directorate

Children's Services, Unity House, Salford Civic Centre, Chorley Road, Swinton Salford, M27 0AP
Tel: 01617 780130 Website: www.salford.gov.uk

ECCLES

Chatsworth High School
Chatsworth Road, Ellesmere
Park, ECCLES M30 9DY
Tel: 01619 211405
Head: Martin Hanbury
Category: SLD PMLD
ASD (Coed 11-19)

New Park High School
Green Lane, ECCLES M30 0RW
Tel: 01619 212000
Head: Ms A Bever-Warren
Category: SEBD LD (Coed 8-16)

Oakwood Academy
Chatsworth Road, Ellesmere
Park, ECCLES M30 9DY
Tel: 01617 861920
Head: Ms Amanda Nicolson
Category: MLD HI VIS SEBD
Complex needs (Coed 10-19)

SWINTON

Springwood Primary School
Barton Road, SWINTON M27 5LP
Tel: 01617 780022
Head: Ms Lesley Roberts
Category: ASD MLD SLD
PMLD (Coed 2-11)

Greater Manchester
STOCKPORT

Metropolitan Borough Council

SEN Team, Town Hall, Edward Street, Stockport, SK1 3XE
Tel: 01612 176028 Email: cyp@stockport.gov.uk Website: www.stockport.gov.uk

STOCKPORT

Castle Hill School
The Fairway, Offerton,
STOCKPORT SK2 5DS
Tel: 01614 946439
Head: Mr John Law
Category: EBD GLD
CLD (Coed 11-16)

Heaton School
St James Road, Heaton Moor,
STOCKPORT SK4 4RE
Tel: 01614 321931
Head: Ms Jo Chambers
Category: SLD PMLD (Coed 10-19)

Lisburne School
Half Moon Lane, Offerton,
STOCKPORT SK2 5LB
Tel: 01614 835045
Head: Ms Samantha Benson
Category: CLD (Coed 4-11)

Oakgrove School
Matlock Road, Heald Green,
STOCKPORT SK8 3BU
Tel: 01614 374956
Head: Mr Rob Metcalfe
Category: SEBD (Coed 5-11)

Valley School
Whitehaven Road, Bramhall,
STOCKPORT SK7 1EN
Tel: 01614 397343
Head: Ms Debbie Thompson
Category: PMLD ASD
SLD (Coed 2-11)

Windlehurst School
Windlehurst Road, Hawk Green,
Marple, STOCKPORT SK6 7HZ
Tel: 01614 274788
Head: Ms Lesley Abercromby
Category: EBD (Coed 11-16)

Greater Manchester
TAMESIDE

Services for Children and Young People

Council Offices, Wellington Road, Ashton-under-Lyne, Tameside, OL6 6DL
Tel: 01613 428355 Fax: 01613 423260 Website: www.tameside.gov.uk

ASHTON-UNDER LYNE

Samuel Laycock School
Broadoak Road, ASHTON-UNDER
LYNE, Tameside OL6 8RF
Tel: 01613 441992
Head: Mrs C Lund
Category: MLD (Secondary)

AUDENSHAW

Hawthorns School
Sunnyside Moss Campus,
Lumb Lane, AUDENSHAW,
Tameside M34 5SF
Tel: 01613 701312
Head: Mrs M Thompson
Category: MLD (Primary)

DUKINFIELD

Cromwell School
Yew Tree Lane, DUKINFIELD,
Tameside SK16 5BJ
Tel: 01613 389730
Head: Mr A Foord
Category: SLD PMLD
MLD (Secondary)

Oakdale School
Cheetham Hill Road, DUKINFIELD,
Tameside SK16 5LD
Tel: 01613 679299
Head: Ms Linda Lester
Category: SLD PMLD (Primary)

White Bridge College
Globe Lane, DUKINFIELD,
Tameside SK16 4UJ
Tel: 01612 148484
Head of Centre: Mr Peter Hartman
Category: BESD (Secondary)

HYDE

Thomas Ashton School
Bennett Street, HYDE,
Tameside SK14 4SS
Tel: 01613 686208
Head: Mr R A Elms
Category: BESD (Primary)

Greater Manchester
TRAFFORD

Family Information Service

c/o Davyhulme Library, Hayeswater Road, Davyhulme, Manchester, M41 7BL
Tel: 01619 121053 Email: fis@trafford.gov.uk Website: www.trafford.gov.uk/sendirectory

ALTRINCHAM

Brentwood School
Brentwood Avenue, Timperley,
ALTRINCHAM, Cheshire WA14 1SR
Tel: 08448 429060
Head: Mrs Hilary Moon
Category: ASD SLD (Coed 11-19)

Pictor School
Grove Lane, Timperley,
ALTRINCHAM, Cheshire WA15 6PH
Tel: 01619 123082
Head: Mrs Beverley Owens
Category: SLCN SPLD ASD
PD MLD (Coed 2-11)

FLIXTON

Delamere School
Irlam Road, FLIXTON, Greater
Manchester M41 6AP
Tel: 01617 475893
Head: Mrs Sally Burston
Category: ASD SLD (Coed 2-11)

**Nexus Education Centre
(Pupil Referral Unit)**
Lydney Road, FLIXTON,
Manchester M41 8RN
Tel: 01619 124766
Category: (Coed 5-16)

Trafford Medical Education Service (Pupil Referral Unit)
The Flixton Centre, 350 Flixton Road, FLIXTON, Manchester M41 56W
Tel: 01619 124766

SALE

Manor High School
Manor Avenue, SALE,
Cheshire M33 5JX
Tel: 01619 761553
Head: Mrs Helen Wilson
Category: ASD SEMH
MLD (Coed 11-18)

STRETFORD

Longford Park School
74 Cromwell Road, STRETFORD,
Greater Manchester M32 8QJ
Tel: 01619 121895
Head: Mr Andrew Taylor
Category: SEMH MLD
ASD (Coed 5-11)

URMSTON

Egerton High School
Kingsway Park, URMSTON,
Greater Manchester M1 7FZ
Tel: 01617 497094
Head: Mr Burgess
Category: SEMH (Coed 11-16)

Greater Manchester
WIGAN

Children and Young People's Services

Access & Inclusion Team, Progress House, Westwood Park Drive, Wigan, Greater Manchester, WN3 4HH
Tel: 01942 486145 Website: www.wigan.gov.uk

ATHERTON

New Greenhall School
Green Hall Close, ATHERTON,
Greater Manchester M46 9HP
Tel: 01942 883928
Head: Ms E Loftus
Category: PD CLD AUT (Coed 2-11)

WIGAN

Landgate School
Landgate Lane, Bryn,
WIGAN WN4 0EP
Tel: 01942 776688
Head: Ms J Sharps
Category: AUT SP&LD (Coed 4-19)

Newbridge Learning Community School
Moss Lane, Platt Bridge,
WIGAN WN2 3TL
Tel: 01942 776020
Head: Mrs E Kucharski

Oakfield High School
Long Lane, Hindley Green,
WIGAN WN2 4XA
Tel: 01942 776142
Head: Mrs C Taylor
Category: MLD SLD PD
SEBD (Coed 11-19)

Wigan Hope School
Kelvin Grove, Marus Bridge,
WIGAN WN3 6SP
Tel: 01942 824150
Head: Mr J P R Dahlstrom
Category: ASD SLD
PMLD (Coed 2-19)

Willow Grove Primary School
Willow Grove, Ashton-in-
Makerfield, WIGAN WN4 8XF
Tel: 01942 727717
Head: Ms V Pearson
Category: SEBD (Coed 5-11)

MEDWAY

Children's Services

Gun Wharf, Dock Road, Chatham, ME4 4TR
Tel: 01634 306000 Email: childrens.services@medway.gov.uk Website: www.medway.gov.uk

CHATHAM

Bradfields Academy
Churchill Avenue, CHATHAM,
Kent ME5 0LB
Tel: 01634 683990
Head: Mr Kim Johnson
Category: MLD SLD
ASD (Coed 11-18)

Inspire Free School
Churchill Avenue, CHATHAM,
Kent ME5 0LB
Tel: 01634 827372
Head: Ms S McDermott
Category: SEMH (Coed 11-16)

GILLINGHAM

Danecourt Special School
Hotel Road, Watling Street,
GILLINGHAM, Kent ME8 6AA
Tel: 01634 232589
Head: Mr John Somers
Category: MLD CLD (Coed 4-11)

Rivermead School
Forge Lane, GILLINGHAM,
Kent ME7 1UG
Tel: 01634 338348
Head: Ms T Lovey
Category: Complex emotional
needs (Coed 11-16)

STROOD

Abbey Court
Rede Court Road,
STROOD, Kent ME2 3SP
Tel: 01634 338220
Head: Ms Karen Joy
Category: SLD (Coed 4-18)

Merseyside
KNOWSLEY

Children & Family Services

SEN Team, The Cordingley Building, Scotchbarn Lane, Prescot, Merseyside, L35 7JD
Tel: 01514 435145 Email: sen@knowsley.gov.uk Website: www.knowsley.gov.uk

HALEWOOD

Finch Woods Academy
Baileys Lane, HALEWOOD,
Merseyside L26 0TY
Tel: 01512 888930
Head: Ms Pam Kilham
Category: SEBD (Coed 6-16)

HUYTON

**Alt Bridge Secondary
Support Centre**
Wellcroft Road, HUYTON,
Merseyside L36 7TA
Tel: 01514 778310
Head: Mr Barry Kerwin
Category: MLD SPLD CLD
ASD SLD PD (Coed 11-16)

**Knowsley Central
Primary Support Centre**
Mossbrow Road, HUYTON,
Merseyside L36 7SY
Tel: 01514 778450
Head: Mrs Patricia Thomas
Category: CLD SEBD (Coed 2-11)

KIRKBY

Bluebell Park School
Cawthorne Walk, Southdene,
KIRKBY, Merseyside L32 3XP
Tel: 01514 778350
Head: Mr John Parkes
Category: PD PMLD SLD
MLD (Coed 2-19)

STOCKBRIDGE VILLAGE

Meadow Park School
Haswell Drive, STOCKBRIDGE
VILLAGE, Merseyside L28 1RX
Tel: 01514 778100
Head: Mr Mike Marshall

Merseyside
LIVERPOOL

City Council

Children's Services (Education), Municipal Buildings, Dale Street, Liverpool, L2 2DH
Tel: 01512 333000 Email: liverpool.direct@liverpool.gov.uk Website: www.liverpool.gov.uk

LIVERPOOL

Abbot's Lea School
Beaconsfield Road, Woolton,
LIVERPOOL, Merseyside L25 6EE
Tel: 01514 281161
Head: Mrs Margaret Lucas
Category: AUT (Coed 5-19)

Bank View High School
Sherwoods Lane, Fazakerley,
LIVERPOOL, Merseyside L10 1LW
Tel: 01515 253451
Head: Mr Jim Pearce
Category: CLD (Coed 11-18)

Clifford Holroyde School
Thingwall Lane, LIVERPOOL,
Merseyside L14 7NX
Tel: 01512 289500
Head: Ms Elaine Dwyer
Category: EBD (Coed 7-16)

Ernest Cookson School
54 Bankfield Road, West Derby,
LIVERPOOL, Merseyside L13 0BQ
Tel: 01512 201874
Head: Mr S Roberts
Category: EBD (Boys 5-16)

Hope School
Naylorsfield Drive, LIVERPOOL,
Merseyside L27 0YD
Tel: 01514 984055
Head: Mr Rohit Naik
Category: EBD (Boys 5-16)

**Millstead Special
Needs Primary**
Old Mill Lane, Wavertree,
LIVERPOOL, Merseyside L15 8LW
Tel: 01517 220974
Head: Ms Michelle Beard
Category: SLD (Coed 2-11)

Palmerston School
Beaconsfield Road, Woolton,
LIVERPOOL, Merseyside L25 6EE
Tel: 01514 282128
Head: Mrs Alison Burbage
Category: SLD (Coed 11-19)

Princes Primary School
Selborne Street, LIVERPOOL,
Merseyside L8 1YQ
Tel: 01517 092602
Head: Mrs Kathy Brent
Category: SLD (Coed 2-11)

Redbridge High School
Sherwoods Lane, Fazakerley,
LIVERPOOL, Merseyside L10 1LW
Tel: 01515 255733
Head: Mr Paul Cronin
Category: SLD (Coed 11-19)

Sandfield Park School
Sandfield Walk, West Derby,
LIVERPOOL, Merseyside L12 1LH
Tel: 01512 280324
Head: Mr J M Hudson
Category: PD HS (Coed 11-19)

Merseyside
SEFTON

Children, Schools & Families, Town Hall, Bootle, Merseyside, L20 7AE
Tel: 01519 343250 Email: special.needs@sefton.gov.uk Website: www.sefton.gov.uk

BOOTLE

Rowan Park School
Sterrix Lane, BOOTLE,
Merseyside L21 0DB
Tel: 01512 224894
Head: Ms K Lynskey
Category: SLD (Coed 3-18)

CROSBY

Crosby High School
De Villiers Avenue, CROSBY,
Merseyside L23 2TH
Tel: 01519 243671
Head: Ms T Oxton-Grant
Category: MLD (Coed 11-16)

Newfield School
Edge Lane, CROSBY,
Merseyside L23 4TG
Tel: 01519 342991
Head: Mrs J Starkey
Category: BESD (Coed 5-17)

SOUTHPORT

Merefield School
Westminster Drive, SOUTHPORT,
Merseyside PR8 2QZ
Tel: 01704 577163
Head: Mrs S Clare
Category: SLD (Coed 3-16)

**Presfield High School
and Specialist College**
Preston New Road, SOUTHPORT,
Merseyside PR9 8PA
Tel: 01704 227831
Head: Ms N Zielonka
Category: ASD (Coed 11-16)

Merseyside
ST HELENS

Community, Education & Leisure Services Department

Additional Needs Team, Atlas House, Corporation Street, St Helens, Merseyside, WA9 1LD
Tel: 01744 671104 Website: www.sthelens.gov.uk

NEWTON-LE-WILLOWS

Penkford School
Wharf Road, NEWTON-LE-
WILLOWS, Merseyside WA12 9XZ
Tel: 01744 678745
Head: Ms Julie Johnson
Category: SEBD (9-16)

ST HELENS

Lansbury Bridge School
Lansbury Avenue, Parr, ST
HELENS, Merseyside WA9 1TB
Tel: 01744 678579
Head: Mrs Jane Grecic
Category: CLD PD MLD
ASD (Coed 3-16)

Mill Green School
Lansbury Avenue, Parr, ST
HELENS, Merseyside WA9 1BU
Tel: 01744 678760
Head: Mr Colin Myers
Category: SLD CLD PMLD
ASD (Coed 6-19)

Merseyside
WIRRAL

Children & Young People's Department

Special Education Support Service, Professional Excellence Centre, Acre Lane, Bromborough Wirral, CH62 7BZ
Tel: 01513 466608 Email: children@wirral.gov.uk Website: www.wirral.gov.uk

BIRKENHEAD

Kilgarth School
Cavendish Street, BIRKENHEAD,
Merseyside CH41 8BA
Tel: 01516 528071
Head: Mr Steven Baker
Category: EBD ADHD (Boys 11-16)

PRENTON

The Observatory School
Bidston Village Road, Bidston,
PRENTON, Merseyside CH43 7QT
Tel: 01516 527093
Head: Mrs Elaine Idris
Category: SEBD LD (Coed 11-16)

THINGWALL

Stanley School
Pensby Road, THINGWALL,
Merseyside CH61 7UG
Tel: 01516 483171
Head: Mr Anthony Roberts
Category: SLD AUT CLD (Coed 2-11)

WALLASEY

Clare Mount Specialist Sports College
Fender Lane, Moreton, WALLASEY,
Merseyside CH46 9PA
Tel: 01516 069440
Head: Mrs Kim Webster
Category: MLD (Coed 11-19)

Elleray Park School
Elleray Park Road, WALLASEY,
Merseyside CH45 0LH
Tel: 01516 393594
Head: Ms Margaret Morris
Category: CLD SLD PD
AUT PMLD (Coed 2-11)

Foxfield School
Douglas Drive, Moreton,
WALLASEY, Merseyside CH46 6BT
Tel: 01516 778555
Head: Mr Andre Baird
Category: ADHD SLD
ASD PD (Coed 11-19)

Orrets Meadow School
Chapelhill Road, Moreton,
WALLASEY, Merseyside CH46 9QQ
Tel: 01516 788070
Head: Mrs Carolyn Duncan
Category: SPLD SP&LD LD
AUT ASD EBD (Coed 7-11)

Wirral Hospitals School
Solar Campus, 235 Leasowe Road,
WALLASEY, Merseyside CH45 8LW
Tel: 01516 376310
Head: Mr Derek Kitchin
Category: HS (Coed 2-19)

WIRRAL

Gilbrook School
Glebe Hey Road, Woodchurch,
WIRRAL, Merseyside CH49 8HE
Tel: 01515 223900
Head: Mr Robert Richardson
Category: EBD DYS (Coed 4-12)

Hayfield School
Manor Drive, Upton, WIRRAL,
Merseyside CH49 4LN
Tel: 01516 779303
Head: Ms Sheena Drake
Category: MLD CLD
ASD (Coed 4-11)

Meadowside School
Pool Lane, Woodchurch,
WIRRAL, Merseyside CH49 5LR
Tel: 01516 787711
Head: Ms Paula Wareing
Category: CLD SLD (Coed 11-19)

The Lyndale School
Lyndale Avenue, Eastham,
WIRRAL, Merseyside CH62 8DE
Tel: 01513 273682
Category: CLD SLD MLD
PMLD (Coed 2-11)

MIDDLESBROUGH

Education and Learning

SEN Team, Civic Centre, P.O. Box 505, Middlesbrough, TS1 9FZ
Tel: 01642 728677 Email: gina_mcbride@middlesbrough.gov.uk Website: www.middlesbrough.gov.uk

MIDDLESBROUGH

Beverley School
Saltersgill Avenue,
MIDDLESBROUGH,
Cleveland TS4 3JS
Tel: 01642 811350
Head: Ms Joanne Smith
Category: AUT (Coed 3-19)

Holmwood School
Saltersgill Avenue, Easterside,
MIDDLESBROUGH,
Cleveland TS4 3PT
Tel: 01642 819157
Head: Mrs Jan Mather
Category: EBD (Coed 4-11)

Priory Woods School
Tothill Avenue, Netherfields,
MIDDLESBROUGH,
Cleveland TS3 0RH
Tel: 01642 770540
Head: Mrs Bernadette Knill
Category: SLD PMLD (Coed 4-19)

MILTON KEYNES

Children and Families Service

SEND Team, Saxon Court, 502 Avebury Boulevard, Milton Keynes, MK9 3HS
Tel: 01908 253414 Email: sen@milton-keynes.gov.uk Website: www.milton-keynes.gov.uk

MILTON KEYNES

Romans Field School
Shenley Road, Bletchley, MILTON
KEYNES, Buckinghamshire MK3 7AW
Tel: 01908 376011
Head: Mr Paul Morton
Category: SEBD (Coed
Day/boarding 5-12)

Slated Row School
Old Wolverton Road,
Wolverton, MILTON KEYNES,
Buckinghamshire MK12 5NJ
Tel: 01908 316017
Head: Ms Liz Bull
Category: MLD Complex
needs (Coed Day 4-19)

Stephenson Academy
Crosslands, Stantonbury,
MILTON KEYNES,
Buckinghamshire MK14 6AX
Tel: 01908 889400
Head: Dr Neil Barrett
Category: EBD (Boys Day/
boarding 12-16)

The Redway School
Farmborough, Netherfield, MILTON
KEYNES, Buckinghamshire MK6 4HG
Tel: 01908 206400
Head: Ms Ruth Sylvester
Category: PMLD CLD
SCD (Coed Day 2-19)

The Walnuts School
Admiral Drive, Hazeley, MILTON
KEYNES, Buckinghamshire MK8 0PU
Tel: 01908 563885
Head: Mr Nick Jackman
Category: ASD SCD (Coed
Day/boarding 4-19)

White Spire School
Rickley Lane, Bletchley, MILTON
KEYNES, Buckinghamshire MK3 6EW
Tel: 01908 373266
Head: Ms Maria Penicud
Category: MLD (Coed
Day & boarding 5-19)

NORFOLK
Children's Services

SEN Team, County Hall, Martineau Lane, Norwich, Norfolk, NR1 2DH
Tel: 03448 008020 Email: cssendlocaloffer@norfolk.gov.uk Website: www.norfolk.gov.uk

ATTLEBOROUGH

Chapel Road School
Chapel Road, ATTLEBOROUGH,
Norfolk NR17 2DS
Tel: 01953 453116
Head: Mrs Karin Heap
Category: SLD ASD
PMLD (Coed 3-19)

CROMER

Sidestrand Hall School
Cromer Road, Sidestrand,
CROMER, Norfolk NR27 0NH
Tel: 01263 578144
Head: Mrs Sarah Macro
Category: MLD (Coed 3-19)

DEREHAM

Fred Nicholson School
Westfield Road, DEREHAM,
Norfolk NR19 1JB
Tel: 01362 693915
Head: Mrs Alison Kahn
Category: MLD SEBD SLD
ASD (Coed 3-19)

GREAT YARMOUTH

John Grant School
St George's Drive, Caister-
on-Sea, GREAT YARMOUTH,
Norfolk NR30 5QW
Tel: 01493 720158
Head: Mrs Pamela Ashworth
Category: SLD ASD
PMLD (Coed 3-19)

KING'S LYNN

Churchill Park School
Winston Churchill Drive, KING'S
LYNN, Norfolk PE30 4RP
Tel: 01553 763679
Head: Mr Paul Donkersloot
Category: Complex
Needs (Day 2-19)

NORWICH

**Eaton Hall Specialist
Academy**
Pettus Road, NORWICH,
Norfolk NR4 7BU
Tel: 01603 457480
Head: Miss Valerie Moore
Category: EBD (Coed 5-16)

Hall School
St Faith's Road, Old Catton,
NORWICH, Norfolk NR6 7AD
Tel: 01603 466467
Head: Mr Keith McKenzie
Category: CLD (Coed 3-19)

Harford Manor School
43 Ipswich Road, NORWICH,
Norfolk NR2 2LN
Tel: 01603 451809
Head: Mr Paul Eteson
Category: ASD PMLD
SLD (Coed 3-19)

The Clare School
South Park Avenue, NORWICH,
Norfolk NR4 7AU
Tel: 01603 454199
Acting Head: Ms Wendy Norton
Category: PH MSI LD Complex
medical needs (Coed 3-19)

The Parkside School
College Road, NORWICH,
Norfolk NR2 3JA
Tel: 01603 441126
Head: Ms Susan Booth
Category: SLD AUT EBD
MLD MSI PD (Coed 3-19)

SHERINGHAM

Woodfields School
Holt Road, SHERINGHAM,
Norfolk NR26 8ND
Tel: 01263 820520
Head: Mr James Stanbrook
Category: CLD (Coed 3-19)

NORTHAMPTONSHIRE
County Council

CYPS, John Dryden House, 8-10 The Lakes, Northampton, NN4 7YD
Tel: 01001 261000 Email: education@northamptonshire.gov.uk Website: www.northamptonshire.gov.uk

CORBY

Maplefields School
Tower Hill Road, CORBY,
Northamptonshire NN18 0TH
Tel: 01536 424090
Head: Mrs Lynda Morgan
Category: BESD (5-19)

KETTERING

Isebrook SEN College
Eastleigh Road, KETTERING,
Northamptonshire NN15 6PT
Tel: 01536 500030
Head: Mrs Denise Williams
Category: MLD ASD SLD
SP&LD PH (11-19)

**Kingsley Special
Academy Trust**
Churchill Way, KETTERING,
Northamptonshire NN15 5DP
Tel: 01536 316880
Head: Mr Tom O'Dwyer
Category: PMLD SLD ASD (3-11)

**Wren Spinney Community
Special School**
Westover Road, KETTERING,
Northamptonshire NN15 7LB
Tel: 01536 481939
Head: Mr Simon Bishop
Category: SLD PMLD ASD MSI (11-19)

NORTHAMPTON

Billing Brook Special Academy Trust School
Penistone Road, NORTHAMPTON,
Northamptonshire NN3 8EZ
Tel: 01604 773910
Head: Mrs Caroline Grant
Category: MLD ASD
SLD SPLD PH (3-19)

Fairfields School
Trinity Avenue, NORTHAMPTON,
Northamptonshire NN2 6JN
Tel: 01604 714777
Head: Ms Karen Lewis
Category: PMLD PH
MSI SLD ASD (3-11)

Greenfields School and Sports College
Prentice Court, Lings Way,
Goldings, NORTHAMPTON,
Northamptonshire NN3 8XS
Tel: 01604 741960
Head: Mrs Lisa-Marie Atack
Category: PMLD SLD ASD MSI (11-19)

Kings Meadow School
Manning Road, Moulton
Leys, NORTHAMPTON,
Northamptonshire NN3 7AR
Tel: 01604 673730
Head: Ms Helen McCormack
Category: BESD (4-11)

Northgate School Arts College
Queens Park Parade,
NORTHAMPTON,
Northamptonshire NN2 6LR
Tel: 01604 714098
Head: Miss Sheralee Webb
& Mike Trundley
Category: MLD SLD ASD (11-19)

TIFFIELD

The Gateway School
St Johns Road, TIFFIELD,
Northamptonshire NN12 8AA
Tel: 01604 878977
Head: Mr Conor Renihan
Category: BESD (11-19)

WELLINGBOROUGH

Friar Academy
Friar's Close, WELLINGBOROUGH,
Northamptonshire NN8 2LA
Tel: 01933 304950
Head: Mrs Suzzanne Ijewsky
Category: MLD SLD ASD (11-19)

Rowan Gate Primary School
Finedon Road, WELLINGBOROUGH,
Northamptonshire NN8 4NS
Tel: 01933 304970
Head: Mrs Laura Clarke
Category: PMLD ASD (3-11)

NORTHUMBERLAND

County Council

Family Services Directorate, SEN Team, County Hall, Morpeth, Northumberland, NE61 2EF
Tel: 08456 006400 Fax: 01670 511413 Email: ask@northumberland.gov.uk Website: www.northumberland.gov.uk

ALNWICK

Barndale House School
Howling Lane, ALNWICK,
Northumberland NE66 1DQ
Tel: 01665 602541
Head: Mr Colin Bradshaw
Category: SLD

BERWICK UPON TWEED

The Grove Special School
Grove Gardens, Tweedmouth,
BERWICK UPON TWEED,
Northumberland TD15 2EN
Tel: 01289 306390
Head: Mrs Elizabeth Brown
Category: SLD

BLYTH

The Dales School
Cowpen Road, BLYTH,
Northumberland NE24 4RE
Tel: 01670 352556
Head: Mr Hugh Steele
Category: MLD CLD PH EBD

CHOPPINGTON

Cleaswell Hill School
School Avenue, Guide
Post, CHOPPINGTON,
Northumberland NE62 5DJ
Tel: 01670 823182
Head: Mr Kevin Burdis
Category: MLD

CRAMLINGTON

Atkinson House School
North Terrace, Seghill,
CRAMLINGTON,
Northumberland NE23 7EB
Tel: 01912 980838
Head: Mr Derek Cogle
Category: EBD

Cramlington Hillcrest School
East View Avenue, CRAMLINGTON,
Northumberland NE23 1DY
Tel: 01670 713632
Head: Mrs Andrea Mead
Category: MLD

HEXHAM

Hexham Priory School
Corbridge Road, HEXHAM,
Northumberland NE46 1UY
Tel: 01434 605021
Head: Mr Michael Thompson
Category: SLD

MORPETH

Collingwood School & Media Arts College
Stobhillgate, MORPETH,
Northumberland NE61 2HA
Tel: 01670 516374
Head: Mr Richard Jones
Category: MLD CLD AUT
SP&LD PH Emotionally fragile
Specific medical conditions

NOTTINGHAM

City Council

The SEN Team, Glenbrook Management Centre, Wigman Road, Bilborough Nottingham, NG8 4PD
Tel: 01158 764300 Email: special.needs@nottinghamcity.gov.uk Website: www.nottinghamcity.gov.uk

NOTTINGHAM

Oak Field School and Specialist Sports College
Wigman Road, Bilborough,
NOTTINGHAM NG8 3HW
Tel: 01159 153265
Head: Mr David Stewart
Category: SCD ASD SPLI
(Coed Day 3-19)

Rosehill Special School
St Matthias Road, St Ann's,
NOTTINGHAM NG3 2FE
Tel: 01159 155815
Head: Mr Andy Sloane
Category: AUT (Coed Day 4-19)

Westbury School
Chingford Road, Bilborough,
NOTTINGHAM NG8 3BT
Tel: 01159 155858
Executive Head: Mr John Dyson
Category: EBD (Coed Day 7-16)

Woodlands Special School
Beechdale Road, Aspley,
NOTTINGHAM NG8 3EZ
Tel: 01159 155734
Executive Head: Mr John Dyson
Category: MLD (Coed Day 3-16)

NOTTINGHAMSHIRE
Children & Young People's Service

SEN Team, County Hall, Loughborough Road, West Bridgford Nottingham, Nottinghamshire, NG2 7QP
Tel: 01159 773779 Email: casework.teamleader@nottscc.gov.uk Website: www.nottinghamshire.gov.uk

COTGRAVE

Ash Lea School
Owthorpe Road, COTGRAVE,
Nottinghamshire NG12 3PA
Tel: 01159 892744
Head: Mrs Dawn Wigley
Category: SLD (Coed Day 3-16)

KIRKBY-IN-ASHFIELD

Bracken Hill School
Chartwell Road, KIRKBY-IN-
ASHFIELD, Nottinghamshire
NG17 7HZ
Tel: 01623 477268
Head: Mr Ron McCrossen
Category: SLD MLD
(Coed Day 3-16)

MANSFIELD

Fountaindale School
Nottingham Road, MANSFIELD,
Nottinghamshire NG18 5BA
Tel: 01623 792671
Head: Mr Mark Dengel
Category: PD (Coed Boarding 3-16)

Redgate School
Somersall Street, MANSFIELD,
Nottinghamshire NG19 6EL
Tel: 01623 455944
Head: Mr Hugh Daybell
Category: MLD (Coed Day 3-16)

Yeoman Park School
Park Hall Road, Mansfield
Woodhouse, MANSFIELD,
Nottinghamshire NG19 8PS
Tel: 01623 459540
Head: Mr Paul Betts
Category: SLD (Coed Day 3-16)

NEWARK

The Newark Orchard School
Appleton Gate, NEWARK,
Nottinghamshire NG24 1JR
Tel: 01636 682255
Head: Ms Margot Tyers
Category: SLD MLD (Coed 3-16)

NOTTINGHAM

Carlton Digby School
Digby Avenue, Mapperley,
NOTTINGHAM NG3 6DS
Tel: 01159 568289
Head: Mrs Glenys Clifton
Category: SLD (Coed 3-16)

Derrymount School
Churchmoor Lane, Arnold,
NOTTINGHAM NG5 8HN
Tel: 01159 534015
Head: Mrs Kathy McIntyre
Category: MLD (Coed 3-16)

RETFORD

St Giles Special School
Babworth Road, RETFORD,
Nottinghamshire DN22 7NJ
Tel: 01777 703683
Head: Mrs Hilary Short
Category: MLD SLD (Coed 3-16)

OXFORDSHIRE
Children, Education & Families

SEN Team, Knights Court, 21 Between Towns Road, Cowley Oxford, OX4 3LX
Tel: 01865 815275 Email: sen@oxfordshire.gov.uk Website: www.oxfordshire.gov.uk

BANBURY

Frank Wise School
Hornbeam Close, BANBURY,
Oxfordshire OX16 9RL
Tel: 01295 263520
Head: Mr Sean O'Sullivan
Category: SLD PMLD (Coed 2-19)

BICESTER

Bardwell School
Hendon Place, Sunderland Drive,
BICESTER, Oxfordshire OX26 4RZ
Tel: 01869 242182
Head: Mr John Riches
Category: SLD PMLD MSI
SP&LD CLD (Coed 2-19)

OXFORD

John Watson School
Littleworth Road, Wheatley,
OXFORD OX33 1NN
Tel: 01865 452725
Head: Mr Stephen Passey
Category: SLD PMLD (Coed 2-19)

Mabel Prichard School
Cuddesdon Way, OXFORD OX4 6SB
Tel: 01865 777878
Head: Mrs Jane Wallington
Category: SLD PMLD (Coed 2-19)

Northfield School
Knights Road, Blackbird
Leys, OXFORD OX4 6DQ
Tel: 01865 771703
Head: Mr Mark Blencowe
Category: BESD (Day/residential
weekday boarding 11-18)

Oxfordshire Hospital School
The Harlow Centre, Raymund Road,
Old Marston, OXFORD OX3 0SW
Tel: 01865 253177
Interim Headteacher: Mr
Gareth Lewis
Category: HS (Coed 3-18)

Woodeaton Manor School
Woodeaton, OXFORD OX3 9TS
Tel: 01865 558722
Head: Mrs Anne Pearce
Category: BESD (Day/residential weekday boarding 7-18)

SONNING COMMON

Bishopswood Special School
Grove Road, SONNING COMMON, Oxfordshire RG4 9RH
Tel: 01189 724311
Head: Mrs Janet Kellett
Category: SLD PMLD (Coed 2-16)

WITNEY

Springfield School
The Bronze Barrow, Cedar Drive, Madley Park, WITNEY, Oxfordshire OX28 1AR
Tel: 01993 703963
Head: Mrs Emma Lawley
Category: SLD (Coed 2-16)

PETERBOROUGH

Families Information Service

2nd Floor, Bayard Place, Broadway, Peterborough, PE1 1FZ
Tel: 01733 864446 Email: fis@peterborough.gov.uk Website: www.peterborough.gov.uk

PETERBOROUGH

Heltwate School
North Bretton, PETERBOROUGH, Cambridgeshire PE3 8RL
Tel: 01733 262878
Head: Mr Adam Brewster
Category: MLD SLD AUT PD SCD (Coed 4-16)

Marshfields School
Eastern Close, Eastern Avenue, PETERBOROUGH, Cambridgeshire PE1 4PP
Tel: 01733 568058
Head: Mrs Janet James
Category: MLD SCD SEBD SLD (Coed 11-19)

Nenegate School
Park Lane, Eastfield, PETERBOROUGH, Cambridgeshire PE1 5GZ
Tel: 01733 349438
Head: Ms Ruth O'Sullivan
Category: EBD (Coed 11-16)

Phoenix School
Clayton, Orton Goldhay, PETERBOROUGH, Cambridgeshire PE2 5SD
Tel: 01733 391666
Head: Mr Phil Pike
Category: SLD PMLD PD SCN ASD MSI (Coed 2-19)

PLYMOUTH

Department for Learning and Communities

Plymouth, Devon, PL1 2AA
Tel: 01752 668000 Website: www.plymouth.gov.uk

PLYMOUTH

Brook Green Centre for Learning
Bodmin Road, Whitleigh, PLYMOUTH, Devon PL5 4DZ
Tel: 01752 773875
Head: Ms Sara Jordan
Category: MLD BESD (11-16)

Cann Bridge School
Miller Way, Estover, PLYMOUTH, Devon PL6 8UN
Tel: 01752 207909
Head: Mr Michael Loveman
Category: SLD (3-19)

Courtlands Special School
Widey Lane, Crownhill, PLYMOUTH, Devon PL6 5JS
Tel: 01752 776848
Head: Mr Lee Earnshaw
Category: MLD BESD (4-11)

Longcause Community Special School
Plympton, PLYMOUTH, Devon PL7 1JB
Tel: 01752 336881
Head: Mrs Anne Thorne
Category: MLD (4-16)

Mill Ford School
Rochford Crescent, Ernesettle, PLYMOUTH, Devon PL5 2PY
Tel: 01752 300270
Head: Mrs Claire Wills
Category: SLD PMLD (3-19)

Mount Tamar School
Row Lane, St Budeaux, PLYMOUTH, Devon PL5 2EF
Tel: 01752 365128
Head: Mr Brett Storry
Category: BESD (4-16)

Woodlands School
Wood View Drive, Tamerton Foliot Road, Whitleigh, PLYMOUTH, Devon PL6 5ES
Tel: 01752 300101
Head: Mrs Andrea Hemmens
Category: PD PMLD MSI (2-19)

BOROUGH OF POOLE

Children, Young People & Learning

Dolphin Centre, Poole, Dorset, BH15 1SA
Tel: 01202 262277 Email: integrated.services@poole.gov.uk Website: www.poole.gov.uk

POOLE

Longspee Academy
Learoyd Road, Canford Heath,
POOLE, Dorset BH17 8PJ
Tel: 01202 380266
Head: Ms Nicky Morton
Category: BESD (5-14)

Montacute School
3 Canford Heath Road,
POOLE, Dorset BH17 9NG
Tel: 01202 693239
Head: Ms Jill Owen
Category: PMLD SLD CLD
PH Medical needs (3-19)

Winchelsea School
Guernsey Road, Parkstone,
POOLE, Dorset BH12 4LL
Tel: 01202 746240
Head: Ms Rachel Weldon
Category: ADHD ASD
ASP MLD (3-16)

PORTSMOUTH

Directorate of Children, Families and Learning

SEN team, Floor 2 Core 1, Civic Offices, Guildhall Square Portsmouth, Hampshire, PO1 2EA
Tel: 02392 841238 Email: sen.education@portsmouthcc.gov.uk Website: www.portsmouth.gov.uk

PORTSMOUTH

Cliffdale Primary Academy
Battenburg Avenue, North End,
PORTSMOUTH, Hampshire PO2 0SN
Tel: 02392 662601
Executive Head: Ms Alison Beane
Category: MLD PD
SLCN (Coed 4-11)

Mary Rose School
Gisors Road, Southsea,
PORTSMOUTH, Hampshire PO4 8GT
Tel: 02392 852330
Executive Head: Ms Alison Beane
Category: SLDCLD PD
MLD (Coed 2-19)

Redwood Park School
Wembley Grove, Cosham,
PORTSMOUTH, Hampshire PO6 2RY
Tel: 02392 377500
Head: Ms Lynda Butt
Category: MLD SP&LD
ASD (Coed 11-16)

READING

Directorate of Education, Adult & Children's Services

SEN Team, Civic Offices, Bridge Street, Reading, RG1 2LU
Tel: 01189 372674 Website: www.reading.gov.uk

READING

Phoenix College
40 Christchurch Road,
READING, Berkshire RG2 7AY
Tel: 01189 375524
Head: Mrs Ekie Lansdown-Bridge
Category: BESD ADHD (Coed 11-16)

The Avenue Special School
Conwy Close, Tilehurst,
READING, Berkshire RG30 4BZ
Tel: 01189 375554
Head: Mrs S Bourne
Category: CLD (Coed 2-19)

The Holy Brook Special School
145 Ashampstead Road,
Southcote, READING,
Berkshire RG30 3LJ
Tel: 01189 375489
Head: Mr Lee Smith

REDCAR AND CLEVELAND

People Services

SEN Service, West Locality Base, Daisy Lane, Ormesby, Middlesborough, TS7 9LF
Tel: 01642 304561 Email: sen@redcar-cleveland.gov.uk Website: www.redcar-cleveland.gov.uk

MIDDLESBROUGH

Pathways School
Tennyson Avenue, Grangetown,
MIDDLESBROUGH TS6 7NP
Tel: 01642 779292
Head: Mr Steve O'Gara
Category: SEBD (Coed Day 7-15)

REDCAR

Kirkleatham Hall School
Kirkleatham Village, REDCAR,
Cleveland TS10 4QR
Tel: 01642 483009
Head: Mrs Karen Robson
Category: SLD PMLD SLCN ASC
PD CLDD (Coed Day 4-19)

SALTBURN-BY-SEA

KTS Academy
Marshall Drive, Brotton, SALTBURN-
BY-SEA, Cleveland TS12 2UW
Tel: 01287 677265
Head: Mr Kevin Thompson
Category: SLD PMLD SLCN ASC
PD CLDD (Coed day 2-19)

RUTLAND

Inclusion Service

Catmose, Oakham, Rutland, LE15 6HP
Tel: 01572 758 331 Fax: 01572 720970 Website: www.rutland.gov.uk

OAKHAM

The Parks School
Burley Road, OAKHAM,
Rutland LE15 6GY
Tel: 01572 722404
Acting Head: Mr Ashley Scott
Category: AUT MLD PMLD
SP&LD VIS SEBD (Coed 2-5)

SHROPSHIRE

SEN Team

Shropshire Council, The Shirehall, Abbey Foregate, Shrewsbury, Shropshire, SY2 6ND
Tel: 01743 254395 Email: senteam@shropshire.gov.uk Website: www.shropshire.gov.uk

ELLESMERE

Kettlemere
c/o Lakelands School, Sports &
langauge College, Oswestry Road,
ELLESMERE, Shropshire SY12 0EA
Tel: 01691 622543
Head: Mr Gary Dean

OSWESTRY

Acorns Centre
Middleton Road, OSWESTRY,
Shropshire SY11 2LF
Tel: 01939 232372
Head: Mr Robin Wilson
Category: EBD (Coed 8-11)

SHREWSBURY

Severndale School
Hearne Way, Monkmoor,
SHREWSBURY, Shropshire SY2 5SL
Tel: 01743 281600
Head: Mr Christopher Davies
Category: SLD PD (Coed Day 2-19)

Woodlands School
The Woodlands Centre, Tilley
Green, Wem, SHREWSBURY,
Shropshire SY4 5PJ
Tel: 01939 232372
Head: Mr Robin Wilson
Category: EBD (Coed 11-16)

SLOUGH

Slough Borough Council

SEN Team, St Martin's Place, 51 Bath Road, Slough, Berkshire, SL1 3UF
Tel: 01753 476589 Email: fis@slough.gov.uk Website: www.slough.gov.uk

SLOUGH

Arbour Vale School
Farnham Road, SLOUGH,
Berkshire SL2 3AE
Tel: 01753 515560
Head: Mrs Debbie Richards
Category: SLD ASD
MLD (Coed 2-19)

**Haybrook College/
Millside School**
112 Burnham Lane, SLOUGH,
Berkshire SL1 6LZ
Tel: 01628 696077/696079
Executive Head: Ms Helen Huntley
Category: BESD (Coed 11-16)

Littledown School
Queen's Road, SLOUGH,
Berkshire SL1 3QW
Tel: 01753 521734
Head: Jo Matthews
Category: BESD (Coed 5-11)

SOMERSET

Children and Young People's Services

County Hall, Taunton, Somerset, TA1 4DY
Tel: 08453 459122 Email: somersetdirect@somerset.gov.uk Website: www.somerset.gov.uk

BRIDGWATER

Elmwood School
Hamp Avenue, BRIDGWATER,
Somerset TA6 6AW
Tel: 01278 456243
Head: Ms Elizabeth Hayward
Category: SLD MLD ASD
EBD (Coed Day 11-16)

Penrose School
Albert Street, Willow Brook,
BRIDGWATER, Somerset TA6 7ET
Tel: 01278 423660
Head: Mrs E Hayward
Category: CLD ASD SLD
(4-10 and Post-16)

**Robert Blake
Science College**
Hamp Avenue, BRIDGWATER,
Somerset TA6 6AW
Tel: 01278 456243
Head: Mrs Ann Winter
Category: AUT EBD CLD
(Coed Day 4-16)

FROME

Critchill School
Nunney Road, FROME,
Somerset BA11 4LB
Tel: 01373 464148
Head: Mr Mark Armstrong
Category: SLD MLD CLD
(Coed Day 4-16)

STREET

Avalon Special School
Brooks Road, STREET,
Somerset BA16 0PS
Tel: 01458 443081
Head: Mrs Alison Murkin
Category: SLD MLD PMLD
ASD (Coed Day 3-16)

TAUNTON

Selworthy School
Selworthy Road, TAUNTON,
Somerset TA2 8HD
Tel: 01823 284970
Head: Ms Karen Milton
Category: SLD PMLD MLD
ASD BESD (Coed Day 4-19)

**Sky College (formerly
The Priory School)**
Pickeridge Close, TAUNTON,
Somerset TA2 7HW
Tel: 01823 275569
Executive Head: Mr Richard Berry
Category: EBD (Boys
Boarding 11-16)

YEOVIL

Fairmead School
Mudford Road, YEOVIL,
Somerset BA21 4NZ
Tel: 01935 421295
Head: Miss Diana Denman
Category: MLD SEBD AUT
SLD (Coed Day 4-16)

Fiveways Special School
Victoria Road, YEOVIL,
Somerset BA21 5AZ
Tel: 01935 476227
Head: Mr M Collis
Category: SLD PMLD ASD
(Coed Day 4-19)

NORTH SOMERSET

Children and Young People's Services

Special Educational Needs Team, Town Hall, Room 119, Weston-Super-Mare, North Somerset, BS23 1UJ
Tel: 01275 888297 Website: www.n-somerset.gov.uk

NAILSEA

Ravenswood School
Pound Lane, NAILSEA, North
Somerset BS48 2NN
Tel: 01275 854134
Head: Mrs P Clark
Category: CLD SLD (3-19)

WESTON-SUPER-MARE

Baytree School
The Campus, Highlands
Lane, WESTON-SUPER-MARE,
North Somerset BS24 7DX
Tel: 01934 427555
Head: Mrs F Richings
Category: SLD (3-19)

Westhaven School
Ellesmere Road, Uphill,
WESTON-SUPER-MARE,
North Somerset BS23 4UT
Tel: 01934 632171
Acting Head: Mrs T Towler
Category: CLD (7-16)

SOUTHAMPTON

City Council

SEN Team, Civic Centre (North Block), Southampton, Hampshire, SO14 7LY
Tel: 02380 833270 Email: sen.team@southampton.gov.uk Website: www.southampton.gov.uk

SOUTHAMPTON

Great Oaks School
Vermont Close, SOUTHAMPTON,
Hampshire SO16 7LT
Tel: 02380 767660
Head: Mr Andy Evans
Category: MLD AUT ASP SLD (11-18)

Springwell School
Hinkler Road, Thornhill,
SOUTHAMPTON,
Hampshire SO19 6DH
Tel: 02380 445981
Head: Ms Jackie Partridge
Category: CLD SP&LD AUT SLD
Challenging behaviour (4-11)

The Cedar School
Redbridge Lane,
Nursling, SOUTHAMPTON,
Hampshire SO16 0NX
Tel: 02380 734205
Head: Mr Jonathan Howells
Category: PD (3-16)

The Polygon School
Handel Terrace, SOUTHAMPTON,
Hampshire SO15 2FH
Tel: 02380 636776
Head: Mrs Anne Hendon-John
Category: EBD (Boys 11-16)

Vermont School
Vermont Close, Off Winchester
Rd, SOUTHAMPTON,
Hampshire SO16 7LT
Tel: 02380 767988
Head: Ms Maria Smyth
Category: EBD (Boys 5-11)

SOUTHEND-ON-SEA

Borough Council

Children's Services, Civic Centre, Victoria Avenue, Southend-on-Sea, Essex, SS2 6ER
Tel: 01702 215007 Email: council@southend.gov.uk Website: www.southend.gov.uk

LEIGH-ON-SEA

The St Christopher School
Mountdale Gardens, LEIGH-
ON-SEA, Essex SS9 4AW
Tel: 01702 524193
Head: Mrs Jackie Mullan
Category: SEBD AUT ADHD (Coed
Day 3-11) ADHD AUT (Coed 11-16)

SOUTHEND-ON-SEA

Kingsdown Special School
Snakes Lane, SOUTHEND-
ON-SEA, Essex SS2 6XT
Tel: 01702 527486
Head: Ms Margaret Rimmer
Category: PNI PD SLD
PMLD (Coed Day 3-14)

Seabrook College
Burr Hill Chase, SOUTHEND-
ON-SEA, Essex SS2 6PE
Tel: 01702 347490
Head: Ms Alice Hexter
Category: SEBD (Coed Day 11-16)

St Nicholas School
Philpott Avenue, SOUTHEND-
ON-SEA, Essex SS2 4RL
Tel: 01702 462322
Head: Mrs June Mitchell
Category: SEBD AUT MLD
(Coed Day 11-16)

WESTCLIFF-ON-SEA

Lancaster Special School
Prittlewell Chase, WESTCLIFF-
ON-SEA, Essex SS0 0RT
Tel: 01702 342543
Head: Ms Melanie Hall
Category: PNI PD SLD PMLD
(Coed Day 14-19)

STAFFORDSHIRE

Children & Lifelong Learning Directorate

Tipping Street, Stafford, Staffordshire, ST16 2DH
Tel: 03001 118000 Email: education@staffordshire.gov.uk Website: www.staffordshire.gov.uk

BURNTWOOD

Chasetown Community School
Church Street, Chasetown, BURNTWOOD, Staffordshire WS7 3QL
Tel: 01543 686315
Head: Dr Linda James
Category: SEBD (Coed Day 4-11)

BURTON UPON TRENT

The Fountains High School
Bitham Lane, Stretton, BURTON UPON TRENT, Staffordshire DE13 0HB
Tel: 01283 239161
Head: Mrs Melsa Buxton
Category: Generic (Coed Day 11-19)

The Fountains Primary School
Bitham Lane, Stretton, BURTON UPON TRENT, Staffordshire DE13 0HB
Tel: 01283 239700
Head: Mrs Melsa Buxton
Category: Generic (Coed Day 2-11)

CANNOCK

Hednesford Valley High School
Stanley Road, Hednesford, CANNOCK, Staffordshire WS12 4JS
Tel: 01543 423714
Head: Mrs Anita Rattan
Category: Generic (Coed Day 11-19)

Sherbrook Primary School
Brunswick Road, CANNOCK, Staffordshire WS11 5SF
Tel: 01543 510216
Head: Mr Clive Lawrence
Category: Generic (Coed Day 2-11)

LEEK

Horton Lodge Community Special School and Key Learning Centre
Reacliffe Road, Rudyard, LEEK, Staffordshire ST13 8RB
Tel: 01538 306214
Head: Mr Charlie Rivers
Category: PD MSI SP&LD (Coed Day/Boarding 2-11)

Meadows Special School
Springfield Road, LEEK, Staffordshire ST13 6EU
Tel: 01538 225050
Head: Mr Christopher Best
Category: Generic (Coed Day 11-19)

Springfield Community Special School
Springfield Road, LEEK, Staffordshire ST13 6LQ
Tel: 01538 383558
Head: Mr Charlie Rivers
Category: Generic (Coed Day 2-11)

LICHFIELD

Queen's Croft High School
Birmingham Road, LICHFIELD, Staffordshire WS13 6PJ
Tel: 01543 510669
Head: Mr John Edwards
Category: Generic (Coed Day11-19)

Rocklands School
Purcell Avenue, LICHFIELD, Staffordshire WS13 7PH
Tel: 01543 510760
Head: Ms Sandra Swift
Category: ASD MLD PMLD SLD (Coed Day 2-11)

Saxon Hill Community Special School and PDSS
Kings Hill Road, LICHFIELD, Staffordshire WS14 9DE
Tel: 01543 414892
Head: Mr Jon Thickett
Category: PD (Coed Day 2-19)

NEWCASTLE UNDER LYME

Merryfields School
Hoon Avenue, NEWCASTLE UNDER LYME, Staffordshire ST5 9NY
Tel: 01782 296076
Head: Mrs Sarah Poyner
Category: Generic (Coed Day 2-11)

STAFFORD

Greenhall Nursery
Second Avenue, Holmcroft, STAFFORD, Staffordshire ST16 1PS
Tel: 01785 246159
Head: Miss Joanne Munro
Category: PD (Coed Day 2-5)

Marshlands Special School
Lansdowne Way, Wildwood, STAFFORD, Staffordshire ST17 4RD
Tel: 01785 356385
Head: Mrs Kim Ellis
Category: Generic (Coed Day 2-11)

STOKE ON TRENT

Cicely Haughton Community Special School
Westwood Manor, Wetley Rocks, STOKE ON TRENT, Staffordshire ST9 0BX
Tel: 01782 550202
Head: Mr Richard Redgate
Category: SEBD (Coed Boarding 5-11)

TAMWORTH

Two Rivers High School
Deltic, off Silver Link Road, Glascote, TAMWORTH, Staffordshire B77 2HJ
Tel: 01827 475690
Head: Mr Anthony Dooley
Category: Generic (Coed Day 11-19)

Two Rivers Primary School
Quince, Amington Heath, TAMWORTH, Staffordshire B77 4EN
Tel: 01827 475740
Head: Mr Anthony Dooley
Category: Generic (Coed Day 2-11)

UTTOXETER

Loxley Hall School
Stafford Road, Loxley, UTTOXETER, Staffordshire ST14 8RS
Tel: 01889 256390
Head: Mr Richard Redgate
Category: EBD (Boys Boarding 11-16)

WOLVERHAMPTON

Cherry Trees School
Giggetty Lane, Wombourne, WOLVERHAMPTON, West Midlands WV5 0AX
Tel: 01902 894484
Head: Mr Paul Elliot
Category: Generic (Coed Day 2-11)

Wightwick Hall School
Tinacre Hill, Wightwick, WOLVERHAMPTON, West Midlands WV6 8DA
Tel: 01902 761889
Head: Mr Paul Elliot
Category: Generic (Coed Day 11-19)

STOCKTON-ON-TEES
Borough Council

Families Information Service, SEN Team, 16 Church Road, Stockton-on-Tees, TS18 1XE
Tel: 01642 527225 Email: fis@stockton.gov.uk Website: www.stockton.gov.uk

BILLINGHAM

Ash Trees School
Bowes Road, BILLINGHAM,
Stockton-on-Tees TS23 2BU
Tel: 01642 563712
Head: Ms Yvonne Limb
Category: SLD PMLD
AUT (Coed 4-11)

STOCKTON-ON-TEES

**Horizons Specialist
Academy Trust,
Abbey Hill School &
Technology College**
Ketton Road, STOCKTON-
ON-TEES TS19 8BU
Tel: 01642 677113
Executive Headteacher: Ms
Elizabeth Horne
Category: SLD PMLD
AUT (Coed 11-19)

**Horizons Specialist
Academy Trust, Westlands
at Green Gates**
Melton Road, STOCKTON-
ON-TEES TS19 0JD
Tel: 01642 570104
Executive Headteacher: Ms
Elizabeth Horne
Category: BESD (Coed
Residential 5-11)

THORNABY-ON-TEES

**Horizons Specialist
Academy Trust,
Westlands School**
Eltham Crescent, THORNABY-
ON-TEES TS17 9RA
Tel: 01642 883030
Executive Headteacher: Ms
Elizabeth Horne
Category: BESD (Coed
Residential 11-16)

STOKE-ON-TRENT
SEND Services

The Mount Education Centre, Mount Avenue, Penkhull, Stoke-on-Trent, Staffordshire, ST4 7JU
Tel: 01782 232538 Email: send@stoke.gov.uk/localoffer@stoke.gov.uk Website: www.stoke.gov.uk

BLURTON

Kemball Special School
Beconsfield Drive, BLURTON,
Stoke-on-Trent ST4 3NR
Tel: 01782 883120
Acting Head: Ms Lisa Hughes
Category: PMLD SLD ASD
CLD (Coed Day 2-19)

BLYTHE BRIDGE

**Portland School and
Specialist College**
Uttoxeter Road, BLYTHE BRIDGE,
Staffordshire ST11 9JG
Tel: 01782 392071
Head: Mr Rob Faulkner
Category: MLD SEBD
(Coed Day 3-16)

STOKE-ON-TRENT

**Abbey Hill School and
Performing Arts College**
Box Lane, Meir, STOKE-ON-
TRENT, Staffordshire ST3 5PR
Tel: 01782 882882
Head: Mr Philip Kidman
Category: MLD AUT
(Coed Day 2-18)

TUNSTALL

Watermill Special School
Turnhurst Road, Packmoor,
TUNSTALL, Stoke-on-Trent ST6 6JZ
Tel: 01782 883737
Head: Mr Jonathon May
Category: MLD (Coed Day 5-16)

SUFFOLK
County Council

Endeavour House, 8 Russell Road, Ipswich, Suffolk, IP1 2BX
Tel: 08456 066067 Email: customerservice@csduk.com Website: www.suffolk.gov.uk

BURY ST EDMUNDS

Priory School
Mount Road, BURY ST
EDMUNDS, Suffolk IP32 7BH
Tel: 01284 761934
Head: Mr Lawrence Chapman
Category: MLD (Coed
Day & boarding 7-16)

Riverwalk School
South Close, BURY ST
EDMUNDS, Suffolk IP33 3JZ
Tel: 01284 764280
Head: Mrs Jan Hatchell
Category: SLD (Coed Day 2-19)

HAVERHILL

**Churchill Special
Free School**
Chalkstone Way, HAVERHILL,
Suffolk CB9 0LD
Tel: 01440 760338
Head: Mrs Georgina Ellis

IPSWICH

Stone Lodge Academy
Stone Lodge Lane West,
IPSWICH, Suffolk IP2 9HW
Tel: 01473 601175
Head: Mr Rick Tracey
Category: MLD ASD
(Coed Day 5-16)

The Bridge School (Primary Campus)
Heath Road, IPSWICH,
Suffolk IP4 5SN
Tel: 01473 725508
Head: Mr Odran Doran
Category: SLD (Coed Day 3-11)

The Bridge School (Secondary Campus)
Sprites Lane, Belstead,
IPSWICH, Suffolk IP8 3ND
Tel: 01473 556200
Head: Mr Odran Doran
Category: SLD (Coed Day 11-16)

Thomas Wolsey School
Defoe Road, IPSWICH,
Suffolk IP1 6SG
Tel: 01473 467600
Head: Ms Rupinder Hosie
Category: PD/Comunication
(Coed Day 3-16)

LOWESTOFT

The Ashley School Academy Trust
Ashley Downs, LOWESTOFT,
Suffolk NR32 4EU
Tel: 01502 565439
Head: Mrs Sally Garrett
Category: MLD (Coed
Day & boarding 7-16)

Warren School
Clarkes Lane, LOWESTOFT,
Suffolk NR33 8HT
Tel: 01502 561893
Head: Mrs Janet Bird
Category: SLD (Coed Day 3-19)

SUDBURY

Hillside Special School
Hitchcock Place, SUDBURY,
Suffolk CO10 1NN
Tel: 01787 372808
Head: Mrs Sue Upson
Category: SLD (Coed day 3-19)

SURREY
County Council

SEN Team, County Hall, Penrhyn Road, Kingston upon Thames, Surrey, KT1 2DN
Tel: 03456 009009 Email: localoffer@surreycc.gov.uk Website: www.surreycc.gov.uk

ADDLESTONE

Philip Southcote School
Addlestone Moor, ADDLESTONE,
Surrey KT15 2QH
Tel: 01932 562326
Head: Mr R W Horton
Category: HI LD (11-19)

CAMBERLEY

Carwarden House Community School
118 Upper Chobham Road,
CAMBERLEY, Surrey GU15 1EJ
Tel: 01276 709080
Head: Mr Jarlath O'Brien
Category: LD (11-19)

Portesbery School
Portesbery Road, CAMBERLEY,
Surrey GU15 3SZ
Tel: 01276 63078
Head: Mr M Sartin
Category: SLD (2-19)

CATERHAM

Clifton Hill School
Chaldon Road, CATERHAM,
Surrey CR3 5PH
Tel: 01883 347740
Head: Ms Andrea Ashton-Coulton
Category: SLD (11-19)

Sunnydown School
Portley House, 152 Whyteleafe
Road, CATERHAM, Surrey CR3 5ED
Tel: 01883 342281
Head: Mr Paul Jensen
Category: ASD SLCN
(Boarding & day 11-16)

CHOBHAM

Wishmore Cross School
Alpha Road, CHOBHAM,
Surrey GU24 8NE
Tel: 01276 857555
Head: Mr J Donnelly
Category: BESD (Boarding
& day 11-16)

DORKING

Starhurst School
Chart Lane South, DORKING,
Surrey RH5 4DB
Tel: 01306 883763
Head: Mr J Watson
Category: BESD (Boarding
& day 11-16)

FARNHAM

The Abbey School
Menin Way, FARNHAM,
Surrey GU9 8DY
Tel: 01252 725059
Head: Mr Nathan Aspinall
Category: LD (11-16)

The Ridgeway Community School
Frensham Road, FARNHAM,
Surrey GU9 8HB
Tel: 01252 724562
Head: Mr D Morgan
Category: SLD (2-19)

GUILDFORD

Gosden House School
Horsham Road, Bramley,
GUILDFORD, Surrey GU5 0AH
Tel: 01483 892008
Acting Head: Ms Fiona Williams
Category: LD (Day 5-16)

Pond Meadow School
Larch Avenue, GUILDFORD,
Surrey GU1 1DR
Tel: 01483 532239
Head: Mr D J Monk
Category: SLD (2-19)

Wey House School
Horsham Road, Bramley,
GUILDFORD, Surrey GU5 0BJ
Tel: 01483 898130
Head: Ms Debra Smith
Category: BESD (Day only 7-11)

LEATHERHEAD

West Hill School
Kingston Road, LEATHERHEAD,
Surrey KT22 7PW
Tel: 01372 814714
Head: Mrs J V Nettleton
Category: LD (11-16)

Woodlands School
Fortyfoot Road, LEATHERHEAD,
Surrey KT22 8RY
Tel: 01372 273427
Head: Mrs Adrienne Knight
Category: SLD (Day 12-19)

OXTED

Limpsfield Grange School
89 Bluehouse Lane, Limpsfield,
OXTED, Surrey RH8 0RZ
Tel: 01883 713928
Head: Ms Sarah Wild
Category: ELD (Boarding
& day 11-16)

REDHILL

St Nicholas School
Taynton Drive, Merstham,
REDHILL, Surrey RH1 3PU
Tel: 01737 215488
Head: Mr Craig Anderson
Category: BESD (Boarding
& day 11-16)

Woodfield School
Sunstone Grove, Merstham,
REDHILL, Surrey RH1 3PR
Tel: 01737 642623
Head: Mrs S Lawrence
Category: LD (11-19)

REIGATE

Brooklands School
27 Wray Park Road,
REIGATE, Surrey RH2 0DF
Tel: 01737 249941
Head: Mr Mark Bryant
Category: SLD (2-11)

SHEPPERTON

Manor Mead School
Laleham Road, SHEPPERTON,
Middlesex TW17 8EL
Tel: 01932 241834
Head: Ms Linda Mardell
Category: SLD (2-11)

WALTON-ON-THAMES

Walton Leigh School
Queens Road, WALTON-ON-
THAMES, Surrey KT12 5AB
Tel: 01932 223243
Head: Ms Linda Mardell
Category: SLD (11-19)

WOKING

Freemantles School
Smarts Heath Road, Mayford
Green, WOKING, Surrey GU22 0AN
Tel: 01483 545680
Head: Mr Justin Price
Category: ASD (4-19)

The Park School
Onslow Crescent, WOKING,
Surrey GU22 7AT
Tel: 01483 772057
Head: Mrs K Eastwood
Category: LD (11-16)

WORCESTER PARK

Linden Bridge School
Grafton Road, WORCESTER
PARK, Surrey KT4 7JW
Tel: 02083 303009
Head: Ms Rachel Watt
Category: ASD (Residential
& day 4-19)

EAST SUSSEX

Children's Services Authority

SEN Team, PO Box 4, County Hall, St Anne's Crescent Lewes, East Sussex, BN7 1UE
Tel: 01273 336740 Fax: 01273 481599 Email: senteam@eastsussex.gov.uk Website: www.eastsussex.gov.uk

BEXHILL-ON-SEA

Glyne Gap School
Hastings Road, BEXHILL-ON-
SEA, East Sussex TN40 2PU
Tel: 01424 217720
Head: Kirsty Prawanna
Category: CLD/ASD (Coed 2-19)

CROWBOROUGH

Grove Park School
Church Road, CROWBOROUGH,
East Sussex TN6 1BN
Tel: 01892 663018
Head: Angela Wellman
Category: CLD/ASD (Coed 2-19)

EASTBOURNE

Hazel Court Special School
Larkspur Drive, EASTBOURNE,
East Sussex BN23 8EJ
Tel: 01323 465720
Head: Ms Sophie Gurney
Category: CLD/ASD (Coed 11-19)

**South Downs Community
Special School**
(West Site), Beechy Avenue,
EASTBOURNE, East Sussex BN20 8NU
Tel: 01323 730302
Executive Head: Remo Palladino
Category: ACLD (Coed 3-11)

The Lindfield School
Lindfield Road, EASTBOURNE,
East Sussex BN22 0BQ
Tel: 01323 502988
Executive Head: Remo Palladino
Category: ACLD (Coed 11-16)

HASTINGS

Torfield School
Croft Road, HASTINGS,
East Sussex TN34 3JT
Tel: 01424 428228
Executive Head: Mr Richard Preece
Category: ACLD (Coed 3-11)

HEATHFIELD

St Mary's School Horam
Maynards Green, Horam,
HEATHFIELD, East Sussex TN21 0BT
Tel: 01435 812278
Executive Head: Mr Frank Stanford
Category: LD EBSD (Boys 9-16)

SEAFORD

Cuckmere House School
Eastbourne Road, SEAFORD,
East Sussex BN25 4BA
Tel: 01323 893319
Executive Head: Mr Frank Stanford
Category: SEBD (Boys 6-16)

ST LEONARDS-ON-SEA

New Horizons School
Beauchamp Road, ST LEONARDS-
ON-SEA, East Sussex TN38 9JU
Tel: 01424 858020
Head: Ms Simone Hopkins
Category: SEBD (Coed 7-16)

Saxon Mount School
Edinburgh Road, ST LEONARDS-
ON-SEA, East Sussex TN38 8HH
Tel: 01424 426303
Head: Mr Richard Preece
Category: ACLD (Coed 11-16)

WEST SUSSEX

Parent Partnership Service

SEN Team, Oriel Lodge, West Street, Chichester, West Sussex, PO19 1RZ
Tel: 08450 751008 Email: localoffer@westsussex.gov.uk Website: www.westsussex.gov.uk

BURGESS HILL

Woodlands Meed Special Educational Needs School
Chanctonbury Road, BURGESS HILL, West Sussex RH15 9EY
Tel: 01444 244133
Head: Ms G Perry
Category: LD (Coed 2-19)

CHICHESTER

Fordwater School
Summersdale Road, CHICHESTER, West Sussex PO19 6PP
Tel: 01243 782475
Head: Mrs S Meekings
Category: SLD (Coed 2-19)

Littlegreen School
Compton, CHICHESTER, West Sussex PO18 9NW
Tel: 02392 631259
Head: Mr R Hatherley
Category: SEBD (Boys 7-16)

St Anthony's School
Woodlands Lane, CHICHESTER, West Sussex PO19 5PA
Tel: 01243 785965
Head: Ms H Ball
Category: MLD (Coed 4-16)

CRAWLEY

Manor Green College
Lady Margaret Road, Ifield, CRAWLEY, West Sussex RH11 0DX
Tel: 01293 520351
Head: Mr G Robson
Category: LD (Coed 11-19)

Manor Green Primary School
Lady Margaret Road, Ifield, CRAWLEY, West Sussex RH11 0DU
Tel: 01293 526873
Head: Mr D Reid
Category: LD (Coed 2-11)

HORSHAM

Queen Elizabeth II Silver Jubilee School
Compton's Lane, HORSHAM, West Sussex RH13 5NW
Tel: 01403 266215
Head: Mrs L Dyer
Category: SLD AUT PMLD (Coed 2-19)

LITTLEHAMPTON

Cornfield School
Cornfield Close, Wick, LITTLEHAMPTON, West Sussex BN17 6HY
Tel: 01903 731277
Head: Ms M Davis
Category: SEBD (Coed 7-16)

SHOREHAM-BY-SEA

Herons Dale School
Hawkins Crescent, SHOREHAM-BY-SEA, West Sussex BN43 6TN
Tel: 01273 596904
Head: Ms T Stepney
Category: LD (Coed 4-11)

WORTHING

Oak Grove College
The Boulevard, WORTHING, West Sussex BN13 1JX
Tel: 01903 708870
Head: Mr P Potter
Category: LD (Coed 11-19)

Palatine Primary School
Palatine Road, Goring-By-Sea, WORTHING, West Sussex BN12 6JP
Tel: 01903 242835
Head: Mrs C Goldsmith
Category: LD (Coed 3-11)

SWINDON

Borough Council

SEN Team, Civic Offices, Euclid Street, Swindon, Wiltshire, SN1 2JH
Email: sendproject@swindon.gov.uk Website: www.swindon.gov.uk

SWINDON

Brimble Hill School
Tadpole Lane, Redhouse, SWINDON, Wiltshire SN25 2NB
Tel: 01793 493900
Head: Mrs Alison Paul
Category: SLD (2-11)

Chalet School
Liden Drive, Liden, SWINDON, Wiltshire SN3 6EX
Tel: 01793 534537
Head: Ms Katherine Bryan
Category: CLD including ASD (2-11)

Crowdys Hill School
Jefferies Avenue, Cricklade Road, SWINDON, Wiltshire SN2 7HJ
Tel: 01793 332400
Head: Mrs M Clarke
Category: CLD & other difficulties (11-16)

Nyland Campus
Nyland Road, Nythe, SWINDON, Wiltshire SN3 3RD
Tel: 01793 535023
Executive Headteacher: Ms Lauren Connor
Category: BESD (5-11)

St Luke's School
Cricklade Road, SWINDON, Wiltshire SN2 7AS
Tel: 01793 705566
Head: Mr Geoff Cherrill
Category: BESD (11-16)

Stratton Education Centre
St Philips Road, Upper Stratton, SWINDON, Wiltshire SN2 7QP
Tel: 01793 828941
Head: Mr Richard Marshall
Category: (Coed 2-11)

Uplands School
The Learning Campus, Tadpole Lane, Redhouse, SWINDON, Wiltshire SN25 2NB
Tel: 01793 493910
Head: Mrs Jackie Smith
Category: SLD (11-19)

TELFORD & WREKIN

IASS

Sen Team, The Glebe Centre, Glebe Street, Wellington Telford, TF1 1JP
Tel: 01952 457176 Email: info@pps-shropshireandtelford.org.uk Website: www.telford.gov.uk

TELFORD

Haughton School
Queen Street, Madeley,
TELFORD, Shropshire TF7 4BW
Tel: 01952 387540
Head: Mrs Gill Knox
Category: MLD ASD SLD
SP&LD BESD (Coed 5-11)

Mount Gilbert School
Hinkshay Road, Dawley,
TELFORD, Shropshire TF4 3PP
Tel: 01952 387670
Head: Mrs Lisa Lyon
Category: SEBD SPLD
AUT (Coed 11-16)

Queensway HLC
Hadley, TELFORD, Shropshire TF1 6AJ
Tel: 01952 388555
Head: Mr Nigel Griffiths
Category: ASD (11-18)

Southall School
Off Rowan Avenue, Dawley,
TELFORD, Shropshire TF4 3PN
Tel: 01952 387600
Head: Ms Jo Burdon
Category: MLD ASD
SEBD (Coed 11-16)

The Bridge
HLC, Waterloo Road, Hadley,
TELFORD, Shropshire TF1 5NU
Tel: 01952 387108
Head: Ms Heather Davies
Category: (3-16)

THURROCK

Council

SEN Services, Children's Services, PO Box 118, Grays, Essex, RM17 6GF
Tel: 01375 652555 Email: sen@thurrock.gov.uk Website: www.thurrock.gov.uk

GRAYS

**Beacon Hill Academy
(Post 16 Provision)**
Buxton Road, GRAYS,
Essex RM16 2WU
Tel: 01375 898656
Head: Mrs Sue Hewitt
Category: SLD PNI PMLD
(Coed 16-19)

Treetops School
Buxton Road, GRAYS,
Essex RM16 2XN
Tel: 01375 372723
Head: Mr Paul Smith
Category: MLD ASD (Coed 3-16)

Treetops School (6th Form)
Buxton Road, GRAYS,
Essex RM16 2XN
Tel: 01375 372723
Head: Mr Paul Smith

SOUTH OCKENDON

**Beacon Hill Academy
(Main Site)**
Erriff Drive, SOUTH OCKENDON,
Essex RM15 5AY
Tel: 01708 852006
Head: Mrs Sue Hewitt
Category: PNI PMLD
SLD (Coed 3-16)

TORBAY

Council

SEN Team, Town Hall, Castle Circus, Torquay, Devon, TQ1 3DR
Tel: 01803 208274 Email: info@sendiasstorbay.org.uk Website: www.torbay.gov.uk

PAIGNTON

Torbay School
170B Torquay Road, Preston,
PAIGNTON, Devon TQ3 2AL
Tel: 01803 665522
Executive Head: Mr James Evans
Category: BESD (11-16)

TORQUAY

Combe Pafford School
Steps Lane, Watcombe,
TORQUAY TQ2 8NL
Tel: 01803 327902
Head: Mr Michael Lock

Mayfield School
Moor Lane, Watcombe,
TORQUAY, Devon TQ2 8NH
Tel: 01803 328375
Head: Mrs June Palmer
Category: SLD PMLD PH
AUT (3-19) BESD (5-11)

Tyne & Wear
GATESHEAD
Council

Learning and Schools, Civic Centre, Regent Street, Gateshead, Tyne & Wear, NE8 1HH
Tel: 01914 333000 Email: customerservices@gateshead.gov.uk Website: www.gateshead.gov.uk

GATESHEAD

Dryden School
Shotley Gardens, Low Fell,
GATESHEAD, Tyne & Wear NE9 5UR
Tel: 01914 203811
Head: Mrs J Bryant
Category: SLD (Coed 11-19)

Eslington Primary School
Hazel Road, GATESHEAD,
Tyne & Wear NE8 2EP
Tel: 01914 334131
Acting Head: Mrs H Stokes
Category: EBD (Coed 5-11)

Furrowfield School
Whitehills Drive, Felling,
GATESHEAD, Tyne & Wear NE10 9RZ
Tel: 01914 954700
Acting Head: Mrs M Richards
Category: EBD (Boys 11-16)

Hill Top School
Wealcroft, Felling, GATESHEAD,
Tyne & Wear NE10 8LT
Tel: 01914 692462
Head: Mrs J Bryant
Category: MLD AUT (Coed 11-16)

The Cedars Academy
Ivy Lane, Low Fell, GATESHEAD,
Tyne & Wear NE9 6QD
Tel: 01914 874595
Head: Mr M Flowers
Category: PD (Coed 2-16)

NEWCASTLE UPON TYNE

Gibside School
Burnthouse Lane, Whickham,
NEWCASTLE UPON TYNE,
Tyne & Wear NE16 5AT
Tel: 01914 410123
Acting Head: Mrs J Donovan
Category: SLD MLD AUT (Coed 4-11)

NEWCASTLE UPON TYNE
City Council

SEN Assessment, Provision & Review Service, Room 213, Civic Centre, Newcastle upon Tyne, Tyne & Wear, NE1 8QH
Tel: 01912 774650 Email: localoffer@newcastle.gov.uk Website: www.newcastlechildrenservices.org.uk

NEWCASTLE UPON TYNE

Hadrian School
Bertram Crescent, Pendower,
NEWCASTLE UPON TYNE,
Tyne & Wear NE15 6PY
Tel: 01912 734440
Head: Mr Christopher Rollings
Category: PMLD SLD
(Coed Day 2-11)

Linhope Pupil Referral Unit
Linhope Centre, Linhope
Road, NEWCASTLE UPON TYNE,
Tyne & Wear NE5 2NW
Tel: 01912 674447
Head: Mr Jeff Lough
Category: (Coed Day 5-16)

Newcastle Bridges School
c/o Kenton College, Drayton
Road, Kenton, NEWCASTLE UPON
TYNE, Tyne & Wear NE3 3RU
Tel: 01918 267086
Head: Mrs Margaret Dover
Category: HS (Coed 2-19)

Sir Charles Parson School
Westbourne Avenue, NEWCASTLE
UPON TYNE, Tyne & Wear NE6 4ED
Tel: 01912 952280
Head: Mr Nick Sharing
Category: SLD PD PMLD
(Coed Day 11-19)

Thomas Bewick School
Linhope Road, West Denton,
NEWCASTLE UPON TYNE,
Tyne & Wear NE5 2LW
Tel: 01912 296020
Head: Ms Diane Scott
Category: AUT (Coed
Day/boarding 3-19)

Trinity School
Condercum Road, NEWCASTLE
UPON TYNE, Tyne & Wear NE4 8XJ
Tel: 01912 986950
Head: Mr Bill Curley
Category: SEBD (Coed Day 7-16)

Tyne & Wear
SUNDERLAND

Children's Services

SEN and Accessibility Team, Sunderland Customer Service Centre, Bunny Hill, Hylton Lane Sunderland, Tyne & Wear, SR5 4BW
Tel: 01915 205553 Email: sen@sunderland.gov.uk Website: www.sunderland.gov.uk

SUNDERLAND

Barbara Priestman Academy
Meadowside, SUNDERLAND, Tyne & Wear SR2 7QN
Tel: 01915 536000
Head: Mrs C Barker
Category: ASD CLD (Coed Day 11-19)

Castlegreen Academy
Craigshaw Road, Hylton Castle, SUNDERLAND, Tyne & Wear SR5 3NF
Tel: 01915 535335
Head: Mr G Shillinglaw
Category: SEBD (Coed Day 11-18)

North View Academy
St Lukes Road, SUNDERLAND, Tyne & Wear SR4 0HB
Tel: 01915 534580
Head: Mr G Mellefont
Category: EBD ASD (4-11)

Portland Academy
Weymouth Road, Chapelgarth, SUNDERLAND, Tyne & Wear SR3 2NQ
Tel: 01915 536050
Head: Mrs M Carson
Category: SLD (Coed Day 11-19)

Springwell Dene Academy
Swindon Road, SUNDERLAND, Tyne & Wear SR3 4EE
Tel: 01915 536067
Head: Mr G Shillinglaw
Category: EBD (Coed Day 11-16)

Sunningdale School
Shaftoe Road, Springwell, SUNDERLAND, Tyne & Wear SR3 4HA
Tel: 01915 535880
Head: Mrs C Wright
Category: PMLD SLD (Coed Day 2-11)

WASHINGTON

Columbia Grange School
Oxclose Road, WASHINGTON, Tyne & Wear NE38 7NY
Tel: 01912 193860
Head: Mrs L Mavin
Category: SLD ASD (Coed Day 3-11)

Tyne & Wear
NORTH TYNESIDE

Children, Young People and Learning Directorate

0-25 Disability and Additional Needs Service (DANS), Quadrant East, Floor 2, Second Left, The Silverlink North, Cobalt Business Park North Tyneside, Tyne & Wear, NE27 0BY
Tel: 01916 437708/07 Fax: 01916 432429 Email: contact.us@northtyneside.gov.uk Website: www.northtyneside.gov.uk

LONGBENTON

Benton Dene School
Hailsham Avenue, LONGBENTON, Tyne & Wear NE12 8FD
Tel: 01916 432730
Head: Mrs Alison McAllister
Category: MLD ASD (Coed 5-11+)

NORTH SHIELDS

Southlands School
Beach Road, Tynemouth, NORTH SHIELDS, Tyne & Wear NE30 2QR
Tel: 01912 006348
Head: Mr D Erskine
Category: MLD BESD (Coed 11-16+)

WALLSEND

Beacon Hill School and Specialist College for Business and Enterprise
Rising Sun Cottages, High Farm, WALLSEND, Tyne & Wear NE28 9LJ
Tel: 01916 433000
Head: Mrs H Jones
Category: ASD SLD PMLD (Coed 2-16)

Silverdale School
Langdale Gardens, WALLSEND, Tyne & Wear NE28 0HG
Tel: 01912 005982
Head: Mr P Gannon
Category: BESD (Coed 7-16)

WHITLEY BAY

Woodlawn School
Drumoyne Gardens, Monkseaton, WHITLEY BAY, Tyne & Wear NE25 9DL
Tel: 01912 008729
Head: Mr Simon Ripley
Category: PD MSI Medical needs (Coed 2-16)

Tyne & Wear
SOUTH TYNESIDE

**Pupil Services, Children, Adults & Families, Chuter Ede Education Centre,
Galsworthy Road South Shields, Tyne & Wear, NE33 2RL
Tel: 01914 247808 Email: lifelonglearningleisure@southtyneside.gov.uk Website: www.southtyneside.info**

HEBBURN

**Hebburn Lakes
Primary School**
Campbell Park Road, HEBBURN,
Tyne & Wear NE31 2QY
Tel: 01914 839122
Head: Mr A S Watson
Category: BESD LD Complex
medical needs

Keelman's Way School
Campbell Park Road, HEBBURN,
Tyne & Wear NE31 1QY
Tel: 01914 897480
Head: Mrs Paula Selby
Category: PMLD SLD
(Coed Day 2-19)

JARROW

**Epinay Business &
Enterprise School**
Clervaux Terrace, JARROW,
Tyne & Wear NE32 5UP
Tel: 01914 898949
Head: Mrs Hilary Harrison
Category: MLD EBD (Coed 5-17)

Fellgate Autistic Unit
Oxford Way, Fellgate Estate,
JARROW, Tyne & Wear NE32 4XA
Tel: 01914 894801
Head: Miss C Wilson
Category: AUT (Coed 3-11)

**Hedworthfield Language
Development Unit**
Linkway, Hedworth Estate,
JARROW, Tyne & Wear NE32 4QF
Tel: 01915 373373
Head: Mrs T Lawton
Category: SP&LD (Coed)

Jarrow School
Field Terrace, JARROW,
Tyne & Wear NE32 5PR
Tel: 01914 893225
Head: Ms J Gillies
Category: HI ASD

Simonside Primary School
Glasgow Road, JARROW,
Tyne & Wear NE32 4AU
Tel: 01914 898315
Head: Ms Bland
Category: HI

SOUTH SHIELDS

**Ashley Child
Development Centre**
Temple Park Road, SOUTH
SHIELDS, Tyne & Wear NE34 0QA
Tel: 01914 564977
Head: Mrs D Todd
Category: Other Early Years

Bamburgh School
Horsley Hill Community
Campus, SOUTH SHIELDS,
Tyne & Wear NE34 7TD
Tel: 01914 274330
Head: Mr Peter Nord
Category: PD MED VIS HI
MLD (Coed Day 2-17)

**Harton Speech and
Language and ASD
Resource Bases**
c/o Harton Technology College,
Lisle Road, SOUTH SHIELDS,
Tyne & Wear NE34 6DL
Tel: 01914 564226
Head: Mr K A Gibson
Category: Speech and
language ASD

Park View School
Temple Park Road, SOUTH
SHIELDS, Tyne & Wear NE34 0QA
Tel: 01914 541568
Head: Mrs Angela Noble
Category: BESD (Coed Day 11-16)

WARRINGTON
Children & Young People

**The Pupil Assessment Support Team, 3rd Floor, New Town House, Buttermarket Street Warrington, WA1 2NJ
Tel: 01925 443322 Email: contact@warrington.gov.uk Website: www.warrington.gov.uk**

WARRINGTON

Fox Wood School
Chatfield Drive, Birchwood,
WARRINGTON, Cheshire WA3 6QW
Tel: 01925 851393
Head: Mrs Val Howarth
Category: SLD (Coed Day 4-19)

Grappenhall Hall School
Church Lane, Grappenhall,
WARRINGTON, Cheshire WA4 3EU
Tel: 01925 263895
Head: Mr Michael Frost
Category: EBD MLD
(Coed Day 11-16)

Green Lane School
Green Lane, Padgate,
WARRINGTON, Cheshire WA1 4JL
Tel: 01925 480128
Head: Mr P King
Category: MLD CLD
(Coed Day 4-19)

WARWICKSHIRE

Children, Young People & Families Directorate

Integrated Disability Service (IDS), Saltisford Office Park, Ansell Way, Warwick, Warwickshire, CV34 4UL
Tel: 01926 413737 Email: ids@warwickshire.gov.uk Website: www.warwickshire.gov.uk

ASH GREEN

**Exhall Grange School
& Science College**
Easter Way, ASH GREEN,
Warwickshire CV7 9HP
Tel: 02476 364200
Head: Mrs Christine Marshall
Category: VIS PD Med
(Coed Day 2-19)

COLESHILL

Woodlands School
Packington Lane, COLESHILL,
West Midlands B46 3JE
Tel: 01675 463590
Head: Mr Iain Paterson
Category: Generic SLD VIS HI AUT
MSI PD MLD PMLD (Coed Day 2-19)

HENLEY-IN-ARDEN

River House School
Stratford Road, HENLEY-IN-
ARDEN, West Midlands B95 6AD
Tel: 01564 792514
Head: Mr Michael Turner
Category: SEBD (Boys Day 11-16)

NUNEATON

Oak Wood Primary School
Morris Drive, NUNEATON,
Warwickshire CV11 4QH
Tel: 02476 740907
Head: Mr Kevin Latham
Category: Generic SLD MLD VIS HI
AUT MSI PD PMLD (Coed Day 2-11)

**Oak Wood Secondary
School**
Morris Drive, NUNEATON,
Warwickshire CV11 4QH
Tel: 02476 740901
Head: Mr Kevin Latham
Category: Generic SLD MLD VIS HI
AUT MSI PD PMLD (Coed Day 11-16)

RUGBY

Brooke School
Overslade Lane, RUGBY,
Warwickshire CV22 6DY
Tel: 01788 812324
Head: Mr Christopher Pollitt
Category: Generic SLD VIS HI AUT
MSI PD MLD PMLD (Coed Day 2-19)

STRATFORD-UPON-AVON

Welcombe Hills School
Blue Cap Road, STRATFORD-UPON-
AVON, Warwickshire CV37 6TQ
Tel: 01789 266845
Head: Mrs Judith Humphry
Category: Generic SLD VIS HI AUT
MSI PD MLD PMLD (Coed Day 2-19)

WARWICK

Ridgeway School
Deansway, WARWICK,
Warwickshire CV34 5DF
Tel: 01926 491987
Head: Ms Debra Hewitt
Category: Generic SLD VIS HI AUT
MSI PD MLD PMLD (Coed Day 3-11)

**Round Oak School
& Support Service &
Sports College**
Brittain Lane, off Myton Road,
WARWICK, Warwickshire CV34 6DX
Tel: 01926 423311
Head: Mrs Fiona Naylor
Category: Generic SLD VIS HI AUT
MSI PD MLD PMLD (Coed Day 11-19)

West Midlands
BIRMINGHAM

Children, Young People & Families

Council House, Victoria Square, Birmingham, B1 1BB
Tel: 01213 031888 Email: senar@birmingham.gov.uk Website: www.birmingham.gov.uk

EDGBASTON

Baskerville School
Fellows Lane, Harborne,
EDGBASTON, Birmingham B17 9TS
Tel: 01214 273191
Head: Mrs Rosemary Adams
Category: ASD (Coed
boarding 11-19)

ERDINGTON

Bridge School
290 Reservoir Road, ERDINGTON,
Birmingham B23 6DE
Tel: 01214 648265
Head: Mr Adrian Coleman
Category: ASD PMLD AUT
(Coed Boarding 2-11)

Queensbury School
Wood End Road, ERDINGTON,
Birmingham B24 8BL
Tel: 01213 735731
Head: Mrs Veronica Jenkins
Category: MLD AUT SLD
(Coed Day 11-19)

Wilson Stuart School
Perry Common Road, ERDINGTON,
Birmingham B23 7AT
Tel: 01213 734475
Head: Mr Stephen Hughes
Category: PD (Coed Day 2-19)

HALL GREEN

Fox Hollies School
Highbury Campus, Queensbridge
Road, Moseley, HALL GREEN,
Birmingham B13 8QB
Tel: 01214 646566
Head: Mr Paul Roberts
Category: SLD PD CLD
MSI (Coed Day 11-19)

Uffculme School
Queensbridge Road, Moseley,
HALL GREEN, Birmingham B13 8QB
Tel: 01214 645250
Head: Mr Alex MacDonald
Category: ASD (Coed day 3-11)

HODGE HILL

Beaufort School
Stechford Road, HODGE
HILL, Birmingham B34 6BJ
Tel: 01216 758500
Head: Ms Fiona Woolford
Category: SLD AUT PMLD
(Coed Day 2-11)

Braidwood School
Bromford Road, HODGE
HILL, Birmingham B36 8AF
Tel: 01214 645558
Head: Mrs Karen Saywood
Category: D HI ASD MLD
(Coed Day 11-19)

Hallmoor School
Hallmoor Road, Kitts Green,
HODGE HILL, Birmingham B33 9QY
Tel: 01217 833972
Head: Mrs Susan Charvis
Category: MLD MSI SP&LD
(Coed Day 5-19)

The Pines Special School
Dreghorn Road, Castle Bromwich,
HODGE HILL, Birmingham B36 8LL
Tel: 01214 646136
Head: Mrs Susan Brandwood
Category: SP&LD ASD (Coed Day 2-11)

LADYWOOD

Calthorpe School & Sports College
Darwin Street, Highgate,
LADYWOOD, Birmingham B12 0TP
Tel: 01217 734637
Head: Mr Graham Hardy
Category: SLD MLD CLD PD
MSI AUT (Coed Day 2-19)

James Brindley Hospital School
Bell Barn Road, Edgbaston,
LADYWOOD, Birmingham B15 2AF
Tel: 01216 666409
Head: Mrs Nicky Penny
Category: HS (Coed Day 2-19)

NORTHFIELD

Longwill Primary School for Deaf Children
Bell Hill, NORTHFIELD,
Birmingham B31 1LD
Tel: 01214 753923
Head: Ms Barbara Day
Category: HI D (Coed Day 2-12)

Victoria School and Specialist Arts College
Bell Hill, NORTHFIELD,
Birmingham B31 1LD
Tel: 01214 769478
Head: Mrs Justine Sims
Category: PD (Coed Day 2-19)

PERRY BARR

Hamilton School
Hamilton Road, Handsworth,
PERRY BARR, Birmingham B21 8AH
Tel: 01214 641676
Head: Mr Jonathan Harris
Category: ASD SP&LD
(Coed Day 4-11)

Mayfield School
Heathfield Road, Handsworth,
PERRY BARR, Birmingham B19 1HJ
Tel: 01214 643354
Head: Mr Paul Jenkins
Category: SLD PMLD
(Coed Day 3-19)

Oscott Manor School
Old Oscott Hill, Kingstanding,
PERRY BARR, Birmingham B44 9SP
Tel: 01213 608222
Head: Ms Joy Hardwick
Category: PMLD ASD MLD
(Coed Day 11-19)

Priestley Smith School
Beeches Road, Great Barr, PERRY
BARR, Birmingham B42 2PY
Tel: 01213 253900
Head: Mrs Helen Porter
Category: VIS (Coed Day 2-17)

REDDITCH

Skilts School
Gorcott Hill, REDDITCH,
West Midlands B98 9ET
Tel: 01527 853851
Head: Mr Charles Herriotts
Category: EBD (Coed
Boarding 5-12)

SELLY OAK

Cherry Oak School
60 Frederick Road, SELLY
OAK, Birmingham B29 6PB
Tel: 01214 642037
Head: Mrs Justine Sims
Category: SLD PMLD
(Coed Day 3-11)

Dame Ellen Pinsent School
Ardencote Road, SELLY OAK,
Birmingham B13 0RW
Tel: 01216 752487
Head: Ms Debbie Allen
Category: ASD EBD SP&LD
HI (Coed day 4-11)

Lindsworth School
Monyhull Hall Road, Kings Norton,
SELLY OAK, Birmingham B30 3QA
Tel: 01216 935363
Head: Mr David McMahon
Category: SEBD (Coed
Boarding 11-16)

Selly Oak Trust School
Oak Tree Lane, SELLY OAK,
Birmingham B29 6HZ
Tel: 01214 720876
Head: Mr Chris Field
Category: MLD (Coed Day 11-19)

SOLIHULL

Springfield House Community Special School
Kenilworth Road, Knowle,
SOLIHULL, West Midlands B93 0AJ
Tel: 01564 772772
Head: Mrs Janet Collins
Category: SEBD (Coed
Boarding 5-11)

SUTTON COLDFIELD

Bridge School - Longmoor Campus
Coppice View Road, SUTTON
COLDFIELD, Birmingham B73 6UE
Tel: 01213 537833
Head: Mr Adrian Coleman
Category: PMLD AUT
ASD (Coed 2-11)

Langley School
Trinity Road, SUTTON COLDFIELD,
West Midlands B75 6TJ
Tel: 01216 752929
Head: Mrs Fiona Woolford
Category: MLD ASD
(Coed Day 3-11)

YARDLEY

Brays School
Brays Road, Sheldon, YARDLEY,
Birmingham B26 1NS
Tel: 01217 435730
Head: Mrs Jane Edgerton
Category: PD SLD EBD
CLD MSI (Coed 2-11)

West Midlands
COVENTRY
Education Authority

SEN & Inclusion, Civic Centre 2.3, Earl Street, Coventry, West Midlands, CV1 5RS
Tel: 02476 831624 Website: www.coventry.gov.uk

COVENTRY

Baginton Fields Secondary School
Sedgemoor Road, COVENTRY,
West Midlands CV3 4EA
Tel: 02476 303854
Head: Mr Simon Grant
Category: SLD (Coed Day 11-19)

Castle Wood
Deedmore Road, COVENTRY,
West Midlands CV2 1EQ
Tel: 02476 709060
Head: Mrs Yvonne McCall
Category: Broad spectrum
(Coed Day 3-11)

Corley Centre
Church Lane, Fillongley, COVENTRY,
West Midlands CV7 8AZ
Tel: 01676 540218
Head: Ms Lisa Batch
Category: Complex
SCD (Coed 11-19)

River Bank Academy
Ashington Grove, COVENTRY,
West Midlands CV3 4DE
Tel: 02476 303776
Head: Mr David Lisowski/
Mrs Jackie Smith
Category: Broad spectrum
(Coed Day 11-19)

RNIB Three Spires Academy
Kingsbury Road, COVENTRY,
West Midlands CV6 1PJ
Tel: 02476 594952
Head: Mr Robert Jones
Category: MLD (Coed Day 3-11)

Sherbourne Fields Primary & Secondary School
Rowington Close, Off
Kingsbury Road, COVENTRY,
West Midlands CV6 1PS
Tel: 02476 591501
Head: Ms Shivaun Moriaty
Category: PD (Coed Day 2-19)

Tiverton Primary
Rowington Close, Off Kingsbury Road,
COVENTRY, West Midlands CV6 1PS
Tel: 02476 594954
Head: Mrs Carolyn Claridge
Category: SLD (Coed Day 3-11)

Woodfield School
Hawthorn Lane Secondary Site,
COVENTRY, West Midlands CV4 9PB
Tel: 02476 462335
Head: Mr Steve Poole
Category: EBD (Boys Day 11-16)

Woodfield School
Stoneleigh Road Primary Site,
COVENTRY, West Midlands CV4 7AB
Tel: 02476 418755
Head: Mr Steve Poole
Category: ESBD (Coed Day 5-11)

West Midlands
DUDLEY

Children's Services

Special Education Needs Team, Westox House, 1 Trinity Road, Dudley, West Midlands, DY1 1JQ
Tel: 01384 814214 Website: www.dudley.gov.uk

COSELEY

Rosewood School
Bell Street, Russells Hall Estate,
COSELEY, West Midlands WV14 8XJ
Tel: 01384 816800
Head: Mr D Kirk
Category: EBD (11-16)

DUDLEY

Old Park School
Thorns Road, Brierley Hill, DUDLEY,
West Midlands DY5 2JY
Tel: 01384 818905
Head: Mrs G Cartwright
Category: SLD (3-19)

The Brier School
Bromley Lane, Kingswinford,
DUDLEY, West Midlands DY6 8QN
Tel: 01384 816000
Head: Mr R Hinton
Category: MLD (5-16)

**The Sutton School &
Specialist College**
Scotts Green Close, Russells
Hall Estate, DUDLEY, West
Midlands DY1 2DU
Tel: 01384 818670
Head: Mr D Bishop-Rowe
Category: MLD (11-16)

The Woodsetton School
Tipton Road, Woodsetton,
DUDLEY, West Midlands DY3 1BY
Tel: 01384 818265
Head: Mr P A Rhind-Tutt
Category: MLD (4-11)

HALESOWEN

Halesbury School
Feldon Lane, HALESOWEN,
West Midlands B62 9DR
Tel: 01384 818630
Head: Mrs J Kings
Category: MLD (4-16)

STOURBRIDGE

Pens Meadow School
Ridge Hill, Brierley Hill Road,
Wordsley, STOURBRIDGE,
West Midlands DY8 5ST
Tel: 01384 818945
Head: Mrs M Bissell
Category: SLD (3-19)

West Midlands
SANDWELL

Children & Families Services

**Special Education Needs Service, PO Box 16230, Sandwell Council
House, Freeth Street Oldbury, West Midlands, B69 9EX
Tel: 01215 698240 Email: children_families@sandwell.gov.uk Website: www.sandwell.gov.uk**

LICHFIELD

Shenstone Lodge School
Birmingham Road, Shenstone,
LICHFIELD, Staffordshire WS14 0LB
Tel: 01543 480369
Head: Mr N C Toplass
Category: EBD (Coed Day 4-16)

OLDBURY

**The Meadows
Sports College**
Dudley Road East, OLDBURY,
West Midlands B69 3BU
Tel: 01215 697080
Head: Mr G Phillips
Category: PMLD (Coed Day 11-19)

The Orchard School
Causeway Green Road, OLDBURY,
West Midlands B68 8LD
Tel: 01215 697040
Head: Mrs G Kew
Category: PMLD(Coed Day 2-11)

ROWLEY REGIS

The Westminster School
Curral Road, ROWLEY REGIS,
West Midlands B65 9AN
Tel: 01215 882421
Head: Mrs C Hill
Category: MLD (Coed Day 11-19)

West Midlands
SOLIHULL

Education Authority

**SEN Team, Council House, Manor Square, Solihull, West Midlands, B91 3QB
Tel: 01217 046690 Email: sen@solihull.gov.uk Website: www.solihull.gov.uk**

BIRMINGHAM

Forest Oak School
Windward Way, Smith's
Wood, BIRMINGHAM, West
Midlands B36 0UE
Tel: 01217 170088
Principal: Mrs A R Mordey
Category: MLD (Coed Day 4-18)

Merstone School
Windward Way, Smith's
Wood, BIRMINGHAM, West
Midlands B36 0UE
Tel: 01217 171040
Principal: Mrs A R Mordey
Category: SLD (Coed Day 2-19)

Northern House School
Lanchester Way, Castle
Bromwich, BIRMINGHAM,
West Midlands B36 9LF
Tel: 01217 489760
Head: Mr Trevor Scott
Category: EBD (Coed Day 11-16)

SOLIHULL

Hazel Oak School
Hazel Oak Road, Shirley, SOLIHULL,
West Midlands B90 2AZ
Tel: 01217 444162
Head: Ms Debbie Jenkins
Category: MLD (Coed Day 4-18)

Reynalds Cross School
Kineton Green Road, SOLIHULL,
West Midlands B92 7ER
Tel: 01217 073012
Head: Mrs Jane Davenport
Category: SLD (Coed Day 2-19)

West Midlands
WALSALL

Walsall Information, Advice and Support Service (IASS)

Blakenhall Village Centre, Thames Road, Blakenhall, Walsall, West Midlands, WS3 1LZ
Tel: 01922 650330 Email: parentpartnership@walsall.gov.uk Website: www.walsall.gov.uk

WALSALL

**Castle Business &
Enterprise College**
Odell Road, Leamore, WALSALL,
West Midlands WS3 2ED
Tel: 01922 710129
Head: Mrs Christine Fraser
Category: MLD, Additional
Needs (Coed Day 7-19)

Elmwood School
King George Crescent, Rushall,
WALSALL, West Midlands WS4 1EG
Tel: 01922 721081
Head: Mr Simon Hubbard
Category: EBD (Coed Day 11-16)

Mary Elliot Special School
Leamore Lane, WALSALL,
West Midlands WS2 7NR
Tel: 01922 490190
Head: Mr Adrian Coleman
Category: SLD PMLD AUT
(Coed day 11-19)

Oakwood School
Druids Walk, Walsall Wood,
WALSALL, West Midlands WS9 9JS
Tel: 01543 452040
Head: Mrs Kay Mills
Category: SLD CLD PMLD
ASD Challenging behaviour
(Coed Day 3-11)

Old Hall Special School
Bentley Lane, WALSALL,
West Midlands WS2 7LU
Tel: 01902 368045
Head: Mrs Lynn Hill
Category: SLD PMLD AUT
(Coed day 3-11)

Phoenix Primary
Odell Road, Leamore, WALSALL,
West Midlands WS3 2ED
Tel: 01922 712834
Head: Mrs Dawn Evans
Category: EBD (Coed Day 4-11)

**The Jane Lane School - A
College for Cognition
and Learning**
Churchill Road, Bentley, WALSALL,
West Midlands WS2 0JH
Tel: 01922 721161
Head: Mr Tony Milovsorov
Category: MLD, Additional
Needs (Coed Day 7-19)

West Midlands
WOLVERHAMPTON

Communities Directorate- Health, Wellbeing and Disabilities

Special Educational Needs Team (SENSTART), Civic Centre, St Peter's Square, Wolverhampton, West Midlands, WV1 1RT
Tel: 01902 555873 Email: city.direct@wolverhampton.gov.uk Website: www.wolverhampton.gov.uk

WOLVERHAMPTON

**Broadmeadow
Nursery School**
Lansdowne Road,
WOLVERHAMPTON, West
Midlands WV1 4AL
Tel: 01902 558330
Head: Miss K Warrington
Category: SLD ASD PMLD
(Coed Day 2-6)

Green Park School
The Willows, Green Park Avenue,
Bilston, WOLVERHAMPTON,
West Midlands WV14 6EH
Tel: 01902 556429
Head: Mrs L Dawney
Category: PMLD SLD
(Coed Day 4-19)

New Park School
Cromer Gardens, Whitmore
Reans, WOLVERHAMPTON,
West Midlands WV6 0UB
Tel: 01902 551564
Head: Ms F Pass
Category: BESD ADHD
(Coed Day 8-16)

Penn Fields School
Boundary Way, Penn,
WOLVERHAMPTON, West
Midlands WV4 4NT
Tel: 01902 558640
Head: Miss E Stanley
Category: MLD SLD ASD
(Coed Day 4-19)

Penn Hall School
Vicarage Road, Penn,
WOLVERHAMPTON, West
Midlands WV4 5HP
Tel: 01902 558355
Head: Mr D Parry
Category: PD SLD MLD
(Coed Day 3-19)

Tettenhall Wood School
Regis Road, Tettenhall,
WOLVERHAMPTON, West
Midlands WV6 8XG
Tel: 01902 556519
Head: Ms S Wewellyn
Category: ASD (Coed Day 5-19)

**Westcroft School Sports
& Vocational College**
Greenacres Avenue, Underhill,
WOLVERHAMPTON, West
Midlands WV10 8NZ
Tel: 01902 558350
Head: Ms A Brown
Category: CLD (Coed Day 4-16)

WILTSHIRE

Children & Education Department

SEN/Disability 0-25 Service, County Hall, Bythesea Road, Trowbridge, Wiltshire, BA14 8JN
Tel: 01225 757985 Email: statutorysen.services@wiltshire.gov.uk Website: www.wiltshirelocaloffer.org.uk

CHIPPENHAM

St Nicholas School
Malmesbury Road, CHIPPENHAM,
Wiltshire SN15 1QF
Tel: 01249 650435
Head: Mr Bruce Douglas
Category: SLD PMLD
(Coed Day 3-19)

DEVIZES

Downland School
Downlands Road, DEVIZES,
Wiltshire SN10 5EF
Tel: 01380 724193
Head: Mr Phil Beaumont
Category: BESD SPLD
(Boys Boarding 11-16)

Rowdeford School
Rowde, DEVIZES, Wiltshire SN10 2QQ
Tel: 01380 850309
Head: Mrs Ingrid Sidmouth
Category: MLD (Coed
Boarding 11-16)

SALISBURY

**Exeter House
Special School**
Somerset Road, SALISBURY,
Wiltshire SP1 3BL
Tel: 01722 334168
Head: Mr Richard Chapman
Category: SLD PMLD SPLD
Del (Coed Day 2-19)

TROWBRIDGE

Larkrise School
Ashton Street, TROWBRIDGE,
Wiltshire BA14 7EB
Tel: 01225 761434
Head: Mr Phil Cook
Category: SLD MLD
(Coed Day 3-19)

WINDSOR AND MAIDENHEAD

Children & Young People Learning & Care Directorate

SEN Team, Town Hall, St Ives Road, Maidenhead, Berkshire, SL6 1RF
Tel: 01628 685878 Email: localoffer@rbwm.gov.uk Website: www.rbwm.gov.uk

MAIDENHEAD

Manor Green School
Elizabeth Hawkes Way,
MAIDENHEAD, Berkshire SL6 3EQ
Tel: 01628 513800
Head: Ms Ania Hildrey
Category: SLD PMLD ASD
MLD (Coed 2-19)

WOKINGHAM

Children's Services

SEN Team, Highwood Annexe, Fairwater Drive, Woodley Wokingham, Berkshire, RG5 3RU
Tel: 01189 746216 Email: sen@wokingham.gov.uk Website: www.wokingham.gov.uk

WOKINGHAM

Addington School
Woodlands Avenue, Woodley,
WOKINGHAM, Berkshire RG5 3EU
Tel: 01189 669073
Head: Mrs Liz Meek
Category: SLD PMLD ASD
MLD (Coed 4-18)

Southfield School
Gipsy Lane, WOKINGHAM,
Berkshire RG40 2HR
Tel: 01189 771293
Head: Mr Dominic Geraghty
Category: BESD (Coed 7-16)

WORCESTERSHIRE

Children's Services Directorate

SENDIASS, PO Box 73, Worcester, WR5 2YA
Tel: 01905 610858 Email: sendiass@worcestershire.gov.uk Website: www.worcestershire.gov.uk

BROMSGROVE

Chadsgrove School & Specialist Sports College
Meadow Road,
Catshill, BROMSGROVE,
Worcestershire B61 0JL
Tel: 01527 871511
Head: Mrs Debbie Rattley
Category: PD PMLD MSI LD (2-19)

Rigby Hall School
19 Rigby Lane, Astonfields,
BROMSGROVE,
Worcestershire B60 2EP
Tel: 01527 875475
Head: Mrs Sarah Radford
Category: SLD MLD ASD (3-19)

EVESHAM

Vale of Evesham School
Four Pools Lane, EVESHAM,
Worcestershire WR11 1BN
Tel: 01386 443367
Head: Mr Stephen Garside
Category: SLD MLD PMLD ASD (4-19)

KIDDERMINSTER

Wyre Forest School
Comberton Road, KIDDERMINSTER,
Worcestershire DY10 3DX
Tel: 01562 823156
Head: Mrs Susan Price
Category: MLD SLD ASD
BESD (Coed 7-16)

REDDITCH

Pitcheroak School
Willow Way, Brockhill, REDDITCH,
Worcestershire B97 6PQ
Tel: 01527 65576
Head: Ms Sheila Holden
Category: SLD MLD AUT (2-19)

The Kingfisher School
Clifton Close, Matchborough,
REDDITCH, Worcestershire B98 0HF
Tel: 01527 502486
Head: Mrs Jodie McCracken
Category: BESD (Coed 7-16)

WORCESTER

Fort Royal Community Primary School
Wylds Lane, WORCESTER WR5 1DR
Tel: 01905 355525
Head: Mrs Jane Long
Category: MLD PD SLD (2-11)

Regency High School
Carnforth Drive,
WORCESTER WR4 9JL
Tel: 01905 454828
Head: Mr Frank Steel
Category: PD MLD SLD (11-19)

Riversides School
Thorneloe Road,
WORCESTER WR1 3HZ
Tel: 01905 21261
Head: Mr Paul Yeomans
Category: BESD (Coed 7-16)

CITY OF YORK

Council

SEN Services, West Offices, Station Rise, York, YO1 6GA
Tel: 01904 554302 Website: www.york.gov.uk

YORK

Applefields School
Bad Bargain Lane, YORK YO31 0LW
Tel: 01904 553900
Head (Until Sept 2015): Mr
G Gilmore
Category: MLD AUT SLD PMLD

Hob Moor Oaks School
Hob Moor Children's Centre, Green
Lane, Acomb, YORK YO24 4PS
Tel: 01904 555000
**Head Teacher (Until Sept
2015):** Mrs Susan Coulter
Category: MLD AUT SLD PMLD

EAST RIDING OF YORKSHIRE
Council

Children, Families & Schools, County Hall, Beverley, East Riding of Yorkshire, HU17 9BA
Tel: 01482 392162 Fax: 01482 392213 Website: www.eastriding.gov.uk

BROUGH

St Anne's Community Special School
St Helen's Drive, Welton, BROUGH, East Riding of Yorkshire HU15 1NR
Tel: 01482 667379
Headteacher: Mrs Lesley Davis
Category: SLD

DRIFFIELD

King's Mill School
Victoria Road, DRIFFIELD, East Riding of Yorkshire YO25 6UG
Tel: 01377 253375
Headteacher: Mrs G Lawton
Category: SLD

GOOLE

Riverside Special School
Ainsty Street, GOOLE, East Riding of Yorkshire DN14 5JS
Tel: 01405 763925
Acting Headteacher: Mr Andrew Hall
Category: MLD and other complex needs

NORTH YORKSHIRE
Education Authority

Access and Inclusion, SEN Team, South Block, County Hall Northallerton, North Yorkshire, DL7 8AE
Tel: 01609 532240 Website: www.northyorks.gov.uk

BEDALE

Mowbray School
Masham Road, BEDALE, North Yorkshire DL8 2SD
Tel: 01677 422446
Head: Mr J Tearle
Category: MLD SP&LD (2-16)

HARROGATE

Forest Moor School
Menwith Hill Road, HARROGATE, North Yorkshire HG3 2RA
Tel: 01423 779232
Head: Mr S Ashby
Category: BESD (Boys 11-16)

Pupil Referral Service
59 Grove Road, HARROGATE, North Yorkshire HG1 5EP
Tel: 01423 536111
Head: Ms S Campbell
Category: PRU

Springwater School
High Street, Starbeck, HARROGATE, North Yorkshire HG2 7LW
Tel: 01423 883214
Head: Mrs S Edwards
Category: SLD PMLD (2-19)

KIRKBYMOORSIDE

Welburn Hall School
KIRKBYMOORSIDE, York YO62 7HQ
Tel: 01751 431218
Head: Mrs H Smith
Category: PHLD (8-18)

KNARESBOROUGH

The Forest School
Park Lane, KNARESBOROUGH, North Yorkshire HG5 0DG
Tel: 01423 864583
Head: Mr P Hewitt
Category: MLD (2-16)

NORTHALLERTON

Hambleton and Richmondshire Pupil Referral Service
East Road, NORTHALLERTON, North Yorkshire DL6 1SZ
Tel: 01609 710443
Head: Mrs F Dodgson
Category: PRU

The Dales School
Morton-on-Swale, NORTHALLERTON, North Yorkshire DL7 9QW
Tel: 01609 772932
Head: Mrs H Barton
Category: SLD PMLD (2-19)

SCARBOROUGH

Brompton Hall School
Brompton-by-Sawdon, SCARBOROUGH, North Yorkshire YO13 9DB
Tel: 01723 859121
Head: Mr M Mihkelson
Category: BESD (Boys 8-16)

Pupil Referral Service
Valley Bridge Parade, SCARBOROUGH, North Yorkshire YO11 2PG
Tel: 01723 330629
Acting Head (until August 2015): Ms Jane Cresswell
Category: PRU

Springhead School
Barry's Lane, Seamer Road, SCARBOROUGH, North Yorkshire YO12 4HA
Tel: 01723 367829
Head: Mrs C D Wilson
Category: SLD PMLD (2-19)

The Woodlands School
Woodlands Drive, SCARBOROUGH, North Yorkshire YO12 6QN
Tel: 01723 373260
Head: Mrs A Fearn
Category: MLD (2-16)

SELBY

The Rubicon Centre
Raincliffe Street, SELBY, North Yorkshire YO8 4AN
Tel: 01609 533951
Head: Mr L Bell
Category: PRU

SKIPTON

Brooklands School
Burnside Avenue, SKIPTON, North Yorkshire BD23 2DB
Tel: 01756 794028
Head: Mrs D Sansom
Category: MLD SLD PMLD (2-19)

North and South Craven Pupil Referral Service
Keighley Road, SKIPTON, North Yorkshire BD23 2QS
Tel: 01756 630495
Head: Mr D Hannah
Category: PRU

South Yorkshire
BARNSLEY

Directorate for Children, Young People & Families

PO Box 634, Barnsley, South Yorkshire, S70 9GG
Tel: 01226 773689 Email: education@barnsley.gov.uk Website: www.barnsley.gov.uk

BARNSLEY

Greenacre School
Keresforth Hill Road, BARNSLEY,
South Yorkshire S70 6RG
Tel: 01226 287165
Head: Mrs Susan Hayter
Category: SLD CLD PMLD
MSI AUT (Coed Day 2-19)

Springwell Learning Community
St Helen's Boulevard, BARNSLEY,
South Yorkshire S71 2AY
Tel: 01226 291133
Head: Mr David Whitaker

South Yorkshire
DONCASTER

Council

Special Educational Needs Service, Civic Office, Waterdale, Doncaster, DN1 3BU
Tel: 01302 737209 Email: sen@doncaster.gov.uk Website: www.doncaster.gov.uk

DONCASTER

Coppice School
Ash Hill Road, Hatfield,
DONCASTER, South
Yorkshire DN7 6JH
Tel: 01302 844883
Head: Mrs L Jarred
Category: SLD ASD BESD
(Coed Day 3-19)

Heatherwood School
Leger Way, DONCASTER,
South Yorkshire DN2 6HQ
Tel: 01302 322044
Head: Mrs Lisa Suter
Category: SLD PD (Coed Day 3-19)

North Ridge Community School
Tenter Balk Lane, Adwick
le Street, DONCASTER,
South Yorkshire DN6 7EF
Tel: 01302 720790
Headteacher: Mrs Christine Djezzar
Category: SLD (Coed Day 3-19)

Pennine View School
Old Road, Conisbrough,
DONCASTER, South
Yorkshire DN12 3LR
Tel: 01709 864978
Head: Ms Jo Barker-Carr
Category: MLD (Coed Day 7-16)

Stone Hill School
Barnsley Road, Scawsby,
DONCASTER, South
Yorkshire DN5 7UB
Tel: 01302 800090
Headteacher: Mr S Leone
Category: MLD (Coed 6-16)

South Yorkshire
ROTHERHAM

School Admissions, Organisation and SEN Assessment Service

Wing A, 1st Floor, Riverside House, Main Street Rotherham, South Yorkshire, S60 1AE
Tel: 01709 822660 Fax: 01709 371444 Website: www.rotherham.gov.uk

MEXBOROUGH

Milton School
Storey Street, Swinton,
MEXBOROUGH, South
Yorkshire S64 8QG
Tel: 01709 570246
Head: Ms Brenda Hughes
Category: MLD ASD

ROTHERHAM

Abbey School
Little Common Lane,
Kimberworth, ROTHERHAM,
South Yorkshire S61 2RA
Tel: 01709 740074
Executive Head: Mr Roger Burman
Category: MLD

Hilltop School
Larch Road, Maltby, ROTHERHAM,
South Yorkshire S66 8AZ
Tel: 01709 813386
Executive Head: Mr N Whittaker
Category: SLD

Kelford School
Oakdale Road, Kimberworth,
ROTHERHAM, South
Yorkshire S61 2NU
Tel: 01709 512088
Head: Mr N Whittaker
Category: SLD

Newman School
East Bawtry Road, Whiston,
ROTHERHAM, South
Yorkshire S60 3LX
Tel: 01709 828262
Head: Ms Julie Mott
Category: PH Medical needs

The Willows School
Locksley Drive, Thurcroft,
ROTHERHAM, South
Yorkshire S66 9NT
Tel: 01709 542539
Head: Mrs A Sanderson
Category: MLD

South Yorkshire
SHEFFIELD

Children, Young People and Families

SEN Assessment & Placement Team, North Wing, Level 5, Moorfoot Building, Sheffield, S1 4PL
Tel: 01142 736394 Fax: 01142 735636 Email: ed-sensupportteam@sheffield.gov.uk Website: www.sheffield.gov.uk

SHEFFIELD

Becton School
Beighton Community Hospital,
Sevenairs Road, SHEFFIELD,
South Yorkshire S20 1NZ
Tel: 01143 053121
Head: Ms Sacha Schofield
Category: Mental health
difficulties (Admissions managed
by Sheffield Children's NHS Trust)

**Bents Green
Secondary School**
Ringinglow Road, SHEFFIELD,
South Yorkshire S11 7TB
Tel: 01142 363545
Category: AUT, Communication
Needs (Day & residential)

**Heritage Park
Community School**
Norfolk Park Road, SHEFFIELD,
South Yorkshire S2 2RU
Tel: 01142 796850
Executive Head: Mr Tony Middleton
Category: BESD (KS 2/3/4)

**Holgate Meadows
Community School**
Lindsay Road, SHEFFIELD,
South Yorkshire S5 7WE
Tel: 01142 456305
Head: Mr Tony Middleton
Category: BESD (KS 2/3/4)

Mossbrook Special School
Bochum Parkway, SHEFFIELD,
South Yorkshire S8 8JR
Tel: 01142 372768
Head: Mr Dean Linkhorn
Category: AUT (Primary
Day/residential)

**Norfolk Park
Primary School**
Park Grange Road, SHEFFIELD,
South Yorkshire S2 3QF
Tel: 01142 726165
Head: Mrs Jane Vickers
Category: SLD PMLD (Primary)

Seven Hills School
Granville Road, SHEFFIELD,
South Yorkshire S2 2RJ
Tel: 01142 743560
Heads: Ms Elaine Everett
& Mr Clive Rockliff
Category: SLD PMLD

Talbot Specialist School
Lees Hall Road, SHEFFIELD,
South Yorkshire S8 9JP
Tel: 01142 507394
Head: Ms Carolyn Sutcliffe
Category: SLD PMLD

The Rowan Primary School
4 Durvale Court, Furniss Avenue,
SHEFFIELD, South Yorkshire S17 3PT
Tel: 01142 350479
Category: AUT (Primary)

**Woolley Wood Community
Primary School**
Chaucer Road, SHEFFIELD,
South Yorkshire S5 9QN
Tel: 01142 327160
Head: Mr David Whitehead
Category: SLD PMLD

West Yorkshire
CALDERDALE

Children & Young People's Services

SEN Team, Town Hall, PO Box 51, Halifax, West Yorkshire, HX1 1TP
Tel: 01422 394141 Fax: 01422 364899 Email: zena.taylor@calderdale.gov.uk Website: www.calderdale.gov.uk

BRIGHOUSE

Highbury School
Lower Edge Road, Rastrick,
BRIGHOUSE, West Yorkshire HD6 3LD
Tel: 01484 716319
Head: Ms Debbie Sweet
Category: All (3-11)

HALIFAX

Ravenscliffe High School
Skircoat Green, HALIFAX,
West Yorkshire HX3 0RZ
Tel: 01422 358621
Head: Mr Martin Moorman
Category: All (11-18)

Wood Bank School
Dene View, Luddendenfoot,
HALIFAX, West Yorkshire HX2 6PB
Tel: 01422 884170
Head: Mr Richard Pawson
Category: All (4-11)

West Yorkshire
KIRKLEES

Directorate for Children & Young People

SEN Assessment and Commissioning Team, Civic Centre 1, High Street Huddersfield, West Yorkshire, HD1 2NF
Tel: 01484 225057 Email: senact@kirklees.gov.uk Website: www.kirklees.gov.uk

BATLEY

Fairfield School
White Lee Road, BATLEY,
West Yorkshire WF17 8AS
Tel: 01924 326103
Head: Ms Anne Tierney
Category: SLD (Coed Day 3-19)

DEWSBURY

Ravenshall School
Ravensthorpe Road, Thornhill Lees,
DEWSBURY, West Yorkshire WF12 9EE
Tel: 01924 325234
Head: Mrs Jeanette Tate
Category: MLD (Coed Day 5-16)

HOLMFIRTH

Lydgate School
Kirkroyds Lane, New Mill,
HOLMFIRTH, West Yorkshire HD9 1LS
Tel: 01484 222484
Head: Mrs Nicola Rogers
Category: MLD (Coed Day 5-16)

HUDDERSFIELD

Castle Hill School
Newsome Road South,
Newsome, HUDDERSFIELD,
West Yorkshire HD4 6JL
Tel: 01484 226659
Head: Mrs Gill Robinson
Category: SLD AUT PMLD
(Coed Day 3-19)

Longley School
Dog Kennel Bank, HUDDERSFIELD,
West Yorkshire HD5 8JE
Tel: 01484 223937
Head: Ms Margaret Burton
Category: MLD AUT EBD
(Coed Day 5-16)

**Nortonthorpe Hall School
(Residential & Day)**
Busker Lane, Scissett,
HUDDERSFIELD, West
Yorkshire HD8 9JU
Tel: 01484 222921
Head: Mrs D Navaratnam
Category: EBD (Coed
Residential & day 7-16)

West Yorkshire
LEEDS

Inclusion Services

SENDIASS, Adams Court, Kildare Terrace, Leeds, West Yorkshire, LS12 1DB
Tel: 01133 951200 Website: www.educationleeds.co.uk

LEEDS

**East SILC - John
Jamieson (main site)**
Hollin Hill Drive, Oakwood,
LEEDS, West Yorkshire LS8 2PW
Tel: 01132 930236
Head: Ms Diane Reynard
Category: Complex physical,
learning and care needs (Coed 2-19)

**North West SILC -
Pennyfields (main site)**
Tongue Lane, LEEDS, West
Yorkshire LS6 4QD
Tel: 01133 368270
Head: Mr Michael Purches
Category: Complex
physical, learning and care
needs (Coed 2-19)

**South SILC - Broomfield
(main site)**
Broom Place, Belle Isle, LEEDS,
West Yorkshire LS10 3JP
Tel: 01132 771603
Head: Mr John Fryer
Category: Complex
physical, learning and care
needs (Coed 2-19)

**West Oaks SEN Specialist
School & College**
Westwood Way, Boston
Spa, Wetherby, LEEDS, West
Yorkshire LS23 6DX
Tel: 01937 844772
Head: Mr Andrew Hodkinson
Category: Complex
physical, learning and care
needs (Coed 2-19)

West Yorkshire
WAKEFIELD

Social Care Direct

SEN Team, Wakefield One, PO Box 700, Wakefield, WF1 2EB
Tel: 08458 503503 Email: social_care_direct@wakefield.gov.uk Website: www.wakefield.gov.uk

BARNSLEY

High Well School
High Well Hill Lane, South Hiendley,
BARNSLEY, West Yorkshire S72 9DF
Tel: 01226 718613
Head: Mr Will Carpenter
Category: EBD (Coed 11-16)

CASTLEFORD

Wakefield Pathways School
Poplar Avenue, Townville,
CASTLEFORD, West Yorkshire WF10 3QJ
Tel: 01977 723085
Head: Ms Dawn Coombes
Category: SLD MLD (Coed 4-11)

OSSETT

Highfield School
Gawthorpe Lane, Gawthorpe,
OSSETT, West Yorkshire WF5 9BS
Tel: 01924 302980
Head: Mrs Pat Marshall
Category: MLD (Coed 11-16)

PONTEFRACT

Oakfield Park School
Barnsley Road, Ackworth,
PONTEFRACT, West Yorkshire WF7 7DT
Tel: 01977 723145
Head: Mr Stephen Copley
Category: SLD PMLD (Coed 11-19)

Maintained special schools and colleges

WAKEFIELD

Kingsland School
Aberford Road, Stanley,
WAKEFIELD, West Yorkshire WF3 4BA
Tel: 01924 303100
Head: Miss Paula Trow
Category: SLD PMLD (Coed 2-11)

**Pinderfields Hospital
(Pupil Referral Unit)**
Wrenthorpe Centre, Imperial
Avenue, WAKEFIELD, West
Yorkshire WF2 0LW
Tel: 01924 303695
Head: Mrs Helen Ferguson
Category: HS PMLD (Coed 2-19)

NEWCASTLE UNDER LYME

Blackfriars Special School
Priory Road, NEWCASTLE UNDER
LYME, Staffordshire ST5 2TF
Tel: 01782 297780
Head: Mr James Kane
Category: PD LD MSI
(Coed Day 5-19)

The Coppice School
Abbots Way, Westlands,
NEWCASTLE UNDER LYME,
Staffordshire ST5 2EY
Tel: 01782 297490
Head: Mr James Kane
Category: MLD PMLD SEBD
SLD ASD (Coed Day 11-19)

STAFFORD

**Walton Hall Community
Special School, a
Specialist Arts Centre**
Stafford Road, Walton, STAFFORD,
Staffordshire ST21 6JR
Tel: 01785 850420
Head: Mr James Kane
Category: LD (Coed Day/
Boarding 11-19)

MANSFIELD

The Beech Academy
Fairholme Drive, MANSFIELD,
Nottinghamshire NG19 6DX
Tel: 01623 623149
Head: Mrs Janice Addison
Category: MLD (Coed Day 3-16)

NOTTINGHAM

Foxwood Academy
Derby Road, Bramcote Hills,
Beeston, NOTTINGHAM NG9 3GF
Tel: 01159 177202
Head: Mr Chris Humphreys
Category: MLD (Coed 3-16)

GUERNSEY

The Education Department

PO Box 32, Grange Road, St Peter Port, Guernsey, GY1 3AU
Tel: 01481 733000 Email: office@education.gov.gg Website: www.education.gg

FOREST

**Le Rondin School
and Centre**
Rue des Landes, FOREST,
Guernsey GY8 0DP
Tel: 01481 268300
Head: Mrs P Sullivan
Category: MLD SLD PMLD (3-11)

ST SAMPSON'S

Le Murier School
Rue de Dol, ST SAMPSON'S,
Guernsey GY2 4DA
Tel: 01481 246660
Head: Mr J Teehan
Category: MLD PMLD
SLD (Coed 11-16)

ST. PETER PORT

Les Voies School
Collings Road, ST. PETER
PORT, Guernsey GY1 1FW
Tel: 01481 710721
Head: Mr J Furley
Category: SEBD (Coed 4-16)

JERSEY

The Department for Education, Sport & Culture

Highlands Campus, St. Saviour, Jersey, JE4 8QJ
Tel: 01534 443500 Email: esc@gov.je Website: www.gov.je/esc

ST HELIER

Mont a l'Abbe School
La Grande Route de St
Jean, La Pouquelaye, ST
HELIER, Jersey JE2 3FN
Tel: 01534 875801
Head: Ms Sharon Eddie
Category: LD (3-19)

ST SAVIOUR

D'Hautree House
St Saviour's Hill, ST SAVIOUR,
Jersey JE2 7LF
Tel: 01534 618042
Category: SEBD (Coed 11-16)

The Alternative Curriculum
Oakside Centre, La Grande
Route de St Martin, Five Oaks,
ST SAVIOUR, Jersey JE2 7GS
Tel: 01534 872840
Category: EBD

NORTHERN IRELAND – BELFAST

Education and Library Board

40 Academy Street, Belfast, Northern Ireland, BT1 2NQ
Tel: 02890 564000 Email: info.belb@belb.co.uk Website: www.belb.org.uk

BELFAST

Belfast Hospital School
Royal Belfast Hospital School
for Sick Children, Falls Road,
BELFAST, Co Antrim BT12 6BE
Tel: 02890 633498
Head: Mrs M Godfrey
Category: HS (Coed 4-19)

Cedar Lodge School
24 Lansdowne Park North,
BELFAST, Co Antrim BT15 4AE
Tel: 02890 777292
Head: Mrs L Little
Category: EPI ASD ADHD
Medical needs (Coed 4-16)

Clarawood School
Clarawood Park, BELFAST,
Co Antrim BT5 6FR
Tel: 02890 472736
Head: Ms J Whyte
Category: SEBD (Coed 8-12)

**Adamís Court8~%,
Fleming Fulton School**
35 Upper Malone Road,
BELFAST, Co Antrim BT9 6TY
Tel: 02890 613877
Head: Ms C Hancock
Category: PH MLD (Coed 3-19)

Glenveagh School
Harberton Park, BELFAST,
Co Antrim BT9 6TT
Tel: 02890 669907
Head: Ms F Leneghan
Category: SLD (Coed 8-19)

**Greenwood House
Assessment Centre**
Greenwood Avenue, Upper
Newtownards Road, BELFAST,
Co Antrim BT4 3JJ
Tel: 02890 471000
Head: Ms K Calvert
Category: SP&LD MLD EBD SLD
Medical needs (Coed 4-7)

Harberton Special School
Haberton Park, BELFAST,
Co Antrim BT9 6TX
Tel: 02890 381525
Head: Mr M McGlade
Category: AUT ASP SP&LD EBD
Medical needs (Coed 4-11)

**Loughshore Educational
Resource Centre**
889 Shore Road, BELFAST,
Co Antrim BT36 7DH
Tel: 02890 773062
Teacher in Charge: Mrs G Cameron

Mitchell House School
1A Marmont, 405 Holywood Road,
BELFAST, Co Antrim BT4 2GT
Tel: 02890 760292
Acting Head: Miss L Matchett
Category: PD MSI (Coed 3-18)

**Oakwood Assessment
Centre**
Harberton Park, BELFAST,
Co Antrim BT9 6TX
Tel: 02890 605116
Head: Mrs P McCann
Category: SLD PMLD
ASD (Coed 3-8)

**Park Education
Resource Centre**
145 Ravenhill Road, BELFAST,
Co Antrim BT6 8GH
Tel: 02890 450513
Head: Ms R McCausland
Category: MLD (Coed 11-16)

**St Gerard's School &
Support Services**
Blacks Road, BELFAST,
Co Antrim BT10 1NB
Tel: 02890 600330
Head: Mrs S McIntaggart
Category: MLD (Coed 4-16)

**St Teresa's Speech &
Language Centre**
Glen Road, BELFAST, Co
Antrim BT11 8BW
Tel: 02890 431871
Teacher in Charge: Miss
N Campbell

St Vincent's Centre
6 Willowfield Drive, BELFAST,
Co Antrim BT6 8HN
Tel: 02890 461444
Teacher in Charge: Mr J McAuley

NORTH EASTERN

Education and Library Board

SEN Team, 182 Galgorm Road, Ballymena, Co Antrim, Northern Ireland, BT42 1HN
Tel: 02825 662560 Email: special.education@neelb.org.uk Website: www.eani.org.uk

ANTRIM

Riverside School
Fennel Road, ANTRIM,
Co Antrim BT41 4PB
Tel: 02894 428946
Head: Mr Colin Ward
Category: SLD

BALLYMENA

Castletower School
91 Fry's Road, BALLYMENA,
Co Antrim BT43 7EN
Tel: 02825 648263
Category: MLD SLD PD SEBD

COLERAINE

Sandelford Special School
4 Rugby Avenue, COLERAINE,
Co Londonderry BT52 1JL
Tel: 02870 343062
Category: SLD

MAGHERAFELT

Kilronan School
46 Ballyronan Road, MAGHERAFELT,
Co Londonderry BT45 6EN
Tel: 02879 632168
Head: Mrs Alison Millar
Category: SLD

NEWTOWNABBEY

Hillcroft Special School
Manse Way, NEWTOWNABBEY,
Co Antrim BT36 5UW
Tel: 02890 837488
Category: SLD

**Jordanstown
Special School**
85 Jordanstown Road,
NEWTOWNABBEY, Co
Antrim BT37 0QE
Tel: 02890 863541
Head: Mrs Ann Magee
Category: HI VIS (Coed 4-19)

Rosstulla Special School
2 Jordanstown Road,
NEWTOWNABBEY, Co
Antrim BT37 0QF
Tel: 02890 862743
Head: Mrs F Burke
Category: MLD (Coed 5-16)

SOUTH EASTERN

Education and Library Board

SEN Team, Grahamsbridge Road, Dundonald, Belfast, Northern Ireland, BT16 2HS
Tel: 02890 566200 Email: info@seelb.org.uk Website: www.seelb.org.uk

BANGOR

Clifton Special School
292A Old Belfast Road,
BANGOR, Co Down BT19 1RH
Tel: 02891 270210
Head: Mrs Stephanie Anderson
Category: SLD

Lakewood Special School
96 Newtownards Road,
BANGOR, Co Down BT19 1GZ
Tel: 02891 456227
Head: Mr Jon Bleakney

BELFAST

Longstone Special School
Millar's Lane, Dundonald,
BELFAST, Co Down BT16 2DA
Tel: 02890 480071
Head: Mr Ioannis Skarmoutsos
Category: MLD

Tor Bank School
5 Dunlady Road, BELFAST,
Co Down BT16 1TT
Tel: 02890 484147
Head: Mr Colm Davis
Category: SLD

CRAIGAVON

Brookfield Special School
65 Halfpenny Gate Road, Moira,
CRAIGAVON, Co Armagh BT67 0HP
Tel: 02892 622978
Head: Mrs Barbara Spence
Category: MLD (Coed 5-11)

DONAGHADEE

Killard House
Cannyreagh Road, DONAGHADEE,
Co Down BT21 0AU
Tel: 02891 882361
Head: Mrs Julie Lavin
Category: MLD

DOWNPATRICK

Ardmore House
95A Saul Street, DOWNPATRICK,
Co Down BT30 6NJ
Tel: 02844 614881
Head: Mr Barry Fettes
Category: EBD

Knockevin Special School
33 Racecourse Hill, DOWNPATRICK,
Co Down BT30 6PU
Tel: 02844 612167
Head: Mrs Anne Cooper
Category: SLD

HILLSBOROUGH

Beechlawn Special School
3 Dromore Road, HILLSBOROUGH,
Co Down BT26 6PA
Tel: 02892 682302
Head: Mrs Barbara Green
Category: MLD

LISBURN

Parkview Special School
2 Brokerstown Road, LISBURN,
Co Antrim BT28 2EE
Tel: 02892 601197
Head: Mr James Curran
Category: SLD

SOUTHERN

Education and Library Board

SEN Team, 3 Charlemont Place, The Mall, Armagh, Northern Ireland, BT61 9AX
Tel: 02837 512200 Email: selb.hq@selb.org Website: www.eani.org.uk

ARMAGH

Lisanally School
85 Lisanally Lane, ARMAGH,
Co Armagh BT61 7HF
Tel: 02837 523563
Head: Ms Sandra Flynn
Category: SLD (Coed)

BANBRIDGE

Donard School
22A Castlewellan Road,
BANBRIDGE, Co Down BT32 4XY
Tel: 02840 662357
Head: Mrs Edel Lavery
Category: SLD (Coed)

CRAIGAVON

Ceara School
Sloan Street, Lurgan, CRAIGAVON,
Co Armagh BT66 8NY
Tel: 02838 323312
Head: Dr Peter Cunningham
Category: SLD (Coed)

DUNGANNON

Sperrinview School
8 Coalisland Road, DUNGANNON,
Co Tyrone BT71 6FA
Tel: 02887 722467
Principal: Miss Paula Jordan
Category: SLD (Coed)

NEWRY

Rathore School
23 Martin's Lane, Carnagat,
NEWRY, Co Down BT35 8PJ
Tel: 02830 261617
Head: Mr Raymond Cassidy
Category: SLD (Coed)

WESTERN

Children and Young People's Services

SEN Team, Headquarters Office, 1 Hospital Road, Omagh, Northern Ireland, BT79 0AW
Tel: 02882 411456 Email: info@welbni.org Website: www.omagh.gov.uk

ENNISKILLEN

Willowbridge School
8 Loughshore Road,
Drumlyon, ENNISKILLEN, Co
Fermanagh BT74 7EY
Tel: 02866 321930
Principal: Mrs J Murphy
Category: SLD MLD (Coed)

LIMAVADY

Rossmar School
2 Ballyquin Road, LIMAVADY,
Co Londonderry BT49 9ET
Tel: 02877 762351
Head: Mr B McLaughlin
Category: MLD (Coed)

LONDONDERRY

**Ardnashee School and
College (Lower Campus)**
15 Racecourse Road,
LONDONDERRY, Co
Londonderry BT48 7RE
Tel: 02871 263270
Head: Dr M Dobbins
Category: SLD (Coed)

**Ardnashee School and
College (Upper Campus)**
17 Racecourse Road,
LONDONDERRY, Co
Londonderry BT48 7RE
Tel: 02871 351266
Head: Dr M Dobbins
Category: EBD MLD (Coed)

OMAGH

**Arvalee School and
Resource Centre**
17 Deverney Road, OMAGH,
Co Tyrone BT79 0ND
Tel: 02882 249182
Acting Principal: Mrs W Winters
Category: MLD SLD (Coed)

STRABANE

**Knockavoe School and
Resource Centre**
10A Melmount Gardens,
STRABANE, Co Tyrone BT82 9EB
Tel: 02871 883319
Head: Ms Martina McCornish
Category: SLD MLD (Coed)

SCOTLAND – ABERDEEN

Education, Culture & Sport

Additional Support Needs, Business Hub 13, Second Floor North, Marischal College, Broad Street Aberdeen, AB10 1AB
Tel: 01224 523449 Email: fis@aberdeencity.gov.uk Website: www.aberdeencity.gov.uk

ABERDEEN

**Aberdeen School
for the Deaf**
c/o Sunnybank School, Sunnybank
Road, ABERDEEN AB24 3NJ
Tel: 01224 261722
Head: Ms Alison Buchan
Category: HI

Cordyce School
Riverview Drive, Dyce,
ABERDEEN AB21 7NF
Tel: 01224 724215
Head: Ms Maureen Simmers
Category: EBD

Hazlewood School
Fernielea Road,
ABERDEEN AB15 6GU
Tel: 01224 321363
Head: Ms Jill Barry
Category: SLD MLD PMLD

**Hospital and Home
Tuition Service**
Royal Aberdeen Children's
Hospital, Lowit Unit, Westburn
Road, ABERDEEN AB25 2ZG
Tel: 01224 550317
Head: Ms Maureen Simmers
Category: HS

Woodlands School
Regent Walk, ABERDEEN AB24 1SX
Tel: 01224 524393
Head: Ms Caroline Stirton
Category: PMLD

*In Scotland, Special Educational Needs are generally referred to as Additional Support Needs (ASN)

ABERDEENSHIRE
Education & Children's Services

St Leonards, Sandyhill Road, Banff, AB45 1BH
Tel: 01261 813340 Email: education.development@aberdeenshire.gov.uk Website: www.aberdeenshire.gov.uk

FRASERBURGH

Westfield School
Argyll Road, FRASERBURGH,
Aberdeenshire AB43 9BL
Tel: 01346 518699
Head: Ms Kerri Dalton
Category: PMLD SCLD
(Coed 5-18, 0-3 Nursery)

INVERURIE

St Andrew's School
St Andrew's Garden, INVERURIE,
Aberdeenshire AB51 3XT
Tel: 01467 621215
Acting Head: Ms Susan Stewart
Category: PMLD SCLD (Coed 3-18)

PETERHEAD

Anna Ritchie School
Grange Gardens, PETERHEAD,
Aberdeenshire AB42 2AP
Tel: 01779 473293
Acting Head: Mrs Brenda Milne
Category: PMLD SCLD (Coed 3-18)

STONEHAVEN

Carronhill School
Mill of Forest Road, STONEHAVEN,
Kincardineshire AB39 2GZ
Tel: 01569 763886
Head: Mrs Glenda Fraser
Category: PMLD SCLD (Coed 3-18)

EAST AYRSHIRE
Education & Social Services

Council Headquarters, London Road, Kilmarnock, KA3 7BU
Tel: 01563 576000 Website: www.east-ayrshire.gov.uk

CUMNOCK

Hillside School
Dalgleish Avenue, CUMNOCK,
East Ayrshire KA18 1QQ
Tel: 01290 423239
Head: Ms Debbie Skeoch
Category: SLD PMLD (Coed 6-17)

KILMARNOCK

Park School
Beech Avenue, KILMARNOCK,
East Ayrshire KA1 2EW
Tel: 01563 549988
Head: Mrs Julie Hope
Category: LD PD (Coed 5-18)

Willowbank School
Grassyards Road, KILMARNOCK,
East Ayrshire KA3 7BB
Tel: 01563 526115
Head: Ms Tracy Smallwood
Category: SLD PMLD

SOUTH AYRSHIRE
Council

ASN Team, County Buildings, Wellington Square, Ayr, KA7 1DR
Tel: 03001 230900 Website: www.south-ayrshire.gov.uk

AYR

Southcraig Campus
Belmont Avenue, AYR,
South Ayrshire KA7 2ND
Tel: 01292 612146
Head: Mrs Lorraine Stobie
Category: SLD CLD (Coed 1-5)

GIRVAN

Invergarven School
15 Henrietta Street, GIRVAN,
South Ayrshire KA26 9EB
Tel: 01465 716808
Head: Mrs Jane Gordon
Category: SLD CLD PD
MSI (Coed 3-16)

*In Scotland, Special Educational Needs are generally referred to as Additional Support Needs (ASN)

CLACKMANNANSHIRE
Council

Educational Development Service, Kilncraigs, Greenside Street, Alloa, Clackmannanshire, FK10 1EB
Tel: 01259 450000 Fax: 01259 452440 Email: education@clacks.gov.uk Website: www.clacksweb.org.uk

ALLOA

Extended Additional Support Needs Provision within Alloa Academy
Bowhouse Road, ALLOA, Clackmannanshire FK10 1DN
Tel: 01259 214979
Principal Teacher of Provision: Linda Brown
Category: CLD MSI PD PH PMLD SLD

Primary School Support Service located in Park Primary School
East Castle Street, ALLOA, Clackmannanshire FK10 1AN
Tel: 01259 212151
Head Teacher: Julie Ann Miller
Category: SEBD EBSD BESD

Secondary Support Service within South School
Bedford Place, ALLOA, Clackmannanshire FK10 1JK
Tel: 01259 724345
Head Teacher: Julie Ann Miller
Category: SEBD EBSD BESD

ALVA

Primary ASD Provision within Alva Primary (from August 2014)
Brook Street, ALVA, Clackmannanshire FK12 5AN
Principal Teacher of Provision: Tracey Howard
Category: ASD AUT ADHD ADD

Secondary ASD Provision within Alva Academy
Academy Avenue, ALVA, Clackmannanshire FK12 5FE
Tel: 01259 760342
Principal Teacher of Provision: Laura Fowler
Category: ASD AUT ADHD ADD

SAUCHIE

Lochies School
Gartmorn Road, SAUCHIE, Clackmannanshire FK10 3PB
Tel: 01259 216928
Head: Rhoda MacDougall
Category: CLD SLD (Coed 5-11)

TILLICOULTRY

Inclusion Support Service located in Tillicoultry Primary School
Fir Park, TILLICOULTRY, Clackmannanshire FK13 6PL
Tel: 01259 452455
Acting Manager: Audrey McCormick
Category: Supports all children with ASN in mainstream schools

COMHAIRLE NAN EILEAN SIAR
Department of Education & Children's Services

SEN Team, Sandwick Road, Stornoway, Isle of Lewis, HS1 2BW
Tel: 08456 007090 Email: enquiries@cne-siar.gov.uk Website: www.cne-siar.gov.uk

SANDWICK

Sandwickhill Learning Centre
East Street, SANDWICK, Isle of Lewis HS2 0AG
Tel: 01851 822680
Principal Teacher: Mrs A Campbell
Category: SLD PMLD (Coed 3-11)

*In Scotland, Special Educational Needs are generally referred to as Additional Support Needs (ASN)

EAST DUNBARTONSHIRE
Council

ASN Team, 12 Strathkelvin Place, Kirkintilloch, Glasgow, Lanarkshire, G66 1TJ
Tel: 01415 788723 Email: education@eastdunbarton.gov.uk Website: www.eastdunbarton.gov.uk

KIRKINTILLOCH

Merkland School
Langmuir Road, KIRKINTILLOCH,
East Dunbartonshire G66 2QF
Tel: 01419 552336
Head: Ms Anne Mulvenna
Category: MLD PH

LENZIE

Campsie View School
Boghead Road, LENZIE, East
Dunbartonshire G66 4DP
Tel: 01419 552339
Head: Mrs Carole Bowie
Category: SCLD

WEST DUNBARTONSHIRE
Council

Educational Services, Council Offices, Garshake Road, Dunbarton, G82 3PU
Tel: 01389 737374 Email: contact.centre@west-dunbarton.gov.uk Website: www.west-dunbarton.gov.uk

CLYDEBANK

Cunard School
Cochno Street, Whitecrook,
CLYDEBANK, West
Dunbartonshire G81 1RQ
Tel: 01419 526614
Head: Jenni Curson
Category: SEBD (Primary)

Kilpatrick School
Mountblow Road,
Dalmuir, CLYDEBANK, West
Dunbartonshire G81 4SW
Tel: 01389 872171/872168
Head: Debbie Queen
Category: SCLD (Primary/
Secondary)

CITY OF EDINBURGH
Council

ASN Team, Waverley Court, 4 East Market Street, Edinburgh, Midlothian, EH8 8BG
Tel: 01312 002000 Email: justask@edinburgh.gov.uk Website: www.edingburgh.gov.uk

EDINBURGH

Braidburn Special School
107 Oxgangs Road North,
EDINBURGH EH14 1ED
Tel: 01313 122320
Acting Head: Ms Morna Phillips
Category: EPI PH (Coed 2-16)

**Edinburgh Secure
Services (Howdenhall)**
39 Howdenhall Road,
EDINBURGH EH16 6PG
Tel: 01316 648488
Head: Gay Smith
Category: BESD (Coed
Residential 10-17)

**Edinburgh Secure
Services (St Katharine's)**
29a Balmwell Terrace,
EDINBURGH EH16 6PS
Tel: 01316 721109
Head: Gay Smith
Category: BESD (Coed
Residential 10-17)

Gorgie Mills Special School
97 Gorgie Park Road,
EDINBURGH EH11 2QL
Tel: 01313 133848
Head: Ms Terri Dwyer
Category: EBD

Kaimes Special School
140 Lasswade Road,
EDINBURGH EH16 6RT
Tel: 01316 648241
Head: Mrs Ros Miller
Category: SP&LD ASD (Coed 5-18)

Oaklands Special School
750 Ferry Road,
EDINBURGH EH4 4PQ
Tel: 01313 158100
Head: Ms Maureen Mathieson
Category: SLD CLD PD MSI

Panmure St Ann's
6 South Grays Close,
EDINBURGH EH1 1TQ
Tel: 01315 568833
Head: Ms Mandy Shiel

Pilrig Park Special School
12 Balfour Place,
EDINBURGH EH6 5DW
Tel: 01314 677960
Head: Ms Ellen Muir
Category: MLD SLD (Coed 11-16)

**Prospect Bank
Special School**
81 Restalrig Road,
EDINBURGH EH6 8BQ
Tel: 01315 532239
Head: Ms Kirsty Rosie
Category: LD SP&LD (Coed 5-12)

*In Scotland, Special Educational Needs are generally referred to as Additional Support Needs (ASN)

Redhall Special School
3c Redhall Grove,
EDINBURGH EH14 2DU
Tel: 01314 431256
Head: Ms Susan Shipway
Category: LD (Coed 4-11)

Rowanfield Special School
67c Groathill Road North,
EDINBURGH EH4 2SA
Tel: 01313 436116
Head: Ms Leanne Hepburn
Category: EBD

St Crispin's Special School
19 Watertoun Road,
EDINBURGH EH9 3HZ
Tel: 01316 674831
Head: Ms Ruth Hendery
Category: SLD AUT (Coed 5-16)

Woodlands Special School
36 Dolphin Avenue,
EDINBURGH EH14 5RD
Tel: 01314 493447
Head: Ms Angelina Lombardo

FALKIRK
Council

Additional Support for Learning, Sealock House, 2 Inchyra Road, Grangemouth, FK3 9XB
Tel: 01324 506649 Email: additionalsupport@falkirk.gov.uk Website: www.falkirk.gov.uk

FALKIRK

Mariner Support Service
Weedingshall, Edinburgh Road,
Polmont, FALKIRK FK2 0XS
Tel: 01324 506770
Acting Head: Ms Gillian Macadam
Category: SEBD (Secondary)

Windsor Park School
Bantaskine Road, FALKIRK FK1 5HT
Tel: 01324 508640
Head: Mrs Catherine Finestone
Category: D (Coed 3-16)

GRANGEMOUTH

Oxgang School
c/o Moray Primary School, Moray
Place, GRANGEMOUTH FK3 9DL
Tel: 01324 501311
Acting Head: Mr David MacKay
Category: BESD (5-11)

LARBET

Carrongrange School
Carrongrange Avenue,
LARBET, Falkirk FK5 3BH
Tel: 01324 555266
Head: Ms Gillian Robertson
Category: CLD MLD (Secondary)

FIFE
Education Service

ASN Team, Rothesay House, Rothesay Place, Glenrothes, Fife, KY7 5PQ
Tel: 03451 555555 (Ext 442126) Email: jennifer.allan@fife.gov.uk Website: www.fifedirect.org.uk/fifecouncil

CUPAR

Kilmaron School
Balgarvie Road, CUPAR,
Fife KY15 4PE
Tel: 01334 659480
Head: Ms Isla Lumsden
Category: CLD PD (Coed 3-18)

DUNFERMLINE

Calaiswood School
Nightingale Place,
DUNFERMLINE, Fife KY11 8LW
Tel: 01383 602481
Head: Ms Deborah Davidson
Category: CLD (Coed 3-18)

Woodmill High School ASN
Shields Road, DUNFERMLINE,
Fife KY11 4ER
Tel: 01383 602406
Category: SEBD

GLENROTHES

John Fergus School
Erskine Place, GLENROTHES,
Fife KY7 4JB
Tel: 01592 583489
Head: Ms Pamela Kirkum
Category: CD PD (Coed Day 3-18)

KIRKCALDY

Rosslyn School
Viewforth Terrace,
KIRKCALDY, Fife KY1 3BW
Tel: 01592 583482
Head: Mr Nick Caiger
Category: SLD PMLD PD (Coed 3-19)

LEVEN

Hyndhead School
Barncraig Street, Buckhaven,
LEVEN, Fife KY8 1JE
Tel: 01592 583480
Head: Ms Agnes Lindsay
Category: SLD (Coed 5-18)

LOCHGELLY

Lochgelly North School
Mcgregor Avenue,
LOCHGELLY, Fife KY5 9PE
Tel: 01592 583481
Head: Ms Mary Sparling
Category: SEBD

GLASGOW

Education Services

40 John Street, Glasgow, G1 1JL
Tel: 01412 872000 Website: www.glasgow.gov.uk

GLASGOW

Abercorn Secondary School
195 Garscube Road,
GLASGOW G4 9QH
Tel: 01413 326212
Head: Ms Patricia McGowan
Category: MLD

Ashcraig Secondary School
100 Avenue End Road,
GLASGOW G33 3SW
Tel: 01417 743428
Head: Mr Danny McGrorry
Category: PH VIS

Broomlea Primary School
Keppoch Campus, 65 Stonyhurst
Street, GLASGOW G22 5AX
Tel: 01413 368428
Head: Ms Fiona Shields
Category: CLD

Cardinal Winning Secondary School
30 Fullarton Avenue,
GLASGOW G32 8NJ
Tel: 01417 783714
Head: Mr Gerard McDonald
Category: MLD

Cartvale Secondary School
3 Burndyke Court,
GLASGOW G51 2BG
Tel: 01414 451767
Head: Ms Pauline Harte
Category: BESD

Croftcroighn Primary School
290 Mossvale Road,
GLASGOW G33 5NY
Tel: 01417 743760
Head: Mrs Margaret McFadden
Category: CLD

Drummore Primary School
129 Drummore Road,
GLASGOW G15 7NH
Tel: 01419 441323
Head: Ms Fiona McLean
Category: MLD

Eastmuir Primary School
211 Hallhill Road,
GLASGOW G33 4QL
Tel: 01417 713464
Head: Mrs Lorraine Campbell
Category: MLD

Glasgow Dyslexia Support Service
Floor 2 Room 9, Thornwood
Primary School, 11 Thornwood
Avenue, GLASGOW G11 7QZ
Tel: 01413 345700
Co-ordinator: Ms
Margaret Glasgow
Category: DYS DYSP

Greenview Learning Centre
384 Drakemire Drive,
GLASGOW G45 9SR
Tel: 01416 341551
Head: Mrs Aisling Boyle
Category: BESD

Hampden Primary School
18 Logan Gardens,
GLASGOW G5 0LJ
Tel: 01414 296095
Head: Ms Mary Cloughley
Category: CLD

Hazelwood School
50 Dumbreck Court,
GLASGOW G41 5DQ
Tel: 01442 79334
Head: Ms Julia Haugh-Reid
Category: HI VIS (2-19)

Hollybrook Academy
135 Hollybrook Street,
GLASGOW G42 7HU
Tel: 01414 235937
Head: Ms Jaqueline Newell
Category: MLD (Secondary)

Howford Primary School
487 Crookston Road,
GLASGOW G53 7TX
Tel: 01418 822605
Head: Ms Karen Keith
Category: MLD

Kelbourne Park Primary School
109 Hotspur Street,
GLASGOW G20 8LH
Tel: 01419 461405
Head: Ms Andrea MacBeath
Category: PH

Kirkriggs Primary School
500 Croftfoot Road,
GLASGOW G45 0NJ
Tel: 01416 347158
Head: Ms Lorraine Booth
Category: MLD

Ladywell School
12A Victoria Park Drive South,
GLASGOW G14 9RU
Tel: 01419 596665
Head: Ms Karen Muir
Category: BESD (10-14)

Langlands Primary School
Glenside Avenue,
GLASGOW G53 5FD
Tel: 01418 920952
Head: Mr Mark Beattie
Category: CLD

Linburn Academy
77 Linburn Road,
GLASGOW G52 4EX
Tel: 01418 832082
Head: Ms Lorna Wallace
Category: CLD (Secondary)

Middlefield School
26 Partickhill Road,
GLASGOW G11 5BP
Tel: 01413 340159
Head: Ms Catherine Gilius
Category: ASD (Day & residential)

Milton School
6 Liddesdale Terrace,
GLASGOW G22 7HL
Tel: 01417 622102
Head: Ms Margaret Mills
Category: CLD

Newhills Secondary School
42 Newhills Road,
GLASGOW G33 4HJ
Tel: 01417 731296
Head: Ms Alison Lochrie
Category: CLD

Parkhill Secondary School
375 Cumbernauld Road,
GLASGOW G31 3LP
Tel: 01415 542765
Head: Ms Evelyn Hill
Category: MLD

St Kevin's Primary School
25 Fountainwell Road,
GLASGOW G21 1TN
Tel: 01415 573722
Head: Ms Elizabeth Murphy
Category: MLD

St Oswald's Secondary School
9 Birgidale Road,
GLASGOW G45 9NJ
Tel: 01416 373952
Head: Ms Margaret MacLeay
Category: MLD

Westmuir High School
255 Rigby Street,
GLASGOW G32 6DJ
Tel: 01415 566276
Head: Ms Pauline Harte
Category: BESD

---

*In Scotland, Special Educational Needs are generally referred to as Additional Support Needs (ASN)

HIGHLAND

Education, Culture & Sport Service

Glenurquhart Road, Inverness, IV3 5NX
Tel: 01463 702801 Website: www.highland.gov.uk

INVERNESS

Drummond School
Drummond Road, Inverness,
INVERNESS, Highland IV2 4NZ
Tel: 01463 701050
Head: Mr Mark Elvines
Category: SLD PMLD
CLD (Coed 3-16)

ROSS-SHIRE

St Clement's School
Tulloch Street, Dingwall, ROSS-
SHIRE, Highland IV15 9JZ
Tel: 01349 863284
Head: Ms Toni Macartney
Category: SP&LD VIS
HI PD (Coed 5-11)

St Duthus School
Academy Street, Tain, ROSS-
SHIRE, Highland IV19 1ED
Tel: 01862 894407
Head: Ms Clare Whiteford
Category: SLD PLD CLD (Coed 3-18)

INVERCLYDE

Council

ASN Team, Municipal Buildings, Greenock, PA15 1LY
Tel: 01475 717171 Email: comment@inverclyde.gov.uk Website: www.inverclyde.gov.uk

GOUROCK

Garvel Deaf Centre
c/o Moorfoot Primary School,
GOUROCK, Inverclyde PA19 1ES
Tel: 01475 715642
Head: Ms Sylvia Gillen
Category: D

GREENOCK

Lomond View Academy
Ingleston Street, GREENOCK,
Inverclyde PA15 4UQ
Tel: 01475 714414
Head: Mr David Peden

PORT GLASGOW

Craigmarloch School
Port Glasgow Community
Campus, Kilmacolm Road, PORT
GLASGOW, Inverclyde PA14 6PP
Tel: 01475 715345
Head: Ms Eileen Stewart

NORTH LANARKSHIRE

Council

Learning and Leisure Services, Municipal Buildings, Kildonan Street, Coatbridge, ML5 3BT
Tel: 01236 812790 Website: www.northlan.gov.uk

AIRDRIE

**Mavisbank School
and Nursery**
Mitchell Street, AIRDRIE, North
Lanarkshire ML6 0EB
Tel: 01236 632108
Head: Mr John Lochrie
Category: PMLD (Coed 3-18)

COATBRIDGE

Buchanan High School
67 Townhead Road, COATBRIDGE,
North Lanarkshire ML5 2HT
Tel: 01236 632052
Category: (Coed Day 12-18)

Drumpark School
Albert Street, COATBRIDGE,
North Lanarkshire ML5 3ET
Tel: 01236 794884
Head: Ms Kathleen Cassidy
Category: MLD PH SP&LD (3-18)

Pentland School
Tay Street, COATBRIDGE,
North Lanarkshire ML5 2NA
Tel: 01236 794833
Category: SEBD (Coed 5-11)

Portland High School
31-33 Kildonan Street, COATBRIDGE,
North Lanarkshire ML5 3LG
Tel: 01236 632060
Head: Mr McGovern
Category: SEBD (Coed 11-16)

Willowbank School
299 Bank Street, COATBRIDGE,
North Lanarkshire ML5 1EG
Tel: 01236 632078
Category: SEBD (Coed 11-18)

CUMBERNAULD

Glencryan School
Greenfaulds Road, CUMBERNAULD,
North Lanarkshire G67 2XJ
Tel: 01236 794866
Category: MLD PH ASD (Coed 5-18)

*In Scotland, Special Educational Needs are generally referred to as Additional Support Needs (ASN)

**Redburn School
and Nursery**
Kildrum Ring Road, CUMBERNAULD,
North Lanarkshire G67 2EL
Tel: 01236 736904
Category: SLD CLD PH (Coed 2-18)

MOTHERWELL

Bothwellpark High School
Annan Street, MOTHERWELL,
North Lanarkshire ML1 2DL
Tel: 01698 274939
Category: SLD (Coed 11-18)

**Clydeview School
and Nursery**
Magna Street, MOTHERWELL,
North Lanarkshire ML1 3QZ
Tel: 01698 264843
Category: SLD (Coed 5-11)

Firpark Primary School
177 Milton Street, MOTHERWELL,
North Lanarkshire ML1 1DL
Tel: 01698 274933
Category: (Coed Day 3-10)

Firpark Secondary School
Firpark Street, MOTHERWELL,
North Lanarkshire ML1 2PR
Tel: 01698 251313
Category: MLD PH (Coed 11-18)

UDDINGSTON

Fallside Secondary School
Sanderson Avenue,
Viewpark, UDDINGSTON,
North Lanarkshire G71 6JZ
Tel: 01698 274986
Category: EBD (Coed 11-16)

SOUTH LANARKSHIRE

Council

Council Offices, Almada Street, Hamilton, ML3 0AA
Tel: 03031 231015 **Email:** customer.services@southlanarkshire.gov.uk **Website:** www.southlanarkshire.gov.uk

CAMBUSLANG

Rutherglen High School
Langlea Road, CAMBUSLANG,
South Lanarkshire G72 8ES
Tel: 01416 433480
Head: Mrs Jan Allen

CARLUKE

Victoria Park School
Market Road, CARLUKE,
South Lanarkshire ML8 4BE
Tel: 01555 750591
Head: Miss Anne Fisher
Category: PMLD SLD

EAST KILBRIDE

Greenburn School
Maxwellton Avenue, EAST KILBRIDE,
South Lanarkshire G74 3DU
Tel: 01355 237278
Head: Mrs Helen Nicol
Category: PMLD

Sanderson High School
High Common Road, St
Leonard's, EAST KILBRIDE,
South Lanarkshire G74 2LP
Tel: 01355 588625
Head: Mr John McEnaney

West Mains School
Logie Park, EAST KILBRIDE,
South Lanarkshire G74 4BU
Tel: 01355 249938
Head: Mrs Rosemary Payne
Category: SLD

HAMILTON

**Hamilton School
for the Deaf**
Anderson Street, HAMILTON,
South Lanarkshire ML3 0QL
Tel: 01698 823377
Head: Ms Eileen Burns
Category: D

LANARK

Ridgepark School
Mousebank Road, LANARK,
South Lanarkshire ML11 7RA
Tel: 01555 662151
Acting Head: Mrs Jane Sludden
Category: EBD

MIDLOTHIAN

Education, Communities & Economy

ASN Team, Fairfield House, 8 Lothian Road, Dalkeith, Midlothian, EH22 3ZG
Tel: 01312 713689 **Email:** asn.officer@midlothian.gov.uk **Website:** www.midlothian.gov.uk

DALKEITH

Saltersgate School
3 Cousland Road, DALKEITH,
Midlothian EH22 2PS
Tel: 01316 544703
Head: F Hume
Category: GLD

---

*In Scotland, Special Educational Needs are generally referred to as Additional Support Needs (ASN)

WEST LOTHIAN
Education & Learning

West Lothian Civic Centre, Howden South Road, Livingston, West Lothian, EH54 6FF
Tel: 01506 775000 Email: customer.service@westlothian.gov.uk Website: www.westlothian.gov.uk

BATHGATE

Pinewood Special School
Elm Grove, Blackburn, BATHGATE,
West Lothian EH47 7QX
Tel: 01506 656374
Head: Ms Pam Greig
Category: MLD SLD

LIVINGSTON

Beatlie School Campus
The Mall, Craigshill, LIVINGSTON,
West Lothian EH54 5EJ
Tel: 01506 777598
Acting Head: Mrs Carol Robbie
Category: CLD MSI PD (Coed 3-16)

Cedarbank School
Cedarbank, Ladywell East,
LIVINGSTON, West Lothian EH54 6DR
Tel: 01506 442172
Acting Head: Ms Carol McDonald
Category: ASD LD (Coed 12-18)

Ogilvie School Campus
Ogilvie Way, Knightsbridge,
LIVINGSTON, West Lothian EH54 8HL
Tel: 01506 777489
Head: Mrs Catriona Grant
Category: EBD (Primary)

LIVINGSTONE

Willowgrove House
1/6 Willowgrove, Craigshill,
LIVINGSTONE, West
Lothian EH54 5LU
Tel: 01506 434274
Head: Mrs Laura Quilter

WHITBURN

Burnhouse School
The Avenue, WHITBURN,
West Lothian EH47 0BX
Tel: 01501 678100
Head: Mrs Laura Quilter
Category: EBD (Secondary)

PERTH & KINROSS
Education & Children's Services

Pullar House, 35 Kinnoull Street, Perth, PH1 5GD
Tel: 01738 476200 Email: enquiries@pkc.gov.uk Website: www.pkc.gov.uk

PERTH

Fairview School
Oakbank Crescent, PERTH,
Perthshire & Kinross PH1 1DF
Tel: 01738 473050
Head: Ms Fiona Gillespie
Category: SLD CLD (Coed 2-18)

RENFREWSHIRE
Education & Learning

ASN Team, Renfrewshire House, Cotton Street, Paisley, PA1 1UJ
Tel: 03003 000170 Email: asn.els@renfrewshire.gov.uk Website: www.renfrewshire.gov.uk

LINWOOD

Clippens School
Brediland Road, LINWOOD,
Renfrewshire PA3 3RX
Tel: 01505 325333
Acting Head: Ms Teresa Brown
Category: ASD CLD PI
MSI (Coed 5-19)

PAISLEY

Kersland School
Ben Nevis Road, PAISLEY,
Renfrewshire PA2 7BU
Tel: 01418 898251
Head: Mrs Carol Jackson
Category: SLD (Coed 5-18)

Mary Russell School
Hawkhead Road, PAISLEY,
Renfrewshire PA2 7BE
Tel: 01418 897628
Head: Ms Julie McCallum
Category: MLD (Coed 5-18)

*In Scotland, Special Educational Needs are generally referred to as Additional Support Needs (ASN)

EAST RENFREWSHIRE

Education Department

ASN Team, Eastwood Park, Rouken Glen Road, Giffnock, East Renfrewshire, G46 6UG
Tel: 01415 773001 Email: customerservices@eastrenfrewshire.gov.uk Website: www.eastrenfrewshire.gov.uk

NEWTON MEARNS

The Isobel Mair School
58 Stewarton Road, NEWTON
MEARNS, East Renfrewshire G77 6NB
Tel: 01415 707600
Head: Ms Sarah Clark
Category: CLD (Coed 5-18)

STIRLING

Council

Education Services, Teith House, Kerse Road, Stirling, FK7 7QA
Tel: 08452 777000 Website: www.stirling.gov.uk

CALLANDER

Callander ASD Provision (at Callander Primary School)
Bridgend, CALLANDER FK17 8AG
Tel: 01877 331576
Head: Ms Audrey Ross
Category: ASD

FALLIN

SEBN Support Service (Primary)
Fallin Primary School, Lamont Crescent, FALLIN FK7 7EJ
Tel: 01786 272330
Acting Head: David McKellar
Category: SEBD EBSD BESD

STIRLING

ASN Outreach Service
Raploch Community Campus, Drip Road, STIRLING FK8 1SD
Tel: 01786 272333
Co-ordinator: Christine Stones

Castleview School
Raploch Community Campus, Drip Road, STIRLING FK8 1SD
Tel: 01786 272326
Head: Mrs Maureen Howie
Category: PD PMLD

Ochil House (at Wallace High School)
Airthrey Road, STIRLING FK9 5HW
Tel: 01786 462166/7
Head: Mr Scott Pennock
Category: CLD SLD PD PH PMLD

Riverside ASD Provision (at Riverside Primary)
Forrest Road, STIRLING FK8 1UJ
Tel: 01786 474128
Head of Provision: Ms Sandra Croug
Category: ASD

SEBN Support Service (S1-S3)
Riverside Base, Forrest Road, STIRLING FK8 1UJ
Tel: 01786 448929
Acting Head: David McKellar
Category: SEBD EBSD BESD

SEBN Support Service (S3-S5)
Chartershall, Fairhill Road, Whins of Milton, STIRLING FK7 0LL
Tel: 01786 812667
Acting Head: David McKellar
Category: SEBD EBSD BESD

St Modan's ASD Provision (at St Modan's High School)
Royal Stuart Way, STIRLING FK7 7WS
Tel: 01786 470962
Head of Provision: Ms Bridget Raeside
Category: ASD

WALES – BLAENAU GWENT

County Borough Council

SEN Team, Anvil Court, Church Street, Abertillery, NP13 1DB
Tel: 01495 311556 Email: education.department@blaenau-gwent.gov.uk Website: www.blaenau-gwent.gov.uk

EBBW VALE

Pen-y-Cwm Special School
Ebbw Fawr Learning Community,
Strand Annealing Lane, EBBW
VALE, Blaenau Gwent NP23 6AN
Tel: 01495 357755
Head: Ms Darya Brill-Williams
Category: SLD PMLD

BRIDGEND

County Borough Council

Access and Inclusion Service, Angel Street, Bridgend, CF31 4WB
Tel: 01656 815230 Email: ais@bridgend.gov.uk Website: www.bridgend.gov.uk

BRIDGEND

Heronsbridge
Special School
Ewenny Road, BRIDGEND CF31 3HT
Tel: 01656 653974
Head: Mrs G James
Category: PMLD VIS AUT (Coed
Day & boarding 3-18)

Ysgol Bryn Castell
Llangewydd Road, Cefn
Glas, BRIDGEND CF31 4JP
Tel: 01656 815595
Head: Mrs H Ridout
Category: EBD LD HI ASD MLD
SLD SP&LD (Coed 3-19)

CAERPHILLY

Inclusion Services

SEN Department, The Octagon Van Court, Caerphilly, CF83 3ED
Tel: 01443 815588 Email: education@caerphilly.gov.uk Website: www.caerphilly.gov.uk

CAERPHILLY

Trinity Fields
Special School
Caerphilly Road, Ystrad Mynach,
CAERPHILLY CF82 7XW
Tel: 01443 866000
Head: Mr H L Jones
Category: SLD VIS HI CLD
SP&LD (Coed 3-19)

CARDIFF

Education Service

SNAP Cymru, County Hall, Atlantic Wharf, Cardiff, CF10 4UW
Tel: 08451 203730 Email: helpline@snapcymru.org Website: www.cardiff.gov.uk

CARDIFF

Greenhill School
Heol Brynglas, Rhiwbina,
CARDIFF CF14 6UJ
Tel: 02920 693786
Head: Mrs Jane Counsell
Category: SEBD (Coed 11-16)

Meadowbank School
Colwill Road, Llandaff North,
CARDIFF CF14 2QQ
Tel: 02920 616018
Head: Mrs Lorraine Felstead
Category: SLCD (Coed 4-11)

Riverbank School
Vincent Road, Caerau,
CARDIFF CF5 5AQ
Tel: 02920 563860
Head: Mrs Amanda Gibson-Evans
Category: MLD SLD (Coed 4-11)

The Court School
Station Road, Llanishen,
CARDIFF CF14 5UX
Tel: 02920 752713
Head: Mr Peter Owen
Category: SEBD (Coed 4-11)

The Hollies School
Brynheulog, CARDIFF CF23 7XG
Tel: 02920 734411
Head: Miss Kath Keely
Category: ASD PMED (Coed 4-11)

Ty Gwyn School
Vincent Road, Caerau,
CARDIFF CF5 5AQ
Tel: 02920 838560
Head: Mr Kevin Tansley
Category: PMLD ASD (Coed 4-19)

Woodlands High School
Vincent Road, Caerau,
CARDIFF CF5 5AQ
Tel: 02920 561279
Head: Mr Russell Webb
Category: MLD SLD (Coed 11-19)

CARMARTHENSHIRE

County Council

The Department for Education and Children, Building 2, St David's Park,
Jobswell Road Carmarthen, Carmarthenshire, SA31 3HB
Tel: 01267 246500 Email: ecs@carmarthenshire.gov.uk Website: www.carmarthenshire.gov.uk

CARMARTHEN

**Rhyd-y-gors School
& Support Services**
Rhyd-y-gors, Johnstown,
CARMARTHEN,
Carmarthenshire SA31 3QU
Tel: 01267 231171
Acting Head: Mrs M Davies
Category: EBD

LLANELLI

Ysgol Heol Goffa
Heol Goffa, LLANELLI,
Carmarthenshire SA15 3LS
Tel: 01554 759465
Head: Mrs N Symmons
Category: SLD PMLD

CONWY

Education Services

Education Services, ALN Services, Government Buildings, Dinerth Road, Colwyn Bay, LL28 4UL
Tel: 01492 575031/032 Email: education@conwy.gov.uk Website: www.conwy.gov.uk

LLANDUDNO

Ysgol Y Gogarth
Ffordd Nant y Gamar, Craig y Don,
LLANDUDNO, Conwy LL30 1YE
Tel: 01492 860077
Head: Mr Jonathan Morgan
Category: General SEN (2-19)

DENBIGHSHIRE
County Council

SEN Team, Middle Lane, Denbigh, Denbighshire, LL16 3UW
Tel: 01745 351205 Email: jeremy.griffiths@denbighshire.gov.uk Website: www.denbighshire.gov.uk

DENBIGH

Ysgol Plas Brondyffryn
Park Street, DENBIGH,
Denbighshire LL16 3DR
Tel: 01745 813914
Head: Dr I Barros-Curtis
Category: AUT SLD (Coed 4-19)

RHYL

Ysgol Tir Morfa
Derwen Road, RHYL,
Denbighshire LL18 2RN
Tel: 01745 350388
Head: Mrs Carol Edwards
Category: MLD SLD (Coed 4-19)

FLINTSHIRE
County Council

Education Department, County Hall, Mold, Flintshire, CH7 6ND
Website: www.flintshire.gov.uk

FLINT

Ysgol Maes Hyfryd
Fifth Avenue, FLINT,
Flintshire CH6 5QL
Tel: 01352 792720
Head: Ms Jane Kelly
Category: (Coed 11-16)

Ysgol Pen Coch
Prince of Wales Avenue,
FLINT, Flintshire CH6 5NF
Tel: 01352 792730
Head: Ms Ange Anderson
Category: (Coed 5-11)

GWYNEDD
Council

SEN Team, Council Offices, Penrallt, Caernarfon, Gwynedd, LL55 1BN
Tel: 01766 771000 Email: education@gwynedd.gov.uk Website: www.gwynedd.gov.uk

CAERNARFON

Ysgol Pendalar
Ffordd Bethel, CAERNARFON,
Gwynedd LL55 1DU
Tel: 01248 672141
Head: Mrs Donna Rees-Roberts
Category: SLD

PWLLHELI

Ysgol Hafod Lon
Lon Caernarfon, Y Ffor,
PWLLHELI, Gwynedd LL53 6UP
Tel: 01766 810626
Head: Mrs Donna Rees-Roberts
Category: SLD

MERTHYR TYDFIL

Integrated Children's Services

Additional Learning Needs Service, Unit 5, Triangle Business Park, Pentrebach, Merthyr Tydfil, CF48 4TQ
Tel: 01685 724616 Fax: 01685 724642 Email: sen@merthyr.gov.uk Website: www.merthyr.gov.uk

MERTHYR TYDFIL

Greenfield Special School
Duffryn Road, Pentrebach,
MERTHYR TYDFIL CF48 4BJ
Tel: 01443 690468
Head: Mr Wayne Murphy
Category: SLD MLD PMLD ASD
EBD MSI SP&LD (Coed 3-19)

MONMOUTHSHIRE

County Council

SEN Department, County Hall, The Rhadyr, Usk, Monmouthshire, NP15 1GA
Tel: 01633 644644 Email: sen@monmouthshire.gov.uk Website: www.monmouthshire.gov.uk

CHEPSTOW

Mounton House School
Pwyllmeyric, CHEPSTOW,
Monmouthshire NP16 6LA
Tel: 01291 635050
Head: Mr P Absolom
Category: EBD (Boys Day/
Boarding 11-16)

NEATH PORT TALBOT

The Child Care (Disability) Team

2nd Floor, Neath Port Talbot CBC, Civic Centre, Neath, SA11 3QZ
Tel: 01639 685862 Email: education@npt.gov.uk Website: www.neath-porttalbot.gov.uk

NEATH

Ysgol Hendrefelin
Heol Hendre, Bryncoch,
NEATH SA10 7TY
Tel: 01639 642786
Head: Mr Jonathan Roberts
Category: GLD (Coed 2-19)

Ysgol Maes Y Coed
Hoel Hendre, Brynoch,
NEATH SA10 7TY
Tel: 01639 643648
Head: Mrs Helen Glover
Category: GLD (Coed 2-19)

NEWPORT
City Council

Education Department, Education Inclusion Department, Civic Centre, Newport, NP20 4UR
Tel: 01633 656656 Email: education@newport.gov.uk Website: www.newport.gov.uk

NEWPORT

Maes Ebbw Bach
St Johns Road, Maindee,
NEWPORT, Newport NP19 8GR
Tel: 01633 815480
Head: Ms Julie Nichols

Maes Ebbw School
Maesglas Road, NEWPORT,
Newport NP20 3DG
Tel: 01633 815480
Head: Ms Julie Nichols
Category: SLD PMLD AUT PH

PEMBROKESHIRE
Education Department

Inclusion and SEN Service, County Hall, Haverfordwest, Pembrokeshire, SA61 1TP
Tel: 01437 775012 Email: nicola.jones@pembrokeshire.gov.uk Website: www.pembrokeshire.gov.uk

HAVERFORDWEST

Portfield School
off Portfield, HAVERFORDWEST,
Pembrokeshire SA61 1BS
Tel: 01437 762701
Head: Mrs S Painter
Category: SLD PMLD CLD
ASC (Coed 4-18+)

POWYS
County Council

Schools Service, Powys County Hall, Spa Road East, Llandrindod Wells, Powys, LD1 5LG
Tel: 01597 826715 Email: pupil.inclusion@powys.gov.uk Website: www.powys.gov.uk

BRECON

Ysgol Penmaes
Canal Road, BRECON,
Powys LD3 7HL
Tel: 01874 623508
Head: Mrs Julie Kay
Category: SLD ASD PMLD
(Coed Day/Residential 3-19)

NEWTOWN

Brynllywarch Hall School
Kerry, NEWTOWN, Powys SY16 4PB
Tel: 01686 670276
Head: Mr Gavin Randell
Category: MLD EBD

Ysgol Cedewain
Maesyrhandir, NEWTOWN,
Powys SY16 1LH
Tel: 01686 627454
Head: Mrs Pippa Sillitoe
Category: SLD ASD PMLD
(Coed Day 3-19)

RHONDDA CYNON TAFF

County Borough Council

Education & Childrenís Service Group, Ty Trevithick, Abercynon, Mountain Ash, CF45 4UQ
Tel: 01443 744000 Email: customerservices@rctcbc.gov.uk Website: www.rctcbc.gov.uk

ABERDARE

Maesgwyn Special School
Cwmdare Road, Cwmdare,
ABERDARE, Rhondda
Cynon Taf CF44 8RE
Tel: 01685 873933
Head: Mr S K Morgan
Category: MLD (Coed 11-18)

Park Lane Special School
Park Lane, Trecynon, ABERDARE,
Rhondda Cynon Taf CF44 8HN
Tel: 01685 874489
Head: Mrs J Davies
Category: SLD (3-19)

PENTRE

Ysgol Hen Felin
Gelligaled Park, Ystrad, PENTRE,
Rhondda Cynon Taf CF41 7SZ
Tel: 01443 431571
Head: Mr A Henderson
Category: SLD (3-19)

PONTYPRIDD

Ysgol Ty Coch
Lansdale Drive, Tonteg,
PONTYPRIDD, Rhondda
Cynon Taf CF38 1PG
Tel: 01443 203471
Head: Ms H Hodges
Category: SLD (3-19)

City and County of
SWANSEA

Education Directorate, Civic Centre, Oystermouth Road, Swansea, SA1 3SN
Tel: 01792 636000 Email: education.department@swansea.gov.uk Website: www.swansea.gov.uk

SWANSEA

Ysgol Crug Glas
Croft Street, SWANSEA SA1 1QA
Tel: 01792 652388
Head: Mr P Martin
Category: SLD PMLD

Ysgol Pen-y-Bryn
Glasbury Road, Morriston,
SWANSEA SA6 7PA
Tel: 01792 799064
Head: Mr Gethin Sutton
Category: MLD SLD AUT

TORFAEN

County Borough Council

Education Service, Civic Centre, Pontypool, Torfaen, NP4 6YB
Tel: 01495 762200 Email: your.call@torfaen.gov.uk Website: www.torfaen.gov.uk

CWMBRAN

Crownbridge School
Turnpike Road, Croesyceiliog,
CWMBRAN, Torfaen NP44 2BJ
Tel: 01633 624201
Head: Mrs Lesley Bush
Category: SLD

VALE OF GLAMORGAN

Council

Learning & Skills, Provincial House, Kendrick Road, Barry, CF62 8BF
Tel: 01446 700111 Website: www.valeofglamorgan.gov.uk

PENARTH

Ysgol Y Deri
Sully Road, PENARTH, Vale
of Glamorgan CF64 2TG
Tel: 02920 352280
Head: Mr C Britten
Category: AUT PMLD MLD SLD
(Coed 5 Day/Residential 3-19)

WREXHAM

County Borough Council

SEN Team, 16 Lord Street, Wrexham, LL11 1LG
Tel: 01978 292000 Email: education@wrexham.gov.uk Website: www.wrexham.gov.uk

WREXHAM

St Christopher's School
Stockwell Grove,
WREXHAM LL13 7BW
Tel: 01978 346910
Head: Mrs Maxine Pittaway
Category: MLD SLD
PMLD (Coed 6-19)

Glossary

ACLD	Autism, Communication and Associated Learning Difficulties
ADD	Attention Deficit Order
ADHD	Attention Deficit and Hyperactive Disorder (Hyperkinetic Disorder)
AdvDip SpecEduc	Advanced Diploma in Special Education
AFBPS	Associate Fellow of the British Psychological Society
ALAN	Adult Literacy and Numeracy
ALCM	Associate of the London College of Music
ALL	Accreditation of Lifelong Learning
AOC	Association of Colleges
AQA	Assessment and Qualification Alliance/ Northern Examinations and Assessment Board
ASC	Autistic Spectrum Conditions
ASD	Autistic Spectrum Disorders
ASDAN	Qualifications for 11-16 age range
ASP	Asperger syndrome
AUT	Autism
AWCEBD	now SEBDA
BA	Bachelor of Arts
BDA	British Dyslexic Association
BESD	Behavioural, Emotional and Social Difficulties
BMET	Biomedical Engineering Technologist
BPhil	Bachelor of Philosophy
BSc	Bachelor of Science
BSL	British Sign Language
BTEC	Range of practical work-related programmes; which lead to qualifications equivalent to GCSEs and A levels (awarded by Edexcel)
C & G	City & Guilds Examination
C(Ed) Psychol	Certificate in Educational Psychology
CACDP	Council for the Advancement of Communication with Deaf People
CAMHS	Child and Adolescent Mental Health Service
CB	Challenging Behaviour
CD	Communcation Difficulties
CertEd	Certificate of Education
CF	Cystic Fibrosis
CLAIT	Computer Literacy and Information Technology
CLD	Complex Learning Difficulties
CNS	Central Nervous System
COPE	Certificate of Personal Effectiveness
CP	Cerebral Palsy

CPD	Continuing Professional Development
CRB	Criminal Records Bureau
CReSTeD	Council for the Registration of Schools Teaching Dyslexic Pupils
CSSE	Consortium of Special Schools in Essex
CSSIW	Care and Social Services Inspectorate for Wales
CTEC	Computer-aided Training, Education and Communication
D	Deaf
DDA	Disability Discrimination Act
DEL	Delicate
DfE	Department for Education
DIDA	Diploma in Digital Applications
DipAppSS	Diploma in Applied Social Sciences
DipEd	Diploma of Education
DipSEN	Diploma in Speial Educational Needs
DipSpEd	Diploma in Special Education
DT	Design and Technology
DYC	Dyscalculia
DYS	Dyslexia
DYSC	Dyscalculia
DYSP	Dyspraxia
EASIE	Exercise and Sound in Education
EBSD	Emotional, Behavioural and/or Social Difficulties
ECDL	European Computer Driving Licence
ECIS	European Council of International Schools
ECM	Every Child Matters (Government Green Paper)
EdMng	Educational Management
ELC	Early Learning Centre
ELQ	Equivalent or Lower Qualification
EPI	Epilepsy
EQUALS	Entitlement and Quality Education for Pupils with Learning Difficulties
FLSE	Federation of Leaders in Special Education
GCSE	General Certificate of Secondary Education
GLD	General Learning Difficulties
HA	High Ability
HANDLE	Holistic Approach to Newuro-DEvelopment and Learning Efficiency
HEA	Higher Educaiton Authority/Health Education Authority
HI	Hearing Impairment
HS	Hospital School
ICT	Information Communication Technology

Glossary

IEP	Individual Education Plan	PGCE	Post Graduate Certificate in Education
IIP	Investors in People	PGCertSpld	Post Graduate Certificate in Specific Learning Difficulties
IM	Idiopathic Myelofibrosis	PGTC	Post Graduate Teaching Certificate
ISI	Independent Schools Inspectorate	PH	Physical Impairment
IT	Information Technology	PhD	Doctor of Philosophy
KS	Key Stage	Phe	Partially Hearing
LA	Local Authority	PMLD	Profound and Multiple Learning Difficulties
LD	Learning Difficulties	PNI	Physical Neurological Impairment
LDD	Learning Difficulties and Disabilities	PRU	Pupil Referral Unit
LISA	London International Schools Association	PSHCE	Personal Social Health, Citizenship and Economics
MA	Master of Arts	RE	Religious Education
MAPA	Management of Actual or Potential Aggression	SAT	Standard Asessment Test
MBA	Master of Business Administration	SCD	Social and Communication Difficulties
MD	Muscular Dystrophy	SCLD	Severe and Complex Learning Difficulties
MDT	Multidisciplinary Team	SEAL	Social and Emotional Aspects of Learning
MEd	Master of Education	SEBD	Severe Emotional and Behavioural Disorders
MLD	Moderate Learning Difficulties		
MS	Multiple Sclerosis	SEBDA	Social, Emotional and Behavioural Difficulties Association
MSc	Master of Science	SEBN	Social, Emotional and Behavioural Needs
MSI	Multi-sensory Impairment	SHB	Sexually Harmful Behaviour
NAES	National Association of EBD Schools	SLCN	Speech, Language and Communicational Needs
NAS	National Autistic Society	SLD	Severe Learning Difficulties
NASEN	Northern Association of Special Educational Needs	SLI	Specific Language Impairment
NASS	National Association of Independent Schools & Non-maintained Special Schools	SLT	Speech and Language Teacher
		SP	Special Purpose/Speech Processing
		SpEd	Special Education
NATSPEC	National Association of Specialist Colleges	SPLD	Specific Learning Difficulties
NOCN	National Open College Network	SP&LD	Speech and Language Difficulties
NPQH	National Professional Qualification for Headship	STREAM	Strong Therapeutic, Restoring Environment and Assesssment Model
NVQ	National Vocational Qualifications	SWALSS	South and West Association of Leaders in Special Schools
OCD	Obsessive Compulsive Disorder		
OCN	Open Course Network	SWSF	Steiner Waldorf Schools Foundation
ODD	Oppositional Defiant Disorder	TAV	Therapeutic, Academic and Vocational
OT	Occupational Therapist	TEACCH	Treatment and Education of Autistic and related Communication Handicapped Children (also sometimes written as TEACHH)
P scales	method of recording the achievements of SEN students who are working towards the first levels of the National Curriculum		
PACT	Parents Association of Children with Tumours	TCI	Therapeutic Crisis Intervention
		ToD	Teacher of the Deaf
PACT	Parents and Children Together	TOU	Tourette syndrome
PCMT	Professional and Clinical Multidisciplinary Team	VB	Verbal Reasoning
		VIS	Visually Impaired
PD	Physical Difficulties	VOCA	Voice Output Communication Aid
PE	Physical Education	WMLG	West Midlands Lupus Group
PECS	Picture Exchange Communication System		

Index

Index

Notes

Notes

Notes